Public Health and Federalism in India

The interface of public health and federalism is increasingly gaining scholarly attention in the fields of comparative federalism and welfare state studies. The authors of this volume explore various facets of public health and governance in India from legal, institutional and policy perspectives.

They explore the regulatory architecture around health care in federal systems of governance; public finance and insurance; and private-sector medical care and the tussle for power between the union and the states. A multidisciplinary volume with essays from scholars working in public health, economics, political science and legal studies, the book is a collection of critical evaluations of India's public policy apparatus for dealing with health crises, inequity and the lack of health infrastructure and resources among other challenges. The authors also look at the impact of the Covid-19 pandemic on federalism and democratic structures as well as the role of institutions such as NITI (National Institution for Transforming India) Aayog and other central agencies in policy formulation and implementation within the broader framework of intergovernmental relations in a federal system.

The book will be of interest to students and researchers of public health, public policy, health administration, medical sociology, constitutional law and political science, as well as of federalism.

Mohan Rao is former professor at the Centre of Social Medicine and Community Health (CSMCH), School of Social Sciences, Jawaharlal Nehru University, New Delhi.

Balveer Arora is Honorary Professor and the Chairman of the Institute of Social Sciences' Centre for Multilevel Federalism, New Delhi. He was previously a professor of political science at Jawaharlal Nehru University (1973–2010) and also the Rector and Pro-Vice Chancellor of JNU (2002–2005).

This ground-breaking volume grapples with one of the most pressing governance conundrums of our day in the world's largest country: how to synergize equity, efficiency, and inclusiveness amid ensuring health justice. Many prominent democracies – Brazil, Mexico, South Africa, the United States, to name but a few – operate under federal models, with shared or devolved responsibilities especially regarding health and other social policies. Each faces its own challenges, but the Indian context is arguably the most complex, geographically, politically, ethno-religiously, culturally, socio-economically, historically, and epidemiologically.

At once timely, jarring, and deeply analytical, Mohan Rao and Balveer Arora's collection critically assesses the never-ending dilemmas of decentralized health governance spanning India's diversity across space and time, from post-colonial disillusion to regulatory abandonment, self-sufficiency ideologies, and mounting, egregious corporate encroachment.

Deftly utilizing the Covid-19 pandemic as a lens on India's over 80-year dalliance with federalism, the book's case studies reveal its double-edged sword: power to the people via responsive, decentralized decision making versus the illusion of control amid budget cuts, bureaucratic constraints, and neoliberal devolved responsibility with limited political power.

Public Health and Federalism is a must-read for health scholars, policymakers, practitioners, and activists.

– **Anne-Emanuelle Birn**, MA, ScD,
Professor of Global Development Studies,
University of Toronto, and author of
The Textbook of Global Health

When federalism is in turmoil, you do not have to be a health expert to benefit from authoritative political economy analyses of centralism, multi-layered governance and the forces of resistance to both; of regulatory variety and principles for standardisation; of pathologies and corruptions of partnership in the public and private spheres; of the power politics of finance and of selective social exclusion. Nor, in what is widely regarded as a poly-crisis, do you have to be an expert on Covid to appreciate the role of a crisis in cracking federalist politics, the way crises invite foreign funds, management, lobbies and policy influence and the way a crisis reveals the class struggle over profits and welfare outcomes.

This book will be treasured as widely relevant both inside and outside its formal remit of public health.

– **Barbara Harris White**, Professor Emerita,
Oxford University

A truly comprehensive and wide-ranging treatment of federalism and public health. Provoked by the Covid-19 pandemic, but going much beyond it, the essays in this volume examine multiple aspects of this relationship – the public and the private in neo-liberal times; centralisation and decentralisation as determinants of state capacity; the social demography of health disadvantage in an unequal society; drugs and pharmaceuticals and the issues of intellectual property and regulatory regimes that they entail; and the role of international organizations in public health emergencies. This promises to be the definitive work on the subject.

– **Niraja Gopal Jayal,** Avantha Chair and Professor of Politics, King's College, London

Public Health and Federalism in India

Dissonant Discourses

Edited by Mohan Rao and Balveer Arora

Routledge
Taylor & Francis Group
LONDON AND NEW YORK

First published 2025
by Routledge
4 Park Square, Milton Park, Abingdon, Oxon OX14 4RN

and by Routledge
605 Third Avenue, New York, NY 10158

Routledge is an imprint of the Taylor & Francis Group, an informa business

British Library Cataloguing-in-Publication Data
A catalogue record for this book is available from the British Library

ISBN: 978-1-032-45168-8 (hbk)
ISBN: 978-1-032-94059-5 (pbk)
ISBN: 978-1-003-56871-1 (ebk)

DOI: 10.4324/9781003568711

Typeset in Sabon
by Apex CoVantage, LLC

Contents

Figures

Tables

Contributors

P.M. Arathi was at the Council for Social Development, New Delhi, before joining the School of Indian Legal Thought, Mahatma Gandhi University, Kottayam, as an assistant professor. Her doctoral research was on *Gendered Bodies, Medicine and Law: A Study of Selected Case Laws from India* and her MPhil dissertation was 'Aborting Gender Justice: Legislating Abortion in Selected Countries of South Asia – A Preliminary Analysis', both from the Centre of Social Medicine and Community Health, School of Social Sciences, Jawaharlal Nehru University, New Delhi. She specialised in health care law for her master's (law) and worked as a research assistant on a collaborative project between the London School of Economics and Jawaharlal Nehru University on spousal violence in India. Her post-doctoral research at the Berlin Social Science Centre was funded by WZB and International Social Science Council, Paris Global Fellowship. She co-edited the book *Universalising Health Services in India*, and she has several academic publications.

Balveer Arora is Honorary Professor and the Chairman of the Institute of Social Sciences' Centre for Multilevel Federalism, New Delhi. He was previously a professor of political science at Jawaharlal Nehru University (1973–2010) and also the Rector and Pro-Vice Chancellor of JNU (2002–2005). He obtained his master's in politics, sociology and public law and his doctorate in political science from Sciences Po Paris at the University of Paris I (Pantheon-Sorbonne) after graduating in history from St. Stephen's College, Delhi. The highest French civilian award, Knight of the Legion of Honour, was conferred on him in 2011. He is also an Officer in the French Order of Academic Laurels and Vice President of the Transcultura International Institute, Paris. He has written extensively on India's politics and governance, especially on public policy and federal democracy. His publications include *Indian Federalism: Origins and Development; Multiple Identities in a Single State*; *Transforming India*; and 'The Changing Role of the All-India Services'. His recent publications include 'Diversity and Unity in the Indian Republic', 'A Survey of Research on Indian Federalism' and 'Political Innovation in the Working of Indian

Democracy'. Dr Arora is President of Water for People, India, and he is currently the Convener of the federal democracy project of the India International Centre, New Delhi.

Rama V. Baru is a professor at the Centre of Social Medicine and Community Health, Jawaharlal Nehru University. She is also an honorary fellow with the Institute of Chinese Studies and an honorary professor at India Studies Centre, Central China Normal University, Wuhan, China. Her research focus is on social determinants of health, health policy, international health, privatisation of health services and inequalities in health. She is the author of *Private Health Care in India: Social Characteristics and Trends* (SAGE Publications). She has edited several volumes of *School Health Services in India: The Social and Economic Contexts* (SAGE Publications) and *Medical Insurance Schemes for the Poor: Who Benefits?* (Academic Publication) and has co-edited a volume with Anuj Kapilashrami titled *Global Health Governance and Commercialisation of Public Health in India: Actors, Institutions and the Dialectics of Global and Local* (Routledge). Her latest is the co-authored book (with Madhurima Nundy) *Commercialisation of Medical Care in China: Changing Landscapes* (Routledge).

Ramila Bisht is a professor at the Centre for Social Medicine & Community Health, Jawaharlal Nehru University, New Delhi. Her research interests comprise health policy and reforms in India; comparative health systems and policies, urbanization, environment and health; health inequalities and the gendered social and cultural determinants of women's health. She was awarded the British Society of Population Studies LEDC visitor award in 2010. She was also an embedded fellow in 2010 in the ESRC Rising Powers Network Award titled India's challenge in a globalizing healthcare economy: social science directions. Her publications include Deepa V, Mohan Rao, Rama V. Baru, Ramila Bisht, Sarojini N. and Susan Murray (2013) *Sourcing Surrogates: Actors, Agencies and Networks* Zubaan: New Delhi and Ramila Bisht (2002) *Environmental Health in Garhwal Himalaya: A Study of Pauri Garhwal.* New Delhi: Indus Publishing.

Biswajit Dhar is a professor in the Centre for Economic Studies and Planning at Jawaharlal Nehru University, New Delhi. Before joining the university, Dr Dhar was the Director General of Research and Information System for Developing Countries, a think tank of India's Foreign Ministry. He also helped in establishing the Centre for WTO Studies of the Government of India. Dr Dhar was a member of the Indian delegation in multilateral treaty negotiations, including the World Trade Organization, the World Intellectual Property Organization and the Convention on Biological Diversity. He also served as a member of the WHO's Working Group on Fair Pricing of Medicines. He has written extensively on the pharmaceutical industry, especially on the impact of intellectual property rights on access to affordable medicines. He has also written extensively on the effects of foreign capital on developing countries.

Sourindra Mohan Ghosh is a consultant with the Council for Social Development, New Delhi. He is also pursuing his PhD from the Centre of Economic Studies and Planning, Jawaharlal Nehru University. His research interests include public health and health policy, food security, nutrition and socioeconomic development. He has several publications in journals and books and is a frequent contributor to popular writings.

Indranil is a professor at Jindal School of Government and Public Policy, Jindal Global University, Sonipat, Haryana. He teaches public health, health economics, development economics, mixed method research, the political economy of health and comparative health systems at JSGP. He has a PhD from Jawaharlal Nehru University, New Delhi. He has more than 16 years of research experience and has led several research studies. Earlier he worked as a research scientist and assistant professor at the Public Health Foundation of India, Delhi. He was a Wellcome Trust Post-Doctoral Fellow (2015–17). He has several international and national publications to his credit. He is the co-editor of *Jindal Journal of Public Policy*.

Kevin James is a research associate at the Centre for Social and Economic Progress and an honorary fellow at the Centre for Multilevel Federalism, Institute of Social Sciences. He works as a legal researcher on interdisciplinary projects in the areas of constitutional law, federalism and public finance. His work has been published in academic journals, by research organisations and in media outlets. Previously, he was a research fellow at Vidhi Centre for Legal Policy, where he co-authored reports for the Fifteenth Finance Commission and advised the Government of India on issues of law and policy through legal research and legislative drafting. Kevin has a B.A.LL.B. (Hons.) degree from Hidayatullah National Law University, Raipur, where he was awarded the University Gold Medal in Jurisprudence & Legal Method. He is also enrolled as an advocate with the Bar Council of Delhi.

K.K. Kailash is with the Department of Political Science, University of Hyderabad. His research interests focus on political parties and elections, coalition politics and processes and issues of federalism in contemporary India. He is a member of the editorial managing team of *Studies in Indian Politics* and on the editorial board of *Commonwealth & Comparative Politics*. He is an honorary fellow at the Centre for Multilevel Federalism, Institute of Social Sciences, New Delhi.

A.K. Shiva Kumar, a development economist, policy advisor and evaluator, has worked on poverty and human development; social policies including education, health and nutrition and the impact of development policies on women and children. He teaches economics and public policy as a visiting faculty member at Ashoka University in the BITS School of Management at Harvard's Kennedy School of Government. Shiv has been a regular contributor to global and national Human Development Reports. He is the co-editor of three books published by Oxford University Press: *Handbook of Human Development*; *Handbook of Population and Development* and *India's Children: Essays on Social Policy*. Shiv earned his master's in economics from Bangalore University and a post-graduate diploma in management from the Indian Institute of Management, Ahmedabad. He is also an alumnus of Harvard University, where he completed a master's in public administration and a PhD in political economy and government.

Harsh Mander is an author, columnist, researcher, teacher, and social activist who started the *Karwan-e-Mohabbat* campaign in solidarity with the victims of communal or religiously motivated violence. He is the director of the Centre for Equity Studies; a founding member of the National Campaign for the People's Right to Information; founder-chairperson of the State Health Resource Centre, Chhattisgarh, which established the Mitanin community health programme (the forerunner of the Asha programme). He has also worked as Country Director, ActionAid India, and the Chairperson of INCENSE (The Inclusion and Empowerment of People with Severe Mental Disorders), and he is a member of the Working Group of the Project on Armed Conflict Resolution & People's Rights, University of California, Berkeley. His books include *The Right to Food Debates: Social Protection for Food Security in India* (with Ashwin Parulkar and Ankita Aggarwal, Orient Blackswan, 2018), *Partitions of the Heart: Unmaking the Idea of India'* (Penguin Vikings, 2019), *Between Memory and Forgetting: Massacre and the Modi Years in Gujarat* (Yoda Press, 2019) and *Looking Away: Inequality, Prejudice and Indifference in New India* (Speaking Tiger, 2015).

Shweta Marathe is a researcher at SATHI, Pune, India. Building on her academic background in health care management and her decade-long experience at SATHI, she now coordinates the organisation's research division. She undertakes various research studies related to the functioning of the public health system, community nutrition and the private health care sector. She is keen to conduct action-oriented, empirical research to improve actions and support advocacy. Her research interests focus on the transformations in the private health care sector. Her recent and ongoing research work includes examining the practices, regulation, and accountability in the evolving private health care sector (with King's College, London); assessing the impacts of community-based monitoring (with the Accountability Research Center at American University); analysing the experiences of patients and examining state regulation of private hospitals during the Covid-19 pandemic. Currently, she holds an India HPSR fellowship (2022).

Manu Raj Mathur is a dental surgeon with more than 15 years of global experience of working in different health systems. He is currently the Head of Health Policy at the Public Health Foundation of India. He has a PhD in epidemiology and population health from University College, London, and a master's in public health from the University of Glasgow. His research focuses on risk factors for non-communicable diseases, especially tobacco cessation. Throughout his career, Professor Mathur has been an advocate for universal health care and has played an active role in ensuring that appropriate quality oral health care is available, affordable and accessible for all.

Dr Mathur is a commissioner on the Lancet Commission on Global Oral Health and President of the Global Oral Health Inequalities Research Network of International Association for Dental Research. He has more than 100 peer-reviewed publications in leading international journals and has been the principal investigator on many projects funded by Government of India, WHO, MRC-UK, The Bill and Melinda Gates Foundation, USAID and NIH-USA. His areas of expertise cover epidemiologic methods, operations, health systems and policy research and health promotion.

Dhvani Mehta is co-founder of the Vidhi Centre for Legal Policy, an independent legal research think tank. She leads Vidhi's work on health law and has special interests in health regulation, the articulation and implementation of the right to health and the intersection of medical ethics and the law. She has worked with the Indian Council of Medical Research and NITI Aayog on clinical trials and medical device regulation, and she has collaborated with the End of Life Care in India Task Force to develop a model law on end-of-life care. She has co-authored a chapter on health care corruption in India for an edited volume. She has also appeared in the Supreme Court on petitions filed by Vidhi on advance medical directives and discrimination against persons affected by leprosy. She has a doctoral degree in law from the University of Oxford.

Daksha Parmar is presently working as an assistant professor of development studies in the Department of Humanities and Social Sciences, Indian Institute of Technology, Guwahati, Assam. She has a doctorate in public health from the Centre of Social Medicine and Community Health, Jawaharlal Nehru University, New Delhi. Her research interests are population policy, public health, human resources in health, social exclusion and inequities in health, gender and health.

Imrana Qadeer, an MD in paediatrics, worked at AIIMS and then shifted to public health and joined the Centre of Social Medicine and Community Health, School of Social Sciences at Jawaharlal Nehru University, New Delhi, to participate in shaping the centre in 1973. Retired as a professor, she joined the Centre for Women's Development Studies as a senior fellow and then served at the Council for Social Development, Delhi, as a Distinguished Professor until 2020. During these five decades, Dr Qadeer has researched and published extensively. She has been engaged in national-level health planning debates as a member of the scientific advisory board of the

Indian Council of Medical Research, the Planning Commission and the Population Commission as well as the academic councils and academic bodies of educational institutions.

K. Sujatha Rao, a 1974 batch IAS officer of the then United AP cadre, is a former Union Secretary of the Ministry of Health and Family Welfare, Government of India. Of her 36 years' service as a civil servant, she spent 20 years in the health sector in different capacities at the state and federal levels. Currently, Ms. Rao is a member of NHSRC, GOI, the board of PRITHVI Asset Reconstruction Company and the boards of a number of NGOs. Prior to her service in these roles, she was the chairperson of the Portfolio Committee of the Global Fund for HIV/AIDS, TB and Malaria; Director General of the National AIDS Control Organization; Vice Chair of WHO's Global Advisory Board on Nursing and Midwifery; Member of the Global Advisory Panel of the Bill & Melinda Gates Foundation and a founding member of the Public Health Foundation of India.

Mohan Rao is a former professor at the Centre of Social Medicine and Community Health, School of Social Sciences, Jawaharlal Nehru University, New Delhi. A medical doctor specialised in public health, he has written extensively on health and population policy and on the history and politics of health and family planning. He is the author of *From Population Control to Reproductive Health: Malthusian Arithmetic* (Sage, New Delhi, 2004), and he edited *Disinvesting in Health: The World Bank's Health Prescriptions* (Sage, New Delhi, 1999) and *The Unheard Scream: Reproductive Health and Women's Lives in India* (Zubaan/Kali for Women, New Delhi, 2004). He edited, with Sarah Sexton of Cornerhouse, UK, the volume *Markets and Malthus: Population, Gender and Health in Neoliberal Times* (Sage, New Delhi, 2010), and with Sarah Hodges, he edited *Public Health and Private Wealth: Stem Cells, Surrogacy and Other Strategic Bodies* (OUP, 2016). His latest work is the edited volume *The Lineaments of Population Policy in India: Women and Family Planning* (Routledge, 2018). He has been a member of the National Population Commission and of several Working Groups of the National Rural Health Mission of the Government of India; he worked on the committee established by the National Human Rights Commission to examine the two-child norm in population policy and he is on the Executive Committee of the Centre for Women's Development Studies. He is also actively involved in the Jan Swasthya Abhiyan (People's Health Movement). Rao is currently an independent researcher based in Bangalore.

K. Srinath Reddy, a cardiologist and epidemiologist by training, is the founder and past president of the Public Health Foundation of India (2006–22). He presently serves as an Honorary Distinguished Professor of PHFI. Under his leadership, PHFI established five Indian Institutes of Public Health to advance multi-disciplinary education and research for multi- sectoral application. He was earlier Head of Cardiology at the All Institute of Medical Sciences, New Delhi. Prof. Reddy was the first Bernard Lown Visiting Professor of Global Cardiovascular Health at Harvard (2009–13) and is presently an adjunct professor at Harvard, Emory, Sydney and Pennsylvania universities.

Prof Reddy is the first Indian to be elected as an International Member of the US National Academy of Medicine. He was President of the World Heart Federation (2013–14) and is co-chair of the Health Thematic Group of the UN Sustainable Development Solutions Network. He chaired the High-Level Expert Group on Universal Health Coverage constituted by the Planning Commission of India (2010–11). He is a member of the Global Panel on Agriculture and Food Systems for Nutrition. He has served on several expert panels of the WHO and of Indian and international scientific agencies. He is a former health advisor to the state governments of Odisha and Andhra Pradesh, with a cabinet rank.

Prof. Reddy has 581 scientific publications in peer-reviewed Indian and international journals. He published *Make Health in India: Reaching a Billion Plus* in 2019, and his second book, *Pulse to Planet: Long Lifeline of Human Health*, was released in September 2023. Among his multiple honours, he has received the WHO Director General's Award and the Luther Terry Medal of the American Cancer Association for outstanding contributions to global tobacco control, the Queen Elizabeth Medal for Health Promotion and Padma Bhushan, the prestigious civilian award conferred by the President of India.

Shreya Shrivastava is Senior Resident Fellow at the Vidhi Centre for Legal Policy. She works in the areas of health regulation, public health governance, right to health and medical law. She has assisted various central and state government departments in drafting laws related to education and health. She is currently involved in an extensive analysis of India's current framework to deal with public health emergencies and preparing a blueprint of India's ideal public health emergency law. She has also been working on projects related to challenges faced by vulnerable patient groups in accessing health care and existing accountability mechanisms against doctors and hospitals. In the past, she worked with NITI Aayog on medical device regulation. She has also been involved in strategic litigation in education and disability rights. She holds a bachelor's degree in law from Hidayatullah National Law University, Raipur.

Abhay Shukla is a public health physician working on community and public health in India for the last 35 years. He is the Senior Programme Coordinator at SATHI Pune and a member of the National Health Mission Advisory Group for Community Action. He is a national co-convenor of Jan Swasthya Abhiyan (People's Health Movement – India). He has co-edited or co-authored the books *Review of Health Care in India*, *Report on Health Inequities in Maharashtra* and *Health System in India – Crisis and*

Alternatives. He is co-author of the popular book *Dissenting Diagnosis*, which exposed malpractices in private health care in India. He played a central role in drafting the Patients' Rights Charter developed by National Human Rights Commission, and is actively involved in campaigns for patient's rights, social regulation of the private healthcare sector, and developing a system for universal health care.

T. Sundararaman completed his MBBS and MD in internal medicine from Jawaharlal Institute of Postgraduate Medical Education & Research, Puducherry (1984) and then served as faculty member and professor in that department for the next 22 years. In 2002 he shifted to full time work in health systems strengthening becoming the first director of the State Health Resource Centre in Chhattisgarh (2002 to 2007) and then the first executive director of the National Health Systems Resource Centre from 2007 to 2014. In these capacities, he pioneered many non-market-based approaches to strengthening public health systems in Chhattisgarh and then offered design and technical assistance to the National Rural Health Mission. His contributions included the design and implementation of the Mitanins and Accredited Social Health Activist programmes and strengthening community participation, district health planning and innovations in human resource management and health management information systems. He has served as a member or chairperson on a number of important health policy committees and joint monitoring missions at the international, national and state levels. He retired as a professor and the dean of the School of Health Systems Studies at the Tata Institute of Social Sciences. He has published a significant number of research papers and books.

Louise Tillin is a professor of politics and currently the director of King's India Institute at King's College, London. Her research interests span federalism, democracy and territorial politics in India and the history and politics of social policy design and implementation. Her books include *Remapping India: New States and their Political Origins* (Hurst & Co/ Oxford University Press, 2013), *Politics of Welfare: Comparisons across Indian States* (with Rajeshwari Deshpande and K.K. Kailash, New Delhi, Oxford University Press, 2015), *Indian Federalism* (New Delhi, Oxford University Press, 2019) and *The Politics of Poverty Reduction in India: The UPA Government, 2004 to 2014* (with James Chiriyankandath, Diego Maiorano and James Manor) (New Delhi, Orient Blackswan, 2020). She was awarded the Leverhulme Research Fellowship (2018–19). She is the King's PI on the Horizon 2020 European Training Network *Global India,* led by Dublin City University.

Acknowledgements

We would like to acknowledge, with many thanks, the Thakur Family Foundation (TFF) for making this project possible. Mr. Dinesh Thakur and Mr. Prashant Reddy, on behalf of the TFF have been both gracious and supportive. We are thankful to all the authors for readily agreeing to be part of the project despite their other commitments. Dr Caroline Netto's assistance towards organizing the conference at the Bangalore International Centre, where drafts of the chapters were first presented, is gratefully acknowledged.

We are entirely responsible for the selection of authors and the editorial suggestions made.

Mohan Rao and Balveer Arora

1 Introduction

Public Health and Federalism: Where Are We and Where Do We Need to Go?

Mohan Rao and Balveer Arora

It is of course a cliché that India is a land of great diversities, and its ecological, demographic and socioeconomic differences reflect in profound epidemiological and health system differences. In this context, a one-size-fits-all health policy is not only ineffective but also significantly wasteful. This is how health policy is normally devolved to lower administrative units, but certain health policy objectives can only be served by centralisation. This is obviously the case for measures to control pandemics, but it also applies in such matters as intellectual property rights and the regulation of drugs and pharmaceuticals. Thus, public health policy always faces a conundrum: what mix of decentralised and centralised policies best serves the people's health? This volume is an effort to address many of the questions this conundrum raises.

This introductory chapter is divided into several parts. First, we spell out the theoretical and conceptual framework that seeks to read federalism into public health policies and practices in independent India. We then lay out how this volume has attempted to address the most pressing issues that confront public health policy in the federal context.

The authors in this volume have tried to weave into their papers on public health issues the two symbiotic concepts of federalism and democracy. Many have tried to go beyond the immediate context of the Covid-19 years to grapple with issues in public health policy that have plagued the country since it began its journey as a republic.

In the next part of this introductory chapter, we tease out the main strands of the arguments that have been developed by the contributors, who were selected to give us their considered assessments of how federalism and public health can be combined for the greater public good. Finally, we will draw some tentative conclusions that emerge from the juxtaposition of these two central concerns of this collection of essays.

I

This curated project was born during the Covid-19 pandemic, and it unquestionably bears the mark of those troubled times. The question that was

DOI: 10.4324/9781003568711-1

asked then in federal systems across the world that grappled with an exceptional global public health emergency was whether federalism was a bane or a boon in dealing with the crisis.[1,2] Public health is a concern that is best handled at its most fundamental level, namely beginning at the local level within districts within states. Epidemics are exceptions to this rule, however, and the principle of subsidiarity clearly applies. National and even global dimensions were superimposed on the health concerns of local populations, and the temptation to centralise decision-making was evident. Some systems were more prone to centralisation than others, and even democratic values were given short shrift in the melee that marked the first phases of the pandemic.

It may be useful, at the outset, to dwell upon some relevant dimensions of the basic structure of Indian federalism that are relevant to our concerns. Being a notable example of the devolutionary model of federal construction, federalism in India, through its downward extension as a cascade of powers, can be visualised as enriching the federal principle in significant ways by introducing multiple levels of democratic self-government institutions. The question arises whether the classical dual-polity framework that was initially adopted for the Indian federal system was the most suitable or whether a multilevel framework would more adequately meet the requirements of the problem at hand by introducing a greater measure of participatory democracy. This question was posed in the following terms by Nirmal Mukarji and Balveer Arora in the context of the Sarkaria Commission Report on Centre-State Relations:

> Should India continue to conform to a two-level federation, or should it (gradually) move towards multilevel federalism? Decentralisation below the State level would thus require a new system of governance which would go beyond mere development – linked administrative decentralisation and enable district and lower institutions to become truly self-governing. India would then have cascading federalism, a federation of federations. . . . Such a radically new approach might help to meet the challenge of pressures from below for effective political participation.[3]

The functional need for multilevel governance and planning gives rise to the concept of a cascading flow of powers and functions. It intersects the demands for self-governance rising from below. Since the lists of powers and jurisdictions of each level of government were borrowed from a centralised unitary state seeking to decentralise, there was an implicit logic of subsidiarity at play. However, overriding powers were liberally strewn across the demarcation of levels. The concurrent list of legislative powers, which is essentially a state list unless the Centre chooses to enact legislation on a particular issue, was transformed over time into an enabling mechanism for central intervention in a wide variety of spheres.

The strong-Centre concept gained currency, but the need for stronger states to effectively shoulder the myriad responsibilities entrusted to them was slower in progressing. The paramount question that needs to be asked when we consider social welfare policies is whether we need a Centre stronger than the one already envisaged in the Constitution or we need to strengthen the capabilities of states. Effective health policy depends on state capacity to provide the basic health care needed, though neoliberal solutions would have it otherwise.

We need to further ask what are the core concepts inherent in multilevel federal systems, their strengths and weaknesses, and what distinguishes them from multilevel governance of the conventional variety in a unitary state? The division of legislative and executive powers is at the core of the federal structure. The 'cascade principle' for the distribution of powers between levels of self-government in devolutionary federal systems is a powerful and persuasive one. It also clearly departs from the multilevel governance principle which characterises many decentralised unitary states seeking more efficient administration. The difference lies in the fact that self-government (*swaraj*) is the foundational principle.

Coping with Covid-19 was a primary concern, and pandemic governance revealed itself to be a stress test for Indian federalism. The public health policy that unfolded sought to deal successively with the measures needed to combat the pandemic and its political and economic consequences. We can distinguish three phases. In the first phase, federalism was suspended, and in the second, there was a relapse into the quasi-federal mode, with the Centre staying in the driving seat. Finally, in the third phase, federalism staged a comeback, albeit in a limited manner and under duress. This is forcefully brought out by T. Sundararaman and Daksha Parmar in their contribution to this volume.

The powers of third-tier governments in multilevel federal systems – the *panchayats* and the municipalities – depend on the extent of delegation of powers by the state legislatures and governments; the initial experience was that the cascade of delegated powers tended to stop at the state level. As K.K. Shailaja, Kerala's former health minister, showed, states with functional local bodies were able to respond more effectively during the pandemic,[4,5,] but the cascade tended to falter and stop at the state level when the flow was reduced from the Centre, in a ripple effect. Federalism also had to confront a counterforce: populism.

Populism is marked by popular appeal over the heads of constituted levels and authorities with a preference for a direct dialogue with the people. The preferred mode of communication was obviously the mass media channels, radio and television, and nationwide addresses with conflicting messages multiplied. The opportunities generated by information technology to directly interface with citizens for the transfer of benefits created what was described as 'hourglass federalism', where the middle level is pinched and squeezed, even bypassed. Health journalist Vidya Krishnan forcefully argued this point in a *Caravan* cover story titled 'Modi's Doctors: How Four Men Botched India's COVID Response".[6]

Here, the centralised regulatory state made its reappearance, whittling away information and accountability mechanisms. Ignoring the fact that lower levels of government meaningfully exercising their powers and responsibilities are valuable operational assets, micromanagerial techniques gain precedence.

The management of the migrant crisis revealed further flaws and weaknesses of interstate coordination. The shrinking of public spaces available to civil society organisations and the voluntary sector dependent on corporate social responsibility spending was evident, as funding was redirected towards schemes and missions favoured by the central ministries. The tightening of Foreign Contribution (Regulation) Act regulations further crippled civil society organisations that provided first relief during the migrant exodus crisis. Bureaucrats were penalised for facilitating the return of migrant labour to their villages, and insensitive handling by state authorities compounded the impression that what we were witnessing was not cooperative but chaotic federalism.[7]

Was the case for federalism lost by default? As Louise Tillin points out in her chapter, federalism was not given a fair chance, and the mechanisms available for making it work were never activated. The centralising impulse was further aggravated by directives emanating from international bodies which showed scant regard for democratic values. Their primary concerns lay elsewhere.

As K.K. Kailash observes in his chapter, the Constituent Assembly was painfully aware of the constraining circumstances in which it functioned, where, post-Partition, the concerns for the unity of the country weighed heavily. In all constitutions, original intent and contemporary content can and do vary with the passage of time. In the Indian case, it is important to revisit the original intent and view it shorn of the pressing concerns of a chaotic institutional ecosystem and the waves of violence at that time. It can be argued that if India has survived as an electoral democracy for so long, it is in no small measure because it has developed a resilient federal architecture of institutions. The checks and balances provided by federalism are superimposed on those put in place at the union level between the three branches of state institutions.

While federalism and democracy are closely intertwined in the institutional ecosystem, there is one type of democratic rule that is incompatible with federalism. That is the absolute majoritarian version of democratic systems, which violates the basic tenets of federalism, namely the right to existence and the protection of minorities.[8] This guaranteed existence is an essential feature of federalism, and no majority can override this fundamental right afforded by a federal constitution. Hence federalism needs to be considered a significant counter-power against majoritarian democracy such that it is inconsistent and incompatible with the federal principles that constitute part of the basic structure of the Constitution.

The original intent of the framers of the Constitution shines through with remarkable clarity. The building of a welfare state respectful of the basic principles that motivated the freedom movement, namely *swaraj* and the respect of democratic values, is the bedrock of the constitutional edifice of responsible government.[9] Disorderly decolonisation imposed an urgent need for the consolidation of the young independent state. The wisdom of the founding fathers in the Constituent Assembly lay in not mistaking the quelling of existing turmoil as their main mission; they transcended the immediate context to lay the foundations of a durable democracy, forsaking neither their principles nor their vision of what the Indian Republic was intended to represent. The unitarian temptation was strong, and so was the urge to situate India ideologically as a reaction to the immediate context and the tragic turn of events. After intense debate, the Constituent Assembly opted for a secular republic with safeguards for the rights of minorities. Justice was the cornerstone, and all state policies were predicated on the principle that they would subserve the cause of equity and justice.

Traumatised by the unprecedented horrors and dislocation of Partition, the Constituent Assembly was naturally focussed on the need to ensure the unity and integrity of the new nation. The fear of excessive federalism was cogently articulated, the risks of centrifugal and fissiparous forces overwhelming the young Republic passionately evoked, and the framework finally adopted departed significantly from all existing models of federalism. The Constituent Assembly devised a system which seemed most suited to the needs of the time and the requirements of a federal society. Political processes generated by the logic of a federal democracy completed this work in course of time.

India's political institutions are now widely recognised as a vigorous albeit hybrid variant of the federal species. Self-rule and shared rule have been combined in unorthodox ways that have enabled the Indian Union to not only survive but also flourish in all its diversity. It is a valuable legacy that must be protected for India to survive as a democracy.

II

Let us begin with some observations that are self-evident truths but of course are not thought so by many people who shape health policy. First, health is far beyond medicine, and we have solid historical and intellectual armoury for believing that. Second, health is a public good to be provided by the state, and here, too, we have strong support, both philosophically and empirically. Third, health is determined, above all, by social, economic and political factors. This is a school of thought in public health that has a long and rich history in social epidemiology, as George Rosen reveals in his classic history of public health.[10]

It is with these in mind that we shall briefly survey what the experience of the Covid-19 pandemic, in India in particular, can teach us. What we shall do is highlight a few salient lessons we might learn, should we wish to, for we seldom learn lessons from history, even if as tragedy. It is these issues that come to the fore now as the Covid-19 pandemic has ripped apart countries all across the globe, exposing all the hidden fissures within our societies, much like pandemics had done earlier. And there is so much interesting historical work on this – as the classic *Epidemics and Ideas* demonstrates.[11] Therefore, we must consider what main lessons we can learn so far from this truly global phenomenon.

First, what the pandemic reveals is a profound disconnect in the popular imagination, and in that of scientists too, about our relationship with nature. Donald Trump, Jair Bolsonaro and Narendra Modi are all dystopic consequences of this blindness. As David Harvey remarks,

> I have long refused the idea of 'nature' as outside of and separate from culture, economy and daily life. . . . Capital modifies the environmental conditions of its own reproduction but does so in a context of unintended consequences (like climate change) and against the autonomous and independent evolutionary forces that are perpetually shaping environmental conditions . . . Viruses mutate all the time, to be sure. But the circumstances in which a mutation becomes life-threatening depend on human actions. . . . But the economic and demographic impacts of the spread of the virus depend upon the preexisting cracks and vulnerabilities in the hegemonic economic model.[12]

Communicable diseases will always exist; viruses mutate, and new diseases will arise both due to global warming and our increasingly extractive invasions of nature that we hope to "conquer". The language of conquest that we use with reference to diseases is neither new nor confined to the military metaphors used during the Covid-19 pandemic. Readers might recall that the malaria eradication programme had a preparatory phase, an attack phase and a consolidation phase. This conquest of nature – of germs – arose when in the late nineteenth and early twentieth century, ideas of public health were drowned in militarist metaphors of the germ theory of disease. This was of course also the heyday of imperialism as countries of the West carved out their colonies across the globe. A broad understanding of how diseases occur in populations, and how social and economic factors shape them, was lost in the individual-based understanding of medicine. This was also the time when doctors consolidated themselves as a profession, following the Flexner Report in the US.[13]

Public health calls for action by the state; clinical medicine, more lucrative to doctors, does not. All such actions by the state involving populations, were, after 1917, labelled "socialistic" especially in the USA. That the Soviet Union became the first nation in the world to promise health care for all, irrespective of people's ability to pay, only fuelled the suspicion. The phrase "public health" was seen as tainted by communism, and the discipline was then variously called community health or preventive health. What was also clear is that curative care, marketised, was lucrative, whereas preventive health was not: there were no profits to be made, although human health improved as did productivity.

As Ed Yong argues,

> germ theory allowed people to collapse everything about disease into battles between pathogens and patients. Social matters such as inequality, housing, education, race, culture, psychology, and politics became irrelevancies. Ignoring them was noble; it made medicine and science more apolitical and objective. Ignoring them was also easier; instead of staring into the abyss of society's intractable ills, physicians could simply stare at a bug under a microscope and devise ways of killing it.[14]

Another factor that led to the decline of public health was the theory of epidemiological transition that gained acceptance in the 1950s. This theory argued that as countries modernised and industrialised, "pre-transition" diseases, primarily diseases of poverty and hunger and communicable diseases, would be replaced by non-communicable, so-called lifestyle diseases, diseases of affluence. That this theory was empirically weak and might not apply to all social settings was ignored, and the USA started shutting down its schools for public health. When the AIDS pandemic struck in the 1970s and 80s, the richest nation in the world found herself completely unaware. The same situation applied with Covid-19, made worse by the last 40 years of neo-liberal reforms.[15]

Second, of course is how even in the West, health systems have failed because of decades of neoliberal cuts in health budgets and consequent reforms involving greater and greater marketisation.[16] It is not the virus, but neoliberalism that is coming home to roost. The welfare state was based on the sound economic argument that health was a public good to be paid for proportionately by everyone so that no one would be deprived of health care or access to its determinants. As[17] argued, it also meant that blood was shared and not sold, attempting to create a community of equals, which also indicated that some things are beyond the picayune calculations of the market. Illness and deaths were not to be determined by matters of birth, caste, class, religion, gender or sexuality.

Imrana Qadeer et al.'s sharp essay in a recent volume traces how neoliberalism not only shaped economies but transformed health systems globally and within India.[18] It is neoliberalism that shaped the abandonment of the idea of the state-led Comprehensive Primary Health Care that had been enunciated at the historic Alma Ata conference of 1978. Qadeer et al. point out that now the idea of universal coverage through public–private partnerships (PPP) is also shaped by neoliberal concerns. As they argue, 'The neoliberal challenge to transform the scope of the medical market compelled governments to ignore Comprehensive Primary Health Care (CPHC) and opting for Universal Health Coverage (UHC)'. While welfare expenditures are cut, defence expenditures mount. They point out that in 2016–17, the budgets for health and defence were 33,000 crore and 246,000 crore, respectively.

Third, the pandemic has shown us that the private sector failed to rise to the challenges. Instead, it was the enfeebled, emaciated, resource-starved public health system that rose to the occasion. As happened earlier during the plague epidemic in Surat in 1994, many private institutions shut shop and melted away.[19] During the Covid-19 crisis, the private sector in medical care indulged in price gouging, refusal of treatment and a host of irregularities. They roped in super-profits, charging up to 10 lakh per person not requiring ICU care.[20] But corporate health care in India is driven not so much by upper class demands as by government concessions and tax write-offs. It is also driven by investments by the World Bank, private equity firms, venture capital and partnerships with foreign hospital chains, all of which demand returns of profits. The Bill and Melinda Gates Foundation, Klynveld Peat Marwick Goerdeler and Boston Consulting have emerged as major influencers, along with the Associated Chamber of Commerce and Industry of India and the Federation of Indian Chambers of Commerce and Industry. Indira Chakravarthi gives us the relevant figures: the International Finance Corporation alone, a member of the World Bank group, had an investment of USD 450 million in 2014, representing 30 per cent of the global investment portfolio. The other 70 per cent comes from private equity companies based in the US, Mauritius, Malaysia, Dubai and so on.[21] Supra-national financial bodies provide an impetus to centralisation.

Neoliberal globalisation has also been described as a global project to restore upper class privileges to the levels that prevailed early in the twentieth century, in a profound trickle up of wealth and resources.[22] Reducing the role of the state and increasing that of the market, irrespective of their social and indeed long-term economic costs, was thus at the centre of this model of therapy. Over this period, of course, the role of the World Bank in health sector development increased enormously, while that of the WHO shrivelled; indeed World Bank loans for one programme, malaria, exceeded the entire budget of the WHO.[23] The Bank is today 'the largest single source of health care finance in developing countries with an unparalleled degree of policy-making authority' (p. 143).[24] The health sector itself emerged as a leading source of multinational profits as the sectors in developing countries was prised open for investment in a range of areas from high-level technologies to insurance and indeed low-level ones such as routine immunisations under the new WTO regimes. All these health programmes are then initiated centrally, with obvious implications for the federal structure, a point made in Sundararaman and Parmar's essay in the volume.

Coming on top of the searing socioeconomic inequalities, the Covid-19 pandemic ripped apart our society and led to the collapse of the public health system. Starved for funds for decades, public institutions are a pale shadow of what they used to be. Beholden to commercial interests, their policy recommendations also arouse profound suspicion. For example, the Bill and Melinda Gates Foundation is a major funder to the WHO and also invests heavily in pharma companies and in vaccine production. Is it any wonder then that vaccination is viewed with suspicion for these commercial interests?

The promise of biomedical panaceas is deeply ingrained in the minds of health policy makers, but Covid-19 should have shown that medical magic bullets lose their power when deployed in a profoundly unequal society. From the USA to the UK, the pandemic has not been the leveller it was said to be: it affected the poor and the marginalised disproportionately. For instance, the Black populations in the UK and the USA had both disproportionate incidence rate, but also a higher case fatality rate.[25],[26] In India, of course, the pandemic was also an excuse for class warfare. While middle class and wealthy Indians stranded abroad were flown in, no arrangements were made for the millions of poor people with insecure jobs, locked in in cities with no wages to move to their villages. Those who started walking over vast distances were subjected to police brutality and sprayed with chemicals as if they were termites our Home Minister called refugees.[27] Hundreds lost their lives in this, the greatest tragic and preventable migration since the Partition.[28]

How did Covid-19 affect the poor, the *dalits*, *adivasis* and Muslims? In India, unfortunately, we do not routinely collect health data in relation to social class. But as Ashwini Deshpande and Rajesh Ramachandran showed, the proportion of employed upper castes dropped from 39 per cent to 32 per cent between December 2019 and April 2020. The fall in employment for the *dalits* was from 44 per cent to 24 per cent, three times that of the upper castes, and for *adivasis*, it went from 48 per cent to 33 per cent.[29] Indeed, reports indicate that the life expectancy declined by two years between 2020 and 2021.[30] Both social and economic marginalisation, have both profound and long-term consequences. Even before the pandemic, *adivasis* had the lowest life expectancy in India. The differences between *adivasis* and Savarna Hindus are almost four years for women and five years for men, and the gap between *dalits* and Savarna Hindus is more than three years for both men and women. Life expectancy among Muslims is about one year lower than that of Savarna Hindus.[31] Even before the pandemic, health care costs alone drove 55 million people below the poverty line each year.

Jean Dreze et al. examined SRS data and found evidence of 'slowdown, pauses and reversals in infant mortality decline in large parts of India in 2017 and 2018'.[32] In urban areas, the infant mortality rate stagnated, but it increased in Chattisgarh, Jharkhand, Madhya Pradesh and Uttar Pradesh. The authors speculate that this could be the outcome of demonetisation. The post-Covid-19 scenario can only be worse with increases in hunger and unemployment.

In the countries of the West, the increasing inequalities in health as a consequence of neoliberal reforms have been well documented.[33] At the height of the second wave, India passed three million cases of Covid-19, adding nearly 70,000 cases every day, although testing levels were abysmally low because of infrastructural constraints.[34] For reasons not definitively known, the case fatality ratio was relatively low, less than 2 per cent. Over the same period, deaths from other causes including tuberculosis and hunger were much higher and are slated to increase as the public health system has had to concentrate on Covid-19.[35] Lack of access to reproductive health care likely increased maternal and child deaths. The fact that we were exporting personal protective equipment when health workers were dying for lack of it is telling of the political economy of health care in India.

Officially, the deaths due to Covid are said to have numbered 5,33,570.[36] However, the demographer Guilmoto[37] estimated the real number to be close to 2.2 million, the highest in the world after adjusting for the young age structure of the population. People by the millions died, and their cries for help were silenced. This is death by neglect.

III

The papers in this volume are by eminent scholars and practitioners of public health and by scholars of political science who have written extensively on federalism. We, the editors, carefully selected the scholars and suggested the chapters they have written. After a wonderful workshop at the Bangalore International Centre, where draft papers were presented and discussed, and suggestions were made to authors by all the scholars at the workshop. The authors then went on to revise their papers and we, editors, are very pleased indeed with what we now have as a volume.

Marked by profound scholarship, one quality that unites these papers is their enormous respect for data. The data has been verified from other sources such as the WHO and triangulated with other data such as on employment and poverty. However, this also means that there is sadly very little by way of qualitative data. We do not have a single ethnographic chapter in this volume, a huge absence. But this is not surprising, given the impact of the pandemic that brought all data collection to a halt. The essays in this volume illustrate the need to innovate on federal principles to achieve the objectives of an inclusive public health policy. They are presented in five parts.

First, we look at the federal context in which health policy is formulated and implemented. From the original intent of the Constituent Assembly to the ways unequal states struggled with the pandemic and other health crises, the framework for addressing these vital issues is laid down as a precursor to the detailed analysis which follows in the second part, dealing with regional variations and asymmetries, the outcome of uneven development on various axes. Not surprisingly, private-sector growth also follows these contours of inequalities.

In the third part, we look at the regulatory architecture that governs public health issues from both the supply side and the maintenance of minimum standards in the provision of medicines and services. In the fourth section, the provision of health security in a federal polity is discussed, from the impact of decentralisation on health outcomes to the control of communicable diseases. Finally, in the fifth and last section, we have powerful testimonies on the pathetic state of the public health systems, the dilemmas of health financing and the distant dream of universal health coverage. We hope that this *tour de horizon* of the vast landscape of public health policy and practice against the landscape of a fractious federal polity will throw light on the ways India can move forward in this sphere so critical to the well-being of its populace, of which a sizeable chunk is made up of the very young.

In a fascinating chapter, K.K. Kailash looks at the debates on health in the Constituent Assembly. There was a consensus that health and education should be priorities for the new state, to distinguish it from the colonial one and also to claim legitimacy. There is consensus as well that provision of health care to all citizens is a responsibility of the state. Indeed, there is explicit concern here that private players and profits have no role to play in health care. What there is no consensus on is the role of the Centre and the provinces, with some arguing for greater centralisation, while others resist this. It is equally clear that good health is a right, not charity. As the Covid-19 pandemic made clear, the fact that the post-colonial state failed to keep its tryst with destiny, neglecting public health profoundly, meant that when the pandemic hit us, our health infrastructure was found woefully inadequate. We failed with infrastructure, human resources and every aspect of a public health system that K. Sujatha Rao addresses in her chapter.

In her chapter, Louise Tillin notes the tensions that exist across all federal systems when it comes to public health, in particular public health emergencies. The first wave of the pandemic saw the stamp of authoritarian centralisation, while the fiercer second wave saw India's leaders react as did other authoritarian populists such as the leaders of Brazil and the USA. Interestingly, she notes that the movement towards greater centralisation also stems from international health governance such as the WHO's revised International Health Regulations and the imperatives of new technological tools for surveillance and data management. This is a matter of enormous importance, that has not received adequate attention in health policy circles. What is neglected, however, is institutional bodies such as the Inter-State Council which could discuss and coordinate responses across states, without eroding states' powers.

Kevin James, in his chapter, examines the laws that govern of public health emergencies in India: The Epidemic Diseases Act (EDA), 1887. A bare-bones colonial-era legislation, the EDA primarily empowers state governments to prescribe temporary regulations to prevent the spread of epidemic diseases and empowers the Centre to inspect certain vehicles and passengers. As a pre-constitutional law, it does not reflect the constitutional commitments to welfare, justice, equality or dignity, and it offers next to no guidance on duties. The Disaster Management Act, which was invoked in the Covid-19 pandemic, does not confer precise authority in matters related to public health emergencies. We thus saw extreme centralisation during the first wave and an abandonment of responsibilities during the second. While a comprehensive guide for such emergencies is in draft form, it has not yet been put out for public discussion. This chapter should act as a framework for that public discussion.

Rama V. Baru in her chapter surveys the growth of the private medical sector in India over the years, identifying four distinct phases. Their growth in the 1980s was facilitated by both public policy and the network of caste and kin associations that stretched from the diasporic Indians in the USA to their home bases in India. These entrepreneurial caste groups, especially in southern and western India, have transformed the medical landscape. Wielding considerable political powers in their respective states, they are able to quell whatever feeble efforts the Centre makes towards regulation. We thus have here forces asserting themselves over the Centre, even as efforts are made to introduce uniformity across disparate states in both medical education and medical care.

K. Srinath Reddy and Manu Raj Mathur in their chapter call for a move away from 'obfuscated' to 'functional' federalism. They note the problematic category of non-communicable diseases (NCDs), which comprises diseases of different causations and pathologies which cannot all be categorised as lifestyle diseases. The states of India differ sharply in terms of epidemiological patterns; while some states have a predominantly NCD burden, other states carry a triple burden of NCDs, communicable diseases and maternal and child health concerns. Thus, India's translating and passing on the attainment of the UN Sustainable Development Goals to these diverse states is problematic and calls for a complete rethink. The states differ not only epidemiologically but also in population distribution and age structure. A one-size-fits-all prescription is both short-sighted and wasteful of resources.

K. Sujatha Rao, former Health Secretary, who should know, says even she has had problems obtaining data. What seems to have happened over the last few years is that officials are either withholding official data or modifying it to render comparisons inapposite. Her chapter attests to the profound lack of infrastructure, human and otherwise, across all states, noting the differences between states. Is it surprising, then, that a woman born in Kerala can expect to live 13 years longer than one born in Uttar Pradesh and nine years longer than one born in Bihar? States have also differing abilities to raise resources for health care: southern states feel they are contributing more to the central pool and do not obtain adequate financial support, straining the federal structure.

Shreya Shrivastava and Dhvani Mehta in their chapter, 'Drug Regulation and Federalism in India', trace the efforts at drug regulation in the country. The deaths of 66 infants in Gambia and 68 infants in Uzbekistan in 2022 due to contaminated cough syrup manufactured in India brought the failure of drug regulation in India into international limelight, but 12 children died in 2019 in Jammu from the same cause, but nothing happened and the matter was ignored.[38] Today, however, at a time of toxic hyper-nationalism, courageous individuals who call attention to these are labelled "anti-national", acting on the behest of the multi-national pharma industry. In their revealing chapter, Shrivastava and Mehta trace the hesitant growth of the regulatory structure and its utter fragmentation across states. Efforts to centralise – evidently necessary in this case – have been thwarted not just by federalist impulses in the states but by drug companies and India's tardy judicial system. This excellent chapter traces historically, the efforts and weaknesses of India's drug regulatory mechanisms in the context of India's federal structure that thwarts regulation and standards.

Abhay Shukla and Shweta Marathe trace the efforts to regulate the private sector in medical care in India. As is well known, India has the world's largest and least regulated medical sector; there is a mountain of literature on the unnecessary tests and investigations, unnecessary surgeries and price gouging practiced here. The Covid-19 pandemic brought this especially to light. While efforts were made through central legislation to enact the Clinical Establishment Act (CEA), states have not accepted or implemented it. Instead, states like Maharashtra and Karnataka – which saw the most egregious behaviour by the private sector during the Covid-19 crisis, enacted laws of their own that were fiercely opposed by the medical community, which succeeded in watering down many stringent regulations. While such regulations are necessary, Shukla and Marathe argue that they are not sufficient. Only strengthening the capacities in the public sector will wean away patients from a rapacious system. This was seen to occur, for example, when Tamil Nadu strengthened maternal and child health services in the primary health centres. There was a sharp decline in admissions of pregnant women in the private sector, accompanied, hearteningly, by a decline in caesarean sections. They also show that market failures in the private medical care industry are subsidised by public funds in the form of insurance schemes.

Even in a federal structure, certain policies and institutions are best served by centralisation. This is certainly the case with drugs and pharmaceuticals. Biswajit Dhar illustrates this in his survey of the growth of this sector. The major impetus for the growth of this sector, to make India self-sufficient, came with establishing public-sector undertakings for the manufacture of pharmaceuticals including vaccines. In the last few decades, however, this policy was abandoned for doctrinaire reasons. The perils of decentralisation were brought home during the Covid-19 pandemic, when the Centre passed on the responsibility of vaccinating the population to the states. Given the financial constraints of some of the states, they were in no position to buy the vaccines from the manufacturers, whereas other states could do so; this led to profound vaccine inequities within the country, even as we were exporting vaccines.

Ramila Bisht in her chapter examines how, if at all, federalism has impacted women's health, marked by diversities across states but with a strong north–south divide. Examining the evolution of health policy, she notes that despite the states pay a larger proportion of health expenditures, the Centre exercises disproportionate policy influence. The National Rural Health Mission (NRHM) represented a positive step towards narrowing gross differences in health outcomes in the states, but it has not been able to reverse these. Indeed, better-off states were able to use more funds than the BIMARU states that sorely needed to catch up, thus increasing interstate differences.

Imrana Qadeer, Sourindra Mohan Ghosh and P.M. Arathi in their chapter point to one important paradox: the average heights of Indians, instead of increasing with increasing wealth of the country, seems to be declining. Yet the fact that obesity is increasing in the country is used to reduce the recommended intake of calories, and this is then utilised to undermine the Public Distribution System for food, while also being used to under-estimate poverty levels in the country. How was this sleight of hand achieved? Through a rigorous critique of the methodology and the assumptions underlying the reworking of the recommended calories, they reveal how the science of nutrition is trimmed to cut the cloth of policy makers. This has been helped by centralisation and the closure of institutions like the National Nutrition Monitoring Bureau, while at the same time data collection in other spheres has also been seriously compromised. Moving from food security to nutrition security thus entails individualising a public health problem, making it amenable to technical interventions such as fortification. In this case, centralisation was instrumentalised to obfuscate the nutritional situation in the country and at the same time seriously underestimate poverty levels.

T. Sundararaman and Daksha Parmar in their chapter review India's tryst with communicable diseases and with federalism. Communicable diseases are on the concurrent list and receive the honour of central funding for vertical programmes. These programmes are usually focussed on a single disease, usually revolve around some technology and have separate funding and staff. Initially, these programmes met with success, but the successes were short-lived, and the programmes did not strengthen public health systems in general.

State health systems are on the state list, which entails fragmented accountability. Towards the end of the 1970s, recognising the limitations of vertical programmes, the WHO gave a call for universal primary health care in 1978. But the world turned upside down soon after and the role of WHO shrank in the neo-liberal world.[39] What shaped health systems globally were the structural adjustment programmes and the health policies they shaped. Vertical programmes made their appearance again, while the public health systems were starved of funds. State policies, dictated by international financial institutions, were towards subsidising the growth of the private sector in health care. While these policies call for a greater role for the Centre – for alignment with global policy and for reasons of technical capacity in technological assessment, patent management, procurement and regulation – the implementation is under state control. Sundararaman and Parmar take the problems with Covid-19 management to show how both over-centralisation and reliance on the private sector boomeranged.

As we know, this centralisation was also one of the features of the Covid-19 response, and what a disaster that was! This is attested by Harsh Mander's searing personal experience of getting Covid-19 and what happened to him at India's premier public health institution. We are infinitely grateful he survived and was nominated, with Karvan-e-Mohabbat for the Nobel Peace Prize, which unfortunately the organisation did not win.

Surveying a whole host of data on finances towards health, at both the central and state levels over a substantial time period from a number of sources, Indranil notes that the initial years of the NRHM did make some attempts to bridge the gap between states. However, with the 14th Financial Commission recommendations coming into force, the share of central funding to states declined. There is also wide variation between the states in their ability to mobilise resources for health. The imposition of the Goods and Services Tax further constrained the fiscal space of states. Schemes such as the Rashtriya Swasthya Bima Yojana and subsequently the Pradhan Mantri Jan Arogya Yojana, he argues, blur constitutional responsibilities and lead to greater fiscal centralisation. Noting that there is a clear inverse – and often impoverishing – relationship between public health spending and personal out-of-pocket expenditures, Indranil makes the argument for greater public spending from both the Centre and the states.

As A.K. Shiva Kumar reveals in his chapter, the Indian government, while neglecting primary health care, has evolved a one-size-fits-all strategy despite the fact that health is a state subject. He shows the marked variation across states in terms of health outcomes and health system strengths. There are also wide variations between the states in terms of health expenditures. In a sharp critique, he shows you how the underfunded system, relying on inadequate and ill-thought-out insurance mechanisms with private provisioning, are not only unsustainable but deeply iniquitous.

We acknowledge many limitations in this volume, not least the fact that we do not have chapters on caste, gender and the utter marginalisation of groups such as transgenders. However, all the rich chapters are based on an amazing review of the literature, a solid mastery of the facts and acute analysis.

IV

In sum, public health in a federal democracy needs to place at the centre of its preoccupations the core republican values that underpin a state wedded to inclusiveness. In this volume, we have attempted to assemble studies that reflect on issues that are likely to dominate thinking on these questions for the foreseeable future. Responses to health emergencies has to be built into the system in a humane and inclusive way, and we need to certainly shore up our humanitarian responses in times of crises. These responsibilities cannot be left to voluntary and charitable organisations alone, particularly when they are viewed with a jaundiced eye by authorities and stymied in their capacity to respond to humanitarian crises through myriad regulations meant to restrict their activities.

An area that is also crying out for action at the central level is the tightening of regulations regarding quality control of drugs and pharmaceutical products. The scandals surrounding spurious and adulterated medicines administered on unsuspecting patients in India and abroad are all too frequent.[40] There are areas in which federalism is a source of strength, and others in which the need for a credible national policy framework demands shared responsibility mechanisms that are capable of yielding results.

In this perspective, it is important to note that the Supreme Court of India, in a unanimous recent judgment, affirmed, 'Our Constitution is federal in character' and further made the following observations:

> The principles of federalism and democracy are interlinked and work together in synergy to secure to all citizens justice, liberty, equality and dignity and to promote fraternity among them. . . . the principles of democracy and federalism are essential features of our Constitution and form a part of the basic structure. . . . Our interpretation of the Constitution must enhance the spirit of federalism and democracy together.[41]

It is important to recall that the original design vested substantial legislative powers and responsibilities in state governments for key developmental activities. A literal reading of the Indian Constitution can, however, be misleading. Multiple overlaps have occurred, not merely in the concurrent spheres of jurisdiction but also in spheres explicitly assigned to the states. New elements of the division of powers and responsibilities have begun to assume importance, overshadowing to a certain extent the issues that dominated the reform agenda of the earlier period. While the issue of distribution of responsibilities and powers in federal political systems is generally contentious, a gross mismatch between the two can lead to serious tensions.

The federal dialogue with the states is often pre-empted by central administrative and policy decisions. The Centre often decides on a particular course of action and only thereafter seeks inputs from the states. Consensus building is after the decision, not before. This mode of decision-making is increasingly contested. In the emerging context of assertive states' rights, mere consultation may not suffice. What is needed is a more proactively inclusive decisional process.

Notes

1 Rupak Chattopadhaya, Felix Knipling, Diana Chebenova, Liam Whittington and Philip Gonzalez (Eds) (2021), "Forum of Federations" in *Federalism and the Response to COVID-19: A Comparative Analysis*, New York: Routledge.

2 The India Forum (Ed) (2021), *India and the Pandemic: The First Year*, Hyderabad: Orient Blackswan.
3 Nirmal Mukarji and Balveer Arora (1992), "Restructuring Federal Democracy" in *Federalism in India: Origins and Development*, New Delhi: Centre for Policy Research/Vikas, page 270.
4 K.K.Shailaja and Manju Sara Rajan (2023), *My Life as a Comrade: The Story of an Extraordinary Politician and the World That Shaped Her*, Juggernaut, New Delhi.
5 Neelanjan Sircar (2020), "The Politics of Vishwas: Political Mobilisation in the 2019 National Election", *Contemporary South Asia*, 26th May.
6 Vidya Krishnan (2022), "Modi's Doctors: How Four Men Botched India's COVID Response, *Caravan*, Vol.14, Issue 3, March.
7 Harsh Mander (2023), *Burning Pyres, Mass Graves and a State That Failed Its People: India's Covid Tragedy*, Speaking Tiger, New Delhi.
8 Partha Chatterjee (1999), "Secularism and Tolerance" in Rajeev Bhargava (Ed), *Secularism and Its Critics*, OUP, New Delhi.
9 Balveer Aroroa and K.K Kailash (2018), "Beyond Quasi Federalism: Change and Continuity in Indian Federalism", *Studies in Indian Politics*, 6(2), 297–302.
10 George Rosen (1993), *A History of Public Health*, The John Hopkins University Press, Baltimore and London.
11 T. Ranger and P. Slack (Eds) (1992), *Epidemics and Ideas: Essays on the Historical Perception of Pestilence*, Cambridge University Press, Cambridge.
12 D. Harvey (2020, March 20), Anti-Capitalist Politics in the Time of Covid-19. *Jacobin*, https://jacobinmag.com/2020/03/david-harvey-coronavirus, accessed 11.10.2021.
13 George Rosen, *op cit.*
14 E. Yong (2021, September 29), We're Already Barreling Toward the Next Pandemic. *The Atlantic*, www.the Atlantic.com/health/archive/2021/09america-prepared, accessed 3.10.2021.
15 Mohan Rao (2022), "The Exsanguination of Public Health in India", *National Medical Journal of India*, 35, 1–2.
16 Leo Panitch and Colin Leys (Eds) (2010), *Morbid Symptoms*, Health Under Capitalism, Monthly Review Press, New York.
17 R.M. Titmuss (1970), *The Gift Relationship: From Human Blood to Social Policy*, The New Press, London.
18 I. Qadeer, P.M. Saxena, and P.M. Arathi (Eds.) (2019), *Universalising Health Care in India: From Care to Coverage*, Aakar Books, New Delhi.
19 G. Shah (1997), *Public Health and Urban Development: The Plague in Surat*, Sage, New Delhi.
20 Harsh Mander, *op cit.*
21 I. Chakravarthi (2019), "Universal Healthcare and Health Assurance Through Healthcare Industry and Market Mechanisms" in I. Qadeer, et al. (Eds) *Universalising Healthcare in India: From Care to Coverage*, Aakar Books, New Delhi.
22 D. Harvey (2005), *A Brief History of Neoliberalism*, Oxford University Press, New York.
23 M. Rao and R. Loewenson (2000), *The Political Economy of the Assault on Health*, Background Paper, People's Health Assembly, Dhaka.
24 J.Y. Kim, J.V. Millen, A. Irwin, and J. German (2000), *Dying for Growth: Global Inequality and the Health of the Poor*, Common Courage Press, Maine.
25 Dielle J. Lundberg, Elizabeth Wrigley-Field, Ahyoung Cho et al (2023), "COVID-19 Mortality by Race and Ethnicity in US Metropolitan and Nonmetropolitan Areas, March 2020 to February 2022", *JAMA*, 6 (5), 2nd May.

26 Mathew L.Bosworth, Tamanna Ahmed, Tim Larsen et al (2023), "Ethnic Differences in COVID-19 Mortality in the Second and Third Waves of the Pandemic During the Vaccine Rollout: A Retrospective, Population-Based, Cohort Study", *BMC Medicine*, 21,13.
27 "Infiltrators Are Termites, Will Throw Them Out: Amit Shah", *The Hindu*, 11th April 2019.
28 Baxi, Upendra (2021), "Exodus Constitutionalism: Mass Migration in Covid-19 Lockdown Times", *India and the Pandemic: The First Year*, Orient BlackSwan, Hyderabad.
29 A. Deshpande and R. Ramachandran (2020, August 22), "Differential Impact of COVID-19 and the Lockdown", *The Hindu*.
30 The Hindu (2021), "Life Expectancy in India in India Dropped by Two Years Due to COVID-19: Study", *The Hindu*.
31 S. Vyas, P. Hathi, and A. Gupta (2022), "Social Disadvantage, Economic Inequality and Life Expectancy in Nine Indian States", *PNAS*, https://doi/10.1073/pnas2109226119, accessed 3/5/22.
32 J. Dreze, et al. (2020), *Pauses and Reversals of Infant Mortality Decline in 2017 and 2018*, https://ssrn.com/abstract-372700, accessed 15.10.2021.
33 P. Townsend, M. Whitehead, and N. Davidson (1992), *Inequalities in Health*, Penguin, Harmondsworth.
34 Mander, Harsh (2023), *op cit.*
35 Mander, Harsh (2023), *op cit.*
36 India COVID – Coronavirus Statistics, *WHO Covid-19 Dashboard*, Geneva.
37 C.Z. Guilmoto (2021), *Estimating the Death Toll of the Covid Pandemic in India*, https://doi.org/10.1101/2021.
38 Dinesh S.Thakur and Prashant Reddy T. (2022), *The Truth Pill: The Myth of Drug Regulation in India*, Simon and Schuster, New Delhi.
39 Rao, Mohan (2009), "Health for All" and Neoliberal Globalisation: An Indian Rope Trick" in Leo Panitch and Colin Leys (Eds) *Morbid Symptoms: Health Under Capitalism*, Merlin Press, London.
40 Dinesh Thakur and Prashant Reddy (2022) *op cit.* See Chapter 8 in this volume.
41 GNCTD v Union of India, 2023.

Part I

The Federal Context

2 Public Health in the Constituent Assembly

K.K. Kailash

As the Covid-19 pandemic spread, the health infrastructure in many parts of the country gave way, and many people lost their lives. To make matters worse, the acute economic and humanitarian crisis resulting from the sudden lockdowns caused continued pain and distress. The crisis raised many questions. Who is best equipped to handle a public health crisis like Covid-19? Is India's scratchy management without unity of purpose a failure of the federal spirit? Who should finance the prevention, mitigation and recovery from the health crisis? Suddenly, everyone was talking about health, but nobody seemed to be doing anything about it.

In this chapter, I examine the Constituent Assembly Debates (CAD) to map the thoughts of the founding minds on public health, which may help us make sense of various questions asked since the spread of the pandemic. While scholarly studies on the CAD have examined issues like democracy, equality, justice, property and secularism, public health has not necessarily received attention. I focus on the basic questions, including the place of health in the Indian Constitution and its commitment to good health services for its citizens. I also attempt to understand how the constitution-makers visualised the public health federal interface.

The chapter is divided into four sections and proceeds as follows. The first section spells out the sources and the methods adopted in the study. The second section maps the different dimensions of health as discussed in the CA. The third section focuses exclusively on the concerns and questions of health in the CA and the documents and reports available around the time of the CA deliberations. The final section summarises and concludes.

Section I
Sources and Methods

In this section, essentially based on explorative desk research, I examine the position of health in the CAD. I did an intensive manual analysis and not a computer-aided exploration of the entire CAD, given that some paragraphs appeared to repeat many times over in the database. The manual route gave me better control over the analysis and enabled me to identify five different dimensions

DOI: 10.4324/9781003568711-3

Table 2.1 Key Health-Related Terms in the Constituent Assembly Debates

S. No	*Subject*
1	Health, Healthy, Unhealthy
2	Disease, Diseased
3	Cholera, Smallpox, Malaria, Malarial, Plague
4	Hospital
5	Nutrition, Malnutrition, Hunger
6	Medical, Medicine
7	Hygiene, Unhygienic
8	Quarantine
9	Sick, Sickness

of health in the CA which I discuss next. My aims included understanding first whether public health was a concern in the making of the constitution; second, how the concept of health was understood; third, which level of government was responsible for health and finally, the issue of resources and finances.

In this study, I rely on the Constituent Assembly's deliberations digitised by the CADIndia project.[1] This is a valuable and user-friendly source for the CAD. Their super-helpful search engine is convenient for filtering searches and locating debates. I also looked at other reports and documents to place health in the context of independent India's developmental agenda. These included the report of the Advisory Planning Board (1946), Congress Ministries at Work by Mitra (ed) (nd), and Comments on the Provisions contained in the Draft Constitution (1948), Grant (1943), Raja (1946).

I followed three steps when examining the CAD. I first searched for the pre-identified terms listed in Table 2.1. Second, I eliminated all references to any individual people. For instance, there was a period when the president of the CA and the home minister, among others, could not attend due to ill health, at which point members expressed concerns over their health.

Third, I placed the identified terms in context, that is, with reference to my four stated aims, as this will enable better making sense of the discussion. In this context, I focused on the CA deliberations on Fundamental Rights, Directive Principles of State Policy and the Seventh Schedule.

Section II
Different Dimensions of Health in the Constituent Assembly

In this section, I explore how health has been used in the CA. Using the key terms identified in Table 2.1 and placing them in context, I was able to identify five dimensions around which health was addressed. These include the use of health as metaphor, health as a persuasive tool, health as a legitimising device, health and the federal dimension and of course health as health. I take up the discussion on health as health in the penultimate section of this chapter.

Health and as a Metaphor

When people speak of health and disease, do they have the lexical meaning of the term in mind, or do they use these terms in other ways? There is a rich field of studies on the use and communication of sophisticated concepts in everyday life (Lakoff and Johnson, 2008). Words are often used not only in the lexical sense but as metaphors. Metaphors structure our arguments, the meanings of what we want to say and how we want others to understand what we are saying. Metaphors are used to convey abstract concepts and supposedly take people closer to the meaning intended by the speaker/author, and this, in turn, allows greater discussion and better understanding (Hills, 2017), and they also help frame arguments (Demjén and Semino, 2016). Finally, metaphors are often normatively loaded and can help us distinguish between the desirable and the undesirable (Ross et al., 1997).

Studies show that using health as a metaphor is common since it easily connects with people. Health is a condition almost everyone can relate to and is an ideal worth moving to, working for and maintaining. Crawford (2006), for instance, notes that in the modern world, a health-valuing culture has developed and being healthy is considered an achievement. Moreover, it is also agreed that governments must do nothing to undermine health and protecting health is one of their most important public duties.

The lexical meaning of the word *health* in the Cambridge dictionary is 'the condition of the body and the degree to which it is free from illness, or the state of being well'.[2] Likewise, for the World Health Organization, health 'is a state of complete physical, mental and social well-being and not merely the absence of disease or infirmity'.[3] Health is lexically associated with a positive valence, and most people want to keep and preserve good health and prevent ill health.

Healthy is therefore a positive, essential and beneficial condition. Being healthy is both a normatively and objectively desirable state of affairs. Ill health, sickness and disease are despised conditions that people seek to avoid. Consequently, health as a metaphor for a desirable condition is politically and emotionally powerful.

Hence, it is not entirely surprising the term health is abundantly used in the CA as a metaphor to judge a given state of affairs or point to a desirable outcome. While health and healthy are repeatedly used in the positive sense of the term, ill health and disease were used to communicate the negative and the undesirable. Healthy and unhealthy were often prefixed to qualify a variety of subjects, including politics, amendment, convention, precedent, sense of responsibility, method, society, opinion, national life, development, restrictions, spirit, seeds of democracy, environment, procedure, principle, functioning and state of affairs among others to spell out distinctive meanings. To illustrate the use of health as a metaphor, I highlight some speeches from the CA.

Purnima Banerjee on religious liberty:

> Therefore, without interfering with the religion of anybody, the state should be perfectly entitled to see that in the formative age of the child, when he is of the school-going age, the religious instruction is controlled and that the syllabus is of such a nature that the child will develop into a *healthy* citizen of India capable of appreciating each other's point of view.[4]
>
> (5.46.67)

KT Shah on fundamental rights:

> I think, Sir, that the freedom of religion being guaranteed by this constitution and promised as one of the Fundamental Rights, the possibility of all religious institutions being accessible and open for all communities is a very *healthy* sign and would promote harmony and brotherhood amongst the peoples following various forms of beliefs in this country, and therefore I think, Sir, that this amendment, at any rate, should find acceptance from those who have sponsored this clause.[5]
>
> (7.67.51)

Shibban Lal Saxena on the Finance Commission:

> If Dr Kunzru's assertion were accepted that there shall be a convention by which the recommendations of this Commission shall be accepted, I personally feel that this convention would be very *unhealthy* and harmful. It will detract from the authority of the Parliament to make allocations.[6]
>
> (9.114.184)

Kishori Mohan Tripathi moving an amendment on the right to property:

> Then, although apparently, the article, as moved by the honourable Pandit Jawaharlal Nehru, does not discriminate between property and property, as facts stand, I feel that it discriminates between industrial property and landed estates. Such a discrimination between property and property, as contained in this article, is, I strongly feel, very dangerous and may create a very *unhealthy* atmosphere in the country, which is already full of discontent.[7]
>
> (9.137.115)

At the same time, undesirable elements like communalism,[8] poverty,[9] untouchability,[10] concentration of power,[11] separate electorates[12] and discontent and oppression[13] among others were treated as diseases that needed to be cured or eliminated. Similarly, unagreeable options put forward by others became remedies that were 'worse than the disease'[14] and successful accomplishments became a 'disease that has been cured'.[15]

When the speakers refer to unhealthy practices or diseases, they draw on an imagined similarity between an improperly functioning body and a bad practice or issue in the real world. Practices like untouchability, the concentration of power, discrimination and oppression have no space in a democratic set-up and are therefore painted in negative colours. In summary, when health is used as a metaphor, it underscores other meanings, practices and beliefs which members believe are beneficial or not beneficial to society.

Health as a Persuasive Tool

Following the proposition that health is a desirable state and that it also grabs everybody's attention, it is not surprising that CA members often use health to reinforce their arguments on other issues. In these discussions, the reference to health is secondary, and other issues have priority. The discussions on the protection of cows, the prevention of cow slaughter and prohibition highlight the use of health as a persuasive tool.

When Seth Govind Das speaks of health during the discussion on cow protection, his primary concern is the cow, and health plays a subordinate role. He moves for an amendment which links agriculture to cow protection, wherein, among other issues, he notes, to 'grow more food and to improve agriculture and the cattle breed are all interdependent and two-sided of the same coin'. Furthermore, he notes, 'besides all these, the best way of increasing the production is to improve the health of human beings and breed of cattle, whose milk and manure and labour are most essential for growing food'.[16] His focus is on the cultural and religious dimension, while the economic and health are ancillary elements in the arguments:

> Cow protection is not only a matter of religion with us; it is also a cultural and economic question. Culture is a gift of history. India is an ancient country; consequently, no new culture can be imposed on it. Whosoever attempts to do so is bound to fail; he can never succeed. Ours is a culture that has gradually developed with our long history. Swaraj will have no meaning for our people in the absence of a culture.[17]
>
> (7.59.103)

His intervention is sophisticated as he also uses data to substantiate his point. Comparing the per capita availability of milk in a couple of countries, Das exhorts members to

> just think what will be the state of health of the people of a country where they get only seven ounces of milk per head. There is a huge

infantile mortality in this country. Children are dying like dogs and cats. How can they be saved without milk?[18]

(7.59.105)

Similarly, Shibban Lal Saxena argued that cow protection had become part of 'the religion of Hindus' because 'of its economic and other aspects'. His primary concerns are still located in the religious and cultural domains. He then uses health to make a case for cow protection:

> The other important evils in our country are infant mortality and tuberculosis, which have their origin in a deficient milk diet. These evils can be remedied only if we preserve our cattle and improve their breed, which is the purpose of this amendment. I, therefore, think that this amendment should be accepted.[19]
>
> (7.59.140)

For the cow protectionists, health concerns added heft to their arguments. A similar line of persuasion is also discerned on the prohibition issue. Speaking on prohibition, BG Kher argued that

> medical research has been made to a considerable extent, and people have come to the conclusion that the consumption of spirituous liquors and injurious drugs (the description which has been used in this clause) is admittedly injurious to health.[20]
>
> (7.59.29)

While this may give us the impression that health was a significant concern, if we examine the preceding and subsequent arguments, it is clear that health concerns arising out of intoxication were not the priority:

> most of those who are interested in the progress of this country have accepted the necessity of protecting our people from going to their ruin by the use of intoxicating drugs and liquor. They believe that humanity will not progress on proper lines unless, along with intellectual and material progress, they give sufficient importance to moral progress, and it is too late in the day now to argue that the use of intoxicating drugs and liquor do not affect the moral sense of a person who uses them. The very lamp which shows to you the distinction between right and wrong is extinguished. . . . Instead of getting a large excise revenue and spending it on education, the best education is to teach people to abstain from drink and drugs.[21]
>
> (7.59.28)

> I am not quoting Mahatma Gandhi in support of my argument, but he has said that he would not attach any importance to any other social

> reform so long as this question of the prevention of consumption of intoxicating liquors and drugs was not taken up by the state. The very first reform that he enjoined upon all the provinces was the stopping of this vicious thing.[22]
>
> (7.59.30)

> I mean sin. The drinking of liquor is one of the five deadly sins which the Smritis have laid down, and that was not a matter of bigotry or prejudice but the result of vast experience. . . . So, though a sin both for the Hindus as also for the Muslim, after the advent of the British, the use of intoxicating liquors became a sign of being fashionable, a sign of progress and culture.[23]
>
> (7.59.32)

While Kher concludes with the hope that members do not encourage 'the use of drinks and drugs which are injurious to the health of the people', the arguments in favour of prohibition are from a moral standpoint.

Frank Anthony and BH Khardekar, among others who opposed prohibition exposed the hollowness of the moral position. Frank Anthony asked if there weren't more pressing matters like education and health that the government should focus on rather than 'idealistic chimaeras':

> Can you create morality through legislation? . . . As long as you have your chawls for workers in the urban areas, and you cannot even provide them with a semblance of decent living conditions, what is the good of trying to make them moral or weaning them from drunkenness by legislation?[24]
>
> (11.165.162)

Here again, we see that health is on the agenda not necessarily as a good in itself. As health is a critical element of modern life, members ride on its significance to push other points.

Health and Regime Legitimation

Promoting the people's well-being is a major concern in the CA and is intrinsically linked to their understanding of democracy. The idea was simple: a democratic government should work for the people's interests, and the people should have some say in deciding what the government does. It might also be valid to note that constitution-making happened in the "golden age" of the welfare state. Previous studies of the Indian constitution note that there were no major arguments in favour of a limited state, and there was a consensus that the state was to ensure the collective good (Austin, 1966; Chaube, 1973).

This understanding gave the CA direction and helped it distinguish between the colonial regime and the government in independent India. For instance, speaking on the issue of filling casual vacancies, a member held that 'the entire basis of the State has changed, and it is no longer a police state, certain social functions such as education and *health* now feature among the major items of the State's development'.[25]

One can discern at least three variations of regime legitimation in the CAD. First, there was concern that the new government needed to prove it was better than the previous regime. Second, the new government had to deliver on the promises made during the national movement. Third, there was also the fear of disappointment and revolution if the new regime did not keep its promises. The members believed that provisioning for health and education would enrich the state of democracy and enhance the legitimacy of the new regime.

The president of the CA speaking on 15 August 1947 declared,

> More than a day of rejoicing, it is a day of dedication for all of us to the India of our dreams. Let us turn our eyes away from the past and fix our gaze on the future.[26]
>
> (5.37.39)

> Let us resolve to create conditions in this country when every individual will be free and provided with the wherewithal to develop and rise to his fullest stature, when poverty and squalor and ignorance and *ill-health* will have vanished, when the distinction between high and low, between rich and poor, will have disappeared.[27]
>
> (5.37.40)

The issue of legitimacy was most eloquently underlined by Biswanath Das, who consistently intervened in the debates on social welfare. He believed that the constitution inadequately addressed the issue of social welfare, especially the operational dimension, and he wanted it to underscore what the government should do and what people should expect from the government. Das argued that it should not be left to the goodwill of government to legislate for the betterment of the conditions of the people:

> Sir, in the fundamental rights, we have not yet ensured that there should be social security for all. Social security means social justice for all, and there should be a certain minimum adequate standard of living for all. There should not only be *public health* and public safety, but there should also be minimum education ensured for all. Unfortunately, Sir, we had an alien government which lived for British domination. Its financial and economic policy was to take all it could take to maintain British Imperialism and British domination not only in India but throughout Asia. It gave nothing to the provinces. If it gave to the

> poorer provinces like Orissa or Assam anything, it was just a sustenance allowance and nothing more.[28]
>
> (4.34.83)

Similarly, Das was unhappy that the preamble to the constitution neither lays down nor defines the main objective of the constitution. Rather,

> [it] should be laid down that the first function of the state is to see to the well-being of the people, – not to rule as the British government have so long ruled India exploited India for England's benefit and for India's misery and death. . . . It is the financial and economic chapter of the Union Constitution that will show what these people really mean, whether they want to ensure social justice or whether they want to evolve another bureaucratic government where power politics will dominate.[29]
>
> (4.34.85)

He reiterates the point during the discussion on fundamental rights, stressing the government's duty to provide basic services to all sections of the population:

> I consider that the fundamental principles of governance mean – Dharma of the Government – the path of duty of the government. But we don't lay down in the Constitution Act what the government should do and what are the responsibilities of government to the citizens and the people of India.[30]
>
> (5.46.29)

> I think it is the primary duty of the government to remove hunger and render social justice to every citizen, and to secure social security. . . . The teeming millions do not find any hope that the Union Constitution that will be passed two months hence will ensure them freedom from hunger, will secure them social justice, will ensure them a minimum standard of living and a *minimum standard of public health*.[31]
>
> (5.46.29)

> I do not find anything that makes it obligatory on the government on the state to discharge their obligatory duties to the people of India about common welfare and well-being of the people.[32]
>
> (5.46.29)

> We are framing our Free Sovereign Constitution. Perhaps ours is the last constitution framed in the 20th century. One would have expected that we would have profited by the knowledge, by the suffering and by the experience of other countries . . . Let us make a more acceptable draft. Let us make the draft fit with the conditions in India. Let

> us tell the world through our draft Constitution that Indians have a civilisation and culture ten thousands of years old. We should draw up a democratic Constitution whereby the state serves the people and the people, the state.[33]
>
> (5.46.30)

A second point Das repeatedly made was about the change of regime and what the new government should be doing. For instance, speaking on the need for a more equitable distribution of resources between the Centre and the states, he drew a sharp contrast between the British regime and the new government. He spoke of the neglect and misplaced priorities of the previous government and pressed that now revenues should be used wisely on social justice and security:

> We will have to conceive of a system of administration so that the largest amount of taxation that will come from the people should go back to the people. It should not be spent in manufacturing armaments or in manufacturing atomic bombs. Sir Ramaswami Mudaliar analysed provincial taxation and showed how provinces are kept merely on sustenance allowances. The foreign government at the centre wanted only cannon fodder from the provinces. People were driven by hunger and starvation to join the army, not a voluntary army, to defend the British Empire, not so much the Indian Empire. This is the third time I am appealing for social justice and social security.
>
> (5.39.65)

Regarding contentment and potential resentment, RK Silva made the point subtly:

> Economic Commission . . . set up so that they may devise ways and means of advancing the nation-building programmes, for instance, *public health*, social security, social co-operation. All these things require immediate attention. If we do not give them immediate attention, I can assure you, Sir, that the people will not be content with any type of constitution that we may make.[34]
>
> (4.34.185)

In these discussions, we see that health took centre stage and providing for or creating conditions for good health was considered an important nation-building activity. However, at the same time, it was a legitimacy-building exercise as the goals of improving and protecting health were necessary to distinguish independent India from the colonial times. Health care here was seen as an important task of a democratic government.

Health and the Federal Dimension

While there was consensus that health is a key nation-building activity and the government had to take responsibility, there were differences as to which level would deal with health. Who was best equipped to handle health and how to finance it were questions that received attention. In my reading of the CA debates, it appears that these discussions were deeply coloured by the centripetal–centrifugal debates on unity and autonomy in the CA. The unionists wanted the central government to be responsible, or at least for health to be in the concurrent list for the benefit of the larger sections of the people. The autonomists preferred that the states be given the resources to handle health-related concerns. It must, however, be mentioned that not all speakers were concerned with the centripetal–centrifugal concerns.

The debates show that members were aware of the great differences between different parts of the country. States and provinces that were doing better were concerned about how they could maintain their existing standards. They were fearful that they would lose in the long run as the quality of services would come down. At the same time, some states were asking for more finances and resources to be diverted to their regions given the abysmal conditions of health care. There was also an understanding that what is in the interests of public health could vary from province to province.[35] For instance, restrictions and quarantine requirements in one state might not make sense in other parts of the country.

Ramaswamy Mudaliar made a strong case for more finances for the states since they not only carry out key nation-building functions which include education and health, but also those activities that are essential for individual happiness of the individual. He was clear that we needed a strong Centre and that it was not a 'tug of war' between the Centre and the states:

> There are problems facing them which in their own sphere are acute, grave, difficult, economic problems of the first magnitude, grievances which it is hard to satisfy, ambitions, hopes, aspirations which it is very difficult to fulfil. Remember, Sir, that much of this sphere of activity which makes for the happiness of the individual man lies with the province or the unit of administration and not with the Central administration. You in the province have the responsibility for free and compulsory education, a goal which you have put before yourself. You have the responsibility for *proper medical aid* for sanitation, for promoting *health*, making the man live a little longer than the average life of 25 or 27 years, which has been so far our lot in this country.[36]
>
> (5.39.45)

I have said before, and I repeat again, that the gravest responsibility is cast on the units for providing what are called nation-building

> activities. These nation-building activities, remember Mr President, are the activities which build up the nation, and these are the direct responsibility of the units and not of the centre . . . the defence activity cannot be strong unless the nation itself the individual who makes the nation is also strong unless they are *healthily* fed unless they are properly educated unless they are in a position to stand up as real stalwart units of the nation and that responsibility again I say is on the provinces and not on the centre.[37]
>
> (5.39.46)

Speaking of the centralisation tendencies and its dangers, K Santhanam observed,

> Then, take the financial distribution. They have put all taxation except land revenue and one or two other diminishing items, like excise on intoxicating liquors, in the federal list. The report says that some provision for assignment should be made. But unless, together with the items, method of allocating the shares of the proceeds is given, the provinces will be beggars at the door of the centre. I do not want any constitution in which the unit has to the centre and say, 'I cannot educate my people; I cannot give sanitation; give me a dole for the improvement of roads, for industries, for primary education'. Let us rather wipe out the federal system and let us have a unitary system.[38]
>
> (5.38.164)

Speaking on the issue of finances, BA Mandloi representing C. P. & Berar underlined the point that the provinces needed money to carry out their responsibilities which are important to the lives of the people:

> While we have attempted to make the centre quite strong, I submit that we have not paid sufficient attention to our Provinces. The Provincial budgets are poor budgets, and there is a chronic poverty prevailing in the provinces. The responsibilities of the provinces are great. We have to fight ignorance, disease, and so many other things, and we have to carry on nation-building departments and the constructive work in the provinces. The allocation from the Central revenues to the provinces should be on an equitable basis so that the provinces may be able to discharge their duties properly and efficiently.[39]
>
> (50.71)

HN Kunzru warned of a peculiar situation with regard to finances and Centre–state relations. This became particularly instructive in the light of the tensions between the Centre and states during Covid-19. He underlined the dangers of modifying financial commitments, which could jeopardise the functioning of states:

> after a financial settlement has been arrived at with the provinces and they have increased their expenditure and have come to depend on the money received by them from the centre for meeting their liabilities, the president may say to them that whatever happens to them, the financial settlement made by them must be modified. What are the provinces to do in these circumstances? So far as I can see, they are to enjoy the blessing of financial nirvana. The Provincial Governments and the people of the provinces may suffer seriously-may, so to say, go about with a loin cloth- but the centre will have little regard for their plight.[40]
>
> (9.119.207)

> there could be no change in them whatsoever in any emergency. The position of the provinces in regard to the other taxes was to remain wholly unaffected by the occurrence of an emergency. It was realised that if the provinces, depending on the money received by them from the centre, extended primary education, or made it compulsory, or increased the *number of hospitals and dispensaries*, or undertook a programme for the improvement of the condition of the rural masses, they could not in justice be asked suddenly to change their budgets and tell their people that the facilities already available to them in respect of education, public *health*, medical relief or rural welfare shall be withdrawn. If such a thing were to be done in future, there would be serious discontent in the provinces, so serious indeed as to create another emergency.[41]
>
> (9.119.207)

At another point, he noted how international obligations entered into by the Centre could increase the burden of the states and may also impact their budgets and commitments. Given the limited resources the states have, they already find it difficult to manage things:

> Do not think that there need be any fear of it because it is well known that the units, whatever financial powers may reasonably be conceded to them at the present time, will not be in a position either to make education free or compulsory or to adopt the measures recommended by Sir, Joseph Bhore's Committee in regard to *public health* or make satisfactory progress in regard to other matters which would lie within the provincial sphere unless they receive generous help from the centre. It is inconceivable to me in these circumstances that the Central Government should, without adequate thought and previous consultation with the units,

> commit them to policies which it would be beyond their resources to implement.[42]
>
> (5.41.56)

On international obligations and states, Ayyangar wanted a council so that there could be consultations on matters including health on which international conferences would be held.[43] This body would ensure that India did not face a situation of not honouring international agreements because certain entities were not consulted and therefore would not comply.

Among the centralisers was DP Khaitan, who came out sharply criticising Mudaliar:

> He has forgotten for the moment the needs of the defence of the country and the requirements that become necessary for the purpose of fighting a war, whether defensive or aggressive. He has forgotten conveniently how the whole country has got to be regimented in times of war, the signs of which are already visible in the world and to which our unfortunate country, not yet fully developed, may become a victim at no distant date. I am no alarmist in this direction, but I do believe that whether it be to protect our freedom, whether it be to spread education and good health or whether it be to produce more goods, it is necessary that the whole country of India must be treated as one.[44]
>
> (5.39.74)

Others took a different line. For instance, Frank Anthony argued that education, health and police should be with the Centre rather than the provinces. Uniformity in nation-building activities would benefit the people and should not be left to the provinces given that they are bound to discriminate between different sections (minorities) of the population, and this could jeopardise national unity.

> the subject which I feel should be also controlled from the centre is the not negligible subject of *health*. Education and *health* are, to my mind, the two paramount problems which this country is faced with. And we cannot begin to liquidate ill-health and malnutrition unless we do it on a uniform scale. I do not believe that we can begin to touch this, perhaps our greatest problem, by allowing it to rest at the mercies of the different provincial Governments, which are, some of them bound to have halting policies; some of them are bound to have disparate policies, some of them are bound to have divergent policies.[45]
>
> (7.49.98)

Others wanted health to be on the concurrent list. TT Krishnamachari argued that he would have preferred that health be in List III, and his fear was the centralising thrust that existed in the constitution:

> There are certain aspects of *public health* where the Central Government could do a lot of good. Actually, disease in this country is universal. It is not the main privilege of Madras, Bombay or U. P. and therefore, in the matter of *public health* legislation and also in the matter of maintaining institutes for purposes of research in *health*, I think some amount of power could be given to the centre, and therefore, that item could come into List 3. But, Sir, while I feel that a strong Centre is necessary because I visualise the most important task before us is the implementing of the economic objectives, I am rather disinclined to pursue that idea to its logical end . . .[46]
>
> (7.49.116)

Similarly, Kamath suggested that public health should ideally be in List III:

> While commending my amendment seeking to transfer *public health*, sanitation, hospitals and dispensaries to the Concurrent List, I should like to state that public health has been the Cinderella of portfolios in the Cabinet of our country. During the British Regime, it was specially so, very sadly neglected and not much provided for: as a result of which the health of the nation has fallen to C-3 standards, it is the object of our government today to raise the health of the nation from C-3 to A-I standard. If this were the aim of our government, we could not do better than make public health a Concurrent subject. It must be accorded top priority if the nation is to rise to its full stature.
>
> (9.130.19)[47]

On the one hand, Bishwanath Das and Rev. J.J.M. Nichols-Roy wanted more finances for the states and highlighted the great disparities between states and their existing spending at the moment. On the other hand, R. Sankar noted that Travancore was spending more on development-related issues and was afraid that the new constitutional provisions would create developmental problems in the state:

> In other words, about 45 per cent of the income of the state will be central revenue from the day this Draft Constitution becomes law. The result would be that a State like Travancore will not be able to maintain, much less improve upon her present administrative efficiency. The States people now look at this picture more or less from this angle . . . The people, after the long struggle, are looking forward to the present responsible governments in the States to find a solution for the

> hundreds of problems, especially economic problems, that they are faced with, and if the States, instead of being in a better position, are in a worse position from tomorrow, they will certainly find it impossible to do anything and to solve any problem that they face.[48]
>
> (7.52.2)

Notwithstanding the discussion being coloured by the centralist–autonomist concerns, there were powerful arguments in favour of and against leaving health to the states. Much of the discussion about the appropriate level for managing health and other such issues as well as the larger question of finances had already taken place in other CA committees. The Union Powers Committee arrived at the division of powers between the Centre and the states, and an expert committee examined the financial provisions of the constitution and also looked at the issue of finances. Consequently, there was not much scope for drastic restructuring during the discussions of specific provisions.

Section III

Health as Health

The discussion thus far might suggest that while health receives attention in various ways, the discussion in the CA does not necessarily match the sheer scope of the challenges India faces on the health front. The provisions surrounding health were quickly done with, and there was no sustained deliberation. Furthermore, by the time the Seventh Schedule of the Constitution, which defines and demarcates functions and powers between the Union and the states, was discussed, the CA was running out of time, and there was a hurry to finish the deliberations. The chair was rationing time, and each speaker was allotted only three minutes.[49] So, does this mean health was not a major concern in the CA?

The absence of lengthy discussions on public health in the CA is primarily because much of the conversation took place outside. This may explain why the discussion in the CA does not get into the details and complexities. At the same time, it also indicates a definitive agreement on public health issues. In this section, I examine the discussion on public health in the CA and other documents and reports that came out around the same time. We see a remarkable consensus on the importance of public health and how it could be improved over time.

While health is understood in many contexts in the CA, there is in particular a sophisticated understanding of health and what it entails that was probably way ahead of its time. Health was not seen in the narrow sense as merely the absence of disease but was associated with well-being and happiness, enabling an individual to live life to the fullest. More importantly, the link between health and poverty was underlined, where health care was a luxury for people on the margins of destitution. Consequently, while health is an individual state of being, it depends on a conducive societal and economic state of affairs, including protection from diseases and adequate prevention and curative facilities and mechanisms.

At the same time, an individual's health also impacts societal well-being. Unhealthy individuals are a drag on society, especially when the development of modern science and medicine has made several diseases preventable. Knowledge and information about disease prevention and cure need to reach different sections for society to advance.

On Independence Day, the president of the CA set the ball rolling speaking of the need to create conditions where every individual will be able to 'develop and rise to his fullest stature' and banish 'poverty and squalor, ignorance and *ill health*'. The focus was on the fullest development of the individual, and a decent and *healthy* life was essential for self-improvement and realisation.[50]

During the discussion on education and the state's duty, Renuka Ray spelt out the complex relationship of health with other dimensions:

> Unless the worker is given the basic opportunities, how can efficiency be increased? This implies that there must be minimum standards for education and health. Unless the men and women who are the builders of society have a minimum standard of education and of *health*, it is not possible for us really to have any increase in efficiency, and unless we have increase in efficiency, it is no use talking about producing more.[51]
>
> (9.128.91)

On another occasion, Lakshminarayan Sahu argued that the constitution was attempting to build a 'new India' based on 'new principles', which would be more equitable than the past. In this context, he underlines the interconnectedness of society and how greater social, political and economic equality India help us realise these goals of new India. Though he is acutely aware of the conditions in his province, his understanding of what is required goes beyond mere survival and embraces a higher-order conceptualisation:

> One man earns Rs. 600, or 800, or 1,000 in a day, but the average income of a person in this country is merely 6 annas daily. Only then can we make the people of free India happy? People say that my province, Orissa, is a very poor province and a very small province. Why is this so? This is the matter that needs consideration. When I talk of Orissa, it may well be that some people may insinuate that it is the spirit of provincialism that makes me do so. It is not provincialism that makes me to talk of my province. It is out of sheer necessity of self-existence; I desire to live. But in order to do so, I must

> also see as to how the people around me keep *healthy* and how they can live happily.[52]
>
> (9.137.384)

There was consensus that health and education should receive the highest priority as the nation-building activities that the state ought to focus on.[53] Similarly, there was the concern that women and children should get special attention.[54] Speaking on the state providing relief and other amenities for the well-being of the people in the Directive Principles, Syamanandan Sahaya insisted that medical relief should also be included as statistics paint a dismal picture of health conditions and life expectancy. The state should therefore give special attention to medical aid in addition to education, unemployment, old age and so on.[55]

The long shadow of the national movement shaped India's developmental goals, and we know that the law and government were invested with the responsibility for social and economic change (Austin, 1966; Chaube, 1973). The transformation of a hierarchic social order into a more egalitarian, pluralist society, along with maintaining democracy and preserving the unity of the nation, formed the foundation of the constitution (Austin, 1999). Given the multidimensional nature of the transformative agenda, it is unlikely that intricate details of different dimensions would have received attention at the time of the framing of the constitution.

Even before the CA came into existence, discussion on the future socio-economic goals and the machinery required was already taking place in different fora. A National Planning Committee (NPC) was in place in 1938, and they set up various subgroups to examine different elements of the national economy. In addition to this effort, there were also specialised groups and committees examining specific sectors. For instance, the Health Survey and Development Committee was set up in 1943 to make recommendations on the health sector after examining the status of health conditions and organisations in the country. Furthermore, alternate plan ideas were being discussed by different ideological persuasions. Subsequently, an advisory planning board was set up in 1946 to review the planning that the government had done, the NPC and other plans and proposals regarding planning and make recommendations regarding the objectives and priorities for planning in independent India.

In its report, the planning board acknowledged the work performed by the Health Survey Committee – popularly known as the Bhore Committee – and decided to go along with its recommendations. The Bhore report spelt out long-term objectives vis-à-vis public health; moreover, provisional governments were already working on them. Consequently, the Bhore report became the country's 'blueprint for health service development' (Baru, 2019).

From the Bhore report and other documents, it is abundantly clear that health was a major anxiety for policymakers. One can discern at least six major points of agreement which also come up in the CA but not necessarily systematically. First, as I established, there was consensus that a healthy individual enjoys a better life and is generally happier and that health is integral to the country's development.[56] Consequently, health was among the priority socioeconomic developmental goals.

It is not surprising that a member even motioned an amendment to include free medical aid among the desirable goals or ideals to be mentioned in the preamble.[57] Disease prevention, early diagnosis and treatment and overall improved health could bring about an attitudinal change in the people, which would benefit general progress and advancement. This also meant that adequate attention had to be given to hygiene, nutrition and general public education.

Second, there was overwhelming consensus that health had been neglected under colonial rule, leading to disastrous consequences. Access to quality health care facilities was unequal in multiple ways, including between states, within states and between different sections of the population.[58] In a more equitable society, good health should not depend on goodwill and charity but is an essential right. Organised health care covering the entire population without distinction is essential for a healthier and happier society.

Third, while available resources are scarce, the current per capita health expenditure is grossly inadequate and has to be increased.[59] The NPC felt that some form of contribution from those who used the services would give people a feeling of self-reliance. At the same time, they noted that the costs of building a robust health infrastructure should be as low as possible.

Fourth, while a national policy or framework would be useful, the process must be democratic and participatory. Health system policies and management require the coming together of the people's representatives, technical expertise and administrative acumen. It was better left to the state than private entities to ensure that everyone would benefit from the infrastructure and advancements.[60] The role of the state in health care was underlined by the Bhore Report as well. In the CA, Loknath Misra went to the extent of asking for medicine to be a 'state business' to ensure proper administration of 'health and disease'.[61]

KT Shah took a similar line, alerting the group of the dangers of monopolies generally and specifically in health and education. He warns that the entry of private players in these areas will not be in the interests of the country, and therefore, the constitution should

> forbid the very possibility of any monopoly emerging, let us say, in the matter of education or educational apparatus, let us say, in regard to health or the production of drugs, or making medicines, or the supply of surgical and other instruments and apparatuses. I would beg to submit to this House that there is every danger of our country being dominated by private monopolists unless, from the very start, in this very constitution, we make it perfectly clear that in this New India,

> there shall be no room for private monopolists, who would be predatory, who would be preying upon their kind as cannibals.[62]
>
> (7.57.68)

Furthermore, health facilities and their administration had to be taken closer to the people. The Bhore report recommended institutions at different levels, from the local to the state. This organisational pattern would not only take care of the needs but also help remove the uneven access to quality health care. For instance, Mahavir Tyagi spoke of the glaring disparities between the rural and urban areas when it came to health:[63]

> Sir, I have had experience of Legislative Assemblies for the last ten or twelve years, and I know that we are not treating the villagers fairly. All budget amounts are mostly spent in towns. Only in the towns you have electricity and all sorts of other amenities. Their roads are cemented. There is public health only in the towns. But the villagers are totally neglected.
>
> (7.58.18)

Fifth, regular and systematic data collection is integral to successful policymaking. Finally, the ratio of trained medical personnel to the population was abysmally low, and it had to be increased over time for the success of the health programme. Among other issues, this meant paying attention to the standards of education and training.[64]

This discussion of health in the CA and other fora shows that providing decent public health facilities is an integral part of democratic governance. Good health is considered an essential right of the citizen, and it was the government's responsibility to cater to the demands and create conditions where citizens could remain healthy so that they could live life to the fullest. Furthermore, they also believed that quality and modern scientific health care should be provided close to the citizens at reasonable cost. Healthy individuals were crucial to the success of the grand development agenda.

Section IV
Summing up and Conclusion

Through my extensive study of the documentation, I find that although public health received attention in the CAD, it is not necessarily in the objective sense of the term, given the use of metaphors to strengthen arguments and the concerns about legitimation. The CAD discussions revolved around five related dimensions. First, health was used as a metaphor to underline the desired state of affairs, and disease was characterised as undesirable. Second, given the relative importance of health, it was often used in other contexts to add weight to an issue that is often incidental to concerns regarding health. Third, while health was a fundamental concern, it appeared to be a tool for legitimising the new regime and underscoring the transition from colonial rule. Fourth, providing good health was considered a key nation-building activity, and it was to be a state-led priority. There were repeated concerns for the inequitable circumstances surrounding health, not only between states and regions and urban and rural but also among different sections of the population. The debates pointed towards fostering a 'health-valuing culture', where being healthy and creating conditions for good health were considered valuable. Fifth, the operational dimension included the level at which health concerns should be addressed and its finances.

While there are discussions on operational dimensions, in my reading of the CAD, the federal dimension is incidental to the discussion on public health. The debate occurs within the unity vs. autonomy and/or centralisation vs. decentralisation debate. Because of the time shortage, there was very little discussion on the benefits of placing health in list II in the Seventh Schedule of the Constitution; instead, much of the discussion on health took place outside the CA. However, this is not to say that public health was not a concern in the CA. These discussions and reports – even though they took place outside of the CA – settled the various questions, including goals and policies surrounding prevention, treatment and management of diseases; health administration; finances and resources, education and training and other issues that were concerns for the CA.

Notes

1 The Friedrich Naumann Foundation for Freedom funded the CADIndia project. It was put together by the Centre for Law and Policy Research, a not-for-profit organisation established to promote law and public policy research, public interest litigation and interventions in legal education. www.constitutionofindia.net/about-us.
2 https://dictionary.cambridge.org/dictionary/english/health.
3 www.who.int/about/governance/constitution.
4 www.constitutionofindia.net/constitution_assembly_debates/volume/5/1947-08-30.
5 www.constitutionofindia.net/constitution_assembly_debates/volume/7/1948-12-06.
6 www.constitutionofindia.net/constitution_assembly_debates/volume/9/1949-08-09.
7 www.constitutionofindia.net/constitution_assembly_debates/volume/9/1949-09-10.
8 www.constitutionofindia.net/constitution_assembly_debates/volume/1/1946-12-19.
9 www.constitutionofindia.net/constitution_assembly_debates/volume/1/1946-12-16.
10 www.constitutionofindia.net/constitution_assembly_debates/volume/3/1947-04-29.
11 www.constitutionofindia.net/constitution_assembly_debates/volume/8/1949-06-16.
12 www.constitutionofindia.net/constitution_assembly_debates/volume/8/1949-05-26.
13 www.constitutionofindia.net/constitution_assembly_debates/volume/10/1949-10-16.

14 www.constitutionofindia.net/constitution_assembly_debates/volume/8/1949-06-03; www.constitutionofindia.net/constitution_assembly_debates/volume/7/1948-11-08; www.constitutionofindia.net/constitution_assembly_debates/volume/11/1949-11-23.
15 www.constitutionofindia.net/constitution_assembly_debates/volume/11/1949-11-24.
16 www.constitutionofindia.net/constitution_assembly_debates/volume/7/1948-11-24.
17 www.constitutionofindia.net/constitution_assembly_debates/volume/7/1948-11-24.
18 www.constitutionofindia.net/constitution_assembly_debates/volume/7/1948-11-24.
19 www.constitutionofindia.net/constitution_assembly_debates/volume/7/1948-11-24.
20 www.constitutionofindia.net/constitution_assembly_debates/volume/7/1948-11-24.
21 www.constitutionofindia.net/constitution_assembly_debates/volume/7/1948-11-24.
22 www.constitutionofindia.net/constitution_assembly_debates/volume/7/1948-11-24.
23 www.constitutionofindia.net/constitution_assembly_debates/volume/7/1948-11-24.
24 www.constitutionofindia.net/constitution_assembly_debates/volume/11/1949-11-25.
25 www.constitutionofindia.net/constitution_assembly_debates/volume/10/1949-10-11.
26 www.constitutionofindia.net/constitution_assembly_debates/volume/5/1947-08-15.
27 www.constitutionofindia.net/constitution_assembly_debates/volume/5/1947-08-15.
28 www.constitutionofindia.net/constitution_assembly_debates/volume/4/1947-07-30.
29 www.constitutionofindia.net/constitution_assembly_debates/volume/4/1947-07-30.
30 www.constitutionofindia.net/constitution_assembly_debates/volume/5/1947-08-30.
31 www.constitutionofindia.net/constitution_assembly_debates/volume/5/1947-08-30.
32 www.constitutionofindia.net/constitution_assembly_debates/volume/5/1947-08-30.
33 www.constitutionofindia.net/constitution_assembly_debates/volume/5/1947-08-30.
34 www.constitutionofindia.net/constitution_assembly_debates/volume/4/1947-07-30.
35 https://www.constitutionofindia.net/debates/01-may-1947/#86417.
36 www.constitutionofindia.net/constitution_assembly_debates/volume/5/1947-08-21.
37 www.constitutionofindia.net/constitution_assembly_debates/volume/5/1947-08-21.
38 www.constitutionofindia.net/constitution_assembly_debates/volume/5/1947-08-20.
39 http://loksabhaph.nic.in/writereaddata/cadebatefiles/C06111948.html.
40 www.constitutionofindia.net/constitution_assembly_debates/volume/9/1949-08-19.

41 www.constitutionofindia.net/constitution_assembly_debates/volume/9/1949-08-19.
42 www.constitutionofindia.net/constitution_assembly_debates/volume/5/1947-08-25.
43 www.constitutionofindia.net/constitution_assembly_debates/volume/5/1947-08-25.
44 www.constitutionofindia.net/constitution_assembly_debates/volume/5/1947-08-21.
45 www.constitutionofindia.net/constitution_assembly_debates/volume/7/1948-11-05.
46 www.constitutionofindia.net/constitution_assembly_debates/volume/7/1948-11-05.
47 www.constitutionofindia.net/constitution_assembly_debates/volume/9/1949-09-02.
48 www.constitutionofindia.net/constitution_assembly_debates/volume/7/1948-11-09.
49 President, CAD Vol 9, Document 130, Paragraph 22. www.constitutionofindia.net/constitution_assembly_debates/volume/9/1949-09-02.
50 www.constitutionofindia.net/constitution_assembly_debates/volume/5/1947-08-15.
51 www.constitutionofindia.net/constitution_assembly_debates/volume/9/1949-08-31.
52 www.constitutionofindia.net/constitution_assembly_debates/volume/9/1949-09-10.
53 www.constitutionofindia.net/constitution_assembly_debates/volume/11/1949-11-25.
54 www.constitutionofindia.net/constitution_assembly_debates/volume/7/1948-12-03.
55 www.constitutionofindia.net/constitution_assembly_debates/volume/7/1948-11-23.
56 www.constitutionofindia.net/constitution_assembly_debates/volume/9/1949-08-31.
57 www.constitutionofindia.net/constitution_assembly_debates/volume/10/1949-10-17.
58 www.constitutionofindia.net/constitution_assembly_debates/volume/5/1947-08-30.
59 www.constitutionofindia.net/constitution_assembly_debates/volume/5/1947-08-20.
60 www.constitutionofindia.net/constitution_assembly_debates/volume/7/1948-11-19.
61 www.constitutionofindia.net/constitution_assembly_debates/volume/7/1948-11-25.
62 www.constitutionofindia.net/constitution_assembly_debates/volume/7/1948-11-22.
63 www.constitutionofindia.net/constitution_assembly_debates/volume/7/1948-11-23.
64 www.constitutionofindia.net/constitution_assembly_debates/volume/9/1949-08-31.

References

Austin, G. (1966). *The Indian Constitution: Cornerstone of a Nation*. Oxford: Oxford University Press.

Austin, G. (1999). *Working a Democratic Constitution: A History of the Indian Experience*. Oxford: Oxford University Press.
Baru, R.V. (2019, February). The Bhore Committee and Recent Debates. *Seminar 719*. www.india-seminar.com/2019/714/714_rama_v_baru.htm, accessed 10.8.2022.
Chaube, S.K. (1973). *Constituent Assembly of India: Springboard of Revolution*. People's Publishing House.
Crawford, R. (2006). Health as a Meaningful Social Practice. *Health*, *10*(4), 401–420.
Demjén, Z., and Semino, E. (2016). Using Metaphor in Healthcare: Physical Health. In *The Routledge Handbook of Metaphor and Language* (pp. 403–417). Routledge.
Hills, D. (2017). Metaphor. In Zalta, E.N. (Ed.), *The Stanford Encyclopedia of Philosophy* (Fall 2017 ed.). https://plato.stanford.edu/archives/fall2017/entries/metaphor/, accessed 10.8.2022.
Lakoff, G., and Johnson, M. (2008). *Metaphors We Live By*. Chicago: University of Chicago Press.
Ross, N., Eyles, J., Cole, D., and Iannantuono, A. (1997). The Ecosystem Health Metaphor in Science and Policy. *Canadian Geographies/Le Géographe Canadien*, *41*, 114–127.

3 What's Ailing Federalism? Health Policy and Strains in Intergovernmental Relations

Louise Tillin

The policy response to the Covid-19 pandemic entailed the activation of emergency powers that strengthened India's central government at the expense of subnational autonomy. This compounded a shift towards greater centralisation that had already been taking place, adding momentum to demands on the one hand for reforms to the distribution of powers to further empower the central government as a force for national coordination, while raising concerns about challenges to states' autonomy on the other.

The fiscal constraints facing state governments, who are constitutionally responsible for health policy, have provided expectations of – and legitimacy for – enhanced central intervention in the fields of public health and social security. However, central interventions during the pandemic were not restricted to these domains: there was a wider set of interventions into fields historically considered the domain of states in Indian federalism. In this chapter, I examine the adaptability or vulnerability of Indian federalism in the face of the pandemic. I ask whether and how Indian federalism will need to adapt to address pressing issues that were not addressed in the original constitutional distribution of powers. Moments of existential crisis such as a pandemic often inspire calls for central coordination but need to be balanced with the risks they pose to fundamental elements of the federal idea in India, which includes the role of federalism in accommodating diversity.

Over the longer term, two features of the changing health policy landscape have contributed to a growing role for the central government in the field of health in India: the strengthening of global health policy and the rapidly evolving data revolution. In different ways, these two developments have brought the landscape of health care into greater tension with India's constitutional landscape, in an already permissive context for central intervention. In addition, in many federal countries, there have been concerns that the decentralisation associated with the adoption of New Public Management reforms in the 1990s and 2000s has undermined equity and driven inequality, weakened relationships of accountability and impeded coordination in health care governance in federal contexts (Fierlbeck and Palley, 2015).

Against this backdrop, the crisis context was also used by policy actors close to India's central government to make the case for more sweeping

DOI: 10.4324/9781003568711-4

changes to the distribution of powers in the Seventh Schedule that would enhance – or regularise – the Centre's ability to exert legislative and executive authority in the field of health. Herein I explore these debates and draw attention to the need to institutionalise spaces for deliberative, intergovernmental policymaking within Indian federalism. In an era of growing partisan Centre–state conflict, it is important to resist the temptation to reduce debates about policymaking to considerations of who has the power to do what. Instead, as the Sarkaria Commission on Centre–State Relations urged in the late 1980s, it is also crucial to strengthen the institutions of intergovernmental relations.

Federalism and the Covid-19 Policy Response

Federalism – given its multiple levels of government and complex distributions of power – is sometimes seen as inherently ill-suited to decision-making during crises. Crises such as pandemics, world wars or climate change have all been used to proclaim the obsolescence of federalism. Such crises generate coordination problems that were not anticipated in original constitutional schemas and can legitimise the use of emergency powers that trample over pre-existing distributions of power. As Harold Laski wrote of the United States in the 1930s following the Great Depression, 'the epoch of federalism is over . . . only a centralized system can effectively confront the problems of a new time'. Writing about the shortcomings of the federal response to the pandemic in the United States, Rozell and Wilcox (2020) concluded 'controlling contagion requires a great deal of national coordination and intergovernmental cooperation'. Starkly different cross-national public health responses to the Covid-19 pandemic opened debates about the effectiveness of the policy response in federal countries in particular.

Observers pointed frequently either to the failure or absence of a nationally coordinated response (for example in Brazil and the United States)[1] or an over-centralised response that used the context of a national emergency to trespass into the domain of states, weakening the federal bargain in the process (such as in India). Both extremes drew attention to a common set of issues in health care federalism in which existing constitutional schema appear to be out of kilter with the changing nature of health care and policymaking in the domain of public health (some of these issues may be unique to health, but others resonate with other policy domains too). The pandemic served as a driver of wider debate about changes to the federal bargain in India.

Federalism in theory offers the opportunity for localised action appropriate for local circumstances and/or shaped by local preferences (e.g. for levels of public goods or expenditure). It enables policy experimentation and diffusion/learning across sub-units. But a crisis such as a pandemic (and complex problems such as climate change) cuts across political borders. Federal sub-units may lack the capacity or policy levers to act alone, or they may be adversely affected if different states adopt different policies. Furthermore, federal initiatives may be 'pre-empted' by subnational initiatives, leaving the potential for confusion and friction arising from local variation.

For these reasons, a crisis such as a pandemic requires intergovernmental cooperation: the effectiveness of policy responses was reduced in countries that saw weak cooperation. Hegele and Schnabel (2021) observed that decision-making in response to Covid-19 in federal settings could be distinguished along two axes: de/centralised and unilateral vs. coordinated (vertical/horizontal). Unilateral responses of either a decentralised or centralised nature were likely to generate 'duplications, contradictions and friction' (Hegele and Schnabel, 2021). The strains on intergovernmental coordination during the pandemic did not simply reflect the ways in which different constitutions distribute powers of policy making and implementation. The response to Covid-19 in major federations from the United States to Brazil to India was also deeply shaped by the growing impact of partisan polarisation on intergovernmental relations (Conlan and Posner, 2016; Birkland et al., 2021).

Covid-19 and Federalism in India: A Play in Two Acts[2]

In terms of Centre–state relations, Covid-19 in India was a play in two acts. Both acts, in their centralising and decentralising tendencies, exposed crucial weaknesses in the infrastructure of Centre–state relations that lie at the heart of India's governance challenges. The pendulum swung from excessively unilateral central action in the first phase of the Covid-19 response as the central government imposed a strict national lockdown overnight to one of an absent Centre as citizens and states were left scrambling to find oxygen supplies and procure vaccines in the second phase. But beyond a debate about the level of centralisation or decentralisation in decision-making, it was the absence of effective Centre–state coordination that was the crucial issue in both stages of the pandemic.

In the first phase, Prime Minister Narendra Modi imposed one of the world's strictest lockdowns overnight, in contrast to fellow nationalist populist leaders in the early months of the pandemic in other large federal countries such as Brazil and the United States. Modi sought to claim credit for the Centre's swift and decisive action against the coronavirus rather than leaving the onus for action on state governments. He traded on his ability to maintain an emotional connection with voters despite the hardships imposed by the lockdown. That India's initial response to the arrival of the Covid-19 pandemic would be highly centralised was, to an extent, over-determined. Following the 2019 elections, the Narendra Modi-led Bharatiya Janata Party (BJP) had intensified its centralised 'one nation' approach to federalism as it sought to consolidate its political dominance (Aiyar and Tillin, 2020).

India's heavily centralised response was criticised by many for imposing a one-size-fits-all approach in a context of high variation in both Covid-19 incidence rates and health system capacity across states (see for instance

Choutagunta et al., 2021). Furthermore, the ability of the centre and states to respond to the social and economic ramifications of a strict lockdown, especially for India's vast informal sector workforce, was severely tested. The sudden, mass movement of migrant workers following the national lockdown revealed the absence of an effective intergovernmental architecture for vertical or horizontal coordination of social security for mobile informal workers in India's federal system.

India's severe second wave of Covid-19, in contrast to the first, saw a marked shift in the Centre's response, characterised by central inaction and decentralisation of key areas of pandemic response such as vaccine procurement and distribution. In the second wave, the Centre's response looked more like that of Brazil or the United States in their first waves; there was no national lockdown but instead localised lockdowns or curfews. The Centre was slow to curtail mass gatherings as evidence of a second wave took shape.

The Centre also effectively ceded oversight of the interstate distribution of critical oxygen supplies to the courts and to citizen activists mobilised via social media. Coming under fire from many state governments for vaccine shortages, the Centre decentralised responsibility for vaccine procurement and distribution for under 45-year-olds to the states. The second wave also saw the Centre shifting blame for mismanagement to the states and the intensification of Centre–state conflict in what was already a hyper-partisan context for intergovernmental relations. For instance, having suddenly decentralised vaccine procurement and distribution, the BJP – in power at the Centre – went as far as to pledge to provide free vaccines if it defeated the incumbent Trinamool Congress government in the West Bengal state elections in late April 2021.[3] In other words, the BJP signalled that Centre–state partisan alignment or what the party dubs "double engine governance" would be essential for ensuring access to vaccines for all citizens of the state.

The decision to decentralise vaccine procurement and liberalise vaccine sales, as well as the failure to construct an infrastructure for coordinating the production and movement of oxygen supplies across states, risked leaving states in a free-for-all in which the Centre was not umpire but another player. Eventually, a Supreme Court intervention pushed the central government to resume responsibility for vaccine procurement, enabling the more effective rollout of India's vaccine programme.

Using the typology developed by Hegele and Schnabel (2021) to categorise federal approaches to decision-making in European federations to Covid-19, India moved from unilateral centralised decision-making in the first wave of Covid-19 to something that approximated unilateral decentralised decision-making – by default – in the second wave.

Taken together, the concerns raised about the effectiveness of the policy response to Covid-19 in federal systems encouraged calls to revisit the effectiveness of federalism as a system for responding to health and other crises. The pandemic also highlighted the potential for political and constitutional tensions to arise as a result of a changing landscape of health care and health

Box 3.1 Four types of federal response to Covid-19

Centralised and unilateral: the Centre decides without consulting states
Centralised and coordinated: the Centre decides but in coordination with states
Decentralised and unilateral: the states decide without coordinating with the Centre or each other
Decentralised and coordinated: the states decide in coordination with the Centre and/or each other

Source: Hegele and Schnabel (2021).

policy that appears increasingly out of kilter with existing constitutional provisions. In the next section, I look at the existing structure of health care federalism and then examine some of the longer-term shifts in the health field that had already begun to prompt reconsideration of the architecture of (de) centralisation before the pandemic.

Currently Existing Health Care Federalism in India

The federal dimensions of health care in India are, to say the least, complex. Health is typically described as a state subject in Indian federalism because public health and sanitation, hospitals and dispensaries fall under the state list of the Seventh Schedule. However, in practice, the Union government has for a long time been heavily involved in health policy design and financing. It also directly exercises legislative and executive powers relating to health via a number of entries in the Union and concurrent lists. These include entry 20A (Population control and family planning) on the concurrent list (under which the National Health Policy 2015 was introduced by the Union government (Mittal, 2021, p. 19). Entries 28, 64 and 66 of the Union List (governing port quarantine and scientific and technical education), and Entries including 16, 25, 26, 29 and 30 (governing 'lunacy and mental deficiency, medical education, medical professions, infectious disease control and vital statistics') of the Concurrent list also relate to the health domain (Mittal, 2021, p. 19).

In the emergency context of Covid-19, the Government of India activated powers to categorise the disease as a national health emergency and impose a national lockdown to control its spread under the Disaster Management Act of 2015. This legislation had been passed under yet another entry under the Concurrent list: Article 23 on Social Security and social insurance.[4] Under the DMA, the orders made by the central government are binding and cannot be contradicted by states or local governments (Singh, 2022, p. 283).

Due to the vertical imbalance inherent to India's fiscal federalism, state governments are fiscally dependent on the Centre; central transfers have always been important for financing state health plans. With the use of Centrally Sponsored Schemes under Article 282 (which provides that 'the Union or a State may make any grants for any public purpose, notwithstanding that the purpose is not one with respect to which Parliament or the Legislature of the State, as the case may be, may make laws'), the Union government has progressively expanded its role (Kumar, 2020). It has used CSS to establish national health priorities and incentivise their adoption by states.

For instance, the pre-eminent national health framework established by the National Rural Health Mission (NRHM), now National Health Mission (NHM), sets priorities and provides funds and grants under several provisions of the concurrent list, and via Article 282. The NRHM was the main vehicle for taking forward the commitments of the Congress-led United Progressive Alliance (UPA) to health policy, which included increasing public health expenditures (to a target of 2 per cent to 3 per cent of GDP by 2009, which was not met) with a focus on strengthening primary health care, health insurance and access to life-saving drugs (Jeffery, 2022). As Roger Jeffery notes in a review of health policy and federalism in India, the NRHM was shaped by powerful new advocacy coalitions at the national level, associated with the shift to embrace a wider range of rights-based social welfare policies under the UPA. 'Significantly,' he writes, 'it is hard to detect any significant contribution by state governments to this process' (Jeffery, 2022, p. 74). The ability of the central government to determine national health priorities was tested in the courts. The Allahabad High Court upheld the central government's authority under these provisions, ruling that state governments do not have the jurisdiction to violate the terms and conditions of the NRHM because the Union government's writ is also justified by numerous entries on the concurrent list.[5] This does not prevent states from adopting their own health policies, but they cannot violate the provisions of NRHM/NHM (Mittal, 2021).

Changing Health Landscape and Implications for Federalism: International Health Regulation

As Fierlbeck and Palley note in a recent volume on comparative health care federalism, and as is clear from the reality of Centre–state entanglements in the field of health in India, the changing nature of health care has been producing changes to health policymaking in federal systems in ways that long predate the Covid-19 crisis. In the next section, I highlight two ways in which the health landscape has changed in ways that are in tension with the constitutional schema of federalism, not just in India: firstly, increasing cross-jurisdictional/global policymaking on global health and secondly, the data revolution.

Over the last two decades, there has been a transformation of global governance with regards to public health. The expanded global jurisdiction is represented by initiatives such as the WHO's revised International Health Regulations (IHRs) 2005, which significantly expanded the powers of the

WHO and placed new obligations on states in terms of surveillance and disease response (Fidler and Gostin, 2006; Feldbaum et al., 2010). In the words of Kumanan Wilson and co-authors, the International Health Regulations grant priority to 'the protection of the international community from public health threats . . .[and do so] over national sovereignty in certain circumstances' (Wilson et al., 2008, p. 215).

The challenge that compliance with the international health regulations posed for federal countries was recognised at the time of their passage. The IHRs apply to all jurisdictions within a country, even if passed under the international treaty signing powers of a federal government in a context in which responsibility for public health, or important elements of it, is decentralised to subnational governments. For instance, the IHRs make all member countries responsible for reporting a public health emergency of 'international concern' within 24 hours; however, in federal countries, a central government may lack authority to collect or force the transfer of data from a region concerned (Wilson et al., 2005). Resolving the 'federalism dilemma' for the implementation of international health commitments led to calls for re-evaluation of constitutional arrangements to ensure that federations can comply. For instance, Canadian health researchers Wilson, McDougall and Upshur concluded,

> It is primarily incumbent upon federations, as responsible members of the international community, to take every measure available to ensure that they can comply with the new IHR. These measures would include using what constitutional means may be available to centralize necessary public health powers concerning surveillance and outbreak response, making efforts to establish effective collaborative intergovernmental arrangements, and developing appropriate public health capacity at the local level. The intergovernmental acrimony to which federations are susceptible would clearly not be acceptable if, at a time of crisis, it produced a dysfunctional response that resulted in the international spread of disease.
>
> (Wilson et al., 2005)

In India, the Union government has used its international treaty making powers to legislate on national health. The preamble to the National Health Bill 2009, introduced by the Ministry of Health and Family Welfare, which – if it had passed – would have recognised health as a fundamental right, asserted the constitutional right to bring the legislation under entry 14 of the Union list (regulating international treaty making) in order to give effect to a host of international treaties signed by the Union government (WHO, 2015, p. 17). These international obligations were listed as follows:

> Universal Declaration of Human Rights (UDHR): Article 25 (1); International Covenant on Economic, Social and Cultural Rights (ICESCR): Article 12; Convention on the Rights of the Child (CRC): Article 24;

Convention on the Elimination of All Forms of Discrimination against Women (CEDAW): Article 12; UN Convention on Rights of persons with disabilities (UNCRPD): Article 25; Declaration of Alma Ata (1978); Principles for the Protection of Persons with Mental Illness and the Improvement of Mental Health Care (1991); Declaration on the Elimination of Violence against Women (1993), Programme for Action of the International Conference on Population and Development, Cairo (1994); Platform of Action for the Fourth World Women's Conference, Beijing (1995) and the Millennium Development Goals (2000); Declaration of Commitment on HIV/AIDS, 'Global Crisis-Global Action' (2001), WTO Doha Declaration on TRIPS Agreement & Public Health (2001), International Health Regulations, 58th World Health Assembly (2005); WHO Framework Convention on Tobacco Control (WHO FCTC, 2005), and several other declarations and conventions on underlying determinants of health.

The international dimension is also important in other ways. The circulation of international ideas has shaped national policymaking in ways that have helped to circumvent the role and authority of state governments in health.

For instance, as Roger Jeffery (2022) writes, international advisors had clear influence on health policy making under the Congress-led UPA governments in India. Jeffery describes how the NRHM was developed in line with ideas emanating from the World Bank, and an international advisory panel set up to help shape the NRHM was chaired by Professor Jeffrey Sachs, Earth Institute at Columbia University. Jeffery notes that in the minutes of the first meeting of this panel, there was clear concern about how the government would 'institutionalise' the emerging national health policy at state level. The panel sought to investigate how to 'institutionalize a 10-year perspective, insulated from politics at State and Union level sufficient to ensure vision reaches the end point', and the minister concerned proposed treating districts rather than state governments as the relevant unit (Jeffery, 2022, p. 76). A strategy of empowering districts was also employed by the Modi administration to bypass state governments (Aiyar and Tillin, 2020).

Changing Health Landscape and Implications for Federalism: Data Management

A second important shift in the landscape of health is technological change, including the data revolution producing data clouds that sit above and beyond territorial boundaries. As Fierlbeck and Palley note, health policy analysts have been slow to consider the ways in which the transition towards large-scale management and analysis of health data at a level above the state will 'shape not only health care but also health care policy and, inevitably the politics of health care policy'.

As part of the new National Health Policy (2017) introduced by the National Democratic Alliance (NDA) government, India adopted a new approach to health data management with the goal to 'regulate, develop and deploy digital health across the continuum of care'. The National Digital Health Blueprint (NDHB) took forward plans to develop an 'integrated health information system which serves the needs of all stakeholders and improves efficiency, transparency, and citizen experience.'[6] The NDHB is centrally controlled and is intended to be interoperable and to enable cooperation of public and private agencies working at different scales. There is no scope for states to depart from this model (Mittal, 2021, p. 20). As Anushka Mittal argues, centralised data collection and management under the NDHB have potentially profound implications for federalism that have not as yet been fully explored:

> Technological federalism or the interface of the landscape of technological and data governance with the federal structure, as enshrined in the Constitution of India, needs to be . . . adjudicated upon. . . . The centralisation of data, digital architectures as well as decision making will be inevitable in the absence of a fresh perspective.
>
> (Mittal, 2021, p. 18)

In the absence of a framework law on the federal governance of data management, the NDHM can variously be seen as a data policy, health policy or insurance policy or as a unique subject not listed in the Seventh Schedule and hence falling under the Union government's residuary powers (Mittal, 2021). As Mittal notes, previous similar policies such as Aadhar Targeted Delivery of Financial and other Subsidies, Benefits and Services were introduced by the Union government under entry 82 covering income tax, as well as residuary powers. Mittal argues that without a clear role for the states, it is also difficult for civil society to draw attention to the other social and privacy concerns that arise from the centralised system of data management: 'This is but one example of the digital disruption of democracy and constitutional structures, as we know them' (Mittal, 2021, p. 21).

Reforms Agendas for Health Federalism in India

These longer-term changes in health federalism, arising from the international context of health governance and the disruptive changes posed by digital technology, in addition to the pandemic, have given momentum to demands for reforms to health federalism. The clearest demand for constitutional reform in the context of Covid-19 was to reconsider the constitutional distribution of powers when it comes to health.

As I have set out, the actual distribution of powers in the health field is hugely complex, and made more so by the pace of technological change, which is generating policy dilemmas for which there is no constitutional framework for decision-making or regulation. Despite this, the clearest call has been simply for a constitutional amendment to the Seventh Schedule to move health from the state list to the concurrent list, mirroring what happened to education via a constitutional amendment in 1976 during the Emergency. A high-level group on the health sector established by the Fifteen Finance Commission (2017–21) recommended that health be formally moved from the state list to the concurrent list to empower the central government. N.K. Singh, Chairman of the Fifteenth Finance Commission, argued in his own public talks that the distribution of powers between the Union, states and the concurrent list in the Seventh Schedule of the constitution should be reconsidered. The 'country's economic progress, global interdependence and the seamless integration through technology have reopened many of these settled contours for further deliberation. . . . Over a period of time the division of functions got increasingly eroded'.[7]

The chairman of the Prime Minister's Economic Advisory Council, Bibek Debroy, made similar arguments in a series of newspaper columns:

> The Spanish Flu, the last major pandemic, triggered governance improvements in many advanced countries, particularly in health. By that logic, as a reaction to covid and lockdown, there needs to be a stronger template for health sector governance across states and districts, breaking down the silos of laws and regulations and driving convergence in how India reacts to an external crisis, health-related or otherwise. More specifically, this requires a relook at the seventh schedule. The Spanish Flu can be dated to 1918–20. Some elements of the Constitution are inherited from the Government of India Act of 1935 and its precursor, the Government of India Act of 1919, which is of the same vintage as the Spanish Flu. There is a message there, one that should not be forgotten once the worst of Covid-19 is out of the way.[8]

He has also argued, as recommended by a report of the Second Administrative Reforms Commission on crisis management, that disaster management ought to become an explicit item on the concurrent list. This would make it much clearer where authority lay during a crisis such as a pandemic, obviating the need – as occurred during Covid-19 – to invoke the Disaster Management Act 2005.[9]

A second set of reform proposals that predate the pandemic have focused on the attempt to develop a national health policy. UPA-era attempts to pass a national health bill did not materialise but they were motivated by an effort to strengthen the broad legal framework and standards within which public and private health were regulated across states. The National Health Bill 2009 (which didn't eventually become law) called for

> broad legal framework for providing essential public health services and functions, including powers to respond to public health

> emergencies, principally through the State and local public health agencies, in collaboration with others in the public health system, including through the cooperation and formal collaborations between the Center and State; And whereas there is need to have an overarching legal framework and a common set of standards, norms and values to facilitate the Governments' stewardship of private health sector as a partner as well as for more effective operation of other existing and future public health related laws enacted at the Central and State levels.

Under the NDA, a National Health Policy was passed in 2017,[10] but it did not squarely address the constitutional questions around the respective roles of the central and state governments in decision making and implementation of health policy.

A number of NITI Aayog reports separately considered these questions. A NITI Aayog paper published in 2019 titled 'Transforming the Indian Health System for the 21st Century' called for the adoption of a 'bottom-up' model of federalism in which the central government would incentivise state-level experimentation:[11]

> Policy change can occur in multiple venues. This is particularly the case in federal systems. For example, the role of the central government in setting an innovative policy agenda can influence policy innovation at the state-level. In the US, this has been done by the federal government through intentional spread strategies such as disseminating information (on innovative policies emerging from the states), issuing mandates ('policy pushes'), and providing grants to support innovative policies at the state-level (such as quality improvement collaboratives). In other words, through creating an 'authorizing environment' and funding stream that encourages experimentation, the central government can serve as a catalyst of state- and local-level learning and policy innovation. Under these conditions, state and local governments as well as healthcare organizations may increase their predisposition (and risk) to innovate.
>
> (NITI Aayog, 2019)[12]

A third theme for debate which has, to date, been less vigorously explored looks less at constitutional reform to the distribution of powers or how to incentivise states to adopt national goals and more at the question of institutionalising spaces for governmental dialogue. As Srinivas Chokkakula observes, the dilemmas of governance during the pandemic share certain similarities with the challenges of addressing the pressing concerns of sustainability. Sustainability and climate change adaptation-related subjects are on the state list or require action by states, for instance, water, agriculture, biodiversity and pollution.

Like health, the Ashok Chawla committee for water argued in its 2011 report that water should be moved to the concurrent list. But Chokkakula argues that more than shifting subjects to the concurrent list, what is needed is the strengthening of spaces for consensus building between the central government and states. He uses the example of the Goods and Services Tax reforms as a 'recent instance of such reworking of the Centre-state roles for a greater and collective goal'.[13] Such an institutional space would allow for the process of consensus building that would enable functional decisions about subsidiarity to be made on a case-by-case basis.

This was the motivation behind the recommendations of the Sarkaria Commission for the creation of an intergovernmental body. The Inter-State Council (ISC) was established in 1990 to serve as a forum to discuss and make recommendations on issues that concern some or all the states or the central government and more than one state. It is constituted by the prime minister, chief ministers of all states and union territories and six union cabinet ministers. However, in the last three decades, the ISC has met only 11 times, largely to discuss the recommendations of the Sarkaria Commission between the mid-1990s and mid-2000s (Pande, 2019). As Amitabha Pande (2019), former Secretary of the ISC, lamented when the Planning Commission was dismantled in 2014, this created the ideal opportunity to 'make the states (and even local governments) vital stakeholders in policy and strategy planning, partners in programme formulation and in designing common standards and measures for evaluating performance and outcomes'. However, that opportunity was lost with the creation of NITI Aayog, which does not have a constitutional or legal mandate equivalent to that of the ISC, which is formally equidistant from both the Centre and the states.

The idea that deliberation is an essential part of a functioning institutional framework for governing health policy in federal settings is forcefully articulated by the Canadian legal scholar Daniel Weinstock. In a recent intervention, Weinstock argued that a judicious health policy requires that policy makers have a framework within which to arrive at different decisions regarding the level of either national or centralised planning, or local autonomy depending on the domain of health concerned. For instance, communicable diseases may require a level of centralised planning that would not be desirable for non-communicable diseases such as diabetes or high blood pressure. Or within the domain of communicable diseases, a different balance between central coordination and local autonomy may be desirable for different elements of disease control. Data collection and reporting may favour a more centralised approach (as reflected in my earlier discussion of international health regulations), but the handling of local outbreaks may require local autonomy. Weinstock argues therefore that policy jurisdictions should be overlapping by design in order to *require* deliberation about the level of jurisdiction best placed to respond:

> Federal partners should . . . be brought together within appropriate deliberative structure to decide how best to apportion responsibilities,

> rather than having distributions of responsibility determined once and for all in an in-flexible constitutional document.
>
> (745)

This framework would enable policy makers to resolve the complicated normative arguments that favour the involvement of different levels of government. Normative arguments favouring centralisation usually invoke equity or coordination concerns; normative arguments favouring decentralisation invoke concerns about democracy (i.e. the ability of local communities to reach different decisions on complex moral questions that are often involved in health, e.g. assisted dying or reproduction, or the allocation of scarce resources) or epistemic concerns (i.e. about the local knowledge that may be essential for making effective public health interventions). These normative considerations may need to be differently balanced in different policy domains. As Weinstock argues, there may be no one-size-fits-all answer; structures likely need to enable flexibility according to the policy domain in question at a given moment.

Conclusion

In this essay, I have explored the growing strains in the federal dimensions of health policy in India as a result of changes that have occurred in multiple streams (international health policy, technological change and health financing) and that came to a head during the Covid-19 pandemic. In all these streams, and in the first phase of the pandemic, the role of the central government in health policy grew as demands for stronger national coordination superseded concerns about local decision-making or regional autonomy. Technological change and the absence of a framework of data regulation also enabled the central government to exploit ambiguities in the constitutional set-up, leaving major questions for what the future of health care federalism will, or should, look like.

As I have demonstrated, the pandemic added momentum to claims that India needs to reform the distribution of powers to empower the central government to coordinate health policy more effectively. However, the question of how to strengthen intergovernmental institutions to enable and require Centre–state debate and dialogue has been less considered. In an era of intense partisan conflict and pressure on all institutions, even regional parties in power at the state level have shied away from advocating stronger mechanisms for intergovernmental coordination. Given the complexity of health policy and – as Weinstock convincingly argues, the need to avoid the temptation to reach for one-size-fits-all policies to determine where power should lie – it is important not to lose sight of the institutions of intergovernmental relations. However challenging it is to imagine in an environment of such political polarisation, spaces for intergovernmental dialogue are going to be crucial in working towards the universalisation of access to health while protecting fundamental elements of the federal idea in India which preserve space for diversity of identities and of values.

Notes

1 On the United States, see Agnew (2022) and Birkland et al. (2021).
2 This section was previously published as part of a special Covid-19 blog series hosted by India in Transition, Center for Advanced Study of India. Louise Tillin (2021, May 24), Center and States Need to Coordinate, not Compete. https://casi.sas.upenn.edu/iit/louisetillin.
3 https://twitter.com/BJP4Bengal/status/1385503786605563912 (accessed 30 August 2022).
4 Report of Rajya Sabha Parliamentary Standing Committee on Disaster Management Bill 2005, Presented to Rajya Sabha 25 August 2005. Rajya Sabha Secretariat. http://164.100.47.5/rs/book2/reports/home_aff/115threport.htm (accessed 31 March 2022). Cited by Bibek Debroy in a number of articles.
5 'The State or its instrumentality lacks jurisdiction to take a decision against NRHM scheme or its operational guidelines. Since broadly the aims and object of the scheme are also covered by List III [concurrent list] of Schedule 7 of the Constitution, now it is well settled law that in case Union of India discharges its obligation under List III of Schedule 7 of the Constitution, then in view of provision contained in Articles 256 and 257 of the Constitution, subject to repugnancy, Union of India will have overriding power with regard to subjects contained in List III of Schedule 7'. *Devendra, Kumar and Others v Union of India 2011*, Allahabad High Court, Lucknow Bench, 8 July 2011. https://indiankanoon.org/doc/29202809/ (accessed 31 March 2022).
6 National Health Policy 2017, p 25. www.nhp.gov.in/nhpfiles/national_health_policy_2017.pdf (accessed 31 March 2022).
7 N.K. Singh (2020, December 11), lecture titled Indian Economy and Reinforcing Federal Trust, Reported in *Business Standard*. www.business-standard.com/article/economy-policy/n-k-singh-for-reviewing-constitutional-provisions-on-federal-structure-120121101155_1.html (accessed 30 August 2022).
8 Bibek Debroy. (2021, March 25), 'Lessons from India's Tryst with Lockdown', *Mint*. See also (2022, February 20), 'India Needs a Unified Public Health Legislation, Writes Bibek Debroy', *The Week*.
9 Bibek Debroy. (2022, January 16), 'How Covid Triggered Changes in India's Disaster Management Framework', *The Week*.
10 www.nhp.gov.in/nhpfiles/national_health_policy_2017.pdf.
11 The authors drew heavily from Shipan and Volden (2006) on policy diffusion in US anti-smoking policies.
12 See also Rajeev Ahuja (2016, July 5), 'NITI Aayog Vision Document: Does India Need a National Health Policy?' *Financial Express*.
13 Srinivas Chokkakula (2020, September 18), 'India's Response to Covid-19 Reflects the Power, Problems, Potential of Federalism', *Indian Express*.

References

Agnew, J. (2022). Failing Federalism? US Dualist Federalism and the 2020–22 Pandemic. *Regional Studies, Regional Science*, *9*(1), 149–171. https://doi.org/10.1080/21681376.2022.2045214.

Aiyar, Y. and Tillin, L. (2020). "One Nation," BJP, and the Future of Indian Federalism. *India Review*, *19*(2), 117–135. https://doi.org/10.1080/14736489.2020.1744994.

Birkland, T.A., Taylor, K., Crow, D.A., and DeLeo, R. (2021). Governing in a Polarized Era: Federalism and the Response of U.S. State and Federal Governments to the COVID-19 Pandemic. *Publius: The Journal of Federalism*, *51*(4), 650–672. https://doi.org/10.1093/publius/pjab024.

Choutagunta, A., Manish, G.P., and Rajagopalan, S. (2021). Battling COVID-19 with Dysfunctional Federalism: Lessons from India. *Southern Economic Journal*, *87*(4), 1267–1299. https://doi.org/10.1002/soej.12501.

Conlan, T.J., and Posner, P.L. (2016). American Federalism in an Era of Partisan Polarization: The Intergovernmental Paradox of Obama's "New Nationalism". *Publius: The Journal of Federalism*, *46*(3), 281–307. https://doi.org/10.1093/publius/pjw011.

Feldbaum, H., Kelley, L., and Michaud, J. (2010). Global Health and Foreign Policy. *Epidemiologic Reviews*, *32*(1), 82–92. https://doi.org/10.1093/epirev/mxq006.

Fidler, D.P., and Gostin, L.O. (2006). The New International Health Regulations: An Historic Development for International Law and Public Health. *Journal of Law, Medicine & Ethics*, *34*(1), 85–94. https://doi.org/10.1111/j.1748-720X.2006.00011.x.

Fierlbeck, K., and Palley, H.A. eds. (2015). *Comparative Health Care Federalism*. Abingdon, Oxon: Routledge.

Hegele, Y., and Schnabel, J. (2021). Federalism and the Management of the COVID-19 Crisis: Centralisation, Decentralisation and (Non-)Coordination. *West European Politics*, 1–20. https://doi.org/10.1080/01402382.2021.1873529.

Jeffery, R. (2022). Health Policy and Federalism in India. *Territory, Politics, Governance*, *10*(1), 67–85. https://doi.org/10.1080/21622671.2021.1899976.

Kumar, A. (2020, August). *Centrally Sponsored Schemes and Centre-State Relations: A Comment*. Dvara Research Working Paper Series WP-2020–05. www.dvara.com/research/wp-content/uploads/2020/08/Centrally-Sponsored-Schemes-and-Centre-state-Relations-A-Comment.pdf.

Mittal, A. (2021). Technological Federalism: A Building Block to Constitutionalise the Digital Sphere. *Economic & Political Weekly*, *LVI*(47), 18–22.

Pande, A. (2019). *Mediating Centre-State Relations. Seminar*. New Delhi. https://www.india-seminar.com/2019/717/717_amitabha_pande.htm.

Rozell, M.J., and Wilcox, C. (2020). Federalism in a Time of Plague: How Federal Systems Cope with Pandemic. *The American Review of Public Administration*, *50*(6–7), 519–525. https://doi.org/10.1177/0275074020941695.

Shipan, C.R., and Volden, C. (2006). Bottom-Up Federalism: The Diffusion of Antismoking Policies from U.S. Cities to States. *American Journal of Political Science*, *50*(4), 825–843. https://doi.org/10.1111/j.1540-5907.2006.00218.x.

Singh, A.K. (2022). Pandemic Governance in India: The Ongoing Shift to "National Federalism". In *Comparative Federalism and Covid-19: Combating the Pandemic* (pp. 279–97). Taylor & Francis. https://library.oapen.org/viewer/web/viewer.html?file=/bitstream/handle/20.500.12657/51022/9781000471311.pdf?sequence=1&isAllowed=y.

Wilson, K., McDougall, C., Fidler, D.P., and Lazar, H. (2008). Strategies for Implementing the New International Health Regulations in Federal Countries. *Bulletin of the World Health Organization*, *86*(3), 215–220. https://doi.org/10.2471/BLT.07.042838.

Wilson, K., McDougall, C., and Upshur, R. (2005). The New International Health Regulations and the Federalism Dilemma. *PLoS Medicine*, *3*(1), e1. https://doi.org/10.1371/journal.pmed.0030001.

World Health Organisation. (2015). International Public Health Hazards: Indian Legislative Provisions. *Regional Office for South East Asia: World Health Organisation*. https://apps.who.int/iris/bitstream/handle/10665/160756/9789290224761-IPT.pdf?sequence=1&isAllowed=y.

4 Towards a Legal Framework for Public Health Emergencies in India

Kevin James

I. Introduction

By now, it is almost trite to say that India's legal framework for public health emergencies (PHEs) requires a complete overhaul (Task Force on Public Health Act, 2012; Rakesh, 2016; Tewari, 2020; Goyal, 2020; Vidhi Centre for Legal Policy [Vidhi], 2021; Gowd et al., 2021). While not a new argument, it now carries a renewed sense of urgency after India's experience with the COVID-19 pandemic.

The Indian Constitution, as interpreted by the Supreme Court, provides a fundamental right to health and assigns several responsibilities and powers relating to public health and epidemics to different organs and levels of the state. But when the pandemic struck, the legal instruments available to mount an adequate multi-level governmental response were severely lacking. Initially, the Epidemic Diseases Act, 1897 (EDA) was resorted to, with the Disaster Management Act, 2005 (DMA) suddenly taking over. A piecemeal framework had to be employed innovatively and expediently, with mixed results and often glaring failures.

While there is substantial literature on the rationale, scope and guiding principles for public health laws, literature that applies these considerations to the complexities of the Indian legal context is limited. Vidhi (2021) is a significant exception. While for this chapter, I draw on Vidhi's (2021) wide-ranging coverage, I present a narrower, more constitutionally grounded attempt to contextualise, conceptualise and analyse a PHE legal framework for India. I aim to inform and contribute to the ongoing discussion on drafting such a legal framework.

This chapter is divided into four sections, with the immediately following section laying the foundations on which any Indian PHE law should be based. The subsequent section frames a set of questions and analyses the existing legal framework accordingly and takes a brief look at some of the applications of these existing laws during the pandemic. The next section gives an overview of past and present attempts to draft PHE legal frameworks. The final section concludes.

DOI: 10.4324/9781003568711-5

II. Foundations of an Indian Public Health Emergency Law

II.A. Public Health Emergencies and the Law

Public health is 'what we, as a society, do collectively to assure the conditions for people to be healthy' (Institute of Medicine, 1988). The term 'public' in public health is seen as referring to the health of populations, not individuals (Parmet, 2009) and to the involvement of government (Rothstein, 2002). Public health is also seen as denoting a self-evident normative reason for taking action (Coggon, 2012). For instance, per the Nuffield Council on Bioethics' (2007) stewardship framework, states have an obligation to secure conditions that allow people to be healthy and take measures to reduce health inequalities.

In this context, laws can help governments by providing tools to protect populations from diseases and also provide frameworks for assessing good public health practice (Martin, 2009). Laws form the basis for organising, empowering and limiting the collective interventions that constitute public health (Institute of Medicine, 1988; Parmet, 2009). Gostin and Wiley (2016) define public health law as

> the study of the legal powers and duties of the state to assure the conditions for people to be healthy (to identify, prevent, and ameliorate risks to health in the population) and the limitations on the power of the state to constrain the autonomy, privacy, liberty, proprietary, or other legally protected interests of individuals for the common good. The prime objective of public health law is to pursue the highest possible level of physical and mental health in the population, consistent with the values of social justice.

This definition's focus on the duties, powers, and limitations of government forms the basis of Gostin's (2001) tripartite duty–power–restraint framework for analysing public health laws.

PHEs constitute an extraordinary subset of public health and have the potential to overwhelm routine capabilities (Nelson et al., 2007). During PHEs, there is an even stronger need for governmental action structured by laws because population health is at the greatest risk. Having an adequate legal framework for PHEs is a significant component of pandemic preparedness (Nelson et al., 2007; WHO, 2021). Public health laws contribute to PHE management by authorising rapid, decisive and coordinated government responses that include accountability mechanisms that safeguard undue infringements of individual rights by emergency powers (WHO, 2017). Extending the main feature of Gostin and Wiley's (2016) definition of public health laws to emergencies, a PHE law must define the powers and duties of, and the restraints to, governmental actions during a PHE.

II.B. The Indian Constitution and Public Health Emergencies

Gostin (2001) asserts that 'No inquiry is more important to public health law than understanding the role of government in the constitutional design'. In India, the three organs of the state – the executive, the legislature and the judiciary – derive their authority from the Constitution. Under the Constitution's federal system, the state also exists at multiple levels: the Centre, the states and the third tier comprising panchayats for rural areas and municipalities for urban areas. Thus, ascertaining the role of government in Indian public health necessarily involves asking the question of which government should act, in addition to questions relating to how it should act. At the same time, the power to enact laws, and the limits of that power, are also derived from the Constitution. Although Gostin's duty–power–restraint framework was originally meant to analyse public health laws, it is useful to analyse the Indian Constitution itself against it, since the Constitution is the source of all the duties, powers, and restraints of the Indian State.

II.B.1. Constitutional Duties of the State

The Constitution's preamble declares that 'JUSTICE, social, economic and political', 'EQUALITY of status and opportunity' and 'FRATERNITY assuring the dignity of the individual' shall be secured to all Indian citizens. This complements the social justice commitment of public health law, the stewardship framework which requires states to reduce health inequalities, and the importance of health in assuring dignity (Gostin and Wiley, 2016; Nuffield Council on Bioethics, 2007). The preamble's goals are supported by the fundamental rights and directive principles of state policy, and its importance in interpreting constitutional provisions has been affirmed by the Supreme Court (*Kesavananda Bharati v. Union of India*, 1973).

Article 21 of the Constitution provides a fundamental right to life, which has been interpreted by the Supreme Court as including the right to health (*Francis Coralie Mullin v. Union Territory of Delhi*, 1981; *Devika Biswas v. Union of India*, 2016). The right to health is part of the constitutional goal of social justice, drawing from the preamble, the directive principles of state policy and international treaties that India has ratified (*Consumer Education & Research Centre v. Union of India*, 1995; *C.E.S.C. Ltd. v. Subhash Chandra Bose*, 1992).

The Constitution's directive principles require the state to promote the welfare of the people, secure the health of workers, ensure that children are given opportunities and facilities to develop in a healthy manner, provide public assistance in case of sickness and regard the improvement of public health as one of its primary duties (India Const. arts. 38, 39 cl. (e) & cl. (f), 41 & 47). While these principles are not directly enforceable, they are fundamental in the governance of the country, and the state has a duty to apply them when making laws (India Const. art. 37).

As for India's international commitments, the UN Universal Declaration of Human Rights (UDHR) provides that everyone has the right to a standard of living adequate for health and well-being (UDHR art. 25, cl. 1). Under the International Covenant on Economic, Social and Cultural Rights (ICESCR), State Parties are expected to recognise the right of everyone to enjoy the highest attainable standard of physical and mental health (ICESCR art. 12, cl. 1). To fully realise this right, they are also required to take steps to prevent, treat and control epidemic diseases (ICESCR art. 12, cl. 2(c)). Similarly, under the WHO's International Health Regulations (IHRs), India is obligated to develop, strengthen, and maintain its capacity to respond promptly and effectively to PHEs (IHR art. 13, cl. 1).

Technically, for implementing such international treaties, Parliament must enact a law under Article 253. However, the Supreme Court has held that international commitments, when not inconsistent with the Constitution and domestic laws, need to be followed and should be read into the fundamental rights to enlarge their meaning and content (*Vishaka v. State of Rajasthan*, 1997; *National Legal Services Authority v. Union of India*, 2014). Moreover, under the Protection of Human Rights Act, 1993, human rights are defined as including the rights to life and dignity that are guaranteed by the Constitution or embodied in international covenants and enforceable by courts. Referring to this statute, the Supreme Court has noted Parliament's legislative desire to implement human rights founded on constitutional values and India's international commitments (*Justice K.S. Puttaswamy v. Union of India*, 2017).

The right to health being included under Article 21, and deriving its meaning and content from the preamble, case law, the directive principles, and India's international commitments, imposes certain obligations upon the state. These include not only a negative obligation to not interfere with an individual's right to health but also, crucially, a positive obligation to take measures to secure the effective enjoyment of this right (*Navtej Johar v. Union of India*, 2018). The Supreme Court has repeatedly imposed obligations on the state to create the conditions that are necessary for good health, viewing the maintenance and improvement of public health as one of the primary constitutional duties of the state (*Modern Dental College and Research Centre v. State of Madhya Pradesh*, 2016; *Vincent Panikurlangara v Union of India*, 1987). In order to fulfil this duty efficiently and effectively in the context of PHEs, there is strong international recognition that adequate legal frameworks are required (Office of the High Commissioner for Human Rights, 2000; WHO, 2017, 2021).

It is worth noting here that the "state" upon which the Constitution and courts have imposed the aforesaid duty refers to several organs and levels of the state, including the central and state governments, Parliament, state legislatures and all local and other public authorities (India Const. arts. 12 & 36).

II.B.2. Constitutional Powers of the State

Constitutional duties give us a sense of why the Indian state ought to take measures regarding public health and a broad indication of what those measures must aim towards. We need to look elsewhere to understand what each level of the State is empowered to do.

The Constitution confers and divides legislative and executive powers between the Centre and the States according to the Seventh Schedule lists, comprising the Union, State, and Concurrent lists (India Const. arts. 73, 162, 245, & 246). The Union List contains matters over which the Parliament and central government have exclusive powers, and similarly, state legislatures and governments have exclusive powers over State List matters. Both the Centre and the states have powers over Concurrent List matters, but any conflict is resolved in favour of the Centre (India Const. arts. 162 & 254). Residuary powers over matters which are not expressly listed rest with the Centre (India Const. art. 248 & sched. VII, list I, entry 97). Additionally, Parliament also has the power to make laws for implementing international agreements (India Const. art. 253 & sched. VII, list I, entries 13 & 14).

For PHEs, relevant entries across the three lists include port quarantine and connected hospitals, and interstate quarantine on the Union List; public health, sanitation and hospitals on the State List and prevention of the interstate spread of infectious diseases on the Concurrent List. (India Const. sched. VII, list I, entries 28 & 81, list II, entry 6, & list III, entry 29). This means that states have exclusive powers over the broad field of public health, whereas they share powers with the Centre over the narrower field of preventing the spread of infectious diseases beyond state borders. This implies the need for coordinated Centre–state action when addressing widespread infectious diseases. The Centre has exclusive powers over only ports and interstate quarantine.

The powers of the third tier are determined by states (India Const. arts. 243G & 243W). The Eleventh and Twelfth Schedules list matters over which the Constitution envisages panchayats and municipalities respectively playing a role, and both include health (India Const. sched XI, entry 23 & sched. XII, entry 6). Even though ultimately, it remains up to the states to decide how to empower local governments, the Constitution indicates that the latter should be empowered 'to function as institutions of self-government' (India Const. arts. 243G & 243W, cl. (a)). This suggests that they should not be treated as mere extensions of the state government or as implementing agencies but as governments in their own right (Aiyar, 2020). In practice, there are considerable differences in the extents to which different states have devolved functions to the third tier (MoPR & TISS, 2016).

II.B.3. Constitutional Restraints on the State

Beyond telling us what the state and its many components must do, and can do, for public health and related emergencies, the Constitution also contains several rights-based and structural limitations to state action.

Article 19 includes the rights to assemble peaceably, to move freely throughout the territory of India and to practise any profession or carry out any occupation, trade or business (India Const. arts. 19, cl. 1(b), cl. 1(d) & cl. 1(g)). PHE measures such as quarantine, contact tracing and movement restrictions can come into conflict with these freedoms. However, the right to assemble is subject to reasonable restrictions in the interests of public order, and the other two aforesaid rights are subject to 'reasonable' restrictions in the interests of the general public (India Const. arts. 19, cl. 2, cl. 5 & cl. 6).

To test whether restrictions are 'reasonable', courts use the proportionality doctrine and look at whether the restriction is meant to achieve a proper purpose, if the measures taken are rationally connected to that purpose and if such measures are necessary (*Modern Dental College and Research Centre v. State of Madhya Pradesh*, 2016). The restrictions cannot be arbitrary or excessive and must be the least restrictive alternative that was available for achieving the desired purpose (*Om Kumar v. Union of India*, 2001; *Teri Oat Estates v. U.T. of Chandigarh*, 2004). Courts also consider whether the restriction is consistent with the directive principles of state policy, and if yes, then it is likely to be upheld as reasonable (*Laxmi Khandsari v. State of Uttar Pradesh*, 1981). In addition to being reasonable and connected to specific purposes, the restrictions must be imposed by executive action that has legislative backing (*Kharak Singh v. State of Uttar Pradesh*, 1963).

Under Article 14, which guarantees equality before law and equal protection of laws, the state needs to afford equal treatment to all individuals who are equally circumstanced and take affirmative action in favour of persons who are unequally circumstanced (*T.M.A. Pai Foundation v. State of Karnataka*, 2002). This requires the law to make classifications, and such classification must be non-arbitrary, reasonable, transparent and based on factors that are related to the object of the law (*John Vallamatom v. Union of India*, 2003). Article 14 prohibits arbitrary discrimination not only by the law but also by executive action (*Onkar Lal Bajaj v. Union of India*, 2003).

The facets of Article 21's right to life that could conflict with PHE measures include the right to privacy, the right to personal liberty, the right to travel abroad and the right to livelihood (*Justice K.S. Puttaswamy v. Union of India*, 2017; *Kharak Singh v. State of Uttar Pradesh*, 1963; *Satwant Singh Sawhney v. D. Ramarathnam, Assistant Passport Officer*, 1967; *Olga Tellis v. Bombay Municipal Corporation*, 1985). PHE measures could also conflict with the right to live with human dignity and the right to social and economic justice (*Francis Coralie Mullin v. Union Territory of Delhi*, 1981; *C.E.S.C. Ltd. v. Subhash Chandra Bose*, 1992).

A person may be deprived of life and personal liberty under Article 21 only in accordance with procedure established by law. Beyond that, the procedure must conform to the principles of natural justice in that it must be fair, just and reasonable and cannot be oppressive or arbitrary (*Maneka Gandhi v. Union of India*, 1978). The Supreme Court has established a relationship between Articles 14, 19 and 21 such that a statutory procedure that deprives a person of her rights under Article 21 must additionally meet the requirements of reasonableness and non-arbitrariness under Articles 14 and 19 as well (*Maneka Gandhi v. Union of India*, 1978).

There are two types of structural limitations imposed by the Constitution on state action. Firstly, restrictions on the rights contained in Articles 19 and 21 require legislative backing, which is effectively a horizontal structural limitation on the executive. Another such limitation, applicable to the executive as well as the legislature, is the power of judicial review (India Const. arts. 32 & 226). Courts can strike down any executive or legislative action that violates fundamental rights and can also issue writs to enforce these rights against any state authority (India Const. arts. 13, 32 & 226).

Secondly, while all levels of the State have the duty to act against PHEs, different levels have different powers. The executive and the legislature at the central and state levels are bound by the constitutional scheme of vertical distribution of powers and cannot overstep their boundaries. Local governments are also bound within the legislative frameworks of their respective states. There are thus clear constitutional rationales for the Indian state to take necessary and balanced measures regarding PHEs. To fulfil this responsibility, existing laws need to be reviewed, and an adequate PHE legal framework with appropriate duties, powers, and restraints needs to be developed.

III. The Existing Legal Framework: On Paper and in Recent Practice

III.A. Asking the Right Questions

To review any existing PHE law against the duty–power–restraint framework, and in a manner that is consistent with constitutional guidance, the following questions need to be asked:

- Does the law clearly define the duties of public authorities, drawing from the broad constitutional commitments to welfare, justice, equality and dignity and the more specific commitments to securing public health and ensuring PHE preparedness?
- Does the law coherently empower the appropriate level of government with adequate and precise authority over different matters relevant to PHEs, consistent with the Constitution's federal scheme that envisages broad public health roles for the state and local governments and a specific coordination role regarding contagious diseases for the Centre?
- Does the law protect the Constitution's fundamental rights by requiring public health restrictions on the former to be reasonable as per constitutional standards such as proportionality, opting for the least restrictive alternative, transparency, affirmative action and accountability?

Other relevant questions include asking whether existing laws are antiquated, ambiguous, or incoherent, have major gaps, and reflect a modern, evidence-based understanding of disease (WHO, 2017). Public health laws tend to reflect scientific and legal standards that were prevalent at the time when they were enacted, and antiquated laws incorporate neither advances in scientific understanding nor advances in constitutional and legal norms (Gostin, 2001; Martin, 2009).

Vidhi (2021) developed a more detailed analytical framework for analysing PHE laws by fleshing out each facet of the duty–power–restraint framework with multiple specific questions:

- Does the law identify a specific set of public actors who are responsible for dealing with a PHE, contain consequences and remedies in case these actors fail to act, set out a duty to coordinate with other specified bodies and create mechanisms for such coordination?
- Does the law confer a power to declare a PHE where defined rights and liberties are suspended; contain specific powers over matters such as quarantine, surveillance, compulsory vaccination, price controls, modifying regulatory requirements linked to clinical research and manufacturing drugs; and include enforcement mechanisms?
- Does the law establish a procedure for determining if a PHE exists and create mechanisms for public participation, appealing restrictions and ongoing review of measures?

These questions give a sense of the contents and standards that need to ground an Indian PHE law for it to be effective, balanced and in keeping with the spirit and text of the Constitution.

III.B. Existing Laws and Recent Application

The two laws that dominated India's COVID-19 response were the EDA and the DMA,[1] but looking at India's public health legal framework more generally, and at provisions relevant to PHEs particularly, reveals a range of scattered provisions.

Vidhi (2021) compiled a comprehensive, but not exhaustive, list of provisions in central laws that are relevant for PHE preparedness and response.[2] These provisions cover aspects such as quarantine, inspection, and travel restrictions; modification of standards and control of supply of essentials and enforcement and include statutes such as the Indian Ports Act, 1908, the Drugs and Cosmetics Act, 1940, the Essential Commodities Act, 1955 and the Indian Penal Code, 1860. At the state level, relevant categories of laws include epidemic disease laws (such as the Rajasthan Epidemics Act, 1957), general public health laws (such as the Assam Public Health Act, 2010) and disaster management laws (such as the Gujarat State Disaster Management Act, 2003).

Another category of state laws containing PHE-relevant provisions are state municipal and panchayat laws. Maharashtra's Mumbai Municipal Corporation Act, 1888 (MMCA), for instance, has a sub-chapter on 'prevention of spread of dangerous diseases' including epidemic diseases (MMCA, S. 3, cl. (aa)). Among state panchayat laws, the Himachal Pradesh Panchayati Raj Act, 1994 (HPPRA), empowers gram panchayats to take curative and preventive measures against epidemics (HPPRA, S. 13, cl. (k)).

III.B.1. The Epidemic Diseases Act, 1897

A bare-bones colonial-era legislation, the EDA primarily empowers state governments to take measures and prescribe temporary regulations to prevent the spread of epidemic diseases and empowers the Centre to inspect certain vehicles and passengers (EDA, S. 2, 2A).

As a pre-constitutional law, the EDA does not reflect the constitutional commitments to welfare, justice, equality and dignity, and it offers next to no guidance on duties. It also does not envisage any duty towards or mechanism for coordination between different governmental entities. When empowering governments, it does not incorporate local governments at all. For the governments it does empower, its provisions are overly broad, leaving too much to governmental discretion and lacking any meaningful guidance or specific powers on relevant PHE matters. It also does not identify any restraints or incorporate any safeguards and has no requirement to opt for the least restrictive alternative, transparency, affirmative action or accountability. There are no specified criteria for determining whether a PHE exists in the first place and no mechanisms for public participation or for appealing or reviewing measures.

The EDA is clearly antiquated and contains major gaps. It reflects the value systems of the era in which it was drafted, in terms of both standards of governance and scientific development (Rakesh, 2021). Until a 2020 amendment, the EDA did not even apply to former princely states, which had their own parallel laws (James and Agarwal, 2021). The inadequacy of the EDA is also reflected in the many epidemic disease ordinances, laws and amendments passed by various states in 2020-21, including Kerala, Karnataka, Rajasthan, Uttar Pradesh and Odisha (James and Agarwal, 2021). Equally, its shortcomings are reflected in the central government's choice of resorting to the more general (but also more comprehensive) DMA.

In an observation that applies perfectly to the EDA, the WHO (2017) notes that outdated public health laws undermine public health in two ways: firstly, by causing governments to lack adequate legal powers to respond to health threats, and secondly, by failing to achieve an appropriate balance between individual rights and public health interests.

III.B.2. The Disaster Management Act, 2005

The DMA addresses several aspects of disaster management. It establishes multi-level authorities, lists measures to be taken by the central and state governments and even specifies functions for local authorities (DMA, ch. II, III, IV, V, & VI).

While the DMA does define a set of duties and public actors, it does not draw from the specific constitutional commitments to securing public health and ensuring PHE preparedness. It does however provide for a degree of coordination and also confers a special power on the central government to issue binding directions to state governments for disaster management (DMA, S. 35, 38, & 62). Similarly, while it does empower multiple levels of government and creates multi-level authorities to act in disasters, it does not confer precise authority over matters relevant to PHEs.

As for restraints, it is worth noting that on the point of providing compensation and relief to disaster victims, it prohibits discrimination on the grounds of sex, caste, community, descent or religion (DMA, S. 61). There is also a requirement of having disaster management plans at all levels of government and for those plans to be reviewed and updated annually (DMA, S. 11, 23, & 31). While these are desirable, the DMA does not incorporate adequate standards of proportionality, affirmative action and accountability.

Even though it is technically possible to include PHEs within the DMA's definition of disaster, this statute was primarily intended for natural calamities affecting particular areas at a time (such as an earthquake). In its essence, the DMA is not a PHE law (Gowd et al., 2021; Bhushan and Agarwal, 2020). However, in the circumstances in which India found itself in early 2020, it is understandable why its provisions were resorted to. More than the DMA's appropriateness for the situation, this only highlights the limitations of the EDA, which nevertheless remains the only dedicated pan-India PHE law to date.

III.B.3. Pandemic Governance

The Centre used the DMA in March 2020 to impose a complete nationwide lockdown over COVID-19. By then, several states were already implementing measures including lockdowns using their EDA powers. The mode of pandemic governance transformed overnight, and the Centre went from encouraging states to use their EDA powers to directing them to submit daily implementation reports of central DMA directives (Home Secretary, 2020; Singh, 2022). After the Centre's DMA lockdown order, states modified their existing EDA lockdown orders to ensure consistency with central directives. This complete executive bypassing of the states by the Centre, outside of a constitutionally regulated state of emergency,[3] was astonishing and unprecedented. Equally astonishing was the timid acquiescence of states to being treated as mere implementing agencies in a matter over which they had substantial constitutional authority of their own.

Gradually, things began to change. Subsequent DMA lockdown orders in 2020 increasingly allowed for more state discretion in implementation, even though decision-making itself remained firmly with the Centre (Saxena, 2022). But in COVID-19's devastating second wave in 2021, the Centre appeared to suddenly rediscover state autonomy. Central intervention was conspicuously absent, and the matter was left almost entirely to state discretion (Sahoo and Ghosh, 2021). This caught the states off-guard, and if the Centre in the first wave was seen as overbearing, in the second wave, it virtually abdicated.

Local governments also played a significant role in states such as Odisha, Rajasthan, Maharashtra and Kerala (Isaac and Sadanandan, 2020; Dutta and Fischer, 2021), but this largely depended on the initiative of individual state and local governments rather than being reflective of any consolidated framework that meaningfully and effectively assigned roles to the third tier (Shringare and Fernandes, 2020). India's multi-governmental pandemic response was ultimately marked by uncertainty, inconsistency, and over-reach. In the extreme centralisation as well as the contrastingly extreme decentralisation of the first and second waves respectively, a common feature was the sheer absence of effective Centre–state coordination (Tillin, 2021). The Supreme Court had to intervene more than once to settle administrative deadlocks in horizontal and vertical governmental relations (*Union of India v. Rakesh Malhotra*, 2021; *In Re: Distribution of Essential Supplies and Services during Pandemic*, 2021; *In Re: Problems and Miseries of Migrant Labourers*, 2021). Despite all this, looking back in August 2022, the Prime Minister singled out states' collective efforts 'in the spirit of cooperative federalism' as the force behind India's emergence from the pandemic (PIB Delhi, 2022). In a sense, this bypassing and subsequent rediscovery of state autonomy revealed both the fragility and the enduring value of the Indian federal system.

Could a clear and consolidated PHE legal framework, comprising appropriate duties, powers, and restraints as argued in this chapter, have made a difference? A late-2020 survey of over 500 Indian civil servants regarding India's COVID-19 response revealed a near-consensus view among them that India had 'enough laws and rules' (Krishnamurthy et al., 2021). Through combinations of different legal instruments, governments did ultimately find the requisite tools to act, but without a consolidated and constitutionally grounded PHE law, there was no framework to guide governmental interventions and none for evaluating and holding entities accountable. Without needing to declare a formal emergency under the Constitution (which carries some safeguards), the Centre could rely on existing statutory instruments to assume vast powers and subvert the federal structure (Bhatia, 2020).

The Centre was initially happy to steal the show, and the states quietly played along. But when this was no longer politically expedient, there was a complete volte-face in the federal configuration of pandemic governance. Such ad hocism by governments ultimately comes at the cost of public health. To some extent, this only reflects the striking lack of political priority afforded to health in India (Venkateswaran et al., 2021), but the absence of a dedicated and modern PHE legal framework is part of what makes such erratic PHE governance permissible and without consequence. In this context, it is perhaps unsurprising that despite being no stranger to epidemics, India has failed to put together such a law to date. The legal status quo is not tenable and was arguably a major contributor to India's lack of pandemic preparedness in 2020-22. Urgent change is needed.

III.C. *Towards a Comprehensive Framework*

Over the last several decades, there have been a few attempts to change this status quo. In 1955, a Model Public Health Act was drafted that was later updated in 1987. However, it was meant not as a national legislation but rather as a model that individual states could adopt and adapt.

In 2009, a National Health Bill (NHB) was framed as a rights-based national legislation for public health as a whole. While it was a comprehensive attempt, informed by constitutional and international commitments and possessing several safeguards, it did not adequately cover PHEs. The next significant attempt came in the form of the Public Health (Prevention, Control, and Management of Epidemics, Bio-Terrorism and Disasters) Bill 2017 (PHEB). It intended to repeal the EDA and was focused on PHEs, unlike the NHB, but it did not identify any duties and came with virtually no safeguards. The powers it conferred, while substantial, varied and vested in multiple levels of government, established a unilateral hierarchy rather than a shared responsibility.

The COVID-19 pandemic may prove to have been the catalyst for the long-overdue overhaul of India's PHE laws. Reportedly, a new national public health bill replacing the EDA is in the works (Sharma, 2022). NITI Aayog (National Institution for Transforming India) was involved in drafting this bill, comments from state governments were sought, and the central government convened a high-level committee in July 2022 to finalise it (Tandon, 2022). The new bill is set to define the situations in which a PHE can be declared and create a four-tier, multi-sectoral health administration architecture (at the national, state, district and block levels), headed by a National Public Health Authority chaired by the union Health Minister. These authorities will be vested with defined powers and functions for addressing PHEs and will be supported by new national- and state-level public health cadres. It is also set to define measures such as isolation, quarantine and lockdown.

With the draft not being in the public domain at the time of writing, it is difficult to comment on the new bill's merits. It is unclear whether this bill will aim to comprehensively cover public health, like the NHB, or focus exclusively on PHEs, like the PHEB and the EDA. To be an adequate solution for the many limitations and gaps in the currently scattered legal framework, the bill would have to meet several requirements and standards, as developed and applied in this chapter. While the creation of multi-level public health authorities and cadres appear to be *prima facie* desirable, much would depend on how they are designed, especially with respect to the need for coordination and cooperation. It also remains to be seen whether the 2022 bill passes muster on duties and restraints especially, which is where the PHEB is notably lacking.

IV. Conclusion

PHEs entail governmental interventions shaped by laws. Applying the duty–power–restraint framework for analysing public health laws to the Indian Constitution itself, I drew out in this chapter a comprehensive set of duties, powers and restraints with respect to PHEs that are applicable to different organs and levels of the Indian state. Accordingly, I framed and posed appropriate questions and standards to relevant existing laws. Analysing these laws against these standards, and surveying some of their applications in the COVID-19 pandemic, revealed major gaps, friction and inconsistencies, especially along federal lines. Previous attempts at reforming this framework through draft bills have also been inadequate. With another such attempt being around the corner, analyses along these lines need to continue.

While the need for reform is urgent, it also requires deep and thorough consideration along with wide-ranging consultation. It is my hope that this chapter's attempt to build the foundations on which the new Indian PHE law should be drafted, and the standards against which it should be evaluated, will help inform legislative attempts going forward.

Acknowledgement

I am grateful to Shaivy Maheshwari for her valuable research assistance and input and to Dhvani Mehta and Balveer Arora for their insightful comments.

Notes

1 Along with Section 144 of the Code of Criminal Procedure, 1973, which was used to enforce lockdowns.
2 A WHO (2015) study also has a detailed analytical matrix that attempts to identify the gamut of Indian legislative provisions relevant to public health hazards across sectors.
3 The Constitution's emergency provisions do not envisage or provide for a PHE and only cover security threats, failure of constitutional machinery in states and financial emergencies.

References

Aiyar, M.S. (2020, May 6). The Panchayati Front: Tap Potential of Local Self-Government to Fight COVID-19. *The Indian Express*. https://indianexpress.com/article/opinion/columns/coronavirus-pandemic-panchayati-front-6395715/

Bhatia, G. (2020, April 13). An Executive Emergency: India's Response to Covid-19. *Verfassungsblog*. https://verfassungsblog.de/an-executive-emergency-indias-response-to-covid-19/.

Bhushan, P., and Agarwal, S. (2020, May 13). Riding Roughshod Over State Governments. *The Hindu*. www.thehindu.com/opinion/op-ed/riding-roughshod-over-state-governments/article62108083.ece.

C.E.S.C. Ltd. v. Subhash Chandra Bose, AIR 1992 SC 573.

Coggon, J. (2012). *What Makes Health Public?: A Critical Evaluation of Moral, Legal, and Political Claims in Public Health*. Cambridge: Cambridge University Press.

Constitution of India, art. 12, 13, 14, 19, 21, 32, 36, 37, 38, 39, 41, 47, 73, 162, 226, 243G, 243W, 245, 246, 248, 253, & 254, sched. VII, XI, & XII.

Consumer Education & Research Centre v. Union of India, AIR 1995 SC 922.

Devika Biswas v. Union of India, (2016) 10 SCC 726.

Disaster Management Act, ch. II, III, IV, V, & VI, S. 11, 23, 31, 35, 38, 61, & 62 (2005).

Dutta, A., and Fischer, H.W. (2021). The Local Governance of COVID-19: Disease Prevention and Social Security in Rural India. *World Development*, *138*, 105234. https://doi.org/10.1016/j.worlddev.2020.105234

Epidemic Diseases Act, S. 2, 2A (1897).

Francis Coralie Mullin v. Union Territory of Delhi, AIR 1981 SC 746.

Gostin, L.O. (2001). Public Health Theory and Practice in the Constitutional Design. *Health Matrix Clevel*, *11*(2), 265–326.

Gostin, L.O., and Wiley, L.F. (2016). *Public Health Law: Power, Duty, Restraint* (3rd ed.). Berkeley, CA: University of California Press.

Gowd, K.K., Veerababu, D., and Reddy, V.R. (2021). COVID-19 and the Legislative Response in India: The Need for a Comprehensive Health Care Law. *Journal of Public Affairs*, e2669. https://doi.org/10.1002/pa.2669

Goyal, P. (2020). The Epidemic Diseases Act, 1897 Needs an Urgent Overhaul. *Economic and Political Weekly*, *55*(45).

Himachal Pradesh Panchayati Raj Act, S. 13 (1994).

Home Secretary. (2020). *DO No. 40–3/2020-DM-I(A)*. New Delhi, India: Government of India. www.mohfw.gov.in/pdf/DOletter_secretary.pdf

In Re: Distribution of Essential Supplies and Services during Pandemic, Suo Motu Writ Petition (Civil) No. 3 of 2021.

In Re: Problems and Miseries of Migrant Labourers, Suo Motu Writ Petition (Civil) No. 6 of 2021.

Institute of Medicine. (1988). *The Future of Public Health*. Washington, DC: National Academies Press.

International Covenant on Economic, Social and Cultural Rights, art. 12 (1966).

International Health Regulations, art. 13 (2005).

Isaac, T.M.T., and Sadanandan, R. (2020). COVID-19, Public Health System and Local Governance in Kerala. *Economic and Political Weekly*, *55*(21), 35-40.

James, K., and Agarwal, A. (2021, November 22). Federal Tensions in India's COVID-19 Response: The Case of the Many Epidemic Acts. *National Law School of India Review Blog*. https://nlsir.com/federal-tensions-in-indias-covid-19-response-the-case-of-the-many-epidemic-acts/

John Vallamatom v. Union of India, (2003) 5 SCALE 384.

Justice K.S. Puttaswamy v. Union of India, (2017) 10 SCC 1.

Kesavananda Bharati v. Union of India, (1973) 4 SCC 225.

Kharak Singh v. State of Uttar Pradesh, AIR 1963 SC 1295.

Krishnamurthy, M., Sanan, D., Sharma, K.R., and Unnikrishnan, A. (2021). *The Pandemic and Public Administration: A Survey of Indian Administrative Service (IAS) Officers*. New Delhi, India: Centre for Policy Research. https://doi.org/10.13140/RG.2.2.20276.17281

Laxmi Khandsari v. State of Uttar Pradesh, AIR 1981 SC 873.

Maneka Gandhi v. Union of India, AIR 1978 SC 597.

Martin, R. (2009). The Role of Law in Public Health. In Dawson, A. (Ed.), *The Philosophy of Public Health*. Farnham and Burlington: Ashgate.

Ministry of Panchayati Raj and Tata Institute of Social Sciences. (2016). *Devolution Report 2015–16: Where Local Democracy and Devolution in India Is Heading Towards*? New Delhi, India: Ministry of Panchayati Raj, Government of India & Mumbai, India: Tata Institute of Social Sciences. www.panchayat.gov.in/documents/20126/0/devolution2015-16.pdf/d5e26984-5783-3a14-e7f7-6113a6cfa7c4?t=1554884884392.

Modern Dental College and Research Centre v. State of Madhya Pradesh, (2016) 7 SCC 353.
Mumbai Municipal Corporation Act, S. 3 (1888).
National Legal Services Authority v. Union of India, (2014) 5 SCC 438.
Navtej Johar v. Union of India, AIR 2018 SC 4321.
Nelson, C., Lurie, N., Wasserman, J., and Zakowski, S. (2007). Conceptualizing and Defining Public Health Emergency Preparedness. *American Journal of Public Health*, 97(S1). www.ncbi.nlm.nih.gov/pmc/articles/PMC1854988/pdf/0970009.pdf
Nuffield Council on Bioethics. (2007). *Public Health: Ethical Issues*. London: Nuffield Council on Bioethics.
Office of the High Commissioner for Human Rights. (2000). *CESCR General Comment No. 14: The Right to the Highest Attainable Standard of Health (Art. 12).* www.refworld.org/pdfid/4538838d0.pdf.
Olga Tellis v. Bombay Municipal Corporation, (1985) 3 SCC 545.
Om Kumar v. Union of India, (2001) 2 SCC 386.
Onkar Lal Bajaj v. Union of India, (2003) 2 SCC 673.
Parmet, W.E. (2009). *Populations, Public Health, and the Law.* Washington, DC: Georgetown University Press.
PIB Delhi. (2022, August 7). Seventh Meeting of Governing Council of NITI Aayog Concludes. *Press Information Bureau.* www.pib.gov.in/PressReleasePage.aspx?PRID=1849410
Rakesh, P.S. (2016). The Epidemic Diseases Act of 1897: Public Health Relevance in the Current Scenario. *Indian Journal of Medical Ethics*, *1*(3), 156-160.
Rakesh, P.S. (2021). Implementing the Epidemic Diseases Act to Combat Covid-19 in India: An Ethical Analysis. *Indian Journal of Medical Ethics*, *6*(1), 13-17.
Rothstein, M. (2002). Rethinking the Meaning of Public Health. *Journal of Law, Medicine and Ethics*, *30*, 144-149.
Sahoo, N., and Ghosh, A.K. (2021). *The COVID-19 Challenge to Indian Federalism.* ORF Occasional Paper No. 322. Observer Research Foundation, New Delhi, India. www.orfonline.org/research/the-covid-19-challenge-to-indian-federalism/.
Satwant Singh Sawhney v. D. Ramarathnam, Assistant Passport Officer, AIR 1967 SC 1836.
Saxena, R. (2022). Federalism and the COVID-19 Crisis: Center-State Apposite Relations in India. In Chattopadhyay, R., Knüpling, F., Chebenova, D., Whittington, L., and Gonzalez, P. (Eds.), *Federalism and the Response to COVID-19: A Comparative Analysis.* Abingdon and New York: Routledge.
Sharma, H. (2022, March 23). New Health Law Draft: Four-Tier System, Clearly Defined Powers. *The Indian Express.* https://indianexpress.com/article/india/new-health-law-draft-four-tier-system-clearly-defined-powers-7828695/#:~:text=The%20proposed%20National%20Public%20Health,and%20nuclear%20attacks%20or%20accidents.
Shringare, A., and Fernandes, S. (2020). COVID-19 Pandemic in India Points to Need for a Decentralized Response. *State and Local Government Review*, *52*(3), 195–199. https://doi.org/10.1177/0160323X20984524
Singh, A.K. (2022). Pandemic Governance in India: The Ongoing Shift to 'National Federalism'. In Steytler, N. (Ed.), *Comparative Federalism and COVID-19: Combating the Pandemic.* Abingdon and New York: Routledge.
Tandon, A. (2022, July 11). New Law to Strengthen Public Health Response. *The Tribune.* www.tribuneindia.com/news/nation/new-law-to-strengthen-public-health-response-411223
Task Force on Public Health Act. (2012). *Approach Paper on Public Health Act.* New Delhi, India: National Health Systems Resource Centre.
Teri Oat Estates v. U.T. of Chandigarh, (2004) 2 SCC 130.

Tewari, M. (2020). *India's Fight Against Health Emergencies: In Search of a Legal Architecture*. ORF Issue Brief No. 349. New Delhi, India: Observer Research Foundation. www.orfonline.org/research/indias-fight-against-health-emergencies-in-search-of-a-legal-architecture-63884/

Tillin, L. (2021, May 24). Center and States Need to Coordinate, Not Compete. *Centre for the Advanced Study of India*. https://casi.sas.upenn.edu/iit/louisetillin

T.M.A. Pai Foundation v. State of Karnataka, (2002) 8 SCC 481.

Union of India v. Rakesh Malhotra, (2021) 9 SCC 222.

Universal Declaration of Human Rights, art. 25 (1948).

Venkateswaran, S., Slaria, S., and Mor, N. (2021). *The Political Pathway to Health System Improvements in India*. CSEP Working Paper No. 18. New Delhi, India: Centre for Social and Economic Progress. https://csep.org/working-paper/the-political-pathway-to-health-system-improvements-in-india/.

Vidhi Centre for Legal Policy. (2021). *What Should a Public Health Emergency Law for India Look Like? A White Paper*. New Delhi, India: Vidhi Centre for Legal Policy. https://vidhilegalpolicy.in/research/what-should-a-public-health-emergency-law-for-india-look-like/

Vincent Panikurlangara v Union of India, AIR 1987 SC 990.

Vishaka v. State of Rajasthan, AIR 1997 SC 3011.

World Health Organisation (WHO). (2015). *International Public Health Hazards: Indian Legislative Provisions*. New Delhi, India: Regional Office for South-East Asia, WHO.

World Health Organisation (WHO). (2017). *Advancing the Right to Health: The Vital Role of Law*. Geneva, Switzerland: WHO.

World Health Organisation (WHO). (2021). *Report of the Review Committee on the Functioning of the International Health Regulations (2005) During the COVID-19 Response*. Geneva, Switzerland: WHO.

5 Interstate Variations in Private-Sector Growth in Medical Care

Rama V. Baru

Introduction

That India is marked by variations in socioeconomic development has been well documented. The federal structure of the Indian polity makes health a state subject with certain limited powers to the Centre. While there is some scholarly writing on federalism and health, it is largely confined to analyses of the public sector; there is very limited reference to the role of for-profit medical institutions in the debates on federalism in health.

For this chapter, I draw on the available analysis to highlight the interstate variations in for-profit medical care; for the purposes of the chapter, I restrict my discussion to nursing homes and hospitals that provide both outpatient and inpatient services. In addition, I examine the growth and distribution of private allopathic medical colleges across major states; the growth of these medical colleges has contributed to the expansion of private medical care provision. I further seek to explain why there is higher growth in the southern and western states than in the north and the east. I explain the reasons for these variations through the lens of political economy and highlight the historical, social and political factors that have fuelled the growth of private medical institutions over the last five decades in terms of type and location. The paper is divided into three sections.

The first section provides the complex and heterogenous structure of private medical care consisting of multiple actors and levels. The second section presents a summary of available data and analysis to capture the magnitude of interstate variations. The third section is my exploration of the historical, social and political factors responsible for these variations. The concluding section highlights the challenges that the interstate variations pose for Centre-state relations and for regulating private health care.

I

There is considerable writing on the large presence of private-sector in the provisioning of health services in India. This has been mostly captured through analyses of National Sample Survey Office (NSSO) utilisation

DOI: 10.4324/9781003568711-6

Table 5.1 Growth of the Private Sector in Health Care in India

NSS rounds	*Description*	*Inpatient*		*Outpatient*	
		Public	*Private*	*Public*	*Private*
42nd 1986-87	Total	60.0	40.0	22.5	77.5
52nd 1995-96	Total	43.5	56.6	19.5	80.5
60* 2004-05	Total	40.0	60.1	20.5	79.5
71st 2014	Rural	41.9	58.1	28.9	71.1
	Urban	32.0	68.0	21.2	78.8

Source: Hooda, S.K. (2017). Growth of Formal and Informal Private Healthcare Providers in India: Structural Changes and Implications. *Health Care Finance*, 44(2), 11. Fall.

data. It is important to point out that analysis of the 42nd Round of the NSSO in the late 1980s highlighted the high dependence of the Indian population on the private sector for outpatient services. For inpatient services that involve hospitalisation, the middle- and lower-income quintiles were mostly dependent on the public sector across states, although this changed almost a decade later as the analysis of the 52nd round of the NSS showed. The dependence on the private sector for inpatient and outpatient care increased in both rural and urban areas for the decade from 2004 to 2014 (see Table 5.1).

Many scholars have observed the growth of private institutions from the 1980s through the 1990s and 2000s, noting the considerable variation in the growth and distribution of public and private institutions across states: specifically there was a clear divide between the better- and less-developed states. The former consisted of southern and western states that performed better in terms of economic and human development outcomes, and the private sectors in these states were largely unregulated and outside the ambit of health services planning. The regulatory framework is weak, and thus, these private-sector providers are not accountable to either the professional associations or any state regulations. The more recent efforts to regulate these institutions have been initiated by the Centre and require ratification and implementation by individual states (Nandraj et al., 2021).

Structure of the Private Sector in Medical Care and Education

The private sector consists of multiple actors of varying sizes, locations and levels of care. The sector is heterogenous, with a large presence of individual private practitioners providing allopathy and indigenous systems of medicine providing primary level care. A substantial percentage of the individual practitioners are informally trained and often referred to as RMPs. According to an estimate based on the Enterprise Survey in the mid-1980s, 80 per cent of the private sector were mostly clinics or dispensaries located mainly in urban areas (Baru, 1998). Analysing the proportion of Own Account Enterprises based on the 67th Round of the NSS, Hooda's estimates show that

> the regional distribution of private facilities shows that the presence of OAEs is greater in rural areas. OAEs held around 61 per cent of the shares in rural areas. In 2010–11, only a marginal 18 per cent of the establishments were reported to be present in rural areas, while the rest 82 per cent were reported to be present in urban areas. This reflects that rural areas have a greater number of small/individual practitioners but lack in formal organised and large facilities as compared to urban areas.
>
> (Hooda, 2017, p. 4; Baru, 1998)

Analysis of OAEs shows that the private sector is dominated by individual practitioners. Medical service providers form the largest share, while only 21.7 per cent are establishments. The remaining 78.3 per cent are Own Enterprises, meaning small, independent practitioners. The private establishments are dominated by small and medium-sized enterprises, while the private and public limited enterprises constitute only around 2 per cent to 4 per cent of the total. The small and medium-sized establishments are located mostly in urban towns of varying sizes, while the corporate hospitals are largely located in metros and Tier I cities.

Growth and Distribution of Private Medical Colleges

The growth of private medical colleges goes back to the late 1970s, mostly in southern and western states. This increase in private medical colleges contributed to the growth of nursing homes and hospitals across states. Doctors graduating from the private medical colleges find employment in nursing homes and hospitals as entrepreneurs, continuing the family business and as salaried employees (Baru, 1998). Baru and Diwate (2022), in their analysis of the growth and distribution of private medical colleges, provide data on the regional distributions of both government and private medical colleges. They confirm the concentration of the private sector medical institutions in mostly southern and western states. Among the northern states, Uttar Pradesh (UP) has a large number of private medical colleges, but the remainder have very few (see Table 5.2).

The Magnitude of Private Establishments in Medical Care

It is estimated that private establishments comprise 62 per cent of all India's health care infrastructure. Over the last three decades, the private sector has expanded, with 43,486 private hospitals and 1.18 million beds contrasted with 25,778 public hospitals and 713,986 beds (Jafferlot and Jumle, 2020). A large percentage of these beds are distributed across several states and cater

Table 5.2 Regional Distribution of Medical Colleges in India

Region	*State*	*No. of Government Colleges*	*No. of Private Colleges*	*Total No of Colleges (% of total region)*
South	Andhra Pradesh	13	18	31 (14.49)
	Telangana	11	22	33 (15.42)
	Karnataka	19	41	60 (28.04)
	Kerala	9	22	31 (14.49)
	Tamil Nadu	25	25	50 (23.36)
	Pondicherry	2	7	9 (4.21)
	Total	79	135	214 (100)
West	Goa	1	0	1 (1.15)
	Gujarat	17	12	29 (33.33)
	Maharashtra	25	31	56 (64.37)
	Daman & Diu	0	0	0
	Dadra & Nagar Haveli	1	0	1 (1.15)
	Total	44	43	87 (100)
Central	Chattisgarh	7	3	10 (10.75)
	Uttarakhand	4	2	6 (6.45)
	Uttar Pradesh	26	29	55 (59.14)
	Madhya Pradesh	14	8	22 (23.66)
	Total	51	42	93 (100)
North	Haryana	5	7	12 (16.90
	Himachal Pradesh	6	1	7 (9.86)
	Jammu and Kashmir	7	1	8 (11.27)
	Panjab	4	6	10 (14.08)
	Rajasthan	15	8	23 (32.39)
	Delhi	8	2	10 (14.08)
	Chandigarh	1	0	1 (1.41)
	Total	46	25	71 (100)
East	Bihar	10	6	16 (25.81)
	Jharkhand	7	1	8 (12.90)
	Orissa	8	4	12 (19.35)
	West Bengal	19	6	25 (40.32)
	Andaman & Nicobar Islands	1	0	1 (1.61)
	Total	45	17	62 (100)

(Continued)

Table 5.2 (Continued)

Region	*State*	*No. of Government Colleges*	*No. of Private Colleges*	*Total No of Colleges (% of total region)*
North-East	Assam	7	0	7 (46.67)
	Manipur	2	0	2 (13.33)
	Tripura	1	1	2 (13.33)
	Meghalaya	1	0	1 (6.67)
	Sikkim	0	1	1 (6.67)
	Arunachal Pradesh	1	0	1 (6.67)
	Nagaland	0	0	0
	Mizoram	1	0	1 (6.67)
	Total	13	2	15 (100)
	Total	**278**	**264**	**542**

Source for Regions in India: Interstate Council Secretariat, Ministry of Home Affairs, Government of India, Zonal Councils Composition as available on http://interstatecouncil.nic.in/zonal_composition.html# subnav2_2.

to around 50 per cent of the population. These states include Uttar Pradesh, Maharashtra, Karnataka, Tamil Nadu, Telangana, West Bengal and Kerala.

There are broadly four phases in the growth of private enterprises. The first phase is from independence to the mid-1970s; the second phase is from the mid-1970s to the mid-1980s; the third phase is from the late 1980s to the 1990s and the fourth phase is from the late 1990s to the present (see Figure 5.1). The first phase consisted of growth of individual private practitioners in rural and urban areas. The second phase consisted of the growth of small and medium-sized nursing homes, mostly urban and promoted by doctor entrepreneurs. The third phase saw the growth of private and public limited enterprises with active involvement of NRI (non-resident Indian) doctors, mostly based in the United States. The fourth phase was a continuation of the same, with an expanded and diversified corporate sector, increased foreign direct investment and partnership with private equity and venture capital (Lefebvre, 2010).

Many of the corporate ventures were either acquiring medium-level enterprises in Tier 2 cities or creating franchises that acted as feeders from the secondary to the tertiary levels. The corporate hospitals often have networks of individuals who refer patients from the primary level. Based on discussions with the RMP Association in Mahbubnagar (a less developed district in Telangana), I learned that there is a well-established system of commissions for referrals through the network of practitioners affiliated with Apollo Hospital in Hyderabad. Specifically, a number of Mahbubnagar clinic practitioners refer their patients for diagnostic testing, consultation and hospitalisation to Apollo Hospital. The business model promotes vertical integration through referrals from the primary to the tertiary level.

We have little information on the phases of growth of these institutions across states. A study of select districts in erstwhile Andhra Pradesh in the mid-1980s

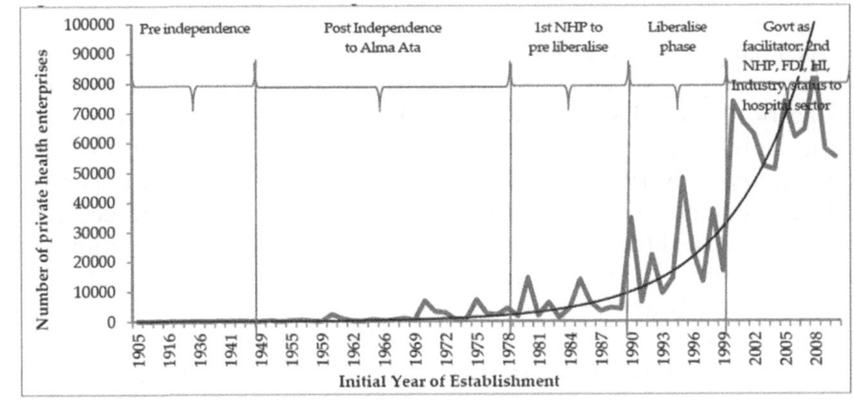

Figure 5.1 Unit-level record of the 67th round of NSS reflecting the growth of private health enterprises.

Source: Hooda, S.K. (2017). Growth of Formal and Informal Private Healthcare Providers in India: Structural Changes and Implications. *Health Care Finance, 44*(2), 4.

revealed that there were more nursing homes in developed districts in coastal Andhra than in the less developed districts of Telangana (Baru, 1987). These nursing homes were mostly small and medium-sized enterprises with from 5 to 40 beds and located in small towns and cities. I later observed a similar pattern in that there were more private institutions in the southern and western states than in the northern states. Gradually the growth of the private sector increased in West Bengal, Haryana and Uttar Pradesh (Baru, 1987).

The 1980s and 1990s saw a spurt in the growth of the middle-level and larger hospitals as financing through bank loans and industrial loans was eased. This was also a period when hospitals were granted the status of an industry, and the government reduced duties for importing high-technology equipment that was an important avenue for increasing profit margins in hospitals; indeed, several of the public subsidies offered to these enterprises came under the jurisdiction of the Ministry of Commerce rather than Health. The 2000s was a period of consolidation and expansion of the tertiary private sector that partnered with venture and private equity capital (Lefebvre, 2010). Again, one could discern regional variations with an active role of NRI doctors and business groups, for instance the NRI Kamma and Reddy doctors in Hyderabad and Chennai; the Chettiar, Mudaliar and Nadar NRIs in Chennai; the Gulf returnees from the Muslim community investing in medicities in Kochi and Calicut and the Gujjar NRI doctor returnees setting up hospitals in UP and Delhi.

Rise of Dominant Castes and Their Diversification Into Medical Care and Education

The growth of the private sector in medical care is marked by interstate variations in India. There are historical, socioeconomic and political factors that have influenced this process. The southern and western states of undivided

Andhra Pradesh, Tamil Nadu, Kerala, Karnataka, Maharashtra and Gujarat are the high private sector growth states.

This can be explained by the level of socioeconomic development, the diversification of surplus from commercialisation of agriculture into entrepreneurial activities that included cinema halls, rice mills, hotels and also nursing homes in the early 1980s. These enterprises were dominated by upper castes and rich peasantry like the Kammas and Reddys in Andhra Pradesh, Marathas in Maharashtra and sections of the middle and OBCs in Tamil Nadu. Many of the doctors from these regions migrated to the United States in the 1960s and 1970s and returned to India during the late 1980s to invest in multi-specialty tertiary hospitals as private limited and corporate enterprises.

The return of NRI doctors transformed the landscape of the private sector in medical care, and these doctors played an important role in shaping health policy through the next three decades. The last three decades saw the growth of the private sector primarily across the southern and western states, with expansion into the eastern and northern states as well over the last decade. It is no longer an urban phenomenon but has expanded into semi-rural and rural areas; the corporate sector has diversified into smaller towns that act as feeders to their tertiary hospitals.

The magnitude and distribution of private institutions has demonstrated regional variations. The reasons for these variations need to be located in their respective historical, socioeconomic and political contexts. For this purpose, the social basis of the private sector needs to be studied. Few researchers have attempted to do this, and the few who have conducted mostly small, location-specific studies.

Almost three decades ago, my research on regional variations in health services development between selected districts in Telangana and coastal Andhra showed the presence of a large number of private nursing homes in the latter (Baru, 1987). I had chosen the districts of Mahbubnagar and Medak in Telangana and Krishna and Guntur in coastal Andhra based on levels of development: the latter two were better developed in relation to social and economic indicators than the former two. For the study, I examined the growth and distribution of public, for-profit and non-profit institutions and found much more variation in the distribution of private-sector than public-sector facilities. I also found less private-sector growth in Telangana than in coastal Andhra, promoted mostly by Reddys; in coastal Andhra, the private-sector nursing homes were owned by doctor entrepreneurs, had from 15 to 40 beds and were located in towns and cities. I also observed that the promoters of the nursing homes were dominated by Kammas in the coastal areas. The investment for these nursing homes was derived from agrarian surpluses (Baru, 1987).

The significance of the rise of private enterprise in health care is that by the late 1970s, there was a significant presence of medical professionals among the Kammas. Several scholars commented on how the Kammas invested in education as a means for social mobility and also to break Brahminical hegemony. This began during the colonial period and provided the base for the rise of Kamma professionals in medicine, engineering and later information technology. Roohi in her study on the mobility of the Kammas discusses the role of caste associations in facilitating access to English education:

> In Andhra, the early 1900s saw the sprouting of caste associations in different parts of the region, under the aegis of caste notables. The famous Kamma Mahajana Sangam was founded in 1914 under the patronage of the Raja of Chellapalli and other prominent Kammas. Various patronage activities, such as building caste hostels, educational institutions and providing scholarships for poor students, were undertaken by the affluent community leaders of that time. Charitable hostels and subsidized or free educational institutions came up in the trading towns of the region and made access to education away from the countryside possible for the rural youth of the community. It paved the way for rural-to-urban migration for those within the community who did not have resources to do so.
>
> (Roohi, 2019, p. 32)

Economists and political scientists have also more broadly studied the diversification of agrarian surplus into agri-based and related commercial activity. Thorner (1980) studied coastal Andhra Pradesh in the 1970s and observed that the rich peasants were investing their agrarian surpluses into setting up oil and rice mills and cinema halls (Thorner, 1980). Krishna Rao also observed and documented growth of the rich peasants and capitalist farmers in the coastal belt of Andhra Pradesh due to the structural changes in the agrarian economy after green revolution technology was introduced during the 1970s. These farmers also invested their agrarian surpluses into a variety of commercial and industrial activities (Rao, 1984).

Upadhya (1988) studied the rise of Kamma entrepreneurs in Visakhapatnam district as rich peasants and how they invested agrarian surpluses into education and subsequently into agri- business such as setting up of rice mills, sugar mills and tobacco trade facilities. Upadhya highlighted the important role that caste and kinship networks played in Kammas' gaining access to higher education and setting up business enterprises. Similarly, Mario Rutten's study of rural Gujarat shows the role of caste and kinship networks in business enterprises.

Upadhya and Rutten argue that there are three domains that are interlinked and require attention in order to explain the regional variations in the returns of NRIs and that the three are exemplified in the case of highly skilled professionals like doctors: (1) the transnational social fields that connect diasporic communities with their home regions; (2) the institutional structures, networks and nodes through which both people and resources move and (3) the specific histories and sociopolitical and socioeconomic conditions of the regions migrants leave and later transmit resources back to (Upadhya and

Rutten, 2012). The flows of ideas, knowledge and technology go beyond the realm of economic transactions because they become integrated within a web of relationships that include regional, caste, class, familial, kinship and institutional ties (Levitt, 1998; Poros, 2011).

This is exemplified in my study of the rise of corporate hospitals in erstwhile Andhra Pradesh (Baru, 1987). By the 1980s, the investments in health care were no longer confined to the towns of Guntur and Krishna but moved to Visakhapatnam, which was emerging as an important centre for commercial activity. The real competition, however, was between Hyderabad and Visakhapatnam. Hyderabad became the preferred location for investments during the 1980s with N.T. Rama Rao (NTR) as chief minister, who was himself a Kamma. For the first time, a Kamma Chief Minister was leading the state, and many of his caste fellows felt that this would open new opportunities to them in the capital city. From 1995 to 2004, under the regime of Chandrababu Naidu, NTR's son-in-law, the economic reforms and the liberalisation process further attracted enterprising businessmen from this particular community to Hyderabad to invest in real estate, corporate health and education or to take up jobs in the new economy (Baru, 1987).

In addition to the traditional upper castes like Brahmins, Kammas were also overrepresented among the software engineers and medical doctors (Roohi, 2019). Investments and promotion of corporate hospitals in Hyderabad were dominated by the Kammas and Reddys, mostly NRI doctors based in the United States. Both these caste groups mobilised their social networks to consolidate the capital – financial, real estate, professional and political – that facilitated the growth of the corporate sector. Examples of the first generation of major corporate hospitals in Hyderabad include K. Suryanarayana's Apollo, Care, Medicity and Kamineni Hospitals; B. Krishnaiah's Bollineni group (Krishna Institute of Medical Sciences), K. Sambasiva Rao's Medwin Hospitals, the Usha Mullapudi Cardiac Centre of Ratnam V. Mullapudi (a US-returned cardio-thoracic surgeon) and the L.V. Prasad Eye Institute (Damodaran, 2008, p. 111).

Reddys and Kammas tapped into their professional networks in the United States to promote their ventures in India. These networks allowed them to persuade NRI doctors to return to India as investors, consultants or employees. Indeed, each of the medical colleges has a US-based alumni association, and searching these associations' websites shows that the doctors are actively engaged with the changing landscape of medical care in the State. By the 1990s, large hospitals with strong NRI links were being established in coastal Andhra in Vijayawada, Bhimavaram and Visakhapatnam (Baru, 1987).

The trend in coastal Andhra was similar to what Omvedt (1981) had observed for the rich peasants, mainly Marathas, in Maharashtra: Omvedt observed that every rich peasant household invested in the professional education of at least one of their sons to become lawyers, engineers or doctors, while others looked after the land. As in coastal Andhra, there was the growth of nursing homes in the prosperous districts of Maharashtra. We do not have detailed studies of the interdistrict variation and social base of the private sector in Maharashtra as a whole. Detailed studies are however available for the growth of private hospitals in Mumbai with investments from big business groups like Tatas and Hindujas. In Maharashtra, the Marathas, who are both economically and politically a powerful caste, diversified from agriculture into a range of commercial ventures that included medical colleges and hospitals.

Diwate systematically delineates Maratha control over sugarcane farming, sugar co-operatives and political institutions and diversification of surpluses into medical education and hospitals, among other commercial activities (Diwate, 2019). Her study shows the domination of the Maratha-Kumbi combine in the setting up of private medical colleges. In Karnataka, the promoters of private medical colleges are dominated by the Brahmins, Shettys, Vokkaligas, Lingayats and sections of OBCs (Diwate, 2016).

Harish Damodaran observed marked variation in the growth of the private sector between southern and western India and the northern and eastern parts of the country. He gives as the reason for this variation the nature of capitalist growth in India, which has diversified

> not just in terms of production profile (spanning a whole lot of industries) but also social base. Capital is not just the bastion of a few mercantile castes the way it was; its base has expanded to incorporate a wide spectrum of communities. However, this 'inclusive capitalism' has been more a feature of southern, and to some extent western India.
> (Damodaran, 2008, p. 312)

He further observes that this is not the case in northern India where the Banias-Marwaris and Khatris tend to dominate. The intermediate castes were engaged in agrarian production but did not make the switch to industrial activity on the same scale as their counterparts in the south and western parts of India. Multiple factors like differences in access to education from the colonial period led to the formation of the middle classes among the intermediate castes in southern India; the non-Brahmin movement in these areas led to the creation of a broad base among these castes to form a middle class and also forced the Brahmins to explore other career opportunities. It is only in recent times that education has become important in the north, although increasingly one sees intermediate and backward castes accessing higher education.

A small-scale study on the caste-class background of promoters of private hospitals in Tirunelveli, Tamil Nadu, shows the dominance of intermediate and backward castes (Ganapathy, 2006). Western Tamil Nadu has seen growth in private-sector medical care and education during the last two decades. The two major caste groups who have diversified into this area are the Naidus and Gounders. The Kongunadu Kammavars Naidus migrated from coastal Andhra and settled in Coimbatore in the early part of the 20th century. They were large landowning *mirasdars* who later diversified into agro-based industries. Subsequent generations diversified into cotton cultivation and set up the cotton mills in Coimbatore. The present generation have set up tertiary hospitals as trusts. Prominent among them is the Aravind Eye Hospital promoted by Govindappa Venkataswamy, who set up the medical venture in 1976 and then expanded to several cities in Tamil Nadu (Ganapathy, 2006).

Another example of diversification is K. Govindaswamy, a Naidu who made forays into textile and iron casting businesses from the 1940s. Subsequently, he set up the Govidaswamy Naidu Medical Trust, which runs a general hospital and an eye hospital. The Trust is now headed by his son, Dr G. Bakthavatsalam, an alumnus of Madras Medical College and a cancer surgeon. He recalls,

> I was doing a post-doctoral fellowship at Mount Sinai, Chicago, in the early 1970s, when my father called me over to start the hospital. He had studied only till the fifth standard but was keen that I become a doctor. We began with 25 beds in 1974 and today it is a 40 crore business on its own.
>
> (Damodaran, 2008, p. 151)

Apart from the Naidus, Gounders have promoted tertiary and specialist private hospitals in Coimbatore:

> Another US-returned entrepreneurial venture is the Coimbatore-based Kovai Medical Centre and Hospital Limited of Nalla G. Palaniswami, an endocrinologist from Wayne State University at Michigan. His group operates colleges offering paramedical courses in nursing, pharmacy, physiotherapy and occupational therapy.
>
> (Damodaran, 2008, p. 159)

Regional Variations in Private Health Services and Centre–State Relations

Under the provisions of the Indian constitution, health is primarily a state subject. However, there are several provisions that come under the purview of the Centre and find place on the Concurrent List. Public health, health service provisioning and sanitation fall under the purview of the State List. The Concurrent List that comes under the purview of the Union government includes national health programmes, medical and nursing education, scientific research, etc. The division of health-related issues between the state and Centre results in fragmented authority and power. Much of the scholarly literature has focused on the financial aspect of Centre–state relations in public health services, but there has been little exploration of those dynamics in private-sector health care.

Given the interstate variations in the growth of the private sector, there are considerable differences in state governments' financing, provisioning and regulation of health care services. States' different sociopolitical contexts are important determinants of their governments' engagement with the private sector – and vice versa – including subsidies offered by state-level public insurance schemes; concessions offered for setting up private health services; human resource deployment and regulation of the private sector. For instance, two central bodies – the National Medical Commission (which replaced the Medical Council of India) and the Nursing Council of India – are the key bodies for registering institutions, standardising syllabi, regulating professional ethics and providing certification. Private institutions are regulated via legislation such as the Clinical Establishments Act and the Pre-Conception and Pre-Natal Diagnostic Techniques Act that is centrally enacted and requires ratification and implementation by states. The extent of compliance by states is influenced by the political clout of the private sector to resist implementation.

The relationship between the private sector and the state government is mediated through the power dynamics between the profession, business interests of promoters of private institutions and local politics. Across levels of the private sector, there is engagement with political parties from the ideological spectrum. An example of this was observed in Mahbubnagar in the early 2000s, where the informal providers had an association that was affiliated with the Marxist Communist Party and were able to put political pressure for recognition on the then-Telugu Desam Party. The association had a presence across districts in Telangana and acted as a pressure group to protect their interests (Baru, field notes, Mahbubnagar district, 2002).

At the secondary level, in several states the promoters of small and medium-sized nursing homes set up associations to protect their interests as efforts were made for registration and regulation. This was seen in Andhra Pradesh, Karnataka, Kerala, Maharashtra and the Bombay Nursing Home Association (1977) and UP, to name a few. These associations lobbied with state governments and used legal measures to resist regulation. At the national level, the Association of Healthcare Providers is led by private and public limited hospitals across states. Several of the hospital members are also members of the associations in their respective states. These multiple organisations represent the interests of the heterogeneous private sector. This gives rise to contestation of the regulatory processes leading to fragmentation of authority and power for its implementation. This undermines effective regulation leading to anarchic behaviour of the private sector in terms of cost and quality of services.

Regulation of private health services is one of the important inputs for availability, quality and cost; it also ensures the protection of patient rights and exploitative practices:

> A regulatory system is made up of the institutions, stakeholders and processes involved in designing, making, implementing, and reviewing the regulation. Good regulations define accountability among the target

> groups and are consistent in action or penalty, irrespective of the position, power, or authority of the person or organisation violating them.
> (Nandraj et al., 2021, p. 3)

However, regulations are implemented differently across India and even within states based on the heterogeneity of the private sector. Many regulations are directed at the middle and small sectors, while the corporate and private limited enterprises are not covered, and there has also been resistance from the Indian Medical Association (IMA), private hospital associations and the state medical councils across states in varying degrees. As a result, large sections of the private sector are beyond the purview of legal and self-regulation. They have set the terms of engagement with the government by wresting public subsidies and supporting the agenda of universal health coverage rather than universal health care.

The government efforts at regulation are fragmented and have many gaps and challenges:

> There is an absence of regulations on the cost of care that practitioners provide, or the fees or charges related to the treatment they may provide. Apart from complaining to the provider specific professional councils such as the State medical council or the Ethics and Registration Board, and the Consumer Protection Act, 2019, which have their own limitations, there are insufficient legal provisions for grievance redressal for patients and consumers. The CEA, 2010, too is deficient on the grievance redressal aspects for the patients/consumers.
> (Nandraj et al., 2021)

A prime example of fragmented regulation is the 2010 Clinical Establishments (Registration and Regulation) Act (CEA). Professional bodies like the IMA placed heavy pressure on state governments not to ratify centrally sponsored legislation like the CEA. States with high private-sector growth like Punjab, Goa and Tamil Nadu have actively resisted the uptake of the centrally sponsored bill and have followed their own existing legislation (see Table 5.3).

In states like Punjab, Goa, Tamil Nadu, Odisha and Rajasthan, the private-sector medical and nursing homes association lobbied actively to keep smaller hospitals from the purview of the CEA (Nandraj et al., 2021), and these regional variations in the growth of health services and the landscape of regulation have created what Arora (2000) described as an intrinsic tension between regional aspirations and the imperatives of national policy cohesion. Indeed, the Covid-19 pandemic amply demonstrated how the combination of professional power and business investments is able to challenge efforts to be regulated by the state and central government: during the crisis, the private sector was more concerned about their decline in demand and wanted concessions from the government. At the height of the first wave, the leadership of the hospital group of the Federation of Indian Chambers of Commerce

Table 5.3 State-Level Acceptance of the Clinical Establishments Act of 2010 (as of March 2021)

Acceptance	*States*
State and Union Territories (UTs) where the CEA took effect on the date of notification, 1 March 2012	Arunachal Pradesh, Himanchal Pradesh, Sikkim, Mizoram and (UTs) Andaman & Nicobar Islands, Dadra and Nagar Haveli and Daman and Diu, Lakshadweep, Chandigarh, Puducherry, Jammu & Kashmir
States which have since adopted the CEA	Assan, Bihar, Haryana, Jharkhand, Rajasthan, Uttarakhand, Uttar Pradesh
States and UTs with their own legislation	Andhra Pradesh, Chhattisgarh, Hoa, Karnataka, Kerala, Madhya Pradesh, Maharashtra, Manipur, Meghalaya, Nagaland, Odisha, Punjab, Tamil Nadu, Tripura, West Bengal, Telangana 1 UT Delhi

Source: Nandraj S, Gupta P, and Randhawa S. (2021). Regulation of Health Care Delivery in India – A Landscape Study, Health Systems Transformation Platform, New Delhi.

and Industry demanded subsidies from the government to protect their fall in profits (Baru and Bisht, 2020). Across states, private associations did not comply with state government orders to free beds for Covid-19 patients, and very few states were able to force compliance.

In the present political environment, there is a tendency to centralise decisions for health through a range of programmes and policies that has reduced spaces for federalism.[1] One might agree with Jeffery (2021) that the

> centre-state relationships in health are the shrinking role of discretional central funding public for health policy; the growing commercialization of health services in large parts of India; and the increasing role of external opportunities and pressures that change the options for all levels of government in the country.

Note

1 The opposition and resistance is coming from largely non-BJP led states. Recent examples of state resistance to centralisation of health legislation include the case of NEET by the Tamil Nadu government and the evoking of the Epidemics Act during the Covid-19 pandemic.

References

Arora, B. (2000). Negotiating Differences: Federal Coalitions and National Cohesion. In F. Frankel, Z. Hasan, R. Bhargav, and B. Arora (Eds.), *Transforming India: Social and Political Dynamics*. Oxford: Oxford University Press.

Baru, R.V. (1987). *Factors Influencing Variations in Health Services: A Study of Selected Districts in Andhra Pradesh* [Unpublished M.Phil Dissertation, Jawaharlal Nehru University, New Delhi].

Baru, R.V. (1998). *Private Health Care in India: Social Characteristics and Trends*. New Delhi: Sage.

Baru, R.V., and Bisht, R. (2020, April 25). The Government Must Stop Appeasing the Private Healthcare Sector. *The Wire*.

Baru, R.V., and Diwate, A. (2022). Private Sector in Medical Education and Allied Health Disciplines. In Varghese, N.V., and Panigrahi, J. (Eds.), *India Higher Education Report 2021: Private Higher Education*. New Delhi: Routledge.

Damodaran, H. (2008). *India's New Capitalists: Caste, Business and Industry in a Modern Nation*. Basingstoke: Palgrave Macmillan.

Diwate, A. (2016). *Social Characteristics of Private Medical Colleges in India: A Study of Select States* [Unpublished PhD Thesis, Submitted to the Centre of Social Medicine and Community Health, Jawaharlal Nehru University, New Delhi].

Diwate, A. (2019). Growth of Private Medical Colleges in Maharashtra and Its Implications for Universal Health Care. In Qadeer, I., Saxena, K.B., and Arathi, P.M. (Eds.), *Universalising Health Care in India: From Care to Coverage*. New Delhi: Aakar Books.

Ganapathy, M. (2006). *Changing Role of the Public and Private Sectors in Health Care: A Case Study of Tirunelveli, Tamil Nadu* [Unpublished PhD Thesis, Submitted to Jawaharlal Nehru University, New Delhi].

Hooda, S.K. (2017, Fall). Growth of Formal and Informal Private Healthcare Providers in India: Structural Changes and Implications. *Health Care Finance*, *44*(2).

Jafferlot, C., and Jumle, V. (2020, November 3). *Public Health in India: Lessons from a Pandemic*. www.institutmontaigne.org/en/blog/private-healthcare-india-boons-and-banes, accessed 20.5.2022.

Jeffery, R. (2021). Health Policy and Federalism in India. *Territory, Politics, Governance*, *10*(1), 67–85. https://doi.org/10.1080/21622671.2021.1899976

Krishna Rao, Y.V. (1984). *Peasant Farming and Growth of Capitalism in Indian Agriculture*. Vijayawada: Visaalandhra Publishing House.

Lefebvre, B. (2010). *Hospital Chains in India: The Coming of Age*? www.ifri.org/sites/default/files/atoms/files/asievisions23blefebvre.pdf January, accessed 22.5.2022.

Levitt, P. (1998, Winter). Social Remittances: Migration Driven Local-Level Forms of Cultural Diffusion. *International Migration Review*, *32*(4), 926–948. Sage Publications.

Nandraj, S., Gupta, P., and Randhawa, S. (2021). *Regulation of Health Care Delivery in India: A Landscape Study*. New Delhi: Health Systems Transformation Platform.

Omvedt, G. (1981). Capitalist Agriculture and Rural Classes in India. *Economic and Political Weekly*, A140-A143+A145-A159.

Poros, M. (2011). *Modern Migrations: Gujarati Indian Networks in New York and London*. Stanford: Stanford University Press.

Roohi, S. (2019). Historicizing Mobility Trajectories of Highskilled Migrants from Coastal Andhra to the United States. *Journal of Interdisciplinary Economics*, *31*(1) 24–41. https://doi.org/10.1177/0260107918770954.

Thorner, D. (1980). Coastal Andhra: Towards an Affluent Society. In *The Shaping of Modern India*. New Delhi: Allied Publishers.

Upadhya, C. (1988). The Farmer-Capitalist of Coastal Andhra Pradesh. *Economic and Political Weekly*, *22*, 27–28.

Upadhya, C. and M. Rutten (2012). Migration, Transnational Flows and Development in India: A regional perspective. *Economic and Political Weekly*. Volume XLVII, No.19. May 12th. Sameeksha Trust.

Part II

Unequal States

6 Responding to the Rising Burden of Non-Communicable Diseases in a Federal Polity

K. Srinath Reddy and Manu Raj Mathur

Introduction

While infectious diseases were the dominant causes of death in all regions of the world till the 19th century, a health transition started to bring other diseases to the fore in the 20th century. These were clustered together under the label of non-communicable diseases (NCDs). This was an unsatisfactory term which described disorders by what they were not (i.e, not infectious) rather than what they were. The label 'lifestyle diseases' was also inappropriate because it attributed the causation to the chosen behaviours of individuals rather than the social, economic, environmental and commercial factors which shaped and steered behaviours and exposures that increased the risk of NCDs. The proposition that all of the disorders labelled as NCDs are non-infectious in origin is also incorrect, since some cancers are clearly linked to infectious agents like viruses (cancers of cervix, liver) or bacteria (stomach).

Another term used to describe this cluster is chronic diseases. This too is not entirely correct, as NCDs may not only present as prolonged ailments but also as acute events (like acute heart attack, stroke or renal failure or sudden cardiac death). None of these terms gives indications of the factors that have been causally linked to NCDs, let alone the upstream social determinants. It would perhaps be more appropriate to call this cluster 'diet, inactivity, tobacco, alcohol' related disorders. Unfortunately, such a label will never become popular in a global environment in which tobacco, unhealthy foods and beverages, alcohol and inactivity-promoting devices are aggressively marketed by powerful commercial interests.

It is not surprising that the rise of NCDs globally coincided with changes in economic systems that transformed the nature of power relationships in society. In the second half of the 20th century, high-income countries of Europe and North America experienced an upswing in NCDs, even as infectious diseases and nutritional disorders receded (Hunter and Reddy, 2013). Propelled by delayed industrialisation, growing urbanisation and globalisation which constituted the tailwind of the 20th century, NCDs also advanced in the low- and middle-income countries (LMICs) towards the end of the

DOI: 10.4324/9781003568711-8

twentieth century. Now, they are the leading causes of death and disability in all parts of the world, including India (Reddy, 2004).

In this chapter, we profile NCDs because they feature in the global health agenda and among India's health priorities (as reflected in policies and programmes), and we discuss how the national response is shaping in the context of federalism. The fact that India is a federal polity, where a Constitution assigns the mandate for delivering health services to the states, is obscured when the central government designs and partly funds national programmes and also undertakes international commitments related to health treaties and development goals. Further, when state leadership is not aligned with the party in power at the Centre, centre–state consensus and coordination on health policies and programmes are constrained by conflicting agendas. It is in that context of obfuscated federalism that India's response to NCDs needs to be studied.

Major NCDs and Risk Factors

In 2011, the World Health Organisation (WHO) assisted the United Nations (UN) in developing and adopting a political declaration on NCDs (United Nations, 2011). This later became the guiding light for WHO's global action plan for prevention and control of NCDs (WHO and others, 2013). They set NCD related targets to be achieved by 2025. These were then adopted, with some modification, in the targets linked to the health and well being goal of the UN Sustainable Development Goals (SDGs) of 2015 (UN Department of Economic and Social Affairs, 2015).

The WHO initially identified four major NCDs as the target diseases based on the high disease burdens associated with them. These were cardiovascular disease, diabetes, cancers and chronic obstructive pulmonary disease, and they were linked to four common risk factors: unhealthy diet, tobacco, alcohol and physical inactivity. Later, WHO expanded this 4 × 4 construct to a 5 × 5 cluster by adding mental health disorders to the disease cluster and air pollution to the risk factor group. These additions reflect the high disease burdens attributable to them and rectify their omission in the earlier priority setting declarations of UN and WHO.

There are other NCDs which demand attention such as kidney and genitourinary disorders; liver and gastrointestinal diseases; musculoskeletal afflictions; eye, ear and oral disorders and a variety of allergic and auto-immune maladies. While they do not explicitly feature in WHO's list of the 'big five', they require the attention and efforts of the health system for prevention, diagnosis and treatment. The risk factors for NCDs also extend beyond the five the WHO lists. It is now well recognised that intra-uterine and early childhood malnutrition are causally linked to early onset of diabetes and cardiovascular disease in adulthood. This is due to a mismatch between metabolic programming for survival, developed during periods of nutrient deprivation, and the rebound adiposity that follows when there is even a slight increase in energy intake during later childhood or adolescence (Bhargava et al., 2004; Barker et al., 2005). Thus, early childhood malnutrition and stress set the stage for adult NCDs. A segmental approach to age and a fragmented approach to labelling health disorders fail to recognise that the life course influences on NCDs extend from pre-conception to late adult life.

The Epidemiological Transitions Which Have Advanced NCDs Globally

The past century has witnessed changes in the dominant disease profiles in different parts of the world. As industrialisation and urbanisation advanced in Europe and North America, sanitation and nutrition security improved to reduce the danger from infectious diseases. However, as life expectancy rose, several risk factors of NCDs also started to become more prevalent in their populations: tobacco use; overconsumption of unhealthy foods and beverages; physical inactivity; harmful use of alcohol and air pollution.

Longer lifetime exposure to NCD risk factors increased the lifetime risk of NCDs, and improvements in scientific knowledge, health care and risk behaviours moved NCD burdens from younger years to the older end of the age spectrum. Changes even occurred in the NCDs themselves: bleeding (haemorrhagic) brain strokes, common in the early stages of the NCD increase, yielded to clotting (thrombotic) brain strokes and coronary heart disease (heart attacks) as the dominant cardiovascular diseases. Cancers also started rising as the population aged.

LMICs followed a more delayed NCD trajectory owing to delayed industrialisation and staccato urbanisation. However, globalisation hastened the process and pitchforked underprepared health systems of LMICS into the vortex of NCDs in the late 20th century. India too has experienced this pattern. Since the NCD burden in India is still maturing, the major impacts related to those diseases are seen in middle age rather than being tilted towards the older ages as seen presently in high-income countries.

As the NCD epidemics mature, there is also a progressive reversal of the socioeconomic gradient in NCD burdens. In early stages of development, more affluent sections of the population have the means to experiment with tobacco, fat- and sugar rich foods, mechanised transport and labour-saving devices. Later, as knowledge of risk factors accrues, the more affluent and educated sections adopt healthier behaviours, giving up tobacco; taking up sports and leisure time physical activity; consuming more fruit, vegetables, fish, lean meat and healthier edible oils. They experience less occupational, economic and social stress. At the same time, contributors to NCD risk become mass produced and become regular features of daily living among those with lower incomes as automation and mass transport reduce physical activity levels. Healthier food products like fruit and vegetables become less accessible to the poor and they also have less access to health information and health services. As NCD epidemics advance across the globe, the poor among countries and the poor within countries become the most vulnerable victims (Reddy et al., 2007; Jeemon and Reddy, 2010).

Global NCD Targets Adopted by India

The UN political declaration of 2011 called for a 25 per cent reduction in 'premature' mortality related to NCDs among those aged 30–70 by the year 2025 from 2010 levels. This was later changed to a target of a one-third reduction in NCD mortality for the same age group by 2030, and India has adopted these targets as well.

These targets have three major limitations. First, NCDs occur outside of the age range of 30 to 70. Rheumatic and congenital heart diseases as well as childhood cancers kill people under age 30 years, and elderly persons have a high risk of NCD-related deaths and also need protection. Second, the focus on only mortality overlooks morbidity (illness) and disability caused by NCDs; these diseases can produce prolonged suffering and loss of function, such as post-stroke disability, reduced exercise tolerance after a heart attack, the debilitating effects of cancer and its treatments or even the pain and impaired mobility of chronic severe arthritis. A health system must not only prevent deaths but also minimise suffering and reduce disability.

Finally, the UN/WHO reduction targets apply uniformly around the world irrespective of marked variations in the current stage and pace of progression of epidemiological transition. In many low-income regions, especially in Africa, high NCD mortality is occurring in those under 30, although it should shift to ages 30–70 over the next decade, whereas in high-income countries, the majority of the NCD deaths presently occur above 70 years of age; in both cases, the target of mortality reduction in the 30–70 year age group is either difficult or not relevant. It is in LMICs that NCD mortality is high in the age range of 30 to 70 years, and a common global target that is insensitive to such variations in current epidemiological profiles, will be unfair to LMICs if used as a performance measure for accountability.

Even within India, different states are at different levels of economic development and stages of epidemiological transition. It would be incorrect to apply the same age 30–70 mortality reduction target to states which are well advanced in epidemiological transition, like Kerala or Tamil Nadu, and states which are at an earlier stage of health transition, like Jharkhand or Chhattisgarh. This is also true of sub-regions in large states. Eastern Uttar Pradesh, for example, is an earlier stage of health transition than western Uttar Pradesh.

India: Burden of NCDs

Over the past three decades, India has experienced demographic, developmental and nutritional transitions which have together resulted in shifting the country's epidemiological profile from predominance of communicable

Table 6.1 Epidemiological Transitions in India

NCDs	*1990 (%)*	*2016 (%)*	*2019 (%)*
Death	35.8	62.1	64.9
Disability-Adjusted Life Years	29.1	54.9	57.9

Source: Institute for Health Metrics and Evaluation. (2019). *GBD Results Tool* (https://vizhub.healthdata.org/gbd-results/).

diseases to one where NCDs are the major contributors to death and disability (Table 6.1).

This change has resulted both through better prevention and control of communicable diseases and a rise in the incidence and prevalence of NCDs, as documented in several population surveys and cohort studies. The risk factors leading to NCDs have also become more widely prevalent in the Indian population, particularly in urban areas. With increasing life expectancy, both lifetime exposure to these risk factors and the risk factor levels themselves rise. With consumption of unhealthy diets (high in salt, sugar, unhealthy fats and carcinogens but low in fruit, vegetables and fibre), tobacco consumption in many forms, exposure to high levels of air pollution, decreased levels of physical activity levels and increased stress of daily living, NCDs have increased in their incidence and impact.

NCD Burdens Vary Across States

While India has moved into a high NCD burden zone, there are variations across different regions. States which have experienced higher levels of demographic transition (longer life expectancy and greater urbanisation) have higher NCD burdens (Table 6.2). These are usually associated with higher levels of economic development. Thus, the pattern of epidemiological transition observed over a century in high-income countries is also being observed in India but in a shorter time frame. Despite the variations based on levels of developmental transition, every state of India has reported an increase in NCD burdens since 1990.

Variations in profiles across states have implications for the health systems of different states. While states like Kerala, Tamil Nadu and Goa can focus their efforts on NCD prevention and control, states like Uttar Pradesh, Bihar, Madhya Pradesh and Jharkhand will have to simultaneously address the challenges that continue to be posed by maternal mortality, child mortality and communicable diseases while striving to stem the rising tide of NCDs. This calls for functional federalism in the countrywide response to NCDs.

Policy and Programme Response

Health is a state subject in India, per constitutional mandate. However, health policy is periodically formulated at the national level. The most recent

Table 6.2 Contribution of NCDs to Deaths and DALYs in Indian States (2019)

State	*DALYs (%)*	*Deaths (%)*
Kerala	76.9	81.8
Goa	74.7	79.3
Punjab	68.9	75.5
Himachal Pradesh	67.8	74.6
Delhi	66.3	73.6
Jammu & Kashmir and Ladakh	63.8	73.1
Other Union Territories	67.9	72.8
West Bengal	66	72.8
Karnataka	65.4	72.5
Tripura	65.3	72.5
Tamil Nadu	68	72.4
Maharashtra	66	71.7
Sikkim	68.2	71.4
Andhra Pradesh	63.3	68.3
Haryana	61	68.3
Telangana	62.7	68
Uttarakhand	61.7	67.9
Gujarat	59.8	67.2
Manipur	61.6	65.4
Mizoram	57.4	64.3
Assam	56	63.3
Arunachal Pradesh	58.6	63.2
Nagaland	56.6	62.5
Meghalaya	56.4	60.9
Rajasthan	51.3	59.9
Chhattisgarh	53.8	59.7
Madhya Pradesh	51.7	59.6
Jharkhand	53.5	58.1
Bihar	50.3	56.9
Uttar Pradesh	49.2	56.7
Odisha	54.3	56.1

Source: Institute for Health Metrics and Evaluation. (2019). *GBD Results Tool*. Available from: https://vizhub.healthdata.org/gbd-results/

version, National Health Policy 2017, recognises the growing burden of NCDs and declares intent to respond with effective strategies for prevention and control (Ministry of Health & Family Welfare, MoHFW, 2017). The national government is also a signatory to the UN Political Declaration on the Prevention and Control of Non-Communicable Diseases, adopted in 2011 (UN, 2011). This commitment was further affirmed in the UN SDGs (UN Department of Economic and Social Affairs, 2015).

The SDG target for NCDs calls for one-third reduction in NCD related mortality, between 2015 and 2030, in the age group of 30–70 years. This is being applied to all countries, irrespective of their current stage of epidemiological transition (Reddy, 2020). India too has adopted this target at the national level and the states will be monitored for their performance in achieving this. This is unreasonable, as states which were in early transition in 2015 are now moving into a stage with high mid-life burdens of NCDs. While every attempt must be made to prevent, detect and treat NCDs at all stages of life, to reduce death and disability, the mid-life mortality cannot be rationally applied to all states for gauging comparative performance.

Some states have developed a State Health Policy, identifying the priority health problems of their populations and indicated the policy and programme responses (Health and Family Welfare Department, Uttar Pradesh, 2018; Health and Family Welfare Department, Tamil Nadu, 2022; Health and Family Welfare Department, Odisha, 2021). Prevention and control of NCDs features in the health priorities identified by all states. However, the indicator for measuring progress is anchored to the 30–70 age group mortality target, reflecting the national target which is in turn tethered to the SDG target. Most states are also identifying mental health services as a priority, although many of them have invested very little so far towards expanding and improving those services.

A national programme for NCDs evolved by expanding the scope of the pre-existing programme for prevention and control of cancer. The National Programme for Prevention and Control of Cancer, Diabetes, Cardiovascular Diseases and Stroke was launched in 2010 (MoHFW, 2010). This was positioned under the umbrella of the National Health Mission (NHM). The funds allocated to this programme, in successive central budgets, have fallen far short of the disease burdens and programme needs of NCDs. The National Mental Health Programme was launched in 1982 (MoHFW, 1982). The District Mental Health Programme was added in 1996 (MoHFW, 1996). The National Mental Health Policy was adopted in 2014, to strengthen the programme and incorporate hitherto neglected areas like urban mental health and disability certification (MoHFW, 2014). The National Tobacco Control Programme was launched during 2007–08 (MoHFW, 2007). Eye health and oral health have their own national programmes.

Until recently, centrally funded health programmes focused on 'selective primary care', which did not include NCDs and mental health, but NHP 2017 called for comprehensive primary health care, and it does include these. Health and wellness centres (HWCs) are to provide these under the umbrella of Ayushman Bharat (MoHFW, 2019). Urban primary health care, long neglected, is also receiving attention through the establishment of urban HWCs. While well intended, limited funding to NHM and health workforce shortages will constrain the scale and speed of establishing functioning HWCs across all states

Integrating the NCD and mental health programmes into the NHM has not been an easy task. Limited budgetary resources, lack of dedicated human resources and inadequate coordination and monitoring have kept these programmes on the slow track. The Covid-19 pandemic further de-prioritised these programmes at the national level, despite the fact that NCDs constitute the co-morbidities that contributed most to severe disease and deaths associated with the SARS CoV-2 virus infection and that mental health disorders are common or get aggravated under the stressful conditions of the pandemic. This adversely affects states with high burdens of NCDs and mental health disorders.

States like Tamil Nadu and Kerala have accorded high priority to NCD prevention and control and to protecting mental health. Two decades ago, Tamil Nadu initiated a district programme for evaluating the impact of a community-centred programme that strengthened health systems to detect and treat hypertension and cervical cancer (The World Bank, 2010). The state now has active NCD and mental health programmes at the district level. Under the recently launched Makkalai Thedi Maruthuvam scheme, the state government aims to provide health care at the doorstep: services include in-home early screening and then regular medication and monitoring of patients with NCDs (Subramanian and Srinivasan, 2021). Kerala, meanwhile, has launched Amrutham Arogyam to identify persons with hypertension or diabetes: in addition to routine NCD screening, subsidiary screening programmes have been incorporated for chronic obstructive pulmonary disease, diabetic retinopathy, diabetic foot, stroke management, adolescent NCD and decentralised cancer management (Health and Family Welfare Department, Kerala, 2020).

While states which have strong primary care systems and reasonably strong district hospitals for providing secondary care have advanced NCD prevention and care without being constrained by the limitations of the national programme, they too are heavily dependent on the private sector for provision of NCD-related tertiary care. Central policies that promote the growth of the private sector and propose an increased role in health care provision further skew tertiary care provision in favour of the organised private sector which runs corporate hospitals. The countrywide scatter of centrally funded and managed new All India Institutes of Medical Sciences will be unable to deliver the needed services due to the severe faculty shortages that are already evident and the lack of a coherent connection with state health systems. Strengthening district and medical college hospitals, linked to state health systems, is an imperative of federalism for the assured provision of health services at all levels of care.

The states' ability to design and implement programmes for NCD prevention and control is partly constrained by the limited mandate and resources of the national programme and by the limited funding available from the central government. The central government's timely sharing of revenues from the Goods and Services Tax with state governments has also become a contentious issue in recent years. The channels for smooth transfer of funds for primary care directly to rural and urban local bodies, as mandated by the Fifteenth Finance Commission of India, have yet to be defined (Finance Commission of India, 2021).

A context-relevant, resource-optimising response to NCDs requires epidemiological information on risk factors and disease patterns at the district level, with clarity on urban–rural differences in each district. Surveillance of NCDs and their risk factors was proposed for inclusion in the Integrated Disease Surveillance Programme, but that has not happened (MoHFW, 2018). Tamil Nadu and Kerala have supported some studies by local medical colleges and research institutes to gather state specific data, but regular periodic surveillance of NCD risk factors is unavailable at the state level. Exceptions have been periodic tobacco surveys: the Global Adult Tobacco Survey (WHO, 2017) and Global Youth Tobacco Survey (WHO, 2009). Indian data are gathered for providing national-level estimates. Prevalence of hypertension, overweight-obesity and elevated blood sugar were only recently incorporated into the National Family Health Survey (IIPS and ICF, 2022). Here too, district-specific prevalence estimates are not available to inform a decentralised programme response.

A pivotal component of the programmes to contain NCDs is the active engagement of communities and locally based civil society partners, and state- and district-level government agencies are best positioned to build such partnerships. Without a strong commitment to federalism, states will not have the freedom to build such partnerships, especially when the central government's ambivalent attitude to community-based organisations impedes active civil society engagement.

References

Barker, D.J.P., Osmond, C., Forsén, T.J., Kajantie, E., and Eriksson, J.G. (2005). Trajectories of Growth Among Children Who Have Coronary Events as Adults. *New England Journal of Medicine*, *353*(17), 1802–1809.

Bhargava, S.K., Sachdev, S., Fall, C.H.D., Osmond, C., Lakshmy, R., Barker, D.J.P., et al. (2004, February 26). Relation of Serial Changes in Childhood Body-Mass Index to Impaired Glucose Tolerance in Young Adulthood. *New England Journal of Medicine*, *350*(9), 865–875.

Finance Commission of India. (2021). *Report of Fifteenth Finance Commission for 2021–26*. New Delhi: GoI.

Health and Family Welfare Department. Government of Kerala. (2020). *Non-Communicable Disease Prevention and Control*. Thiruvananthapuram. Government of Kerala.

Health and Family Welfare Department. Government of Odisha. (2021). *Health Policy*. Bhubaneshwar. Government of Odisha.

Health and Family Welfare Department. Government of Tamil Nadu. (2022). *Policy Note*. Chennai. Government of Tamil Nadu.

Health and Family Welfare Department. Government of Uttar Pradesh. (2018). *Towards Building a Robust, Resilient and Responsive Health System*. The Uttar Pradesh Health Policy.

Hunter, D.J., and Reddy, K.S. (2013, October 3). Noncommunicable Diseases. *New England Journal of Medicine*, *369*(14), 1336–1343.

Institute for Health Metrics and Evaluation. (2019). *GBD Results Tool*. https://vizhub.healthdata.org/gbd-results/

International Institute for Population Sciences (IIPS) and ICF. (2022 March). *National Family Health Survey (NFHS-5), 2019–21*. Mumbai. Ministry of Health and Family Welfare, Government of India.

Jeemon, P., and Reddy, K.S. (2010). Social Determinants of Cardiovascular Disease Outcomes in Indians. *Indian Journal of Medical Research*, *132*(5), 617–622.

Ministry of Health and Family Welfare. Government of India. (1982). *National Mental Health Programme (NMHP)*. New Delhi: GoI.
Ministry of Health and Family Welfare. Government of India. (1996). *District Mental Health Programme (DMHP)*. New Delhi: GoI.
Ministry of Health and Family Welfare. Government of India. (2007). *National Tobacco Control Programme (NTCP)*. New Delhi: GoI.
Ministry of Health and Family Welfare. Government of India. (2010). *National Programme for Prevention & Control of Cancer, Diabetes, Cardiovascular Diseases & Stroke (NPCDCS)*. National Health Mission. Government of India.
Ministry of Health and Family Welfare. Government of India. (2014). *National Health Mental Policy*. New Delhi: GoI.
Ministry of Health and Family Welfare. Government of India. (2017). *National Health Policy*. New Delhi: GoI.
Ministry of Health and Family Welfare. Government of India. (2018). *Integrated Disease Surveillance Programme(IDSP)*. New Delhi: GoI.
Ministry of Health and Family Welfare. Government of India. (2019). *Ayushman Bharat – Health and Wellness Centres*. New Delhi: GoI.
Reddy, K.S. (2004, June 10). Cardiovascular Disease in Non-Western Countries. *New England Journal of Medicine*, *350*(24), 2438–2440.
Reddy, K.S. (2020, April 1). Measuring Mortality from Non-Communicable Diseases: Broadening the Band. *Lancet Global Health*, *8*(4), e456–e457.
Reddy, K.S., Prabhakaran, D., Jeemon, P., Thankappan, K.R., Joshi, P., Chaturvedi, V., et al. (2007, October 9). Educational Status and Cardiovascular Risk Profile in Indians. *Proceedings of the National Academy of Sciences U S A*, *104*(41), 16263–16268.
Subramanian, M., and Srinivasan, R. (2021). Giving Healthcare Teeth to Fight Non-Communicable Diseases. *Chennai News – Times of India*. https://timesofindia.indiatimes.com/city/chennai/giving-healthcare-teeth-to-fight-non-communicable-diseases/articleshow/88200973.cms.
United Nations. (2011). High Level Meeting on the Prevention and Control of Non-communicable Diseases. In *High Level Meeting, 2011*. New York: United Nations.
United Nations Department of Economic and Social Affairs. (2015). *Transforming Our World: The 2030 Agenda for Sustainable Development*. Department of Economic and Social Affairs. United Nations General Assembly.
The World Bank. (2010). *The Tamil Nadu Health System Project*. New York: World Bank.
World Health Organization. (2009). *Surveillance of Noncommunicable Diseases. India*. Global Youth Tobacco Survey (GYTS): India.
World Health Organization. (2017). *Surveillance of Noncommunicable Diseases. India*. Global Adult Tobacco Survey (GATS): India.
World Health Organization and Others. (2013). *Global Action Plan for the Prevention and Control of Noncommunicable Diseases 2013–2020* (p. 55). New York: World Health Organization.

7 Public Health Infrastructure and Human Resources in Primary Health Care

K. Sujatha Rao

Introduction

India is unique for the immense diversity in all factors – economic, social, cultural – that directly impact the type, quality and nature of the health system. Therefore, reference to 'India's health system' is a travesty of sorts: the interstate differences are substantial in terms of governance, financing and outcomes. While health indicators in Kerala and Tamil Nadu (TN) are comparable with those a developed country, those in Uttar Pradesh (UP), Assam and Bihar are similar to those for sub-Saharan Africa (see Table 7.1). Wide disparities make formulating policies that enable standardisation without glossing over the underlying inequities a challenge.

To address interstate differences and the imperative of building health systems in accordance with local realities, the National Rural Health Mission (NRHM) launched in 2005 and developed guidelines that enabled states to design their own approaches and strategies; the programme also provided funding based on the states' individual action plans. To ensure a measure of equalisation, the poorer states were provided an additional third of resources. However, in reality, neither differential planning nor financing helped substantially. This was and continues to be largely because of the structural architecture of financing that has contributed to the poor development of the public health infrastructure and human resources (HR), making our health system broken, costly and inaccessible.

The Financial Architecture – A Brief Overview

India is neither a unitary nor a purely federal state; it has a complex governance framework within which the Union (normally addressed as the Centre) and states function. According to the Seventh Schedule of the Constitution, which distributes the legislative powers, functions and responsibilities between the Union and the States, maternal care, infectious disease and population control and medical and technical education are on the Concurrent List, while public health and hospitals fall under the State List, and this demarcation of subjects has not been without consequences. For example, while the responsibility of building the health delivery system is solely that of the state,

DOI: 10.4324/9781003568711-9

Table 7.1 Interstate Differences in Health Indicators in Some Sample States in India

S. No	*Health Indicator*	*All India*	*Kerala*	*TN*	*Assam*	*UP*	*Bihar*	*Reference Year*
1.	CD% to DB*	27.5	13.6	20.4	38.5	40.5	42.6	2016
2.	NCD% to DB	61.8	74.6	65.3	51.2	47.9	47.6	2016
3.	MMR/1 lakh births**	113	43	60	215	197	149	2021 (2016–18)
4.	IMR/1000*** live births	30	6	15	40	41	29	2021
5.	CBR/1000**	22.12	14.1	14.5	22.2	18.1	26.7	2017
6.	LE**	69	75.2	71.7	66.2	65	68.9	2020
7.	Stunting ****	35.5	23.4.7	25	35.3	39.7	42.9	2019–21
8.	Per capita income: INR in lakh constant prices *****	0.86	1.49 (2019–20)	1.50	0.6 lakh (2019–20)	.0.4	0.3	2021

Sources: *ICMR Disease burden Study; **RGI; ***SRS 2021; ****NFHS2019–21; *****RBI 2021.

making available the appropriately trained personnel in required numbers is split between the Centre and the states. This division of powers and the lack of clarity regarding two critical drivers of a health system – infrastructure and HR – have created distortions, calling for revisiting this framework by the 15th Finance Commission and bringing the whole health sector under the Concurrent List.

Beyond the division of powers and responsibilities, the apportionment of resources has resulted in horizontal and vertical asymmetries. The Constitution provides overriding powers of taxation and financial controls to the Centre, leaving the states with limited taxation powers that are not commensurate with their responsibilities; this state of affairs increases their dependence on the Centre, as can be seen in the fact that most national interventions and programmes are today being implemented with the grant in aid from the central government under the National Health Mission.

At the state level, public investment in the health sector consists of three sources: (1) own resources (excise duties on alcohol, petrol, etc.); (2) financial transfers – proportion of direct income taxes centrally collected and 60 per cent of the total NRHM outlay and (3) the mandated devolutions from the Finance Commission spread over five years. Though states are responsible for the bulk of expenditures involved in service delivery and 40 per cent of the centrally designed schemes, they do not get any share of the 3 per cent health cesses levied by the Centre. Levied at 4 per cent since 2018–19 as Education and Health Cess, the Centre mobilised INR 35,221 crore during 2020–21 and proposed to mobilise INR 54,715 crore in the next financial year.[1]

Given the fact that public health spending is an abysmal 1.2 per cent of GDP with less than 30 per cent accounted for by the Centre, the health sector is grossly underfunded. Doubling such spending levels would require states to also double their spending to 8 per cent of the revenue expenditure. Low public spending is the main reason for the poor development of the health sector (particularly infrastructure development and HR) and the dominance of the inflationary fee-for-service mode of financing. Due to partial financial risk protection, household out-of-pocket expenditures account for nearly 55 per cent to 60 per cent of total health spending against the SDG target of 20 per cent to be achieved by 2030.

Infrastructure Development: Status of Primary Care

Since 1947, India has been attempting to build its health infrastructure within available resources. With initial focus on disease control, primary health care services were provided through a two-tiered structure consisting of a subcentre for every 5,000 population manned by an auxiliary nurse midwife (ANM) and a variety of male workers (malaria surveillance workers, basic health workers, vaccinators) and then block primary health centres (PHCs) for every 1 lakh population; following the Kartar Singh Committee Report of 1973, these were upgraded as community health centres (CHCs) with 30 beds manned by four specialists. An additional PHC was established for a population of 30,000.

The NRHM 2005 was an opportunity for revamping, redesigning and re-evaluating the continued efficacy of the existing multi-tiered primary health system from the viewpoint of access to primary care as well as emergency services. It did, but only partially. To address the spatial spread, the new mission introduced an additional norm of ensuring a facility within half hour access, and to ensure access to life-saving maternal and child care, HR were increased. The NRHM also included capital investments for physical infrastructure – buildings, equipment, transport services, etc. – but these amounted to less than 10 per cent of the total spending. The 2005 mission funded 9378 subcentres, 1682 PHCs (largely in Rajasthan, Chattisgarh, Gujarat, Kerala and Madhya Pradesh) and 1837 CHCs (mainly in TN, UP, West Bengal, Rajasthan and Odisha).[2]

In 2019, the Government of India introduced the Ayushman Bharat, which had two components, one of which was to strengthen the subcentres and PHCs as health and wellness centres (HWCs) for providing 12 guaranteed services including reproductive and child health services; management of communicable and non-communicable diseases; basic oral, eye, ear and mental health services; geriatric and palliative care and emergency medical services. Funds were released to strengthen both infrastructure (toilets, additional rooms, water supply, etc.) and HR. An estimated 1.13 lakh HWCs had been established as of March 2021.[3]

As of this writing, there are 157,921 subcentres (155,404 rural, R, and 2517 urban, U) 30,813 PHCs (24,918 R and 5895 U) and 5649 CHCs (5183 R and 466 U). In accordance with the policy of integrating different disciplines to offer a wider choice to patients, Ayush practitioners are co-located with allopathy doctors in primary health care centres.

Significant shortfalls could be identified in 2019. For instance, Jharkhand, UP and Bihar together had a deficit of over 7000 subcentres; on average, the populations covered in each state by its subcentres, PHCs and CHCs are 5729, 35,730 and 1.71 lakh, respectively. About a fifth of the PHCs have no road connectivity, electricity or water supply. Overall, the mean distance a subcentre should cover is about 19.87 km, and for a PHC, it is 123.93 km; for CHCs, it is 595.8 km with radial distances of 2.52 km, 6.28 km and 13.77 km, respectively, in the three states.[4] In the absence of good all-weather roadways and an efficient and affordable transport system, these distances are a severe deterrent to accessing emergency care.

Table 7.2 clearly shows the massive shortfalls in the physical infrastructure in the public sector. In Bihar, only a third to a half of the PHCs and subcentres are in their own buildings, while one CHC serves 18 lakh population against the norm of 1.2 lakh population. In rural areas, which are particularly backward and poor and in turn need the most attention and health care services, it is conversely impossible to obtain decent rented spaces for subcentres; instead, clinics must work out of thatched huts, verandas of big houses or single rooms, making them virtually non-functional. Likewise, PHCs are supposed to have four beds in theory for addressing emergencies, but only 16,658 PHCs have the required four beds, and only 4026 CHCs have the required 30 beds. In other words, from 20 per cent to 50 per cent of the facilities are inaccessible to patients because of distance, lack of road connectivity and inadequate infrastructure.

The interstate differences persist between southern and northern states not only in terms of spatial spread but also lack of infrastructure: beds, operation theatres, laboratories and appropriate accommodation required to provide emergency or even routine basic care. Until a few years ago, not a single PHC in Kerala had a laboratory, and even today, hardly a third of the facilities in Bihar have one. Laboratories are the most basic of facilities that ought to be provided at decentralised levels close to the people.

Table 7.3 compares CHC infrastructure across several thousand clinics in a few sample states in India; the table unfortunately reflects the priority accorded to health care at decentralised levels. Under every indicator that defines a CHC, the shortfalls are remarkable, except in TN. In Bihar, CHCs are virtually non-existent, not even for the limited function of conducting deliveries. Of concern is that after nearly one and half decades of the NRHM, only 9080 – less than 5 per cent of the total – are functioning in accordance with the Indian Public Health Standards (IPHS) of 2012.

Human Resources: Primary Care

HR availability is one issue that public policy has failed to resolve. The findings in Table 7.4 show critical personnel in position in three facilities as of

Table 7.2 Public Health Infrastructure Shortfalls in Sample States in India

S. No	*Health Indicator*	*India*	*Kerala*	*TN*	*Bihar*	*Assam*	*UP*
1.	Subcentre shortfall (%)	157,921 (155,404 R and 2517 U) (24%)	5410 (0)	8713 (0))	9112 (58)	4659 (28)	20,778 (41)
	Without own buildings %	31.7	30	28	59	22	18
2a.	Primary Health Centres (Rural + Urban) shortfalls (%)	30,813 (24,918 R + 5895 U) (29% R+) 38.2 %U)	784 + 148 (R + U) (0% R + 70% U)	1420 + 464 (R + U) (0% R + 42% U)	1702 +375 (R + U) (53% R)	946 + 56 (R + U) (10% R + 47% U)	2880 + 593 (R + U) (51% R + 45% U)
b.	Without own buildings %	12.7	1.2	2.2	42	0	48.2
c.	No Laboratory/OT (rural areas)		0*/270	1,349/124	548/356	762/66	2,205/988
d.	No. with the 4 beds (notional)	16,658 (66,632 beds)	113	1005	483	418	1644

Source: Rural Health Statistics, 2021 * Need updating by RHS as over 550 PHCs have been converted into family health centres equipped with laboratories.

Table 7.3 Interstate Differences in Infrastructure at 5649 CHCs in India

S. No	*Health Indicator*	*India*	*Kerala*	*TN*	*Bihar*	*Assam*	*UP*
1.a.	Community Health Centres R + U shortfalls (%)	5183 R + 466 U (38%)	211 R +16 U (0%)	385 R + 15 U (0%)	57 R +7 U (94%)	192 R + 2 U (27%)	711 R + 12 U (51%)
b.	Operating theatre	4899	133	368	45	186	626
c.	Laboratory	4459	211	381	36	187	625
d.	Labour room	4075	1	276	34	115	418
e.	Newborn corner	4458	1	326	49	180	617
f.	30 beds	120,780 (4026 CHCs)	69	376	43	101	676
g.	X-ray machines	2679	28	202	27	100	364
3.	SC/PHC/UPHC per IPHS norms – number	5363/3218/439	0/0/0	2845/1211/349	18/100/0	0/5/8	0/0/0

Source: Rural Health Statistics, 2021.

Table 7.4 Interstate Differences in Human Resources in Indian Primary Care – Subcentres and PHCs

SNo	*State*	*@1ANM –*	*P*	*@1.Doctor-*	*P*	*@4.Specialists*	*P*	*@7Nurses*	*P*
		R		*R*		*R*		*R*	
1.	Assam	4659	7494	1002	1424	876	188	1533	1824
2.	Bihar	9112	13,425	2077	1745	256	124	448	462
3.	Kerala	5410	5147	932	1028	908	173	1589	615
4.	TN	8713	7562	1884	2708	1600	228	2800	2999
5.	UP	29,778	20,389	3473	2759	2892	816	5061	5795
6.	India	157,921	183,999	30,813	28,516	22,596	4957	39,543	41,874
7.	Specialists at CHC	Surgeons	Paediatricians	Physicians	Gynaecologists	Anaesthetists	Eye care	Required 33,894 (5649 CHC*6 specialists)	Total with 4 specialities
	No Available	1096	1140	1130	1591	1314	733	7004	304
	Shortfall %	79	78	79	70	59 (against sanctioned posts)	29 (against sanctioned posts)	79% against norm of 4 specialists and 80% against norm of 6	6.4%

Source: Rural Health Statistics, 2021. R required; P in position.

March 2020; it does not include state data for accredited social health activists (ASHAs), who number 10.66 lakh for the country as a whole. Rather, the table shows the personnel requirements to give an estimate of the actual shortfall and not shortfall against posts sanctioned, which are usually lower than requirements. The HWCs are now required to have two nurses, which means low ANM/nurse availability: of the 3.14 lakh ANMs who are required, only 1.83 are working, and the situation is the same with doctors, specialists and other support staff. This said, it can be the case that positions in some centres are being filled by contractual appointees and are not captured by the RHS.

Clearly the current model of rural health care has not worked and requires a serious re-evaluation. The CHCs function suboptimally due to the huge numbers of vacancies. UP has a severe lack of human resources, and Kerala's deployment policies are biased towards urban areas. In Kerala in particular, population density, the excellent transport network and peoples' preference for higher-level facilities where more comprehensive care is available have influenced choice and partly explain the low demand for PHCs and CHCs.

Notwithstanding these findings, recent surveys are indicating an improvement in public health facilities and people's return to public facilities for care, thereby increasing the proportionate share of public facilities in the delivery of health care services. That said, it is however also a fact that for emergency and specialist care, use of private-sector facilities and hospitals continues to be quite high, even though these cost three times more per service. Likewise, for minor ailments, people still tend to access locally and easily available private providers who are largely quacks. This seeking of private care is one reason for ongoing high out-of-pocket expenditures (MoPSI, 2018b). To address these anomalies, both Kerala and TN are in the process of reviewing the infrastructure design and human resource policies in PHCs and CHCs to align the primary health care architecture to respond to the changed epidemiology and prevailing ground realities.

Infrastructure Development: Secondary and Tertiary Care

In the current architectural design, secondary care is provided in the sub-district and district hospitals. These are monitored for achieving present standards in terms of beds, facilities and/or services in accordance with the IPHS laid down in 2012. Per the RHS 2019, there are an estimated 1,193 sub-district hospitals. District and sub-district hospitals account for 1.43 lakh and 2.87 lakh beds, respectively, or about 0.4 beds per 1000 population.

At the apex are medical colleges providing tertiary care and hospitals such as regional cancer centres, for example, or NIMHANS for highly specialised treatment. No data is available on the number of beds, services or human resources being provided in these tertiary care facilities. India has 595 medical colleges with 88,170 seats, with 274 of those owned by the government. The southern states and Maharashtra with 30 per cent of the population account for 54 per cent of the seats.

Table 7.5 Interstate Differences in Indian Secondary and Tertiary Care

S. No	*Health Indicator*	*India*	*Kerala*	*TN*	*Bihar*	*Assam*	*UP*
1.	Population in Cr./no of districts	135.3	3.53	7.6	12.18	3.47	22.89
a.	No. of districts	705	14	32	38	27	75
b.	Rural %	65.8	30.5	47.5	87.9	84.8	76.4
2.	Sub-district hospitals	1193	86	278	35	14	0
b.	Beds	143,538	8730	42,170	1837	745	0
3.	District hospitals (total districts)	810	48	32	36	24	168
b.	Beds	287,025	21,363	12,242	10,279	10,563	30,443
4.	Medical colleges	274	7	29	8	7	19
5.	Other hospitals (Taluk, specialist, etc.)		1284	2507	2132	1239	4683
6.	Bed to population ratio per 1000	0.6	1	1.3	0.1	0.20	0.2

Source: Rural Health Statistics, 2021.

Together, it is estimated that there are, in all, 40,900 hospitals and 8.18 lakh beds in the public sector providing secondary and tertiary care (Table 7.5). This is a major improvement since 2004, when India only had 5,500 hospitals and 3.80 lakh beds. Also important to note is the significant increase in rural areas from 3,700 hospitals and 1.19 lakh beds in 2004 to 31,000 hospitals with 2.95 lakh beds: a tenfold increase in hospitals and two and half times increase in beds. The result, however, is that even though by location, there are more facilities in rural areas – estimated to be 83 per cent – they only account for 37 per cent of the total beds in the country.[5] Overall, the bed-to-population ratio is about 0.6 per 1000 population, far less than the WHO norm of 5/1000, and of this, fewer than half are in rural areas – which have double the population of urban areas.

Service Delivery Capacity

Health infrastructure is about the complement of inputs that enable service provisioning, but there are no reliable estimates of the services being provided by hospitals in India. In 2021, NITI Ayog undertook an analysis of district hospitals to develop a baseline on 10 key performance indicators, of which five pertain to infrastructure and five to HR. Table 7.6 presents some of the findings for all of India and for a sample of states. The findings for 707 hospitals assessed (out of an estimated 810 in the country) highlight the existing wide differences in five of the 10 key indicators.

The situation is dismal, particularly the fact that even in diagnostics, we do not have district hospitals that are fully functional. The importance of good laboratories at the district level came up sharply during the Covid-19 pandemic, when in March 2020, only a handful of states, and none of the

Table 7.6 Status of District Hospitals Against Five Key Performance Indicators

SNo	*Indicator KPI*	*All India*	*Assam*	*Bihar*	*Kerala*	*TN*	*UP*
1.	Beds/1 lakh pop – IPHS norm 22	24	18	6	22	22	13
2.	Support services* Norm 14	89	0	1	1	18	9
3.	Core services** Norm 14	101	1	0	10	17	1
4.	Diagnostic services*** Norm 14	21	0	0	0	1	0
5.	Hospitals with bed occupancy Norm 80%	182	2	6	2	6	27
a.	Current bed occupancy	66	60.5	56.3	60	73.3	45.4
	Surgeries Norm 205/Surgeon	177 (average of 194/surgeon)	2	8	5	10	39

Source: NITI Ayog (2021). *Pharmacy, blood bank, ambulance, OPD, IPD, etc. **Specialities – surgery, critical care emergencies, gynae, etc. *** sputum, haemotology, microbiology, serology, biochemistry, etc.

well-developed states like TN and Kerala, had enough laboratories to conduct RTPCR tests; the lack of such laboratories was the main reason for the initial delay in scaling up testing and being ahead of the virus. Indeed, inadequate laboratory and diagnostic services make the functioning of specialists suboptimal and also force people to travel long distances and incur substantial out-of-pocket expenditures to access those specialist services.

With the growing surge of cancers and cardiac diseases, the demand for advanced diagnostics is growing, but for the most part, only urban and semi-urban metros have diagnostic labs. Overall, India's use of medical devices, although it is growing, is still much lower than in other countries. Per capita spending on medical devices is reportedly USD 3 in India (National Medical Devices Policy) compared with USD 622 in the United States (Estimates of Medical Device Spending in the United States Gerald Donahoe June 2021). India is also one of the world's lowest consumers of radiological and oncological devices (e.g. MRI, CT SCANS, PET) despite the country's rapidly increasing cancer burden. With the private sector having more than six times more of this technology than the government, the current proportion of out-of-pocket expenditures for diagnostics is an estimated 7.6 per cent compared with 2.2 per cent in 1993–94 (NSSO 93–94; NSSO 2017) (MoPSI, 2018a; MoPSI, 2018b).

Similarly, during the Covid-19 pandemic, shortages emerged of life-saving oxygen-supported beds and ICUs, and the lack of such critical infrastructure, including emergency transport, was among the reasons for the losses of thousands of lives. However, overall, the scale-up of critical infrastructure during the two years of 2020 and 2021 was impressive. Although there is no readily available data by state, it is reported that government-owned dedicated Category 1 Covid-19 hospitals increased in number from 163 to 4,522, a 28-fold increase; dedicated Category 2 Covid-19 health centres increased from 0 to 9,403; dedicated Category 3 Covid-19 centres increased from 0 to 9,777; ICU beds increased from 2,500 to 139,412, a 56-fold increase; oxygen-supported beds increased 10-fold from 50,583 to 494,253; and isolation beds (excluding ICU) increased from 41,000 to 1,809,266 (44-fold). By position, the report is that nearly 3.26 lakh personnel are employed at different levels by state governments: 5346 specialists; 11,672 medical officers; 72,293 nurses; 20,929 multipurpose workers; 75,139 lab technicians and other staff and 141,541 community volunteers and ASHAs.[6] Funding was mobilised from the World Bank, the Asian Development Bank (ADB) and the central and state governments including non-formal channels like PM Cares.

To further bridge the inadequacies of the health infrastructure in the public sector, the Government of India in October 2021 launched the Pradhan Mantri Ayushman Bharat Health Infrastructure Mission (PM-ABHIM) with the objective of strengthening institutions and systems for preventing, detecting and responding to future pandemics alongside expanding delivery of high-quality client-centric primary health care services. The PM-ABHIM is proposed to have an outlay of INR 64,180 crore (including both central sector and centrally sponsored scheme components) to be implemented over the period 2021–26 with assistance from the World Bank and ADB.

Human Resources: Secondary and Tertiary Care

India has a deficit of doctors, nurses and allied staff.[7] A granular analysis will show a more severe problem, with shortages among disease specialists such as oncologists, surgeons, orthopaedists and radiologists and equally importantly public health specialists such as epidemiologists and biostatisticians.

In the absence of updated registries of doctors and nurses by their respective regulatory authorities, it is difficult to estimate the number of active and practicing human resources in the country including rural versus urban and public versus private. In 2021, the WHO estimated in the Global Health Observatory that there were 9.28 doctors/10,000 population in 2019 against 5.7 in 2004 but observed that this was far short of the 23 in Brazil, 19.8 in China and 11.5 in Sri Lanka.[8] India also has 3.12 million nurses, which amounts to 23.89 per 10,000 population, compared with 74 in Brazil, 26.6 in China and 31.5 in Thailand, but this reflected a steady increase from 12.59 in 2004. There are 29.6 lakh nurses registered, in addition to another 8.6 lakh ANMs. Of these so far 10.4 lakh nurses have enrolled in the NCI, and 8.3 lakh have been approved. Once this drive is completed, the actual position of nurses in active practice in India will be known.

Likewise, there is no reliable data regarding availability of human resources – doctors, nurses and paramedical support staff – in medical colleges and specialist hospitals. The NITI Ayog assessment, based on the IPHS

Table 7.7 District Hospitals That Meet IPHS Personnel Norms: All India and Some States

S. No.	*Indicator*	*All India*	*Assam*	*Bihar*	*Kerala*	*TN*	*UP*
1.	No. of hospitals assessed	707	25	36	21	32	150
2.	Doctors	189	3	3	6	6	24
a.	% of total hospitals	26.73	12	8.33	28.57	18.75	16
3	Nurses	88	0	6	1	0	10
a.	% of total hospitals	12.45		16.67	4.76		12.45
4.	Paramedics	399	13	19	7	14	83
a.	% to total hospitals	56.44	52	52.7	33.33	43.7	55.4

Source: NITI Ayog, 2021.

norms, is the only reliable source of the numbers of doctors including specialists, nurses and paramedical staff available in the district hospitals and the gaps thereof. The IPHS assigns norms for doctors, nurses and paramedics according to number of beds: for facilities with 100, 200, 300, 400 and 500 beds, there should be, respectively, 105, 166, 251, 319 and 393 staff members across the three types of personnel. Against that, the assessment of 707 hospitals reflected in Table 7.7 revealed that only 189, 88 and 399 hospitals meet the norms for, respectively, doctors, nurses and paramedics.

While the information in the table is useful, further research would be required to assess outcomes and specialist services at these hospitals. For example, among the indicators for doctors, it is not known how many are gynaecologists and anaesthetists to assess the outcomes related to, for example, C-sections. NITI Ayog's report shows that of the 707 hospitals assessed, 450 were performing fewer than 35 per cent of total C-sections. The general norm is 15 per cent C-sections against all deliveries. Against that norm, district hospitals in UP and Bihar were performing only 8.35 per cent and 5.85 per cent, whereas Assam, TN and Kerala hospitals were performing 35 per cent, 55 per cent and 34 per cent, respectively, reflecting a clear case of too little service in states that lack affordable alternatives and too much in other states, indicating need for regulation. The implications are critical as lack of life-saving C-section services could imply higher maternal mortality.[9]

Way Forward

While I have given evidence for the need to increase capital investments in public health care delivery at the district level and below to reach IPHS standards, an additional issue that needs attention is ensuring that the summer of 2021 does not recur. An estimated 5 lakh people died from Covid-19, and this does not include people who died during that time for want of access to life-saving surgeries or treatment due to lockdowns and diversion of hospital resources to Covid-19 patients. There is a need to balance surges due to pandemics with managing essential health care, and I argue for a three-pronged approach: one, timely fill gaps and bring all primary and secondary care facilities to IPHS; two, rationalise the infrastructure through a stringent process of weeding out dead facilities and three, build a resilient public health system consisting of strong surveillance and laboratory capacity alongside the data analytical capabilities.

Pursuing this three-pronged approach would require good-quality, reliable data, but examining the data reveals extensive variance between program data and data published in the Rural Health Statistics. There appear to be far more beds than are being reported, and there are HR discrepancies as well; there is also no information of even reasonable acceptability regarding the private sector due to the absence of rigorous reporting systems. Fully implementing the CEA could have been of some help in that context, but in the absence of credible state and district data on infrastructure and disease burden, planning is based more on national and state aggregates that hide the inter- and intra-district variations.

A second issue is related to the IPHS. The Government of India first came up with standards in 2007, and these were revised in 2012. Most recently, the standards were revised again in 2021 to conform with the HWC policy. The difference between the first two sets of standards and the most recent one is ambition: while the IPHS of 2007 and 2012 aimed to ensure the barest minimum, the 2021 standards are very idealistic and highly resource intensive. Authors of a 2019 report[10],[11] estimated that based on the 2007–12 IPHS, INR 1.6 lakh crore would be required to fill the current infrastructure gaps and a similar amount for bridging the HR gaps. These amounts would be vastly greater if the resource estimates were based on IPHS 2021. Given this situation, inroads are being made with funds being mobilised from external donors like the ADB and the World Bank.

Redesigning the Primary Care Model

What is needed is a sturdy primary health care approach anchored within communities that gives equal focus to preventive, promotive health and curative services based on trust between the communities and the health care teams within the framework of accountability.

In 2014, MoHFW convened a committee that examined the issue and produced a report that highlighted the urgency of strengthening the subcentres and PHCs, which were renamed family health centres (FHCs) to drive focus to family well-being and make local health teams more accountable for the health of the families under their charge. While the central government ignored the report, Kerala, with grant support from the UK Department for International Development and technical support from the Imperial College London, established FHCs at three existing PHCs. Modelled along the GP system in the UK, the PHCs were designed around patient needs, convenience and engagement by providing an expanded set of services in keeping with their disease profiles. As of today, over 550 PHCs have been refurbished and strengthened as FHCs.

Delivering comprehensive primary care requires new skills and competencies and an intersectoral approach that brings together counsellors, physiotherapists, nurse midwives and public health nurses and family medicine physicians to work as teams with departments implementing nutrition and sanitation programmes, etc. While the idea driving the HWCs is laudable, inattention to human competencies can end in a case of new wine in old bottles. For example, even the limited design is problematic. Under this scheme, every subcentre must have a community health officer (CHO) and a graduate nurse and be assisted by two ANMs with 18 months of training. The flaw in this design is that the graduate/diploma nurse is trained in hospital settings and clinical bedside care, not community or public health. To make up this deficiency, nursing school tutors provided a six-month public health training, but they themselves had no field experience in public health. Additionally, CHOs have been appointed in the backward pockets of districts that lack even the supporting infrastructure for normal service delivery. That is, hospitals lack graduate nurses because the available nurses are being appointed to perform tasks at facilities where ANMs are already performing equally competently.

I conclude from the state of affairs I have been describing that it is critical for the current three-tiered primary health care – as the foundation for the health system – to be revamped from passive to active facilities run by health teams headed by doctors qualified in family medicine and consisting of public health nurses and midwives, auxiliary staff and community workers like ASHAs. In particular, these facilities need to be held to no more than 2000 families per doctor. Based on a baseline survey of the demographic and morbidity profiles, it should be possible to hold the team accountable for achieving certain preset targets and also monitor patients for quality of outcomes. A related issue in the context of expanding access to services is partnering with the private sector. The private sector is not a homogenous entity in terms of quality or price. It ranges from untrained quacks at the community level to single doctors providing outpatient services to corporate facilities in large cities.

The outpatient environment is highly competitive and is the main reason for fewer footfalls in public facilities. It could therefore be worthwhile for the government to partner with not-for-profit and missionary entities to supplement and complement the public system, particularly in hard-to-reach areas. Forming such partnerships, however, must not be confused with mindless outsourcing essential activities to private contractors. This was done in Andhra Pradesh during the years 2017–19, and it resulted in balkanising primary care with multiple unconnected public–private partnerships: school health by one agency, eye care by another, simple laboratory tests by a third, urban health outsourced to a fourth and so on. With shoddy contracting and shoddier enforcement, there has been much waste of resources without any substantial gain to the health and wellness of the people. India also needs to move away from a doctor-centric approach and broaden the use of paramedical personnel who possess new skills and competencies, as well as retraining existing personnel in new skills. This new training focus would require significant funding for both training and the new posts.

The success of the reform agenda I propose requires two key policies: doubling health budgets and shifting or weeding out ineffective allocations. Prioritising strengthening health infrastructure at the district level and below would alone require more than 2 per cent of GDP, although some savings can be achieved by weeding out inefficient and superfluous facilities. Separately, money collected as cesses and taxes on tobacco, alcohol, equipment import and health infrastructures should be earmarked for health programmes alongside the amounts being mobilised from the World Bank and ADB under the PM-ABHIM project. Yet another source of funding could be allocating three quarters of the funds that come in from government-sponsored insurance schemes to improving the infrastructure with only one quarter put aside for incentives. Tamil Nadu and Kerala have done this successfully, and both have steadily improved their infrastructures through such demand-side financing by giving government hospitals the maximum reimbursement and thereby making them competitive with the private sector.

Reforming Medical Education

Political will is required for optimising investments and introducing vital reforms in medical education. Stakes are very high as is the money. Under medical education, two policies require urgent review: one, establishing a link between disease burden and producing specialists and two, the need to strengthen and develop public health cadres in the country.

Regarding the first matter, in the UK, the government annually indicates to the British Medical Council the disciplines in which specialists are required. India has no such reporting, and often the government is 'requesting' the regulator to 'sanction' seats where it urgently needs specialists. For example, with the increasing burden of cancers, demand for radiologists is increasing, but there are far fewer MD seats than the demand, meaning higher capitation premiums, making it impossible for expensively educated specialists to work in the government; this is the case for other disciplines as well such as surgery. Increasing seats would require examining several options and some out-of-the-box thinking such as expanding training sites from medical colleges to specialist institutions.

The second issue requiring urgent review is creating public health specialists. A large number of institutes offer master of public health programmes that need standardisation of both curricula and quality of instruction. It is also necessary to create cadres of subspecialists in the broad fields of public health and family medicine with competencies in the real-time analysis of surveillance data and epidemic intelligence, supported by a laboratory network to monitor emerging and re-emerging pathogens towards managing public health.

While producing such specialists and skills is one aspect, without changing the structure of medical education, the problem of shortages of human resources may still not be resolved. Of the 595 medical colleges, only 274 are government owned and therefore have affordable fees; the rest are private, and fees can follow market forces. Medical education has been commercialised, and the exorbitant capitation fees have made access impossible for the majority of aspirants, while those who can afford may not necessarily be committed to pursuing a medical career.

More importantly, very few people are willing to specialise in public health or other potentially low-paying fields because of the lack of available positions are the likelihood that remuneration will not be sufficient to repay the loans needed to pursue the higher education. Additionally, doctors who paid large amounts to earn their degrees are not likely to work in rural areas or in government service where salaries are half of what corporations could be offering. All these reasons make compelling arguments against the further commercialisation of medical education and for the NMC to introduce badly needed reforms. Reforms need to be comprehensive and range from weeding out bogus and substandard colleges to changing curricula to be in line with India's contemporary health needs; introducing career pathways such as clinical specialisation, public health and family medicine; moderating fees and admission standards and providing financial incentives in disciplines like public health to motivate students to choose these disciplines. Without these reforms, health goals cannot be achieved as alongside finances, infrastructure and technology, human resources is a key driver of health system cost and efficacy.

Conclusion

The three main takeaways from my work for this chapter are the need to strengthen the public delivery system at the district level and below, reset the financing system to allocate more funds to states to invest in health and education and redesign the health delivery system – both public and private – within an accountability framework. I argue for removing infrastructure redundancies, dedicating 2 per cent GDP exclusively for this purpose over the next five years and bringing in crucial reforms related to medical education to ensure a strong and resilient primary and secondary health care system. In addition, I argue that the policy focus needs to shift from state-level aggregate data to district levels to accommodate local disease burdens. The goal should be for all states to be able to deliver basic health care and emergency services in accordance with national norms as a universal right, where place of birth is not a disadvantage.

Health systems are driven by certain determinants such as quality of governance, adequacy of financing, availability of human resources with appropriate skills and competencies, enforcement of regulations to minimise market distortions, the nature of financial incentives driving provider behaviour, a demanding population and access to technology. While these factors help determine the nature of the health system, what is important is to understand the underlying political economy that drives policy choices. Such an understanding combined with the ability to negotiate the muddy waters of conflicting interests will determine whether India will ever achieve a system that is equitable, affordable and accessible.

Notes

1 Receipt Budget, 22–23, Ministry of Finance.
2 Rural Health Statistics, MoHFW, 2021.
3 RHS, 2021.
4 MoHFW, 2021.
5 Selvaraj et al., 2022.
6 Author's sources.
7 The WHO norm for HR for health was 23/10,000 in 2006, revised to 44.5/10,000 in 2016. It is believed that there are about 20.8/10,000 health personnel in India: 8.4 doctors and 14.4 nurses and midwives.
8 Shakthivel et al., 2021.
9 NFHS5 has shown a disturbing increase in C-sections that is not advisable. In Kerala and TN, respectively, 38.9 per cent and 44.9 per cent of deliveries are by C-section, while in UP and Bihar, the rates are 13.7 per cent and 9.7 per cent, also respectively. There is concern, however, that poor reporting means there might be large numbers of missing cases.
10 Report of Subgroup IV of the Expert Committee on Enhancing Resource Investment in Health, May 2018.
11 A background paper from the Centre for Economic and Social Studies of Hyderabad submitted to the 14th Finance Commission on Health reiterates these findings.

References

Donahoe, G. (2021, June). Estimates of Medical Device Spending in the United States. *Advamed.* www.advamed.org/wp-content/uploads/2021/12/Estimates-Medical-Device-Spending-United-States-Report-2021.pdf

Government of India, Ministry of Finance. *Receipt Budget 2022–23.* www.indiabudget.gov.in

Government of India, Ministry of Health & Family Welfare (MoHFW). (2021). *Rural Health Statistics.* https://main.mohfw.gov.in/newshighlights-90

Ministry of Statistics and Programme Implementation. (2018a). *India – Household Consumer Expenditure, July 1993–June 1994, NSS 50th Round.* National Data Archive. https://microdata.gov.in/nada43/index.php/catalog/76

Ministry of Statistics and Programme Implementation. (2018b). *India – Household Social Consumption: Health, NSS 75th Round Schedule-25.0: July 2017–June 2018.* National Sample Survey Office. https://mospi.gov.in/NSSOa

Planning Commission, PEO Evaluation Studies. (1999). *Functioning of Community Health Centres (CHCs).* New Delhi: GoI.

Report of Sub-Group IV: Expert Committee on Enhancing Resource Investment in Health (ECERIH). (2018, May 13). *Human Resources and Infrastructure for Health Sector in India.* New Delhi: MoHFW.

Sarwal, R., Kalal, S., and Iyer, V. (2021). *Best Practices in the Performance of District Hospitals.* Niti Aayog. New Delhi: GoI. ISBN 978-81-953811-0-4

Selvaraj, S., Karan, K.A., Srivastava, S., Bhan, N., and Mukhopadhyay, I. (2022). *India Health System Review.* New Delhi: World Health Organization, Regional Office for South-East Asia.

Part III

Regulatory Architecture

8 Drug Regulation and Federalism in India

Shreya Shrivastava and Dhvani Mehta

I. Introduction

The deaths of children in Gambia and Uzbekistan that have been linked to Indian-made cough syrups reveal the devastating impact that India's weak drug regulatory system has on people's lives.[1] There are multiple contributors to the state of drug regulation in India: inadequate financial and human resources, poor infrastructure and capture by the pharmaceutical industry.[2] A key aspect of this is the fragmentation of regulatory powers across the Centre and states. State Drug Regulatory Authorities (SDRAs) exercise significant powers under the Drugs and Cosmetics Act, 1940 ("Drugs Act") in relation to licencing and enforcement. In this chapter, we argue that SDRAs are not best equipped to perform some of these functions, in part because they lack capacity and in part because the promise of investment by the pharmaceutical industry prejudices stringent enforcement of the Drugs Act. The discretion vested in these 36 SDRAs leads to wide variations in regulatory approaches across India. Despite the increasing centralisation of drug regulatory functions since the enactment of the Drugs Act, there is no common, minimum guarantee of protection from unsafe and ineffective drugs.

While there is much to be done to strengthen the regulatory capacity of both the Central Drugs Standards Control Organisation (CDSCO) and the SDRAs, we also make the case for the creation of a more powerful central regulator, vested with licencing functions that are key to ensuring the uniform implementation of the Drugs Act. There are broader implications of this argument in the context of public health and federalism. The objective of drug regulation is to ensure that only safe and effective drugs are available in the market. This requires a set of uniform, minimum standards, with states having the flexibility to determine how to demand compliance with these standards and to set more stringent standards. The potential impact of drug regulation on human health and on the right to safe, efficacious medicines[3] means that there is a greater imperative to achieve uniformity than to secure autonomy for the states in the context of drug regulation.

In this chapter, we discuss the non-uniform implementation of the Drugs Act across states through the lens of three important drug regulatory

DOI: 10.4324/9781003568711-11

functions – standard-setting, licencing and enforcement. In the first part of the chapter, we provide an overview of these functions and how they are currently divided between the Centre and the states. In the second part, we trace the historic evolution of the Drugs Act from the initial emphasis on state (at the time, provincial) autonomy to a gradual concentration of powers in the Centre. In the third part of the chapter, we use case studies to highlight the variations in regulation by SDRAs and their consequent impacts on public health. In the fourth part, we describe prior and recent centralising mechanisms and their limitations for attaining appropriate drug regulation standards, in contrast with the model of pharmaceutical federalism in the United States of America (US). In the conclusion, we discuss potential reforms against the backdrop of the draft Drugs, Medical Devices and Cosmetics Bill, 2022. We argue that centralising key functions must go hand in hand with transparency and accountability at both the Centre and state levels. However, until sufficient regulatory capacity is built, centralising certain aspects of drug regulation is necessary to protect public health.

II. Drug Regulatory Architecture in India Across the Centre and States

In India, pharmaceutical products – drugs, biologicals, and medical devices – are regulated by the Drugs Act. This part provides an overview of key drug regulatory functions under the Drugs Act, standard setting, licencing and enforcement, and their division between the Centre and the states.

A. Drug Regulatory Authorities

Modern regulatory bodies in India, like the Telecom Regulatory Authority of India and the Food Safety and Standards Authority of India are independent, statutory entities. The Drugs Act, which was enacted before independence, does not, however, create such an entity. Instead, it grants certain powers to the central and state governments, including the power to prescribe rules for the implementation of the Act. The Centre and states, in turn, have assigned these powers to their respective agencies, the SDRAs for the states and the CDSCO under the authority of the Drugs Controller General of India (DCGI) for the Centre.

This means that drugs in India are regulated by more than three dozen state regulators, plus the CDSCO, and these regulators are not part of a unified system. SDRAs work independently of each other as well as of the CDSCO, with the former housed under their state health departments, and the CDSCO under the Ministry of Health and Family Welfare (MoHFW). Unlike other central regulatory bodies like the Food Safety and Standards Authority of India, CDSCO does not work as an oversight and coordination body for SDRAs. The only statutory bodies under the Drugs Act are the Drugs Technical Advisory Board, which advises the central and state governments on technical matters, and the Drugs Consultative Committee that comprises representatives of the central government and all state governments and advises on matters tending to secure uniformity.[4] Drug regulation lacks a unified enforcement cadre as well; the Act empowers both the central and state governments to appoint analysts and inspectors independently. This fragmentation of regulatory authorities inevitably leads to fragmentation in the exercise of powers and performance of duties under the Drugs Act.

B. Drug Regulatory Functions

The primary aim of drug regulation is to protect the public from harmful drugs and ensure that only those with a favourable benefit–risk balance are approved and made available.[5] For this, the law must set mandatory standards both for drugs themselves and for drug manufacturers based on which regulatory authorities can approve drugs and grant licences to manufacturers. Finally, to complete the regulatory cycle, compliance with these standards must be enforced. In short, standard setting, licensing and enforcement are the three key regulatory activities that are needed to ensure the safety and effectiveness of drugs. Next we discuss how these functions are divided between the Centre and states.

1. Standard setting

The Drugs Act prescribes the minimum standards of quality that imported and domestically manufactured drugs must comply with before they can be marketed. It is a benchmark that all drugs must meet before being approved for sale or distribution. The Drugs Act prohibits the import and manufacture of drugs that are not of standard quality (for the purposes of this chapter, we will refer to these as substandard drugs).[6] The Act considers a drug to be of standard quality if it complies with the standards set out in Schedule II of the Act.[7]

Schedule II refers to the India Pharmacopoeia (IP) – a text published by the Indian Pharmacopoeia Commission (IPC) – an autonomous institution under the MoHFW that lists mandatory quality standards every four years for all drugs sold in the country. The central government has the power to amend or add to Schedule II. Standard setting, therefore, is seen to be largely a central function, although as we describe next, this was not always the case.

2. Licencing

The licencing of drugs refers to the approval granted by regulatory authorities for the import or manufacture of drugs for sale and distribution. Compliance with Good Manufacturing Practices ("GMP"), assessed through an annual inspection, is a necessary precondition for the grant of a manufacturing licence.[8]

The Drugs Act prohibits the import of any drug for which a licence is prescribed except in accordance with such licence.[9] It also prohibits the manufacture, sale or distribution of any drug except under the conditions of a licence.[10] However, the Act does not have any other substantive provisions on licencing. These are delegated to the central government to be prescribed in the rules, including the conditions governing the issuance of such licences and the authority empowered to issue them.[11]

The central government, via the Drugs and Cosmetics Rules, 1945 (Drugs Rules), established the DCGI as the authority to issue licences for importing drugs and manufacturing new drugs,[12] for drugs notified by the central government and for certain biological and special products specified[13] under the Drugs Rules.[14] However, the power to issue licences for manufacturing all other drugs rests with the SDRAs. The respective powers of the central and state governments to issue manufacturing licences have varied over the years, and next, we discuss this in more detail.

3. *Enforcement*

The enforcement process under the Drugs Act entails randomly drawing samples and testing them in government laboratories to assess compliance with mandatory standards. As mentioned earlier, annual inspections for GMP compliance are mandated under the law.

In case of non-compliance, the Drugs Act provides for two kinds of enforcement actions against violators: administrative actions like suspending or cancelling licences and criminal prosecutions. Both central and state drug inspectors have the power to test drug samples and initiate criminal prosecutions, but the power to suspend or cancel licences rests only with the relevant licencing authority. However, this division of the regulatory functions between the Centre and the states has been in flux since the enactment of the Drugs Act in 1940. As it stands today, the power related to standardisation currently rests with the Centre, licencing powers are fragmented between the Centre and the states and enforcement is vested primarily with states with a limited role for central drug inspectors.

The next part of this chapter helps understand this division and its impact on the current state of drug regulation by tracing the history of the enactment of the Drugs Act and its subsequent evolution.

III. Evolution of Drug Regulation in India

In the early 20th century, the Indian drug market was largely dependent on imported drugs for modern medicine.[15] In the aftermath of World War I, European manufacturers began trading in fake and adulterated drugs at throwaway prices. The Indian market became susceptible to such drugs between 1919 and 1926, especially in the absence of any regulatory framework or authority.[16]

A. *Beginning of Drug Regulation: Drug Enquiry Committee, 1930–31 and the Need for a Central Law*

This issue was highlighted in the Legislative Assembly, and later in the Council of States. The Drugs Enquiry Committee was appointed in 1930 under the chairmanship of RN Chopra to investigate adulterated and substandard drugs, both imported and indigenously manufactured, and to recommend steps to control them.[17]

This marked the beginning of drug regulation in India. The Chopra Committee recommended central legislation to regulate both the import and manufacture of drugs and to secure effectiveness and uniformity in control throughout India. The committee suggested that the enforcement of the Act in the provinces should generally rest with the local governments concerned,[18] but its three major recommendations focused on centralisation: (1) centralise control by vesting it with the Governor-General in Council without detracting from provincial responsibility, (2) maintain uniformity in essentials by instituting a strong advisory board and (3) create a well-equipped central laboratory with efficient branch laboratories in states under its direction and control.[19]

Details that were 'purely local in character' could be left to provincial governments, although it is unclear today what such details might have been. One critical recommendation of the commission was to compile an Indian pharmacopoeia that would set uniform standards for therapeutically active substances and pharmaceutical necessities.[20] This laid the ground for today's Second Schedule to the Drugs Act. The committee also recognised the need to centralise certain aspects of regulation to achieve the objective of weeding out substandard drugs from the market. It recommended that prescribing standards for the composition, strength, purity and quality of drugs, as well as setting the terms for licences to be granted to manufacturers, importers and retail dealers, rest with the Governor-General in Council, in consultation with the advisory board.[21]

B. *The 1937 Bill: Provincial Autonomy Stakes a Claim*

In 1937, a truncated version of the bill that diluted the centralising focus of the Chopra Committee recommendations was finally introduced in the Legislative Assembly. The Government of India Act, 1935 had introduced a certain degree of provincial autonomy. In deference to this, the Centre was seen as having legislative competence only in relation to importing drugs and the 1937 Bill was introduced to give effect to this aspect of the Chopra Committee recommendations.[22] Under the Government of India Act, "public health" was within the exclusive legislative competence of Provincial Governments, with "drugs" understood as a facet of public health (the Act did not provide a separate legislative entry for drugs).

Although the option of legislating on other aspects of drugs was also available to the Centre – s. 103 of the Government of India Act permitted the

Centre to legislate on provincial subjects after the provinces passed resolutions to this effect – it limited itself to import regulation. This is to be understood in the context of the political and legal atmosphere at that time that determined the course of division of power between the Centre and provinces,[23] with the Government of India Act conferring greater provincial autonomy than its predecessor, the Government of India Act, 1919.[24] This unanimous consensus towards greater provincial autonomy is the context in which the restrained approach of the Indian legislature while regulating drugs must be understood.

C. *The 1940 Act: Balancing Uniformity and Provincial Autonomy*

The 1937 Draft Bill was, however, rejected by the Select Committee appointed by the Legislative Assembly, which recommended a more comprehensive law uniformly regulating the manufacture, distribution and import of drugs. Accordingly, a central Drugs Bill of 1940 was passed after provincial governments passed resolutions in this regard, allowing the Central Legislature to legislate even on the domestic manufacture of drugs.[25] However, despite the enactment of a central law, the preference for provincial autonomy continued to be reflected in its structure.

Further, the Statement of Objects and Reasons of the 1940 Act limited the Centre's control to the standardisation of imported drugs, while amending the standards for domestic drugs remained within the control of provincial governments. This contrasted with the recommendations of the Drugs Enquiry Committee, which had recommended uniform, centralised standard setting. However, the Statement specifically stated that it would be *ultra vires* to assign standard-setting and rule-making powers for domestic drugs to any authority other than the provincial governments that had exclusive legislative competence in this regard.[26] Similarly, the Statement conferred rule-making power on provincial governments, including the power to set the terms for manufacturing, sale and distribution licences and to nominate the authority empowered to issue such licences, again, at variance with the recommendations of the Drugs Enquiry Committee report. This thinking ruled out the possibility of a single regulatory body.

This was the beginning of the tension between federalism and imperatives of regulation, sowing the seeds for non-uniformity in the standard of drugs available throughout the country. The Act did attempt a nod to uniformity by constituting the Drugs Consultative Committee (DCC) and requiring the central and provincial governments to consult DTAB before modifying standards and making rules. However, these were mere advisory bodies that have not proved to be effective, an issue that we will discuss in more detail later in the chapter. As a result, the 1940 Act, as it was originally passed, walked the tightrope between attempting to achieve uniformity and accommodating the competing claim of autonomy. There was an implicit recognition that uniformity, and as a corollary, centralisation, was needed to achieve effective drug regulation, but the legislative distribution of powers to the provinces limited the extent of centralisation.

D. *Enactment of the Constitution: Towards Centralisation*

The post-independence period saw a general deviation from provincial autonomy towards centralisation, especially after the enactment of the Constitution of India. This also had an impact on drug regulation. One of the major developments regarding drugs was that it was added as a separate subject under Entry 19 of the Concurrent List,[27] which gives both the Centre and states the power to legislate on this subject, most likely in recognition of the need for uniformity in drug regulation.

Thus, the political landscape in which the Drugs Act was enacted in 1940 changed to a great extent after the enactment of the Constitution. K.L. Sharma, former Joint Secretary, Drug and Food Regulation, Government of India, in his book *Healing the Pharmacy of the World* describes the discord between the 'pre-independence governmental architecture' under the Drugs Act and modern constitutional provisions.[28] As a result, there have been post-independence attempts to bridge this discord and prioritise uniformity in drug regulation. These are discussed in the next section.

E. *Post-independence Reforms to Drug Regulation: Attempts Towards Centralisation*

Post-independence, the Pharmaceutical Enquiry Committee was set up in 1954 to undertake a comprehensive investigation into the working of the pharmaceutical industry. One of its key findings was that the Drugs Act was being poorly administered across states, with neither states nor manufacturers exercising control over drug quality.

As a result, the Committee strongly recommended centralising drug administration by bringing SDRAs, which controlled manufacture, sale and distribution, under the authority of the Drugs Controller (India) to ensure uniform implementation of the Drugs Act throughout the country. To facilitate this, the Committee recommended setting up a centralised Drugs Control Administration.[29] It believed that these reforms were in keeping with India's federal scheme, given the placement of drugs in the Concurrent List.

These recommendations were reflected in the Drugs (Amendment) Bill, 1954. This bill, with the objective of maintaining uniformity throughout the states, proposed transferring the power to make rules under section 33 with respect to the manufacture, sale and distribution of drugs from the state governments to the central government.[30] This received support in the Rajya Sabha[31] and the Lok Sabha[32] during discussions on the bill. The Drugs (Amendment) Act, 1955 brought this into being. Additionally, the power to amend standards for imported and domestic drugs, which was originally split between the central and state governments, was now consolidated only in the

Centre, cementing the move towards uniformity. Further attempts at centralising the administration of drugs continued in the 1960s. The Drugs (Amendment) Act, 1960 gave the central government the power to issue directions to any state governments to execute any of the provisions of the Act or rules.[33]

While some of the reforms like centralised standardisation have lasted, others have been diluted over the years either through subsequent amendments or in practice. For instance, through an amendment to the Drugs Rules in 1960, the central government delegated its powers to issue manufacturing licences to state governments,[34] in effect, nullifying the amendment made to Section 33 of the Drugs Act, which had specifically transferred this power from state governments to the central government.[35] It has been argued that this is an excessive delegation of power, on the grounds that the power to make secondary legislation, once assigned to the executive by Parliament under a primary statute, cannot be further delegated.[36]

Since then, India has had a federally fragmented regulatory system, particularly in terms of issuing manufacturing licences. Failed legislative attempts were made in 2007[37] and 2013[38] to create a central drugs authority, as recommended by the Hathi Committee and more structurally by the Mashelkar Committee in 2003, and to centralise manufacturing licencing. The most recent revision to the Drugs Act in the form of the draft Drugs, Medical Devices and Cosmetics Bill, 2022 continues to duplicate the existing regulatory architecture without making any attempts to streamline it.

Next, we discuss the effects of this fragmented architecture on the safety and quality of drugs.

IV. The Effects of a Fragmented Drug Regulatory Framework

The federal division of powers under the Drugs Act complicates the performance of essential regulatory functions. When more than three dozen regulators function independently and exercise their individual interpretations in implementing the provisions of the Act, non-uniformity and a lack of coordination are inevitable. Here we discuss the specific manner in which this plays out and how different kinds of non-uniformity weaken the drug regulatory system in India.

A. Non-uniformities in Standardisation

As we have discussed, drug standardisation is a centralised function. Standards that determine the identity, strength, quality and purity of drugs are prescribed centrally by the IPC and then purchased both by industry and government laboratories that are responsible for testing samples sourced from the market by drug inspectors through random sampling. Despite this centralisation, they are not necessarily applied uniformly and coherently during drug testing. There are multiple reasons for this.

First, the IP does not have specifications for certain new drugs or impurities, particularly for fixed-dose combinations (FDCs). Currently, 4046 FDCs are approved FDCs in India,[39] but the 2022 IP prescribes standards for only *157*.[40] For the remainder, the Second Schedule to the Drugs Act calls for referring to standards prescribed in any other country's official pharmacopoeia. However, India is a hub for many FDCs that are not approved anywhere else in the world or do not find mention in any other pharmacopoeia. The specifications for these FDCs are then approved by SDRAs, which lack necessary skills and infrastructure, resulting in major discrepancies in quality standards.

SDRAs do not necessarily test drugs against all prescribed standards, particularly impurity tests. It has been reported that government drug laboratories in at least seven states and one union territory have either never conducted impurity tests or do not perform them as a matter of routine. The non-availability of materials needed to conduct impurity tests is often cited as the reason for not conducting them.[41] The IP also does not contain up-to-date standards for certain drugs because it is published only once every four years, and the SDRAs have sole discretion over whether to even conduct testing for impurities. Agencies not conducting drug testing is one way that substandard drugs are never identified and instead get released to the market, with a detrimental impact on public health.

Case Study: Variations in the Application of Quality Standards and the Case of Remdesivir

A recent investigation revealed stark variations in how SDRAs apply quality standards. When the drug remdesivir caused severe adverse effects in Bihar, Uttar Pradesh, Rajasthan, Maharashtra and Gujarat during the second wave of the Covid-19 pandemic, hospitals tested batches and found some to be tainted.[42] While the concerned hospitals informed their respective SDRAs of these adverse effects, none of the SDRAs declared the drug to be of substandard quality except Bihar's. In Gujarat, where the drug was being manufactured, and where the SDRA had the duty to be the most vigilant, it conducted no quality testing and did not recall tainted batches despite being informed by local hospitals. The Rajasthan SDRA did not act due to a failed adverse event reporting system. In Uttar Pradesh, while the SDRA decided to test the concerned batches, it did not have the appropriate infrastructure.[43]

Maharashtra and Bihar achieved different regulatory outcomes despite both testing the drug. Maharashtra did not conduct an endotoxin test[44] because this test was not required under outdated specifications for the drug under the IP. As a result, Maharashtra did not find the drug to be substandard. Bihar, on the other hand, lacked its own testing facilities and thus sent its batches of remdesivir to the Central Drugs Laboratory, which conducted the endotoxin test based on international specifications. This case study reflects that even where standards are uniformly set, the flexibility afforded to SDRAs in interpreting them and applying them means that an objectively substandard drug may not be classified as such in all states. It also demonstrates that variations in state capacity impact the ability to enforce uniform standards.

B. Non-uniformities in Granting Manufacturing Licences

India has a common market for drugs: drugs manufactured in one state can be sold in another state. However, the manufacturing licenses for these drugs are not granted by a single regulator; 36 different SDRAs have significant discretion in granting drug licences despite the existence of centrally prescribed standards. For instance, compliance with GMP is one of the conditions of receiving a licence, and an Indian version of the current World Health Organisation (WHO)-GMP was incorporated in Schedule M of the Drugs Rules, 1945, but different SDRAs interpret Schedule M differently. Authors of a 2015 study on drug quality and safety issues in India found that although appropriate rules and guidelines are in place for granting manufacturing licences, different states interpret them differently, particularly Schedule M.[45]

Another reason for non-uniformity in how states grant licences is that they do not all have access to the same information before making their decisions. A relevant criterion to consider is the manufacturer's past record, but there is no central database of this information. This allows some States to be more lenient than others, especially given the fact that there is competition among them to attract investments.[46] The knock-on effect of this is forum shopping because manufacturers only need to find one SDRA that will grant them a manufacturing licence; then they may sell their drugs throughout the country even if other SDRAs denied them the licence.[47]

Case Study: Illegally Approved FDCs

The power vested in SDRAs to issue manufacturing licences proved to be a regulatory roadblock in the context of approving FDCs. FDCs are considered new drugs under the Drug Rules[48] and therefore require the approval of the CDSCO. Despite this, manufacturing licences have been issued for a spate of FDCs without central approval, with suspicion of corruption on the part of both state regulators and manufacturers.[49] As a result, there are thousands of irrational FDCs on the market whose effectiveness has not been proved. While the DCGI has advised SDRAs to cancel manufacturing licences for such FDCs, it has never acted directly to withdraw these drugs from the market in the exercise of its powers under section 26A of the Drugs Act, even though the 59th Report of the Parliamentary Standing Committee on Health and Family Welfare flagged the public health risk presented by these drugs.[50]

Manufacturers themselves exert considerable pressure to prevent enforcement of the standards and press instead for regularising unapproved FDCs. When issuing licences for unapproved FDCs was raised in meetings of the DCC, some SDRAs mentioned political pushback because industries were relocating to other states that willingly issued licences to manufacture unapproved FDCs.[51] In response, instead of immediate withdrawal, the central government first issued directions under Section 33P[52] to states not to grant licences to manufacture FDCs that fell under the definition of new drugs. The central government then invited applications from the manufacturers of unauthorised drugs on the market, and MoHFW set up an expert committee (the Kokate Committee) to review these applications. Following the review, 344 irrational FDCs were finally recommended for withdrawal from the market, and it was only after this that section 26A was used to ban these 344 drugs.[53]

This ban was promptly challenged in the Delhi High Court,[54] Madras High Court, Karnataka High Court and ultimately the Supreme Court.[55] This long battle to remove unsafe or ineffective FDCs from the market reveals weak links in the regulatory process. The fact that SDRAs have the power to issue manufacturing licences allowed such drugs to enter the market in the first place despite not having central approval, and although the central government had the power to act unilaterally to remove them, the fact that SDRAs had already issued licences dictated the regulatory path that the CDSCO chose. Today, India has more than 4000 FDCs on the market, including those regularised by the Kokate Committee. However, many of them are not on the WHO's list of rational FDCs,[56] nor have standards been prescribed for them in the IP or other global pharmacopoeia, once again, leaving more room for discretion to SDRAs.

C. *Non-uniformities in Enforcement*

The 2003 Mashelkar Committee report observed that the enforcement of drug laws was weak and non-uniform even after 56 years since their enactment and that the issue of non-uniformity of enforcement at the state level was serious and needed to be addressed immediately.[57] This problem persists even two decades after this report was published.

1. *Lack of Standard Operating Procedures*

In India, until 2016, drug inspectors essentially relied on a system of random sampling. In the absence of uniform metrics to determine inspection targets, there is huge statewide variation in drugs inspections.[58] In 2016, a comprehensive tool was designed to conduct risk-based inspections of drug manufacturing units in India, which are preferred by other drug regulatory agencies like the US Food and Drug Administration (FDA) and the European Medicines Agency. However, this tool is yet to yield results and will require changes before inspection becomes more effective. For instance, risk-based inspections require information about manufacturers' track records, but SDRAs do not maintain such records. Additionally, inspectors in India unhelpfully focus more on products than processes; focusing instead on GMP compliance across states, in line with global best practices, would be more effective.

Beyond inspections, states show tremendous variation in how drug laws are enforced when inspections or testing reveal drugs to be substandard or reveal non-compliance with GMP processes. In the absence of a central standard, each state is free to determine how to respond when a drug fails testing or inspection. Further, there is no standard for how to withdraw the substandard drug from the market. While there are Guidelines on Recall and Rapid Alert System for Drugs,[59] these are more in the nature of directions to individual SDRAs than a formal nationwide mechanism for recalling bad batches of drugs across the country once they fail a quality test in a particular state.[60]

2. *Operating in Silos*

Non-compliance with the Drugs Act can result in suspension or cancellation of licences as well as criminal prosecution. However, the power to suspend/cancel licences lies only with individual SDRAs.[61] This presents three problems: First, the SDRA which reports a substandard drug in its state has to rely on the SDRA of the manufacturing state to suspend or cancel that drug's licence. Second, the reporting SDRA can neither raid a manufacturing unit outside its territorial jurisdiction nor stop the drugs from a non-compliant manufacturing unit from entering its state. Third, the Drugs Act and Rules lack substantive provisions for exactly when and how to suspend or cancel a non-compliant manufacturer's licence, again leaving too much to the SDRAs' discretion.

In January 2020, 12 children died in Jammu after consuming adulterated cough syrup manufactured by Digital Vision, a manufacturing unit situated in Himachal Pradesh and licensed by that state's SDRA. Different SDRAs and the Central Drug Laboratory had already found that Digital Vision had manufactured and sold substandard drugs on 19 different occasions,[62] but the Himachal Pradesh SDRA took no appropriate action, allowing Digital Vision to continue its operations. This is an unfortunate example of how poor coordination between different SDRAs allows non-compliant manufacturers to continue their business operations, with adverse effects on public health.

This lack of coordination also hampers the launch of prosecutions, which are the only tools available to SDRAs against manufacturers located outside their jurisdiction. To launch a prosecution against a manufacturer, SDRAs need updated information regarding the constitution of its firm and other relevant details, but in a DCC meeting, some SDRAs raised the issue that states are not sharing this information. Therefore, the DCC recommended that states nominate a contact officer to provide such information, to be assisted by branch offices of the CDSCO.[63] Rajasthan in fact used the courts, relying on provisions of the Indian Penal Code, when other state government officers refused to cooperate in providing the necessary information.[64] The DCC endorsed this approach at its next meeting for clear cases of non-communication but urged states to use this only as a matter of last resort.[65]

The aim of this section was to demonstrate the impact that the division of powers between the Centre and the states has had on three major drug regulatory functions – standardisation, licencing and enforcement. This division of powers shows that even uniform standard setting through centralisation is insufficient in preventing fragmentation. The fragmented regulatory architecture and the vesting of licencing and enforcement in SDRAs results in the uneven implementation of the Drugs Act throughout the country because SDRAs have too much discretion and different regulatory capacities.

Next we examine the mechanisms that have been used to address this non-uniformity and the extent of their effectiveness.

V. Weak Central Coordinating Mechanisms

A. *Uniformity Without Authority*

The framers of the Drugs Act established the DCC because they anticipated some of the non-uniformity we just discussed given the fragmented distribution of drug regulatory powers between the Centre and the states.[66] The DCC has representatives from the CDSCO and all SDRAs and advises the central government, state governments and DTAB on any matter tending to secure uniformity throughout the country in the administration of the Drugs Act.[67]

The DCC, however, does not have any legal or binding authority to enforce its decisions. It only issues non-enforceable guidelines like *Guidelines for taking action on samples of drugs declared spurious or not of standard quality in the light of enhanced penalties under the Drugs and Cosmetics (Amendment) Act, 2008*. However, given the non-uniform implementation of these guidelines across states, there was a recommendation to convert the guidelines themselves into rules under the Drugs Act.[68]

B. *Joint Inspection – A Move Towards Cooperative Pharmaceutical Federalism*

Another attempt at ensuring uniformity was made through the Drugs and Cosmetics (Tenth Amendment) Rules, 2017, which mandated a joint inspection by central and state drug inspectors before a manufacturing unit received a licence.[69] The amendment was aimed at streamlining uniform inspection procedures regarding conforming with the GMP. However, it received huge backlash from the industry as well as SDRAs on the ground that the CDSCO did not have adequate capacity or manpower to carry out joint inspections, so the amendment would only lead to delays which in turn would encourage competitive, rent-seeking interest.[70]

Joint inspections were even challenged in the Madras High Court by the All India Drug Control Officers Confederation on the ground that it overreached and surpassed the defined division of powers between the central and state governments under the Drugs Act and that the Act granted exclusive power to the states regarding inspections. However, the Court dismissed these challenges, stating that the purpose of joint inspections by both central and state inspectors was to ensure uniform quality compliance by the entire pharmaceutical industry, including ensuring that there were no differences in the quality of inspections from state to state. While the Court ultimately held that the joint inspection was not contrary to the distribution of powers under the Act, it was clearly also persuaded by the merits of the amendments and the potential of cooperative pharmaceutical federalism in bringing uniformity in drug quality across the country.

In both these examples, attempts were made to introduce uniformity that was lacking in the structure of the Drugs Act. In the first instance, this proved to be ineffective because the Act does not confer sufficient powers on the DCC. The second example takes a different approach from the first: rather than impose a top-down *diktat*, decision-makers attempted to solve the question of non-uniformity by requiring the Centre and states to cooperate with each other, an imperative given the lack of overall coordination in the existing framework. This is discussed in the next section.

C. *Lack of Overall Coordination, Oversight and Accountability*

The Drugs Act is the only legislation that aims to regulate the quality of products marketed across India through multiple regulators functioning independently of each other. The WHO multi-country Study on Effective Drug Regulation observed that when drug regulatory functions are assigned to two or more agencies, at either the same or different levels of government, regulatory effectiveness is usually impeded by fragmentation and uncoordinated delegation. For countries with a federal system of government that grant some drug regulatory powers to states, the study authors noted that uniformity would require a concerted effort across agencies at all levels to attain the same regulatory objectives for the whole country. This type of organisational structure eventually lacks unity of command over drug regulatory functions, which undermines the overall effectiveness of regulation.[71]

In India, the lack of hierarchy between the CDSCO and the SDRAs due to their autonomous functioning leads to a huge gap concerning overall coordination between the Centre and states. Since there is no single statutory body that is ultimately responsible for ensuring the regulatory effectiveness of the system, with clear duties and powers substantively laid down under the Act, it is hard to demand accountability for deficiencies in regulation. CDSCO officials, despite being aware of the challenges that undermine the regulatory functioning of SDRAs, do not consider it their responsibility to address such problems.[72] The Estimates Committee of the Seventh Lok Sabha in its report pointed out that the division of drug regulatory responsibilities between the

Centre and states fails to take into account the role of overall coordination and control that the CDSCO should play.[73]

To address this, one token provision under the Drugs Act is section 33P, which gives the central government the power to issue directions to state governments to carry out any of the provisions of this Act or the Drugs Rules, but it is rarely used, and the CDSCO does not have the power to enforce these directions.[74] The 59th Parliamentary Standing Committee Report on the functioning of the CDSCO also expressed concerns about the serious shortcomings in Centre–state coordination in enforcing the Drugs Act and Rules and commented on the reluctance of the central government to exercise its powers under section 33P and section 26A to protect the public interest. There is an argument to be made that states are reluctant to use these tools because no centralised administration has explicit regulatory oversight across states.

VI. Reimagining Pharmaceutical Federalism in India

The right to the highest attainable standard of health includes the right to access safe, efficacious and quality essential medicines.[75] This can be achieved by appropriately regulating the manufacturing and marketing of drugs as well as by making available accurate and appropriate information on drugs. For effective regulation, appropriate and adequate structures must be in place.

The WHO report on effective drug regulation sets out certain recommendations in this regard.[76] The most relevant in the Indian context is that one single central agency should be accountable for the overall effectiveness of drug regulation. The report suggests that drug regulatory structures should be designed in such a way that there is a central coordinating body with overall responsibility and accountability for all aspects of drug regulation for the entire country.[77] This aspect is currently missing in India, as is highlighted in the following examination of the drug regulatory architecture in the US – a country with one of the most effective drug regulatory systems in the world – from a federal lens.

A. *Pharmaceutical Federalism in the United States*

Looking at the history of drug regulation in the US, considerable commonalities can be drawn with India. While the FDA is today a powerful federal drug regulator and has extensive control over drugs, this was not always the case. The FDA emerged in response to disparities in state drug regulatory laws.

Just like India, the US initially attempted only to regulate imports federally by means of the Import Drug Act of 1848, while states continued to enact their own laws on drug regulation, leading to divergent and sometimes unreasonably severe state laws.[78] This led to the enactment of two significant federal laws, the Biologics Act of 1902 and the Pure Food and Drugs Act of 1906. The Pure Food and Drugs Act led to the establishment of the FDA but did not end state regulation; instead, states enacted laws that mirrored the federal law. Yet the existence of unsafe and fake drugs continued in the US culminating in a public health scandal in 1937 involving adulterated drugs.[79] This finally led to the enactment of the federal Food, Drug, and Cosmetic Act of 1938, the statute that forms the basis for the FDA's drug regulation. This did not, however, spell the end of state regulation.

As part of modern-day regulation, no new drug can be marketed in the US without the approval of the FDA, which determines the safety and efficacy of the drug.[80] The FDA now dominates the sphere of national drug regulation, and states only complement it by employing product liability schemes to provide compensation under their tort laws. States may impose certain requirements under their food and drug laws parallel to the federal law, but these are almost identical to the federal law.[81] In some cases, state laws have interfered with the FDA's authority by either prohibiting the prescription or dispensing of an approved drug or establishing more permissive policies than federal ones for certain drugs on the ground that FDA oversight is too restrictive. However, in both cases, courts concluded that these actions were pre-empted by the 1938 Act.[82]

In effect, under the US model of drug regulation, the FDA regulates drugs through the life cycle of the product while state laws only complement this.

B. Suggested Reforms to the Indian Drug Regulatory Framework

This section identifies reforms that are key to strengthening Indian drug regulatory architecture with emphasis on a cooperative spirit between the Centre and states. Of these, the most important is giving a statutory basis to the performance of regulatory functions, by either creating a new central statutory regulatory body or making the CDSCO itself a statutory body. The latter is in line with the recommendations of the Pharmaceutical Enquiry Committee in 1954; the Hathi Committee in 1975; the National Drug Policies of 1986, 1994 and 2002 and, more structurally, the Mashelkar Committee in 2003. Whichever route is adopted, it is vital that the authority have oversight over SDRAs, which should function as its counterparts across states. Ideally, this should be accompanied by a fundamental overhaul of the existing Drugs Act, with the new law creating transparency and accountability mechanisms for the regulator.

The second major reform that is needed is streamlining fragmented drug regulatory functions between the Centre and states. Regulatory functions ought to be divided, keeping in mind the spirit of cooperative pharmaceutical federalism. For instance, standard setting should remain vested in the Centre in line with Entry 51 of the Seventh Schedule, which gives the Centre the power to set standards for the quality of products moved from one state to another.

The power to issue manufacturing licences should be entirely centralised with the central regulator being the sole authority to grant licences across India. This has already been suggested by expert groups and committees. The National Human Rights Commission, in a 1999 order, stated that the present dual system of control did not appear to have achieved the desired effects and that the central government should immediately take steps to bring the entire system of licencing under its effective control.[83] The Mashelkar Committee also recommended a single central agency to regulate the manufacture and quality control of drugs in the country.

Enforcement, meanwhile, should be carried out jointly between the Centre and the states. SDRAs should continue to exercise powers alongside the central regulator to test drugs marketed in their states and to launch prosecutions against non-compliant manufacturers irrespective of their location, as a check on the central regulator. Where the central body fails to enforce GMP compliance, substandard drugs will be detected by SDRAs during their testing and sampling.[84]

VII. Conclusion

Drug regulation poses interesting challenges for federalism. In India, the peculiar historical context has meant that there is path dependence in favour of the involvement of state governments in regulation, even though the constitutional scheme has changed since the enactment of the Drugs Act. There are no legislative or constitutional barriers to centralising drug administration; in fact, it has even been argued that transferring licencing power back to the Centre requires only an amendment of the Drugs Rules, not the Act.[85] The question, then, is one of political will, which no government appears to have been inclined to exercise so far. The new draft Drugs, Medical Devices and Cosmetics Bill, 2022, which replicates the existing architecture, confirms this.

However, what appears to emerge from the discussion in this chapter is that in areas like drug regulation, it appears almost impossible to achieve minimum levels of safety and quality in an equitable manner across the country without a certain degree of centralisation. This suggests that in areas where human life and health are at stake, there is less room for the exercise of state discretion. This has been the experience across similar areas like food and environment, where centralisation has already taken place to a much greater degree than under the Drugs Act. The Food Safety and Standards Act, 2006 created the central, statutory Food Safety and Standards Authority of India in part to address weak enforcement under the Prevention of Food Adulteration Act, 1954. Most environmental legislation is also central, with the Central Pollution Control Board having standard-setting authority and the power to issue directions to state pollution control boards.

This is not to say that effective regulation is incompatible with a distribution of powers across different levels of government. Centralisation, especially as regards standard setting and licencing in drug regulation, is necessary for achieving uniformity. It can also act as a check against the weak implementation of the Drugs Act by states that see strong enforcement as a deterrent to investment. However, no effective regulation is possible without investing in regulatory capacity at both the Central and state levels, or without a modern drug law that provides substantive guidance to regulators and creates accountability mechanisms for them.

Acknowledgement

The authors would like to thank Nihal Sahu for providing research assistance for this chapter.

Notes

1 Dutta (2022, December 24; 2022, December 29).
2 Thakur and Reddy T (2022).
3 Committee on Economic, Social and Cultural Rights, General Comment No. 14: The Right to the Highest Attainable Standard of Health (Article 12), (Adopted on 11 August 2000).
4 Section 5, Section 7, Drugs and Cosmetics Act, 1940.
5 Callréus and Schneider (2013).
6 Sections 10, 18.
7 Sections 8, 16.
8 Schedule M, Drugs and Cosmetics Rules, 1945.
9 Section 10.
10 Section 18.
11 Sections 12, 33.
12 Per Rule 122E, drugs are considered to be "new drugs" for a period of four years after their first approval, when they have not been approved to be safe and effective by the licensing authority before and have not been used in the country to any significant extent. This includes fixed-dose combinations of two or more drugs, vaccines and recombinant DNA.
13 Under Schedule C and C1.
14 Rule 68A, Rule 122B, Rule 122D and Rule 69 of the Drugs and Cosmetic Rules, 1945.
15 Bhatia et al. (1954).
16 Bhatia et al. (1954), 146.
17 Bhatia et al. (1954).
18 Chopra et al. (1931).
19 Chopra et al. (1931), 173–174.
20 Chopra et al. (1931), 170.
21 Chopra et al. (1931), 171–173.
22 Drugs Bill 1940, Statement of Objects and Reasons.
23 Chatterjee et al. (2019).
24 See Government of India Act, 1919, Section 1(1)(d), Section 4(3) and Section 10(3).
25 Government of India Act 1935, s 103.
26 Drugs Bill 1940, Statement of Objects and Reasons.
27 Constitution of India, *Seventh Schedule, List III:* '19. Drugs and poisons, subject to the Provisions of Entry 59 of List I with respect to opium'.
28 Sharma (2021).
29 Bhatia, et al. (1954).
30 Drugs (Amendment) Bill 1954, Statement of Objects and Reasons.
31 Discussion in the Rajya Sabha by the Minister of Health while introducing the Bill on 31 August 1954.
32 Lok Sabha Debates 28 February 1955.
33 The Drugs and Cosmetics Act 1940, s 33P.

34 Rule 69 as amended by Notification F. 1–22/59-D dated 9 April 1960. The amendment allowed state governments to appoint authorities to issue manufacturing licenses.
35 The Drugs (Amendment) Act, 1955.
36 Thakur and Reddy T (2016).
37 The Drugs and Cosmetics (Amendment) Bill, 2007.
38 The Drugs and Cosmetics (Amendment) Bill, 2013.
39 List of FDC & Subsequent New Drugs Approved in India, Central Drugs Standard Control Organisation. https://cdsco.gov.in/opencms/opencms/en/Approval_new/FDC-New-Drugs-Marketing/ (accessed 29 August 2022).
40 Indian Pharmacopoeia (2022).
41 Pulla (2021, November 5).
42 Pulla (2021, December 23).
43 Pulla (2021, December 23).
44 Endotoxins are compounds present in the protective envelopes of bacteria that cause fever, chills and life-threatening septic shock in humans. Low endotoxin levels are a key quality requirement for drugs that are injected into humans.
45 Chokshi et al. (2015).
46 See note 36.
47 Jeffery and Santhosh (2009).
48 Rule 122E.
49 Sharma (2021, p. 121).
50 Section 26A of the Drugs and Cosmetics Act confers on the central government the power to regulate, restrict or prohibit the manufacture, sale or distribution of a drug in the public interest if it involves any risks, does not have any therapeutic value or does not have any therapeutic justification for its ingredients.
51 Sharma (2021, p. 123).
52 Under Section 33P, the central government 'may give such directions to any State Government as may appear to the central government to be necessary for carrying into execution in the State any of the provisions of this Act or of any rule or order made thereunder'.
53 'Complete list of 344 drugs banned by the Ministry of Health Family Welfare', National Health Portal. www.nhp.gov.in/Complete-list-of-344-drugs-banned-by-the-Ministry-of-Health-Family-welfare_pg (accessed 29 August 2022).
54 *Pfizer Limited and Ors. v. Union of India and Ors.*, W.P.(C) No.2212/2016, Delhi High Court.
55 *Union of India and Anr. v. Pfizer Limited and Ors.*, Civil Appeal No. 22972 of 2017 Supreme Court.
56 Mehta et al. (2022).
57 Mashelkar et al. (2003).
58 Choudhary et al. (2015).
59 Central Drugs Standard Control Organisation (2017).
60 See note 36.
61 Rule 85(2), Drugs and Cosmetics Rules, 19145.
62 Pulla (2021, September 28).
63 42nd DCC Meeting, Agenda No. 7: Non-Cooperation between the States in Providing Information in Respect of Manufacturers Located Under Their Jurisdiction (15th February 2011).
64 Under Sections 175 and 176 of Indian Penal Code, every public servant is legally bound to produce or give information or deliver any document to another public servant.
65 43rd DCC Meeting, Agenda No. 4: Providing Constitutions of Licensed Firms and Other Relevant Documentary Evidences by Licensing Authorities When Required for Launching Prosecution Against Offending Firms (14 November 2011).

66 Drugs Bill 1940, Statement of Objects and Reasons.
67 Drugs and Cosmetics Act 1940, s 7.
68 Minutes of the 77th Meeting of the Drugs Technical Advisory Board (2017, June 16).
69 Drugs and Cosmetics Rules 1945, r 73AB.
70 Shankar (2018, June 13).
71 Ratanawijitrasin and Wondemagegnehu (2002).
72 See note 58.
73 Committee of Estimates of the Seventh Lok Sabha (1983–84).
74 See note 58.
75 Sharma (2021, p. 15).
76 See note 71. https://iris.who.int/bitstream/handle/10665/42470/9241562064.pdf?sequence=1&isAllowed=y.
77 See note 71. https://iris.who.int/bitstream/handle/10665/42470/9241562064.pdf?sequence=1&isAllowed=y. See also, *Fifty-fifth Report* (2021).
78 Young (1989).
79 Ballentine (1981).
80 21 USC § 355(d).
81 Zettler (2017).
82 *Ouellette v Mills, 91 F Supp 3d 1, 9 (D. Me. 2015)*; *Zogenix, Inc v Patrick, No 14–11689-RWZ, 2014 WL 1454696, *1* (D Mass. 15 April 2014).
83 Mashelkar et al. (2003).
84 Citizens for Affordable, Safe & Effective Medicine (2022).
85 See note 36.

References

Ballentine, C. (1981, June). *Sulfanilamide Disaster.* United States Food & Drug Administration. www.fda.gov/files/about%20fda/published/The-Sulfanilamide-Disaster.pdf.

Bhatia, S.L., et al. (1954). *Report of the Pharmaceutical Enquiry Committee.* Ministry of Commerce & Industry, Government of India. https://ia802800.us.archive.org/25/items/dli.csl.2136/2136.pdf.

Callréus, T., and Schneider, C.K. (2013). The Emergence of Regulatory Science in Pharmaceutical Medicine. *Pharmaceutical Medicine*, *27*, 345–351. https://doi.org/10.1007/s40290-013-0039-x.

Central Drugs Standard Control Organization. (2011, February 15). *Report of the 42nd Meeting of Drugs Consultative Committee Agenda No. 7: Non-Cooperation between the States in Providing Information in Respect of Manufacturers Located under Their Jurisdiction.* Central Drugs Standard Control Organization. www.cdsco.gov.in/opencms/resources/UploadCDSCOWeb/2018/UploadCommitteeFiles/42dcc.pdf.

Central Drugs Standard Control Organisation. (2017). *Guidelines on Recall and Rapid Alert System for Drugs (2017).* https://cdsco.gov.in/opencms/export/sites/CDSCO_WEB/Pdf-documents/biologicals/4GuidelineRecalRapidAlert.pdf, accessed 20.8.2022.

Central Drugs Standard Control Organisation. *List of FDC & Subsequent New Drugs Approved in India.* Ministry of Health & Family Welfare. https://cdsco.gov.in/opencms/opencms/en/Approval_new/FDC-New-Drugs-Marketing/, accessed 29.8.2022.

Central Drugs Standard Control Organization. (2011, November 14). *Report of the 43rd Meeting of Drugs Consultative Committee Agenda No. 4: Providing Constitutions of Licensed Firms and Other Relevant Documentary Evidences by Licensing*

Authorities When Required for Launching Prosecution against Offending Firms. Central Drugs Standard Control Organization. https://cdsco.gov.in/opencms/resources/UploadCDSCOWeb/2018/UploadCommitteeF iles/43dcc.pdf.

Chatterjee, S., et al. (2019, October 8). *Cleaning Constitutional Cobwebs: Reforming the Seventh Schedule.* Vidhi Centre for Legal Policy. https://vidhilegalpolicy.in/research/cleaning-constitutional-cobwebs-reforming-the-seventh-schedule.

Chokshi, M., Mongia, R., and Wattal, V. (2015). *Drug Quality and Safety Issues in India.* Indian Council for Research on International Economic Relations. https://icrier.org/pdf/Working_Paper_310.pdf.

Chopra, R.N., et al. (1931). *Report of the Drugs Enquiry Committee.* Government of India, 162. https://indianculture.gov.in/rarebooks/report-drugs-enquiry-committee-1930-31.

Choudhary, N., Joshi, P., Patnaik, A., and Saraswathy, B. (2015). *Administrative Structures and Functioning of Drug Regulatory Authorities in India.* Indian Council for Research on International Economic Relations. https://icrier.org/pdf/Working_Paper_309.pdf.

Citizens for Affordable, Safe & Effective Medicine. (2022, August 20). *Comments on Draft of New Drugs, Medical Devices and Cosmetics Bill, 2022.* Casem. https://casemindia.org/wp-content/uploads/2022/08/CASEM-FInal-Comments-on-DC-Amendment-2022.pdf.

Committee on Economic, Social and Cultural Rights. (2000, August 11*). General Comment No. 14: The Right to the Highest Attainable Standard of Health (Article 12).* New York: United Nations. https://www.ohchr.org/sites/default/files/Documents/Issues/Women/WRGS/Health/GC14.pdf.

Constitution of India. (1950). *Seventh Schedule, List III, Entry 19 ("Drugs and Poisons, Subject to the Provisions of Entry 59 of List I with Respect to Opium").*

The Drugs (Amendment) Act of 1955, Act 11 of 1955. www.indiacode.nic.in/repealed-act/repealed_act_documents/A1955-11.pdf

Drugs (Amendment) Bill of 1954, Bill 14 of 1954, Statement of Objects and Reasons [PDF downloaded from Manupatra, a legal database which is not open source].

Drugs Bill of 1940, Statement of Objects and Reasons. *Indian Penal Code of 1860*, Act 45 of 1860. www.indiacode.nic.in/bitstream/123456789/4219/1/THE-INDIAN-PENAL-CODE-1860.pdf

The Drugs and Cosmetics (Amendment) Bill of 2007. Bill 57 of 2007. https://prsindia.org/files/bills_acts/bills_parliament/2007/1188536330_DRUGS_20BILL_2007.pdf

The Drugs and Cosmetics (Amendment) Bill of 2013. Bill 58 of 2013. https://prsindia.org/files/bills_acts/bills_parliament/2013/Bill%20Text_11.pdf

Dutta, A. (2022a, December 24). 70 Kids' Deaths: Gambian Panel Holds Cough Syrup Manufacturer Maiden Culpable, Seeks Legal Action. *The Indian Express.* https://indianexpress.com/article/india/70-kids-deaths-gambian-panel-holds-cough-syrup-manufacturer-maiden-culpable-seeks-legal-action-8341367/.

Dutta, A. (2022b, December 29). After Gambia, an Indian Syrup Linked to the Deaths of 18 Kids in Uzbekistan. *The Indian Express.* https://indianexpress.com/article/india/uzbekistan-children-died-consumption-of-india-made-syrup-8349555/.

Indian Pharmacopoeia Commission. (2022). *Indian Pharmacopoeia 2022.* https://indianpharmacopoeia.in/Salient_Features_of_IP_2022.pdf.

Jeffery, R., and Santhosh, M.R. (2009). Architecture of Drug Regulation in India: What Are the Barriers to Regulatory Reform. *Journal of Health Studies*, 2, 13–32.

Mashelkar, R.A., et al. (2003). *Report of the Expert Committee on a Comprehensive Examination of Drug Regulatory Issues, Including the Problem of Spurious Drugs. 2003(27).* Department of Pharmaceuticals. https://pharmaceuticals.gov.in/sites/default/files/MashelkarCommitteeReport.pdf

Mehta, A., et al. (2022, August 22). Systemic Antibiotic Sales and WHO Recommendations, India. *Bulletin of the World Health Organization*, Article ID: BLT.22.287908.

https://cdn.who.int/media/docs/default-source/bulletin/online-first/blt.22.287908.pdf?sfvrsn=d89d46fb_1.
Ministry of Health and Family Welfare. (1955, February 28). *Lok Sabha Debates*. https://eparlib.nic.in/bitstream/123456789/55782/1/lsd_01_09_28-02-1955.pdf
Ministry of Health and Family Welfare. *Rajya Sabha Debates, 31 August 1954* [PDF downloaded from the RS website].
Ministry of Health and Family Welfare, Complete List of 344 Drugs Banned. *National Health Portal*. www.nhp.gov.in/Complete-list-of-344-drugs-banned-by-the-Ministry-of-Health-Family-welfare_pg.
Ministry of Health and Family Welfare, Department of Health. (1940). *Drugs and Cosmetics Act, 1940*. https://cdsco.gov.in/opencms/export/sites/CDSCO_WEB/Pdf-
Ministry of Health and Family Welfare, Department of Health. (1945). *Drugs and Cosmetics Rules of 1945*. https://cdsco.gov.in/opencms/export/sites/CDSCO_WEB/Pdf-documents/acts_rules/2016DrugsandCosmeticsAct1940Rules1945.pdf.
Minutes of the 77th Meeting of the Drugs Technical Advisory Board. (2017, June 16). The Health Master. https://thehealthmaster.com/wp-content/uploads/2021/03/77th-DTAB-held-on-16.06.2017.pdf.
Ouellette v Mills, 91 F Supp 3d 1, 9 (D. Me. 2015); Zogenix, Inc v Patrick, No 14-11689-RWZ, 2014 WL 1454696, *1 (D Mass, 15 April 2014).
Pfizer Limited and Ors. v. Union of India and Ors. W.P.(C) No.2212/2016. Delhi High Court.
Pulla, P. (2021, November 5). With Officials Rarely Checking for Impurities, India's Drug Testing Has a Big Blind Spot. *The Wire*. https://thewire.in/health/with-officials-rarely-checking-for-impurities-indias-drug-testing-has-a-big-blind-spot.
Pulla, P. (2021, September 28). How Weak Drug Laws Are Costing Lives. *Mint*. www.livemint.com/politics/policy/how-weak-drug-laws-are-costing-lives-11632761831130.html.
Pulla, P. (2021, December 23). The Dangerous Failure to Stop Tainted Remdesivir. *Mint*. www.livemint.com/science/health/the-dangerous-failure-to-stop-tainted-remdesivir-11640197634967.html.
Ratanawijitrasin, S., and Wondemagegnehu, E. (2002). *Effective Drug Regulation: A Multicountry Study*. World Health Organization. https://apps.who.int/iris/handle/10665/42470.
Shankar, R. (2018, June 13). Fears of Joint Inspections. *Pharmabiz.com*. www.pharmabiz.com/NewsDetails.aspx?aid=109429&sid=3.
Sharma, K.L. (2021). *Healing the Pharmacy of the World*. Notion Press, 50. https://notionpress.com/read/healing-the-pharmacy-of-the-world.
Sixtieth Report (1983–84) on the Ministry of Health and Family Welfare (1983, December 22). Parliament of India, Lok Sabha, Digital Library. https://eparlib.nic.in/handle/123456789/58595?view_type=search.
Thakur, D.S., and Reddy, P. (2016). *A Report on Fixing India's Broken Drug Regulatory Framework*. https://spicyip.com/wp-content/uploads/2016/06/Report_India-Drug-Regulatory-Framework_June-2016.pdf.
Thakur, D.S., and Reddy, P. (2022). *The Truth Pill*. Simon & Schuster.
Union of India and Anr. v. Pfizer Limited and Ors., Civil Appeal No. 22972 of 2017 Supreme Court.
United States Code, Title 21, § 355. (2010). www.govinfo.gov/content/pkg/USCODE-2010-title21/pdf/USCODE-2010-title21-chap9-subchapV-partA-sec355.pdf
World Health Organization. (2021). *Fifty-Fifth Report WHO Expert Committee on Specifications for Pharmaceutical Preparations: Annex 11 Good Regulatory*

Practices in the Regulation of Medical Products. https://apps.who.int/iris/bitstream/handle/10665/340323/9789240020900-eng.pdf.

Young, J.H. (1989). *Pure Food: Securing the Federal Food and Drugs Act of 1906*. Princeton, NJ: Princeton University Press.

Zettler, P.J. (2017). Pharmaceutical Federalism. *Indiana Law Journal*, 92, 845.

9 Federalism and Regulation of Private Health Care in India

Unfolding Contradictions Between Centre, States and People in Times of Authoritarian Neoliberalism

Abhay Shukla and Shweta Marathe

Federalism is a major expression of democracy that seeks to accommodate diversity and power sharing and has the potential for decentralising power. However, in many countries including India today, there is tension between the push for growing power centralisation and the pull towards due power sharing between the central and state governments. Combined with these tensions on the political plane are powerful processes at the economic level, where strengthened neoliberal capitalism since the 1990s has diluted or stalled state regulation in various sectors, including the private health care industry. There is growing influence of health care corporations along with rising transnational investments in health care, which have gathered steam under accelerated pro-corporate regimes at the national level since 2014. This has been accompanied by the current central government largely stalling legal regulation of private health care.

However, unregulated privatisation and commercialisation has serious consequences for users and patients, resulting in financial barriers to health care access and other violations. In the current constitutional and sociopolitical framework, some state governments have addressed these adverse social consequences directly, proactively exercising their autonomy to develop mechanisms for negotiating the public interests of large masses of health care uses and the commercial interests of private health care providers. These ongoing tensions between the central government, state governments and health care users regarding regulation of private health care were brought into sharp focus during the Covid-19 pandemic. In the absence of central government initiative, several state governments took measures to regulate rates for COVID care in private hospitals to ensure affordability, with mixed results.

With this background, in this chapter, we give an overview of the trajectories of central and state governmental approaches to regulating private health care since the initiation of neoliberal policies in the 1990s. We seek to understand how during and following the Covid-19 pandemic, contradictions between the central government, various state governments, and ordinary people unfolded in terms of potentially regulating the private health

DOI: 10.4324/9781003568711-12

care sector. Under the shadow of authoritarian neoliberalism, state power is increasingly pulled towards serving the globalised corporate-dominated market to the detriment of popular constituencies, and these tensions are also reflected in Centre–state relations in a federal polity which is increasingly under siege. Given this context, there is a need for sharper articulation of public interests regarding private health care, as well as health systems as a whole, to ensure that public health and welfare remain paramount at all levels of governance.

The Ongoing Commercialisation of Health Care and the Diversity of Health Systems

Commercialisation of Health Care From the 1990s Onwards

Due to the adoption of neoliberal economic policies in India from the early 1990s, both the public and private health care sectors have undergone significant transformations. The commercialisation of health care was promoted systematically, with the industry marketed as a lucrative business opportunity. Health care was increasingly converted from a social good to an industry with the potential for double-digit growth and substantial revenues for investors (Chakravarthi et al., 2017). These include private equity funds, high net-worth individuals and global investment firms including transnational financial institutions such as the International Finance Corporation. Foreign investment in the hospital sector in India increased from merely INR 31 crore in 2001–02, to INR 3995 crore in 2013–14, an over hundred-fold increase in little more than a decade (Hooda, 2015). This influx of capital resulted in a burgeoning corporate health care sector across India, particularly during the 2010s, that displaced the earlier model of health care professionals running small and medium-sized hospitals and individual-run clinics (Shukla et al., 2021).

Since the 1990s, the private sector has grown to occupy a larger share of the health care market, becoming the dominant player in both inpatient and outpatient care utilisation. In a report on the 75th round of the National Sample Survey (NSS), conducted in 2017–18, 70 per cent of all patients were treated in the private health care sector, including 58 per cent of all inpatients being registered in private hospitals (National Sample Survey Organisation, NSSO, 2019). One critical reason for the overall growth of the private health sector has been both the central and most states' governments' major neglect of public health systems including inadequate public spending on health. India presently spends barely 1.2 per cent of its gross domestic product on public health, much lower than the global norm of 5 per cent and the averages for both lower-middle-income (2.4 per cent) and upper-middle-income (3.8 per cent) countries (WHO Global Health Observatory, 2023).

Although health care privatisation during the neoliberal period was promoted across all states, state-specific analysis reveals differing levels of privatisation among the states. Mapping the health systems in major Indian states

Table 9.1 Per Capita Total Health Expenditures and Public Hospitalisation Rates by State

Low spenders (< Rs. 3500)	THE per capita (Rs.)	Govt. hospitalistion%
Assam	2461	70.9
Bihar	1389	37.8
Jharkhand	2726	40.7
MP	2422	47.9
Uttarakhand	2963	35.7
CG	3061	54.0
J&K	3109	91.2
Odisha	3130	72.2
Rajasthan	3406	50.5
UP	3296	27.1
Medium spenders (Rs.3500- 4500)		
Gujarat	3534	31.1
Tamil Nadu	3955	49.9
Haryana	4329	31.1
Punjab	4231	29.4
W Bengal	4460	69.2
Telengana	4267	21.0
High spenders (> Rs. 4500)		
AP	4628	27.8
Karnataka	4533	26.6
Kerala	9264	38.3
Maharashtra	5236	22.2
HP	6541	77.3

Sources: Ministry of Statistics and Programme Implementation, 2019 and National Health Systems Resource Centre, 2021.

based on per capita total health expenditure (THE), an indicator of overall health system development that includes both public- and private-sector health care spending, and share of public hospitalisation (SPH), which is inverse to the degree of privatisation, shows that major Indian states can be broadly classified into one of the following five categories (see also Table 9.1 and Figure 9.1):

a) **Poor privatisers** – Uttar Pradesh (UP), Uttarakhand, Bihar, Chhattisgarh, Jharkhand, Madhya Pradesh (MP) and Rajasthan have both low per capita THE and low SPH, indicating less developed health care sectors within which private-sector utilisation dominates.
b) **Better-resourced privatisers** – Andhra Pradesh, Karnataka, Maharashtra, Gujarat, Haryana, Punjab and Telangana show high THE and low SPH, with predominantly private health care providers.
c) **Poor votaries of public services** – Although Assam, Odisha and Jammu and Kashmir have low THE, the dominant mode of hospitalisation is from the public health system.
d) **Better resourced, balanced public–private care** – Two southern states, Kerala and Tamil Nadu, uniquely balance the public and private health care sectors, showing relatively high THE and moderate SPH.

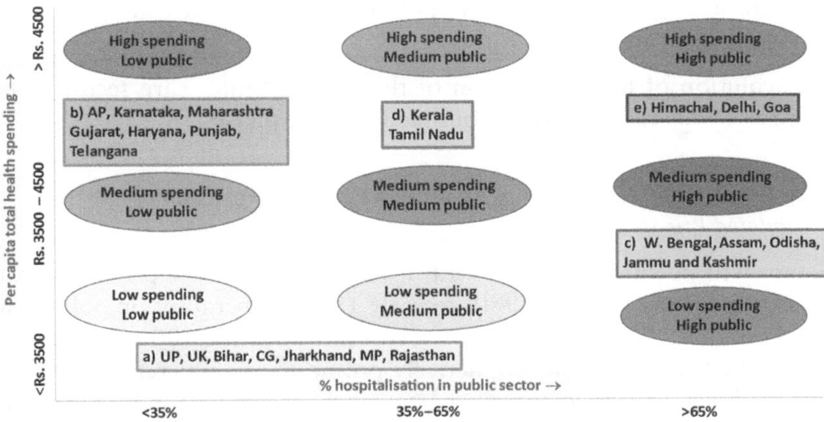

Figure 9.1 State health care system mapping by public health care utilisation and total health spending.

e) **Better resourced, majority public hospitalisation** – Although Himachal, Delhi and Goa show high THE, most of the hospital use is interestingly within the public health system.

West Bengal appears as an outlier in this classification with moderate THE and historically higher public hospitalisation but emerging as a 'late privatiser' with high out-of-pocket (OOP) spending.

Expansion of Private Medical Colleges in Southern States Drives State-Supported Health Insurance Schemes

The southern states of Karnataka, Maharashtra, AP, Telangana, Tamil Nadu and Kerala have a large number of medical colleges, and collectively, these six states alone contribute 50 per cent of the MBBS (Bachelor of Medicine, Bachelor of Surgery) seats and 49.8 per cent of all allopathic medical course seats in the country (CBHI, National Health Profile, 2021). The expansion of private medical colleges in these states and presence of more doctors in proportion to population seems to have been associated with the launch of state-supported health insurance schemes, which preceded the central government's 2018 enactment of Pradhan Mantri Jan Arogya Yojana (PMJAY), the national health care coverage scheme. Such state-specific schemes had been launched prior to PMJAY in all mentioned states except Kerala, which had previously made extensive modifications for implementing RSBY (Rashtriya Swasthya Bima Yojana) but subsequently adopted PMJAY.

Brief Chronology of the Regulation of Private Health Care in the Neoliberal Period

The evolution of legal regulation of the private health care sector in India since the 1990s can be broadly outlined in three phases.

Early 1990s–2004: Launching of Neoliberal Policies, Expansion of Unregulated Private Health Care

The growth in number and spread of private health care providers started picking up during the mid-1980s to early 1990s. Liberalisation policies were rolled out in the Indian health care sector like allowing 100 per cent foreign direct investment in hospitals, actively promoting commercial health insurance, rolling out public–private partnerships, providing industry status to the hospital sector, reducing customs duties on medical equipment and giving tax exemptions to hospitals for opening branches in rural or semi-urban areas. Such pro-business policies boosted the private health care sector significantly. The analysis of successive rounds of NSS data related to 42nd and 60th rounds shows a clear reversal of the ratio of public versus private hospitalisation utilisation from the mid-1980s to mid-2000s (NSSO, 1989, 2006).

During the same period, hospitals in India began to be set up as private and public limited companies. This was linked with growing transnational investments and corporatisation of health care in India. The National Health Policy (NHP) 2002 (Ministry of Health and Family Welfare, MoHFW, 2002) explicitly recognised the need to promote and standardise the private health care sector, pointing to the rising significance of private provisioning.

2005–13: An Interlude of Social Liberalism

The next phase, from 2005 to 2013 during the two United Progressive Alliance governments, can be regarded as an interlude of social liberalism, the variant of neoliberal policies which attempts to balance continued capital accumulation with some social entitlements and welfare; socially oriented legislation and programs combined fulfilling some social needs with ongoing expansion of the business sector. In the health sector, there were two notable initiatives, the 2005 launch of the National Rural Health Mission to strengthen rural public health services (later expanded to include urban health services to form the National Health Mission) and the enactment of the Clinical Establishments Act (CEA) in 2010 (Act No. 23 of 2010) (MoHFW, 2010) by the Union government under Article 252 of the Constitution. While CEA was a significant step in regulating the private sector, only 11 states and 6 Union Territories (UTs) have adopted it so far; the Indian Medical Association (IMA) and other medical associations have persistently resisted its implementation, including vehemently opposing including rate regulation and centralised minimum standards in the 2012 CEA Rules.

2014 Onwards: Accelerated Private-Sector Engagement Under the Shadow of Authoritarian Neoliberalism

Following the central regime change in 2014, there was a major shift in Union government policies, making the policy environment favourable for accelerated privatisation and foreign investments in health care. With the explicit promotion of privatisation and corporatisation at the policy level, regulation of private healthcare was moved off the Union government's agenda. NHP 2017 (MoHFW, 2017) included the objective of aligning the growth of private health care with public health goals, with emphasis on strategic purchasing:

> Strategic purchasing would play a stewardship role in directing private investment . . . main mechanisms of strategic purchasing are insurance and through trusts. . . . To encourage the participation of private sector, the policy advocates incentivising the private sector through financial and non-financial incentives.

On these lines, the PMJAY, the flagship health scheme of the current Union government, was launched in 2018, taking political priority over the existing National Health Mission. This scheme publicly subsidises market-based access to health care for the poor rather than providing expanded public health services or effectively regulating private health care. It is implemented with the involvement of private hospitals, which currently treat more than half of the total patients benefitting from the scheme. The Union government has been strongly persuading nearly all state governments to adopt PMJAY, even though the scheme is widely publicised as a centrally led initiative of the Prime Minister.

The Troubled Trajectory of the CEA

A Step Towards Transparency and Accountability of Private Health Care With Certain Limitations

The Union government enacted the CEA to provide for registration and regulation of clinical establishments in the country, with the purpose of prescribing minimum standards for facilities and services provided by them. Following this landmark legislation in 2010, CEA rules were notified in 2012. While CEA focusses on registration, the 2012 rules include detailed regulatory provisions like transparency in rates, standardisation of rates and standard treatment guidelines. Given the fact that public health, hospitals and dispensaries are placed in the State list of the Seventh Schedule of the Indian Constitution (Constitution of India, 2022), there has been limited scope within a federal framework for the central government to pass regulations on private hospitals and clinical establishments. The enactment of CEA signalled an intent by the Union government to create such a framework for regulating private health care providers, although it was not binding on the states.

CEA applies to all public and private clinical establishments, which are eligible for permanent registration once there has been notification that the facility meets the minimum standards. While enactment of CEA is indeed a step towards private-sector regulation, there are also significant gaps and challenges related to this legislation. Firstly, emphasising physical infrastructure standards may make it difficult for smaller hospitals to fulfil the provisions; while the act focuses on structural standards of clinical establishments, it does not address process standards related to health care settings, which are more important from the patient's viewpoint. Secondly, standards formulation is highly centralised at a national level, constraining the space for states to devise context-specific standards, which is much needed in a highly diverse country like India. States have no power to amend the act or rules, except for limited flexibility to customise the state-level rules. Thirdly, CEA is not accompanied by dedicated resources and mechanisms for its enforcement, and it is therefore likely that it will remain primarily registration-driven and will not positively reshape the functioning of private providers. Fourthly, CEA lacks key provisions like a multi-stakeholder appellate body at district level and patient grievance redressal mechanisms.

Deceleration of Momentum in CEA Implementation After 2014

The momentum behind CEA decelerated after 2014, which is evident from the decreasing frequency of meetings of the NCCE, the governing body. After the notification of the NCCE, a total of only 12 meetings took place through 2022; Table 9.2 visibly displays how momentum tapered off with time. Due to delays in critical notifications at the national level, states have so far only provisionally registered clinical establishments since the passage of CEA.

Massive Delay in Notification of Minimum Standards – Time Lag of Nearly a Decade

Under CEA, the National Council was supposed to release the first set of minimum standards within two years of its constitution. However, it took almost eight years for the council to formulate draft minimum standards. Finally, on 17 July 2019, MoHFW circulated the draft notification of standards. However, these critical standards, which are essential for ensuring permanent registration of clinical establishments, are yet to be finally notified. This has effectively kept the ground-level implementation of this important regulation in a state of prolonged suspension.

Table 9.2 Meetings of the National Council for Clinical Establishments

2012	*2013*	*2014*	*2015*	*2016*	*2017*	*2018*	*2019–2020*	*2021*
1, 2	3	4, 5, 6	7	8, 9	10	11	–	12

Source: https://web.archive.org/web/20151106214438/http://clinicalestablishments.nic.in/cms/Home.aspx#

National Council Sub-committee on Rate Standardisation Dissolved, Responsibility Shifted to States

Rate transparency and standardisation are among the most critical and contentious aspects of regulating clinical establishments in India. There is pressing need for transparency in health service rates given the arbitrary and often inflated pricing of services by many commercial private health care providers in India, and it is also one of the reforms that health care users most commonly demand. The CEA Rules prescribe that the clinical establishments registered under CEA must display the rates charged for various services/facilities available and that the rates must be fixed within the range determined by the Union/state governments. The NCCE shared a list of standard procedures and a template for the costing of these procedures with the states and UTs that have adopted the Union Government Act, advising them to use these for determining the standard cost of any procedure, taking into consideration all including pertinent local factors.

However, the NCCE has yet to develop a concrete framework for standardising service rates. In fact, the Council dissolved its sub-committee on rate standardisation, which was active during 2013, and shifted the responsibility for this complex task to the 11 states and 6 UTs that had adopted CEA. This move could be interpreted as a negative use of federalism as a pretext for allowing the Union government to shrug off its larger responsibility for regulating service rates in the private health care sector.

Varying CEA Implementation Across States

Since hospitals and dispensaries are under state government jurisdiction per the Indian Constitution, there were two options for state governments: adopt the CEA or enact their own similar state-level legislation. Few of India's states or UTs had adopted CEA by 2020, and there was significant delay in issuing notifications of the state rules to the individual state councils and the District Registering Authority. These notifications are still pending in the states of UP, Haryana and Bihar.

The major obstacle to implementing CEA has been stiff resistance from the private health care lobby, often spearheaded by the Indian Medical Association (IMA). IMA state chapters have filed public interest litigations to block CEA implementation and disseminated systematic propaganda among members, fuelling exaggerated fears about regulation among medical professionals. In this 'regulatory stalemate', there are currently four broad scenarios of implementation among Indian states:

- States such as Bihar, UP, Rajasthan, Jharkhand, Assam and Haryana adopted the CEA but have not moved beyond the provisional registration of establishments.
- Karnataka and West Bengal have implemented their own state-specific regulatory acts while adding some notable additional features beyond the CEA.

- Tamil Nadu, Kerala, Punjab, AP and Chhattisgarh have enacted their own state-specific acts which are largely similar to CEA but with some dilutions and modifications.
- In Maharashtra, Gujarat, Delhi, MP and Odisha, regulation remains weak with outdated acts limited mostly to registration because of opposition to regulation from private health care providers.

This status of CEA implementation reflects that although the federal system provides spaces for states to promote regulation, the level of political will within states is critical in deciding how such regulation will actually unfold. CEA as a legal instrument had significant potential to create a framework for regulating private health care, but with declining sociopolitical support from governments at both Central and state levels, its adoption was patchy, and its implementation has so far been largely ineffective.

Notable State-level Regulatory Acts in Karnataka and West Bengal

Karnataka State Initiative Stymied by Private Health Care Lobby: The 2017 KPME Amendment Bill

The Karnataka Private Medical Establishments (Amendment) Bill 2017 was proposed as an amendment to the existing KPME Act 2007 which the state government had adopted for regulating private medical establishments. The proactive health minister at the time championed certain pro-patient amendments in the KPME Act that were actively supported by civil society but met with fierce criticism from private doctors' associations. Calling it a draconian act, private doctors protested certain recommendations including price capping on various procedures, setting up district-level and metropolitan grievance redressal cell phone lines and not including public health care facilities in the bill. In response to this agitation, the government constituted an 18-member joint select committee of the legislature to investigate the issues that concerned the doctors' lobby, but the committee ignored most of the doctors' demands and recommended retaining most of the original provisions.

However, bitter resistance by the IMA and other private health care associations included circulating misinformation about provisions in the bill that exaggerated apprehensions among private doctors. Some high-profile, influential doctors from corporate hospitals lobbied politicians to support the demands of the private health care sector. Finally, the state government was forced to make four important modifications in the bill, diluting its initial intent (Shukla et al., 2021). The clause of cost regulation was restricted to publicly funded health insurance schemes. Imprisonment for medical negligence was scrapped, and deterrent clauses for filing baseless complaints of medical negligence were included. Finally, the district-level grievance redressal authority was reconstituted to include more representation from the private sector. The KPME Amendment experience points to the disproportionate influence of powerful private health care providers on India's regulatory framework: ultimately, the interests of medical associations prevailed over public interests.

West Bengal Initiatives for Regulation (2017 Onwards) – A Regulatory Commission to Convert Rules Into Action

The state-specific West Bengal Clinical Establishments Act (2010) was mostly focused on registration and licensing, similar to other such registration acts, but 2017 amendments added significant provisions for rate transparency, grievance redressal mechanism, patient's rights and an autonomous regulatory commission (Health and Family Welfare Department, West Bengal, 2017). Major change came with the formation of the West Bengal Clinical Establishment Regulatory Commission with backing from Chief Minister Mamata Banerjee. This 13-member commission chaired by a retired High Court judge, is armed with powers to receive grievances, inspect establishments, ask for documents, serve notices, etc.

However, the IMA and other private doctors' associations have resisted the implementation of the amended act and called for protests against penalties for doctors. There have been allegations of arbitrariness and corruption in regulating private hospitals, but the Commission seems to have established some kind of countervailing mechanism to deal with the established clout of private hospitals, although the manner in which these powers are used needs further scrutiny. Based on examination of various Commission orders, it appears intended to resolve disputes between patients/caregivers and private hospitals within the framework of the WBCE Act and Rules 2017. Although West Bengal's CEA is a limited measure which has its own share of controversies, it can be regarded as a significant step when most states lack effective grievance redressal mechanisms for patients concerning private hospitals.

State Differences in Public Engagement With Private Health Care

In keeping with the diverse character of health systems in the different Indian states (outlined in 'Ongoing Commercialisation of Health Care' earlier in this chapter), it is clear that the Union government interacts differently with different state governments regarding engagement with the private health care sector. The two major levers of direct government engagement with the private healthcare sector have been legal regulation like CEA and large-scale public purchasing of care from the private sector, often through state-specific health insurance schemes and PMJAY. The balance between these two modes of involvement has varied over time with change in political contexts and is also differentiated from state to state. Of course, the greatest pull away from private-sector health care use is an effective public health care delivery system to be the first option for people seeking health care.

In observing trends, it becomes clear that state government responses to central initiatives concerning the private sector depend on how much the states themselves depend on the Union government for financial support. Following the privatisation categories on pages 148-149, type a) states (the poor privatisers: UP, UK, Bihar, CG, Jharkhand, MP, Rajasthan) show low public health spending and weaker health systems and depend heavily on the central government for health system resources; therefore, they are more likely to toe the central government's line. In contrast, states with more developed health systems exhibit more autonomy from the central government. Many type b) states (better-resourced privatisers: AP, Karnataka, Maharashtra, Gujarat, Punjab, Telangana) also have large private-sector lobbies that heavily resist regulation. Many of these states instead launched their own insurance schemes or engaged statewide public–private partnerships (PPPs) that arrange state-subsidised markets for private health care providers.

Keeping this background in view, we can analyse differential state government responses to central government policies related to private health care, as these have evolved from the UPA period to the current National Democratic Alliance government, commonly called NDA-II. As we have noted, during the UPA period (2010–14), Central government attempts to convince state governments to adopt the CEA evoked mixed responses. Several northern states including Rajasthan, UP, Bihar, Jharkhand, Himachal Pradesh, Uttarakhand and later, Haryana have adopted the Central CEA, while most southern states either adopted their own acts or stalled CEA-type legal regulation.

However, during NDA-II (2014 onwards), as we described, the central government's emphasis shifted away from implementing the CEA towards actively engaging private health care providers through PMJAY. Implementing PMJAY has often involved piggybacking on existing state health insurance schemes in southern states even as it is being promoted as a significant new initiative in many northern states that lacked earlier state-supported health insurance schemes.

Within this entire context, it is clear that there are not neatly delineated patterns in Indian state governments' engagement with the private health care sectors in their states; in the next sections, we discuss some loose patterns that can be discerned.

Significant influence of the Union government in shaping state engagement with private health care

During the UPA era, UP, Uttarakhand, Bihar, Jharkhand and Rajasthan adopted the CEA; Chhattisgarh did not, but in 2010, state leaders adopted an act that was similar to the CEA. MP has an outdated nursing home registration act, and regulatory processes have largely been stalled. Now all these states have adopted PMJAY and are proceeding with public purchasing of private health care through this Union government scheme.

- *State-specific health insurance, state-level regulations, etc.*

AP, Telangana, Karnataka and Maharashtra avoided adopting the CEA because they have health insurance schemes which predate PMJAY, and this seems to have been their major mode of public engagement with the private sector. Gujarat and Punjab also have their own regulatory acts, but neither had a state-level health insurance scheme which predated PMJAY.

- *Weak engagement with the private sector, historically dominant public provisioning*

Assam, Odisha, Jammu and Kashmir have historically higher public health system utilisation. While Assam adopted the CEA in 2015, Odisha still has an outdated nursing home registration act. Jammu and Kashmir also had older, limited registration acts that dated to 1963, but this has recently become a Union Territory and are now subject to the CEA. Overall, these states show weak engagement with the private health care sector.

- *Robust public health care utilisation balanced by significant private provisioning, state-led models for purchasing private health care*

Delhi, Tamil Nadu and Kerala are characterized by relatively large proportion of public hospitalisation combined with significant OOP spending in private health care facilities, which reflects significant utilisation of the private sector also. Given this situation, these states have developed state-specific models for engaging with the private sector, including purchasing care. Both Tamil Nadu and Kerala adopted their own CEAs, while Delhi has an outdated nursing home registration act and is yet to adopt CEA-type legislation. While Tamil Nadu launched its own health insurance scheme, Kerala modified and expanded RSBY to purchase care from private providers for covering poorer sections of the population. Delhi has been experimenting with different PPPs, including outsourcing certain surgical care and diagnostic tests to empanelled hospitals, while also implementing innovative models like Mohalla clinics which insource private practitioners.

In this tracing of broad patterns, West Bengal is somewhat of an outlier state in that it has historically higher levels of public sector hospitalisation but is now a late privatiser of health care. The autonomy exercised by state-level political actors seems to have played a role both in launching the state's Swasthya Sathi health insurance scheme (Health and Family Welfare Department, *West Bengal*, 2016) and in creating the West Bengal Clinical Establishment Regulatory Commission, which helps to operationalise the state's own regulatory act, which has certain additional provisions relevant for health care users.

Activating Federalism to Regulate Private Health Care During Covid-19 as NITI Aayog Pushes for Further Health Care Commercialisation

During the unprecedented Covid-19 pandemic, the hitherto stalled agenda of private health care regulation became reactivated due to the crisis of bed availability in public hospitals. Although the Union government did not issue specific orders for private-sector regulation related to Covid-19 care, the threat of public unrest and muted resistance from the private sector impelled 15 State governments to move further and impose regulations on rates for Covid-19 treatment by private health care providers, often invoking the Disaster Management Act, 2005 (DMA) and Epidemic Diseases Act, 1897 (EDA; Table 9.3).

Although sociopolitical conditions seemed to be conducive for regulation during the pandemic, the available legal instruments were weak due to inherent limitations of the DMA and EDA; therefore, the different states' measures were somewhat ineffective. Nevertheless, state government regulatory measures implemented during the pandemic highlighted a positive aspect of federalism: despite the largely centralised response to Covid-19 pandemic and the Union government's lack of initiatives for regulation of private health care, multiple state governments took independent initiatives to ensure that critical emergency care was affordable. In the wider context of aggressively neoliberal policies adopted at the central level, the central government was

Table 9.3 Proportions of Private Hospital Beds Brought Under Rate Capping for Covid-19 by State and Month of Decision

	State	*Proportion*	*Month*
1	Maharashtra	80%	April 2020
2	Andhra Pradesh	50%	April 2020
3	Delhi	60%	June 2020
4	Tamil Nadu	25%	June 2020
5	Karnataka	50%	June 2020
6	Goa	20%	June 2020
7	West Bengal	Not specified	June 2020
8	UP	50%	August 2020
9	Punjab	25%	August 2020
10	Odisha	10 %	August 2020
11	Chhattisgarh	Not specified	September 2020
12	Kerala	10%	October 2020
13	Gujarat	Not specified	April 2021
14	Bihar	10–25%	April 2021
15	Jharkhand	50%	April 2021

Source: Compilation by authors from various media reports

reluctant to rein in powerful private health care interests even during the pandemic. On the other hand, state governments directly faced public discontent due to widespread profiteering, denials and violations by commercial private hospitals, and being more directly answerable on the ground, many were forced to respond.

These measures also unveiled the potential of state governments to regulate private health care in the public interest given the crystallisation of requisite political will. State-level interim regulatory measures taken during the Covid-19 period could be treated as a precedent to take forward more comprehensive regulation of private health care, including implementing CEA-type acts in various states (Marathe and Shukla, 2022).

Maharashtra Nursing Homes Registration Act

Maharashtra state has persisted with the outdated Bombay Nursing Homes Registration Act (1949), which is minimalist in content, despite constant demands from civil society for more comprehensive and effective CEA-type legislation. This act was somewhat modified in 2005 and 2013 with only minor changes in content, and now the act has been renamed the Maharashtra Nursing Homes Registration Act.

During Covid-19, Maharashtra was the worst-affected state in the country in terms of numbers of deaths and cases, and there were widespread reports of denial as well as overcharging by private hospitals. Perhaps with belated recognition of the need to regulate private health care and keeping in view people's harrowing experiences in private hospitals during the pandemic, the state government modified MNHRA rules in January 2021 to now require all clinical establishments to display key rates and implement the patients' rights charter, along with mandating patient grievance redressal cells in all cities and districts. Until now no publicity has been given to these provisions, and there seems to be little official initiative for their implementation, but now, civil society organisations are demanding that these significant pro-people provisions be effectively implemented on the ground (*The Indian Express*, 2023).

No Lessons Learned From the Covid-19 Experience? NITI Aayog Advocates for Accelerated Commercialisation in Midst of the Pandemic

In March 2021, in the midst of the world's worst pandemic in a century, the national official think-tank NITI Aayog launched the report *Investment Opportunities in India's Healthcare Sector* (Sarwal et al., 2021), which effusively invited multinational investors and domestic capitalists to further invest in India's already highly privatised health care industry and contains not even a single sentence on private providers' overcharging and exploitative behaviours during the pandemic, which were widely experienced and documented. Instead, it presents the situation emerging from Covid-19 as a fantastic business opportunity to be further exploited, for instance via accelerated foreign and domestic investments in private health care and expanding private hospital players to Tier 2 and Tier 3 locations. Even though state government leaders had faced the ground level situation and reluctantly realized they needed to regulate private hospital rates during the Covid-19 care crisis, the leading national think-tank NITI Aayog seems to have learned no lessons from the pandemic, perhaps expressing in concentrated form the overall policy direction of the Union government.

Using Centre–State Spaces to Further a People-centred Health Care Agenda in the Context of Tensions with Neoliberal Health Care

As we have discussed, the neoliberal period has witnessed growing commercialisation and corporatisation of health care in India. However, health care does not behave like a typical commodity; even while it is shaped by the market, it also remains deeply socially embedded. To paraphrase Polanyi, health care is a 'contentious commodity' (Mackintosh, 2006), due to which attempts to accelerate commodification beyond a point create major contradictions and social reactions.

In India, there is an ongoing aggressive push by capital to deregulate the health care market for profit maximisation, accompanied by promoting both passive and active privatisation. However, if access to health care is left purely to market mediation, then the effective market remains constricted given that most of the Indian population cannot afford private health care. With neoliberal policies leading to weak public care provisioning in most states, rising prices in the commercialised private sector have led to critical gaps in access to health care with adverse social consequences. It is partially in response to this conundrum that states launched their own health insurance schemes and the central government subsequently instituted PMJAY. These schemes provide state-supported markets to private providers and partially subsidise hospitalisation care to poorer sections of the population.

Another emerging problem is that health care corporations with no social roots in Indian communities – often backed by global financial investments – are seeking to expand their share in India's national health care market. The corporate hospitals offer glittering new technologies and an attractive 'consumer experience' to members of the upper middle class who can afford their services, often mediated by higher-end commercial insurance coverage. However, many small and medium hospitals and individual clinics have historically been run by doctors themselves, occupying local market niches and enjoying certain confidence of families and communities due to greater social embeddedness. Today with the onslaught of corporatisation, these smaller and individual-run health care providers are finding it difficult to defend their local market segments; many are being forced to become franchisees or agents of corporate chains or are shutting down their establishments entirely to become consultants or just work for corporate hospitals.

These challenges reflect the different approaches to private health care between the central government and different state governments, which as we discussed show diversity in their approaches. Since 2014, the central government's approach could be called 'authoritarian neoliberalism'; along with overall tendencies for centralisation of governance, leaders have nearly completely sidelined efforts to regulate private health care through CEA. As we identified in their published report, NITI Aayog – the chosen think-tank of the central government – is promoting accelerated foreign and domestic investments linked with further privatisation and corporatisation of the health sector.

Meanwhile, although some state governments are politically aligned with the central government, others are less aggressively pro-corporate and balance commercial interests of private providers (including non-corporate providers) with the need to ensure some access to care for large sections of the population. Their diverse approaches can be broadly categorised as examples of 'social-liberalism', a variant of neoliberal policies which balances the drive for capital accumulation with promotion of some social entitlements and welfare. Some examples include the attempt by Karnataka government to effectively regulate private health care providers through the KPME Amendment (which was significantly rolled back due to backlash from the private sector), the creation of the clinical establishments regulatory commission in West Bengal, and modification in MNHRA rules by Maharashtra government in 2021, creating some legal spaces for patients' rights and redressal systems. Higher public allocations for health care accompanied by launching of Mohalla clinics in Delhi, and various initiatives for strengthening public health services (especially at primary level) in states like Kerala and Tamil Nadu are notable state-level efforts to strengthen publicly delivered health services. In all such instances federalism can provide significant spaces to shape health care policy in pro-people directions.

Experiences on the ground such as the unique participatory audit of private hospital bills in Maharashtra in 2022, leading to dozens of substantial refunds to overcharged patients from private hospitals, show that new alliances between state and civil society actors can emerge in the post-Covid-19 recovery scenario (Shukla, 2023). Recent state-level developments like the Right to Healthcare act in Rajasthan and the draft Right to Health policy in Tamil Nadu are examples of significant pro-people federal initiatives in the health sector, even in an era of overall centralisation of governance.

Hence in the unfolding contention between central authoritarian neoliberalism and state-level social-liberalism, some spaces can emerge to push a pro-people agenda, including advocating to expand public health services to fulfil health rights, and meeting demands for effective state regulation of private hospitals in the wake of the Covid-19 pandemic. However, to move further and transcend the neoliberal, capital-driven framework itself which prevails today in the health sector, there is an outstanding need for organised social forces to develop a popular 'third strand' distinct from existing central and state governments that would aim to detach health care from the market and convert it into a publicly organised social good which is accessible to all. This would require combining strong, expanded and socially responsive public health services with socially accountable, comprehensive regulation of health care providers, socialised under a publicly managed universal health care system.

As we noted at the outset of this chapter, federalism is an important expression of democracy. Today, people-centred health movements definitely need to defend and utilise the democratic spaces mandated in a federal framework to promote health sector reforms. Yet there is also a need to maintain the vision of expanding democracy to encompass socioeconomic rights, so that striving for universal access to health and social entitlements becomes an important rallying point in the wider struggle to safeguard the future of democracy in India.

References

Central Bureau of Health Intelligence. (2021). *National Health Profile 2021* (pp. 364–365). New Delhi: Ministry of Health and Family Welfare, Government of India. www.cbhidghs.nic.in/showfile.php?lid=1160

Chakravarthi, I., Roy, B., Mukhopadhyay, I., and Barria, S. (2017). Investing in Health: Healthcare Industry in India. *Economic & Political Weekly*, *52*(45), 50–56.

Constitution of India. (2022). *Seventh Schedule (Article 246)* (pp. 310–324). Constitution of India, Government of India. https://cdnbbsr.s3waas.gov.in/s380537a945c7aaa788ccfcdf1b99b5d8f/uploads/2023/05/2023050195.pdf

Health and Family Welfare Department. (2016). *West Bengal Swasthyasathi Health Insurance Scheme*. Government of West Bengal. https://swasthyasathi.gov.in

Health and Family Welfare Department, West Bengal. (2017). *West Bengal Clinical Establishment (Registration, Regulation and Transparency) Rules, 2017*. Government of West Bengal. www.wbhealth.gov.in/pages/acts_rules

Hooda, S.K. (2015). Foreign Investment in Hospital Sector in India: Trends, Pattern and Issues. *Working Paper No. 181*. New Delhi: Institute for Studies in Industrial Development.

The Indian Express. (2023, January 22). Nursing Homes Registration Rules: Will Set Up Grievance Redressal Cell, Assures PMC. *The Indian Express*. https://indianexpress.com/article/cities/pune/nursing-homes-registration-rules-will-set-up-grievance-redressal-cell-assures-pmc-8396535/

Mackintosh, M. (2006). Commercialisation, Inequality and the Limits to Transition in Health Care: A Polanyian Framework for Policy Analysis. *Journal of International Development*, *18*, 393–406.

Marathe, S., and Shukla, A. (2022). Lessons from Private Sector Engagement with COVID-19 for Universal Health Care. *The Leaflet*. https://theleaflet.in/lessons-from-private-sector-engagement-with-covid-19-for-universalhealth-care/.

Ministry of Health and Family Welfare. (2002). *National Health Policy 2002*. Government of India. https://main.mohfw.gov.in/sites/default/files/18048892912105179110National.pdf

Ministry of Health and Family Welfare. (2010). *The Clinical Establishments (Registration and Regulation) Act, 2010*. Government of India. https://web.archive.org/web/20151106214438/http://clinicalestablishments.nic.in/cms/Home.aspx#

Ministry of Health and Family Welfare. (2017). *National Health Policy 2017.* Government of India. https://main.mohfw.gov.in/sites/default/files/9147562941489753121.pdf

Ministry of Statistics and Programme Implementation. (2019). *Key Indicators of Social Consumption in India: Health, National Sample Survey 75th Round.* National Statistical Office, Ministry of Statistics and Programme Implementation, Government of India. www.mospi.gov.in/sites/default/files/publication_reports/KI_Health_75th_Final.pdf

National Health Systems Resource Centre. (2021). *National Health Accounts Estimates for India 2017–18.* Ministry of Health and Family Welfare, Government of India. https://nhsrcindia.org/sites/default/files/2021-11/National%20Health%20Accounts-%202017-18.pdf

National Sample Survey Organisation. (1989). *Morbidity and Utilisation of Medical Services, 42nd Round, National Sample Survey.* New Delhi: Department of Statistics, Government of India.

National Sample Survey Organisation. (2006). *Morbidity, Health Care and the Condition of the Aged, 60th Round National Sample Survey.* New Delhi: Ministry of Statistics and Programme Implementation, Government of India.

National Sample Survey Organisation. (2019). *Key Indicators of Social Consumption in India: Health, 75th Round National Sample Survey.* New Delhi: Ministry of Statistics and Programme Implementation, Government of India.

Shukla, A. (2023). Regulation of Private Hospitals During COVID Gets a 'Booster' of Social Accountability. *The Leaflet.* www.theleaflet.in/regulation-of-private-hospitals-during-covid-gets-a-booster-of-social-accountability

Shukla, A., Pawar, K., and More, A. (2021). *Analysing Regulation of Private Healthcare in India.* New Delhi: Oxfam India.

World Health Organisation. (2023). *Global Health Observatory Data Repository.* https://apps.who.int/gho/data/view.main.GHEDGGHEDGDPSHA2011WBv?lang=en

10 Ensuring the Availability of Pharmaceutical Products

A Critical Evaluation of the Role of the Central Government

Biswajit Dhar

I. Introduction

The growth of the Indian pharmaceutical industry is among the few highpoints of the country's manufacturing industry during the past four decades. Several key characteristics of the industry are well documented, including its ability to provide affordable medicines not only in India but in many countries, especially in the advanced economies (Dhar and Joseph, 2019).

These achievements notwithstanding, the Indian pharmaceutical industry suffers from one major weakness, which is its unacceptably high reliance on imported active pharmaceutical ingredients (APIs), including those for antibiotics and several major therapeutic areas. Thus, its abilities have remained limited largely to the formulations segment alone. To meet the requirements of its critical intermediates, the APIs, the formulations manufacturers increasingly relied on imports. Not only have imports of APIs risen consistently since 1996–97, the last year from which consistent data are available from the Department of Commerce, Government of India, there have been increasing reliance on a single source country, namely, China. Interestingly, a similar situation prevailed in the Indian pharmaceutical industry at the dawn of independence, when most of the production units were engaged in the mere processing of imported APIs and producing formulations; almost 80 per cent of the imports comprised antibiotics, sulpha, drugs, vitamins, hormones and other chemotherapeutic products.

Based on the recommendations of at least two expert committees and the central government's endeavour to establish a viable manufacturing sector, a strategy for the holistic development of the country's pharmaceutical industry anchored in the public sector was adopted from the 1950s. Although the industry had made its beginnings at the turn of the 20th century with the establishment of the Bengal Chemicals and Pharmaceutical Works, steps were taken in the early 1950s for a systematic development of the industry starting from the production of APIs. Efforts were made to set up state-owned enterprises to produce 'antibiotics and other essential drugs' and 'basic and intermediate products required for by chemical industries such as the

DOI: 10.4324/9781003568711-13

manufacture of drugs'. The Industrial Policy Resolution of 1956 included the pharmaceutical industry in Schedule B, 'for whose future development, the State will increasingly establish new undertakings' (Government of India, 1956a, paragraph 9).

Given that India had once begun to develop the pharmaceutical industry with a focus on establishing a robust API segment, what led to the retrogression of the industry and its heavy dependence on imports of APIs? This chapter is an attempt to explain the vicissitudes of the Indian pharmaceutical industry over the past seven decades that have resulted in inadequate availability of critical intermediate products. In the first three decades following the country's independence, the central government had taken the responsibilities of developing a resilient domestic industry by establishing several public sector undertakings (PSUs) that would supply APIs. However, when it initiated market-oriented reforms in the 1980s, support for the PSUs began to be pruned in keeping with the ideological underpinnings of the new policy orientation.

Its lack of commitment to ensuring long-term sustainability of the pharmaceutical industry, was not the only instance where the central government had fallen short of realising a crucial public policy objective. Ensuring Covid-19 vaccine access during the pandemic was yet another major instance. A series of policy changes on vaccine roll-out has meant that the target of getting the country's entire population vaccinated is yet to be met.

II. Genesis of a Domestic Pharmaceutical Industry

Phase I: Establishment of the Industry

In the initial post-independence period, the policy of industrialisation by way of import substitution was not applicable to the pharmaceutical industry, and foreign capital was encouraged. This was because, on the one hand there was no alternative available to the drug technology held by foreign companies (Narayana, 1984), and on the other, the government expected that foreign companies would help in building a strong industry within the new environment. The Industrial Policy Resolution of 1948 read that 'it should be recognised that participation of foreign capital and enterprise, particularly as regards industrial technique and knowledge, will be of value to the rapid industrialisation of the country' (Ministry of Industry and Supply, 1948, para10). This liberal approach resulted in many foreign pharmaceutical companies opening subsidiaries in India alongside companies with Indian ownership (Government of India, 1975, p. 17).

The indigenous sector at the time was mainly engaged in medicine processing and formulation based on imported fine chemicals and bulk drugs 'with little or no programme for undertaking their production in basic chemicals' (Government of India, 1954, p. 9). This just perpetuated the country's dependence on imports. In 1949–50, India's imports of pharmaceutical products were nearly INR 7.9 crore, which increased quickly to INR 15.6 crore in 1951–52. Almost 80 per cent of the imports were antibiotics, sulpha, drugs, vitamins, hormones and other chemotherapeutic products (Government of India, 1954, p. 9).

With the private sector, and especially the foreign companies, inclined to maintain the status quo, the government decided to establish domestic production facilities in the public sector to manufacture penicillin, paludrine and three sulpha drugs: sulphathiazole, sulphamerazine. and sulphanilamide.[1] In 1951, the government agreed to accept monetary and technical assistance from the World Health Organization and the United Nations International Children's Emergency Fund for the setting up of penicillin manufacturing facilities of the Hindustan Antibiotic Ltd (HAL). This facility became functional in 1955, a year later than was scheduled.

Simultaneously, the Pharmaceutical Enquiry Committee headed by General Bhatia was appointed in 1953 with a detailed mandate to study the state of the Indian industry and issues relating to pricing of pharmaceutical products. The committee was mandated to study the following: (1) the working of the existing pharmaceutical manufacturing concerns in India; (2) operations of foreign and/or Indian companies that import drugs and pack them in the country; (3) extent of link between Indian concerns and those of foreign companies; (4) recommended steps for encouraging the domestic manufacture of important drugs that are currently imported; (5) the distribution of pharmaceutical products, both imported and domestically manufactured and packed and (6) the profit margins for trade and industry (Government of India, 1954, p. 2).

Two committee recommendations would reverberate for most of the next two decades with respect to capacity creation in the pharmaceutical industry. The first was that Indian manufacturers should produce 'as many fine chemicals and drugs starting from basic chemicals, and/or intermediates as close to the basic chemicals as practicable', aiming to minimise the country's dependence on imported APIs (Government of India, 1954, p. 14). The second was that the committee expected that HAL would meet most of the demand for pharmaceuticals, and the government would encourage the private sector to be actively involved only if the public sector enterprise failed to meet the rising demand (Government of India, 1954, p. 37).

The Second Five Year Plan (1956–61) gave another boost to expanding a domestic pharmaceutical industry. The plan underlined that the 'progress of the industry will be in the direction of increased production as well as development from basic primary organic chemicals and intermediate products in place of the present operations based on penultimate products' (Government of India, 1956b, Chapter 19). The plan further underlined that beyond the establishment of HAL to develop the public sector, specific 'efforts initiated by private enterprise to establish the production of penicillin are expected to bear fruit'. This was entirely consistent with the Industrial Policy Resolution of 1956, which had placed the pharmaceutical industry in Schedule B, giving a role also to the private sector in its expansion, albeit a lesser one.[2]

Almost simultaneously, the government began engaging with the USSR to explore ways to expand the industry and made two suggestions: (1) build four plants to produce antibiotics, synthetic drugs, organic intermediates for drugs, dyestuffs and endocrines and (2) expand HAL and research facilities (Lok Sabha Secretariat, 1966, p. 1). The foundation was thus laid for the establishment of the Indian Drugs and Pharmaceuticals Ltd (IDPL) in 1961.

The setting up of the drug manufacturing units in the public sector was intended to meet three sets of objectives: (1) to reduce prices through large-scale production of high-quality life-saving drugs, (2) to provide facilities for medical relief on a mass scale in consonance with declared government objectives and (3) to not only achieve self-sufficiency in life-saving drugs but to also produce an exportable surplus and earn foreign exchange (Lok Sabha Secretariat, 1966, p. 47). However, it was only towards the mid-1960s, that IDPL's production facilities began to stabilise, and this was not before the company experienced several problems in providing adequate supplies of pharmaceuticals at affordable prices (Lok Sabha Secretariat, 1966, p. 15).

Phase II: Planning for the Future

The decade of the 1970s marked a turning point in the Indian pharmaceutical industry as the government enacted two policy initiatives to strengthen the industry. Firstly, it constituted the Committee on Drugs and Pharmaceutical Industry (better known as the Hathi Committee) in 1974 following a suggestion by Parliament to provide a comprehensive framework for developing a domestic pharmaceutical industry (Government of India, 1975). Secondly, the Drug Policy of 1978 was adopted essentially to implement the recommendations of the Hathi Committee. Preceding these initiatives, the Parliament gave its approval to enact the Patents Act, 1970, replacing the colonial Indian Patents and Designs Act, 1911. The Patents Act played a vital role in the subsequent development of India's pharmaceutical industry (Dhar and Rao, 2002).

The Hathi Committee

The Hathi Committee was the first and the only comprehensive policy initiative for developing a pharmaceutical industry that could truly be self-reliant by producing from the 'basic' stage (implying APIs). The committee dwelled on a key issue concerning the pharmaceutical industry, namely, measures necessary for ensuring that the public sector attained a leadership role in the manufacture of basic drugs and formulations and in research and development.[3]

The Hathi Committee pointed out that the public sector had 'achieved an overall production of substantial capacity particularly in the field of synthetic drugs' and had also 'demonstrated the competence of this sector to handle the growing needs of the country in this highly technology-intensive area of drug production' (Government of India, 1975, p. 54). The committee alluded to the fact that when public sector began producing synthetic bulk drugs in the late-1960s, it had to meet the challenge of modifying the production technologies to meet India's growing need for pharmaceuticals, which it effectively did by adapting the technology for producing of almost all their products and working out the technology for several others. The initial licensed capacity of the public sector was 857 tonnes covering 16 bulk drugs, but by 1973, it produced 1212 tonnes spread over 17 bulk drugs. Of this production, the public sector distributed to other formulators about 600 tonnes in 1973, accounting for about 50 per cent of their total production of bulk drugs (Government of India, 1975, p. 61).

However, questions were raised regarding the utilisation of the bulk drugs produced by the public sector units by the private sector formulators, both by the Hathi Committee and the Committee on Public Undertakings (COPU). The Hathi Committee argued that the formulation activity represented the 'high pay-off sector of the pharmaceutical industry', while the API manufacturing sector had comparatively low profits (Government of India, 1975, p. 55). Thus, the committee argued that the maximum benefits from the then existing division of labour between the public and private sector would 'accrue to the subsidiaries of multinational companies in this country who have the capacity to out-do the public sector units'. The committee pointed out that while the government's policies were against 'concentration of the industry in the hands of foreign branches/subsidiaries and larger industrial group but the result achieved is just the contrary' (Government of India, 1975, p. 94).

The government argued before the COPU that the public sector 'must play its role in developing the drug industry as a whole in the country and particularly in the small-scale sectors'. It added that 'supplying to the small-scale sector *is a social objective, for which the public sector must pay a price* by producing smaller quantities of the higher priced formulations' (emphasis added) (Lok Sabha Secretariat, 1974, pp. 134–35). According to the COPU, the public sector's higher volumes of API sales 'became a substantial factor contributing toward losses which the public sector companies had suffered' (Lok Sabha Secretariat, 1976, p. 258). The COPU concluded that

> by showing excessive concern for the requirements of private viallers and by keeping HAL's formulation capacity under-utilised all through this period, the administrative Ministry as well as HAL have not acted as the guardian and promoter of the interests of the public sector but has rather helped the private firms, particularly the foreign firms to

earn huge profits at the expense of the public sector and national interest.

(Lok Sabha Secretariat, 1976, p. 142)

In order to obviate the anomalous situation, the Hathi Committee determined that at least 60 per cent of the bulk drugs produced by the public sector units must be formulated by the public sector industry, and while disposing of the remaining 40 per cent, first preference must be given to 'meet the needs of the Indian sector particularly small-scale units' (Government of India, 1975, p. 69). The committee insisted that the government must 'take an early decision in the matter so as to ensure that the public sector does not have to continue to supply bulk products to formulators, more particularly foreign drug companies' (Lok Sabha Secretariat, 1976, p. 269). In the same vein, the COPU argued that IDPL 'should increase the quantity of its formulation so as utilise 50 per cent or more of the bulk drugs produced by it' (Lok Sabha Secretariat, 1974, p. 137).

The Hathi Committee stated also that the 'public sector should be given the major role for the production of capital and technology intensive bulk drugs . . . as are needed in high tonnage quantities and where large-scale production would be economically preferable' (Government of India, 1975, p. 67). In other words, the committee's view was that the public sector must play the dominant role in consolidating India's pharmaceutical industry. The committee also stated that 'wherever possible public sector units for drugs and pharmaceuticals should also produce bulk intermediates which may not either be produced indigenously or may be produced in insufficient quantity'. This would ensure the minimum dependence on imports (Government of India, 1975, p. 66).

Drug Policy, 1978

Based on the recommendations of the Hathi Committee, a new drug policy was announced in 1978 with the following five broad objectives: (1) develop a strong Indian pharmaceutical sector with the public sector playing a leading role; (2) channel the activities of the foreign firms in accordance with the national priorities and objectives; (3) ensure that drug production took place from as basic a stage as possible; (4) encourage research and development and improve the technological sinews of the industry and (5) provide drugs to consumers at reasonable prices (Dhar and Rao, 2002).

The Drug Policy (DP) thus became an industrial policy instrument by linking production to profitability and the essentiality of medicine. To promote indigenous production from basic stages, the policy mandated that all firms producing formulations based on imported bulk drugs or bulk drugs manufactured from the penultimate stage instead indigenously produce the bulk drug from the basic stage within a period of two years. These firms were also required to supply 50 per cent of the total production of bulk drugs to non-associate formulators. The policy also restricted the value of a firm's formulation production to five times the value of its total bulk drug production.

All these measures meant that any significant increase in the production of formulations depended on increasing the indigenous production of bulk drugs. Companies were forced to engage in bulk drug production, which is the technology-intensive phase in drug manufacturing. The DP also prohibited the practice of loan licensing, firms selling products under their own name that they had acquired from other firms and selling them under their own name. The policy required the foreign firms operating in India with a turnover in drugs exceeding INR 50 million per year to have research and development (R&D) facilities in India and spend at least 4 per cent of their turnover as recurring expenditure on R&D. The policy also liberalised licenses for the production meant for exports: A company could produce any amount for export and had flexibility in the use of foreign exchange.

All these policy measures had a profound impact on developing a strong indigenous pharmaceutical sector. The investment in the pharmaceutical industry increased from INR 240 million in 1952 to INR 2.3 billion in 1973 and further to INR 6 billion in 1982 (Hamied, 1988). The share of the domestic sector in total pharmaceutical production in India increased from 27 per cent in 1975–76 to 52 per cent in 1980–81 (Narayana, 1984). The indigenous production of drugs grew from INR 100 million in 1947 to INR 1.7 billion in 1965–66 and to INR 82 billion in 1993–94 (Narayana, 1984). These measures also made a significant contribution towards self-reliance and self-sufficiency, using appropriate technology and based essentially on indigenous raw materials. In the production of bulk drugs, the share of the domestic sector had reached 82 per cent in 1987 (Hamied, 1988).

The drug prices in India became among the lowest in the world (Ghosh and Keayla, 1998), the time lag for introducing a drug in India after its launch in the global market was reduced to less than five years (Keayla, 1994) and the industry transformed from a net importer to a net exporter. By the beginning of the 1990s, the Indian pharmaceutical industry was globally recognised as a powerhouse in reverse engineering. It substantially facilitated access to medicines in a number of countries other than India through its supply of drugs that are compliant with good manufacturing practices at low prices.

Phase III: Liberalisation From the 1980s

The expectations of establishing a robust pharmaceutical industry, built on the foundations of public-sector API production capabilities, did not last very long. From the early 1980s, there were signs that the government's commitment to promoting the public sector had begun to wane. Evidence of this tendency was provided in the government's presentations before the COPU of negative assessments of public-sector functioning, which I highlight in the following discussion. The most cogent articulation of its assessments of the public sector was the adoption of the Drug Policy of 1986.

This policy marked the first departure from the policy of reserving the essential APIs for the public sector as the private sector was allowed to produce penicillin and polio vaccines (Government of India, 1986). The government's justification for the dereservation of these two APIs was two-fold. First, public-sector units had underperformed and had not met the burgeoning demand for critical APIs like penicillin (Lok Sabha Secretariat, 1986, p. 20). The second argument of the government was that even if the public sector units had expanded their production, they could not have produced enough to meet the entire national requirements for penicillin and polio vaccines: the companies' past production 'did not at all look healthy enough . . . to assume that these two public sector companies will be able to meet the entire demand of the country'. However, the government insisted that penicillin had only been 'dereserved', 'not delicensed' (Lok Sabha Secretariat, 1986, p. 20).

The government argued that in 1989–90, penicillin demand was estimated to be as high as 2470 mmu as against the existing installed capacity of 637 mmu inclusive of 390 mmu in the public sector. This gap between the demand and production of this crucial drug would have further widened by the end of the seventh plan period unless corrective steps were taken to narrow it. To meet the requirements of this essential drug, the country had to bear significant costs of importing them, resulting in a substantial outgo of foreign exchange of INR 24 crores in the year 1985–86.

The Government of India argued that it was dereserving these two drugs for 'some very valid reasons'. Its statement that domestic facilities simply did not seem sufficiently healthy almost anticipated the next step, namely, delicensing of the pharmaceutical industry in 1993. However, the arguments for diluting the role of the public sector seemed quite contentious given the additional facts that were placed before the COPU. Firstly, the two major public-sector companies, namely, HAL and IDPL, were functioning without approved corporate plans, which had to be developed in keeping with the recommendations of the Administrative Reforms Commission that 'Government should make a comprehensive and clear statement on the objectives and obligations of Public Undertakings' (Lok Sabha Secretariat, 1986, p. 12). In the absence of these plans, it was 'difficult to have a clear direction for the [companies'] growth consistent with its objectives and obligations and the national plans' (Lok Sabha Secretariat, 1982, p. 7).

Secondly, the Department of Chemicals and Petrochemicals admitted that the IDPL had very low capacity to produce some of the essential bulk drugs for reasons, including shortages of funds, raw materials and resources such as electricity and water (Lok Sabha Secretariat, 1986, p. 12). The third and the most significant argument that the government's dereservation was hasty was that the Ministry did not consult IDPL or HAL before finalising the new drug policy. That is, where the Hathi Committee expected that the public sector would provide direction to the pharmaceutical industry, the sector was not even consulted when a major change in extant policy was effected.[4]

The COPU's response was to 'deprecate the casual manner in which the question of dereservation of penicillin [had] been decided by Government even without consultation with their own public undertakings' (Lok Sabha Secretariat, 1986, p. 32). The committee's view was that this was 'not a step in the right direction as it will in the ultimate analysis give concessions to the multinationals and undermine the capacity of penicillin production available with IDPI, and HAL'. The COPU instructed that in

> light of claim made by IDPL to meet the entire penicillin demand of the country, the Government should appoint a Committee to assess thoroughly the capacity and capability of Public Units and if that Committee feels satisfied with the claim of IDPL, the Government should then reconsider the policy of de-reservation.
>
> (Lok Sabha Secretariat, 1986, p. 32)

The COPU advised that the 'Government should proceed with caution on the question of issuing licences for the manufacture of or for the import of penicillin' (Lok Sabha Secretariat, 1986, p. 24).

In hindsight, it seems obvious that the 1986 DP was a precursor to the 1991 industrial policy that reflected a re-think in ideas about the industrial sector in keeping with the spirit of economic reforms. The 'priority areas for growth of public enterprises in the future' did not include the pharmaceutical industry (Government of India, 1991). That the government had decided to hand over the reins of the industry to the private sector was made explicit in the Modified Policy for Drugs and Pharmaceuticals Industry, introduced in 1994, in which the bulk drugs reserved for the public sector were reduced from 17 to five (Government of India, 1994). The remaining five bulk drugs were delicensed in 1999 (Government of India, 1999).

III. Globalisation of the Indian Pharmaceutical Industry

In the four decades since the government took the first steps to establish a domestic pharmaceutical industry, Indian companies have been able to supply cheap generic products to much of the world, especially to the developing countries. But the expansion of the industry has an important downside: the domestic producers of APIs were unable to match the expansion of the formulations that supplied the generics, and, consequently, India became a significant importer of these intermediate products. Table 10.1 provides the data on growth of imports of APIs from 1996–97, the last year from which official data on trade are publicly available. The table reflects what I discussed at the outset: that one of the disquieting aspects of India's imports of APIs has been the increasing reliance on China.

Table 10.1 India's Imports of APIs Including China's Share

Years	*Total ($ billion)*	*China ($ billion)*	*China's share (%)*
1996–97	0.6	0.1	17.1
1997–98	0.7	0.1	18.6
2003–04	1.6	0.4	26.4
2004–05	1.9	0.5	28.3
2008–09	3.7	2.0	52.8
2009–10	3.9	2.1	52.9
2014–15	7.3	4.1	56.9
2015–16	6.9	4.1	58.9
2018–19	9.6	5.8	60.2
2019–20	8.9	5.6	62.4

Source: Author's calculations using data from the Directorate General of Commercial Intelligence and Statistics, Department of Commerce.

Table 10.1 shows that API imports increased steadily, especially from the second half of the 2000s. Thus, during the period in which the production of pharmaceuticals in the organised sector increased from USD 10 billion to USD 44 billion, imports of APIs expanded from less than USD 2 billion to almost USD 89 billion.

The more striking aspect of API imports was the increasing reliance on China. From less than 18 per cent in 1996–97, China's share increased to 62 per cent in 2019–20, and the overall figures do not even fully convey the reality of India's dependence. Understanding the reality would require analysing the detailed data on imports of major APIs and China's share in total imports for four recent years (see Table 10.2). The APIs included in the Annex Table had import values of more than USD 10 million in each of the four years for which data are presented.

In recent years, India's dependence on several critical APIs has been unacceptably high. Among the medicines for whose APIs India has been relying heavily on China is paracetamol, the common antipyretic and anti-inflammatory medicine. During the four years reflected in the Annex Table, China was the sole supplier of API for this medicine. India has also been significantly dependent on Chinese exports for several broad-spectrum antibiotics, including ampicillin, azithromycin, doxycycline, tetracycline, erythromycin and 6-aminopenicillanic acid (6-APA). For tetracycline and 6-APA, China was the source of over 99 per cent of India's import requirements in 2019–20 and more than 90 per cent for ampicillin.

India increasingly relied on imports to meet the API requirements for ciprofloxacin, the widely prescribed quinolone antibiotic for a range of bacterial infections, and China provided over 96 per cent of India's imports. China was also a dominant supplier for India's steep increase in API imports for rifampicin, an anti-tuberculosis drug. However, for the cephalosporin

Table 10.2 Major Active Pharmaceutical Ingredients Imported by India

ITCHS Code	*Active Pharmaceutical Ingredient*	*Specific therapeutic uses/products*	*Total Imports ($ million)*		*China's Share (%)*		*Total Imports ($ million)*		*China's Share (%)*	
			2019–20	*2018–19*	*2019–20*	*2018–19*	*2015–16*	*2014–15*	*2015–16*	*2014–15*
28051100	Sodium		23.9	24.4	85.5	77.4	16.1	14.7	85.6	86.4
28051200	Calcium		15.9	20.3	88.2	86.0	11.9	16.1	79.6	74.5
29124999	Pioglitazone hydrochloride	Antidiabetic	13.4	12.1	81.3	86.1	22.7	21.8	42.2	33.6
29142990	Other cyclanic and other ketones without other oxygen function (1,1 cyclohexane di-acetic acid)	Antidepressant (Gabapentin)	80.8	105.3	53.7	67.7	47.2	44.2	63.4	66.3
29146100	Anthraquinone	Antimicrobial and anti-inflammatory	18.1	17.1	85.1	87.1	5.4	6.6	88.1	78.6
29152100	Acetic acid		385.9	603.6	35.9	29.1	316.3	384.7	30.2	17.7
29152990	Other salts of acetic acid		87.7	99.3	86.1	81.4	54.8	63.7	85.2	78.0
29156020	Pentanoic acids, their salts and esters	Anti-stress	5.1	5.8	66.9	58.7	4.0	2.8	56.0	33.3
29156010	Butanoic acid, their salts and esters	Irritable bowel syndrome	42.4	46.7	42.9	42.5	27.3	31.0	88.1	78.6
29159090	Other saturated acrylic monocarboxylic acids	anti-inflammatory	194.9	185.5	39.2	34.9	178.8	163.7	30.2	17.7
29163110	Benzoic acid	Antimicrobial	11.7	17.3	64.4	81.5	9.1	6.4	73.5	74.7
29163190	Other salts and esters of benzoic acid	Antimicrobial	26.0	26.3	77.6	68.0	19.8	32.5	75.3	74.6
29163990	Monocarboxylic acid		128.3	107.9	94.7	90.0	58.6	51.5	87.5	84.6
29181200	Tartaric acid	Antioxidant	15.8	17.7	86.1	94.2	12.0	12.0	94.6	91.4
29181400	Citric acid	Antioxidant	54.3	64.7	96.9	98.1	55.3	54.4	97.8	98.0
29181690	Other gluconic acid its salts and esters	Maintains cation–anion balance on electrolyte solutions	26.9	22.9	91.7	90.2	10.3	12.0	54.7	59.5

29182110	Salicylic acid	Treatment of skin conditions	35.0	35.5	92.4	95.9	18.1	16.7	88.9	93.3
29182190	Other salicylic acid and its salts	Treatment of skin conditions	19.0	18.2	61.0	66.9	4.9	8.9	64.2	69.0
29182990	Other carboxylic acid	Antimicrobial	43.9	37.9	63.7	58.2	28.3	35.4	64.2	69.0
29183090	Other carboxylic acids with aldehyde/ketone function		77.7	77.0	62.1	68.6	76.8	71.6	73.4	85.5
29213090	Other cyclanic, cyclenic/ cycloterpenic mono or polyamines and their derivatives, salts	Anticancer/ antituberculosis drugs	30.0	26.1	65.4	59.5	51.7	56.6	85.2	90.4
29214110	Aniline	Paracetamol	75.5	116.7	91.6	72.9	41.5	60.6	93.5	66.8
29214190	Other aniline salts		20.1	36.1	98.5	98.1	35.0	28.7	98.5	98.3
29215990	Other aromatic polyamines	Anticancer	29.1	42.1	62.5	82.9	32.4	42.1		
29221190	Other salts of monoethanolamine	Antidiabetic	10.3	11.1	59.5	56.4	7.0	14.9	59.7	77.1
29221990	Other		99.6	97.2	44.1	54.1	44.8	49.0	56.4	45.6
29222913	Para aminophenol	Paracetamol	76.3	98.6	100.0	100.0	48.0	59.8	100.0	100.0
29222933	Para acetyl aminophenol	Paracetamol	14.1	6.0	91.1	85.6	9.5	18.7	84.6	95.6
29222990	Other amino-naphthol and other amino- phenols, their esters and salts	Antioxidants	101.4	80.5	93.8	95.5	31.0	37.7	91.8	94.6
29223900	Other amino aldehydes etc containing more than oxygen function; salts		11.3	16.4	90.2	88.4	23.9	24.3	95.5	84.1
29224290	Other glutamic acid and its salts	Gliclazide IP (antidiabetic)	13.6	18.5	59.7	56.7	4.0	5.4	65.2	72.4
29224100	Lysine and its esters and salts		64.6	65.9	26.7	13.2	59.4	64.8	9.8	16.6
29224990	Other amino acids and their esters	Biopharmaceuticals	97.8	104.6	72.0	82.7	87.5	98.3	62.8	57.9
29225090	Other frusemide aminodial domperidone	Nausea	56.3	62.6	61.3	66.5	72.9	144.2	77.3	53.3

(Continued)

Table 10.2 (Continued)

ITCHS Code	Active Pharmaceutical Ingredient	Specific therapeutic uses/products	Total Imports ($ million)		China's Share (%)		Total Imports ($ million)		China's Share (%)	
			2019–20	2018–19	2019–20	2018–19	2015–16	2014–15	2015–16	2014–15
29239000	Other quaternary ammonium salts and hydroxide lecithin	Levocarnitine USP (treatment of kidneys)	22.4	22.8	54.5	47.0	13.6	15.4	60.7	47.1
29241900	Other acyclic amides and their derivatives, salts (Sabam HCl)		56.4	76.7	60.9	63.9	55.1	61.9	62.2	65.9
29242990	Other cyclic amides and their derivatives and salts	Levetiracetam (anti-epilepsy)	143.3	112.5	78.6	82.2	95.9	109.6	72.7	50.0
29251900	Other imides and their derivatives salts thereof		15.4	23.7	76.4	79.7	11.0	8.2	82.7	75.3
29269000	Other nitrile-function compounds –	Metformin (diabetes)	259.3	189.9	79.1	70.8	110.9	105.1	64.4	59.3
29280090	Other organic derivatives of hydrazine/hydroxylamine	Marimastat (anti-cancer)	70.7	63.9	43.9	33.1	29.4	26.9	27.8	20.9
29304000	Methionine	Building blocks for proteins	86.4	102.6	7.5	9.1	157.4	115.1	4.3	5.0
29309040	L-cystine (alpha-amino beta-thio propionic acid)-sulphur containing amino acid	Anti-arthritis	19.3	15.5	28.8	26.7	13.3	15.8	27.8	20.9
29309099	Other organo-sulphur compounds	Meropenem (abdominal infections)	121.4	136.4	72.2	75.6	75.6	95.7	70.9	82.4
29321990	Other compounds containing unfused furan ring		55.6	53.7	85.8	81.2	13.9	11.2		
29322090	Other lactones	Spironolactone USP (hypertension)	66.1	59.9	52.6	40.6	39.9	41.5	35.0	36.7
29329900	Other heterocyclic compounds with oxygen hetero – atom/s)	Artesunate (antimalarial)	158.4	170.1	71.1	73.5	93.4	88.7	44.9	52.8
29331990	Unfused pyrazole ring in structure	Analgesic and febrifuge	145.9	98.2	67.5	76.2	81.0	88.0	94.4	91.8
29332990	Other compounds containing an unfused imidazole ring (w/n hydrogenated) in structure	Ketoconazole (antifungal)	84.6	90.0	83.5	85.9	54.5	97.2	84.6	89.5

29372100	Cortisone, hydrocortisone, Prednisone (dehydrocortisone) and Prednisolone (dehydro hydrocortisone)	Corticosteroids	36.6	45.9	80.3	71.4	41.0	44.6	69.9	74.3
29372300	Oestrogens and progestogens	Hormones	60.1	45.3	24.3	24.6	38.0	36.2	45.5	37.8
29372900	Other Steroidal hormone, their derivatives and structural analogues	Hydrocortisone Aceponate	71.1	85.2	70.1	75.7	86.1	87.3	65.5	60.0
29379090	Other	Lidocaine (local anaesthetic)	78.2	77.3	67.9	54.0	35.2	40.2	63.8	69.5
29389090	Other glycosides	Diamine (anti-allergic)	61.7	68.7	44.7	53.8	33.5	42.9	30.9	30.5
29411010	Penicillin and its salts		100.2	164.6	95.8	94.5	100.6	102.8	95.7	94.3
29411030	Amoxycillin and its salts	Antibiotic	27.2	36.7	90.0	89.6	23.3	33.9	92.8	94.6
29411050	6-aminopenicillanic acid	Antibiotic	174.2	225.9	99.5	98.6	169.3	176.0	100.0	100.0
29411090	Other penicillin and their derivatives with a penicillanic acid structured salts thereof	Azithromycin (antibiotic)	166.2	189.6	73.0	72.9	33.4	46.5	87.5	86.4
29413010	Doxycycline and its salts	Antibiotic	21.6	16.7	73.8	57.8	15.2	11.0	68.1	77.6
29413020	Tetracycline/oxytetracycline	Antibiotic	13.1	13.7	99.0	99.9	10.0	9.6	99.4	99.7
29413090	Other tetracyclines and their derivatives and salts	Antibiotic	19.1	39.4	16.1	3.5	12.9	22.6	21.6	23.1
29415000	Erythromycin/azithromycin	Antibacterial	124.7	150.7	82.9	63.0	137.2	102.1	62.8	73.1

(Continued)

Table 10.2 (Continued)

ITCHS Code	*Active Pharmaceutical Ingredient*	*Specific therapeutic uses/products*	*Total Imports ($ million)*		*China's Share (%)*		*Total Imports ($ million)*		*China's Share (%)*	
			2019–20	*2018–19*	*2019–20*	*2018–19*	*2015–16*	*2014–15*	*2015–16*	*2014–15*
29419011	Rifampicin	Antibiotic	31.0	18.1	97.4	94.7	12.4	11.9	92.9	91.3
29419019	Other rifampicin and its salts	Cefuroxime Axetil (anti-bacterial)	107.7	134.2	71.1	67.4	29.0	29.3	92.6	95.5
29419020	Cephalexin and its salts	Antibiotic	19.5	12.2	7.4	12.4	10.3	13.8	20.7	31.1
29419030	Ciprofloxacin and its salts	Antibiotic	15.0	6.8	96.3	95.0	3.5	3.7	92.6	95.5
29419090	Other antibiotics	Azithromycin, clarithromycin, tobramycin	484.4	410.5	80.1	71.0	419.2	407.6	82.7	78.8
29420012	Ibuprofen	Ant-inflammatory	29.6	24.4	95.2	98.8	17.7	18.0	95.8	96.9
29420090	Other Diloxanide furoate	Cimetidine, ornidazole, ritonavir, carbidopa	404.0	371.3	67.3	68.3	838.6	831.0	67.2	61.4

Source: Directorate General of Commercial Intelligence and Statistics. Government of India. Ministry of Commerce and Industry.

antibiotic Cephalexin, although its API imports were great, China was not among the major suppliers in recent years.

India's reliance on penicillin imports is actually one of the more disconcerting aspects of a country that has established itself as a major producer of pharmaceutical products. In 2018–19, the import value of these APIs was over USD 350 million, and although their imports declined to below USD 300 million in 2019–20, there was excessive reliance on Chinese suppliers. API imports were also high for antimicrobials and anti-inflammatories such as ibuprofen, a common medicine.

India's excessive dependence on China was confirmed by the Drug Security Committee, which examined the issue of drug security in the country in the context of Covid-19. The committee identified 58 APIs for which India had heavy import dependence on China, including 100 per cent dependence for 45 APIs. Of the 58 APIs, 45 per cent are antibiotics (Government of India, 2020a).

I find that two observations emerge from this scenario of India's import dependence on APIs and unacceptably high reliance on supplies from China. First, the dependence of India's pharmaceutical industry on China shows that the "pharmacy of the world" has fairly weak foundations that can be problematic for two reasons: disruptions in supplies from China can cause serious bottlenecks, and there is no assurance that the Chinese suppliers of APIs maintain product quality in conformity with the global standards. My second observation is that since India imports from China more than 90 per cent of the APIs for several antibiotics and vitamins, it is not plausible that India can easily find an alternate source for meeting its API requirements. These observations are strong indicators that if India is going to become a world supplier of high-quality pharmaceutical products and – more critically – at sustainable prices, the Indian pharmaceutical industry must deepen its production base to produce all the critical APIs.

IV. Undermining 'Vaccination for All'

Just when the spread of Covid-19 had reached catastrophic proportions in April 2021, with the daily caseload rising faster than that seen anywhere in the world, the Government of India unveiled a completely revamped vaccine strategy with two key elements. First, the phased roll-out of the vaccination drive initiated in January 2021 under which the vaccine-eligible sections of population were gradually increased was extended to the entire adult population above 18 years. Second, and more importantly, the vaccine market was significantly deregulated, and vaccine manufacturers were given the freedom to sell 50 per cent of their product to state governments and private hospitals at prices that could be substantially higher than the fixed government prices. A third element of the vaccine strategy that was not announced formally was a INR 45 billion grant to two vaccine manufacturers to boost their capacities: the Serum Institute of India (SII) and Bharat Biotech.

Handing Over the Reins

The new vaccine strategy raised a number of questions, not least concern that the central government surrendered its control over the vaccine market, a key feature of the vaccine roll-out plans. This issue assumed further significance since the Government of India was well aware – as were all public authorities around the world – of the significance of vaccinating every citizen in the country: 'none of us will be safe until everyone is safe'. It was therefore vitally important that public health authorities in the country take an objective view of the realities of the country before adopting strategies for vaccine availability, for this was vitally important for resetting lives and livelihoods disrupted by the pandemic. Several facts suggest that this was not done while rejigging the extant vaccine strategy.

Vaccine Exports

The phased roll-out of the government's ambitious vaccination drive, beginning with health care and frontline workers in January followed by the gradual inclusion of senior citizens and people above 45 years in March and April 2021, respectively, was in sync with the availability of vaccines in the country. Although SII, the largest vaccine producer, had initially promised to supply 100 million doses a month, it could actually only provide between 50 and 60 million doses. However, Indian residents were not immune to vaccine scepticism, and the Government of India found itself able to promise vaccine exports to 95 countries, mostly in Africa and Asia.

The worrying facet was a demand–supply mismatch began to appear as the vaccine-eligible population expanded. The largest supplier, SII, gave two explanations for its inability to meet its commitments. The first was that the US government had used a Cold War piece of legislation, the Defense Production Act, to restrict exports of vaccine culture and other essential materials. Second, the company complained that it lacked the financial capacity to expand its production and requested a grant of INR 30 billion from the government.[5]

Onus on States

It is in the face of this vaccine supply crunch that the government announced the new vaccine strategy: by opening vaccination to all adults in the country and allowing vaccine producers to sell 50 per cent of their production directly to state governments and private hospitals. The new strategy shifted the onus onto the state governments, which had to take decisions regarding free vaccination for people above 18 years, while the central government undertook vaccination for people over 45 and health care and frontline workers. The government did not fix the vaccine prices and allowed the producers to pre-declare the prices they would charge the State governments and private hospitals, a sharp departure from the extant strategy.

Until the change in policy, government facilities provided vaccines free of cost, while private facilities were allowed to charge no more than INR 250 per dose. The central government played the role of a sole procurement agency that helped drive down prices, making vaccines affordable. However, the new strategy abandoned this mechanism and fragmented the market into three layers: central government, state government and private hospitals. This layering of the market allowed the producers to charge the state governments and private hospitals high prices; indeed, both SII and Bharat Biotech immediately announced their intentions to raise vaccine prices. SII announced that it would sell Covishield to state governments and private hospitals at INR 400 and INR 600 per dose, respectively,[6] while the corresponding figures for Bharat Biotech's Covaxin were INR 600 and INR 1200 per dose.[7]

The new strategy shifted the burden of vaccinating the population between 18 and 44 years entirely onto the state governments, which meant that vaccinating a significant section of the population depended on the financial health of each state government, resulting in inequitable access to vaccines across states. For instance, given their poor state of finances, most state governments could not procure sufficient vaccine doses to meet demand. Instead, 50 per cent of domestic vaccine production that had been earmarked for the state governments and the private hospitals ended up with the latter.

In the US

The decision to substantially deregulate the vaccine market raised serious questions in view of the reported advance of INR 45 billion made by the Government of India to the two vaccine producers in India for expanding their production capacities.[8] The US government did the same thing by providing financial support to vaccine producers, which in turn raked in billions by charging high prices. Several public interest groups in the US asked why the tax-paying public should bear the high prices of vaccines when federal taxpayer funds were used to support the vaccine producers, and this question was more pertinent in India, where access to affordable vaccines was critical for ensuring 'vaccination for all'.

More Open Licensing Is Needed

It is somewhat ironic that a country that had long championed the cause of access to affordable medicines in international forums adopted a strategy that actually could undermine the vaccination for all aim. Rather than hand over the reins of price determination to the duopoly in the vaccine market, the government should have urgently addressed the serious concerns about vaccine affordability by ensuring a competitive market. However, one positive step that the government took to ease vaccine supplies was to involve the public sector, including the Haffkine Institute, in helping to increase the production of Bharat Biotech's vaccine. This was the right step forward as there was a need for more open licensing of vaccines to scale up production and to ensure that vaccines reach every citizen in the country.

V. The Way Forward

I have just discussed recent government initiatives to strengthen API production in India, but here I discuss two inherent flaws in these policy initiatives. The first is that new government polices ignore the reality that although private enterprise had established a strong base for producing formulations domestically, it was seriously lacking in API production capacity. Interestingly, the architects of India's industrialisation strategy anticipated the present situation in the years immediately after Independence. They took initiative by establishing public sector enterprises (PSUs) to produce APIs in the country, recognising that producing formulations was the profitable segment of the drug industry. Therefore, the private sector would not be inclined to manufacture bulk drugs and would instead produce formulations to rake in the profits. Based on this understanding, the government took the decision to manufacture bulk drugs in the public sector.

The PSUs have been the bedrock of the pharmaceutical industry since the HAL was established in 1954. In subsequent years, this segment of the industry was expanded with the coming of Indian Drugs and Pharmaceuticals Ltd and its subsidiaries, while Bengal Chemicals & Pharmaceuticals Limited was nationalised in 1980. But despite having these production units that are designed to meet the domestic API requirements, the government chose the path of whittling down the public-sector companies.

The second flaw is that the government decided to attract private investors to create capacities for API production during a phase when investor sentiments were the worst in decades[9] and investors may not have been inclined to invest in higher-risk activities. It is by now well established that API production involves higher risks and lower profits than the formulations sector, which determined the pattern of private investment participation in the pharmaceutical industry. As mentioned earlier, the Hathi Committee (the Committee on Drugs and Pharmaceutical Industry) documented for the first time in 1975 that risks are higher in API production. The pattern of development seen in the pharmaceutical industry in the subsequent decades, with its emphasis on formulations production, vindicated the Committee's point.

Despite the obvious case for greater public-sector participation in API production, successive governments have decided otherwise. The government's deep antipathy towards the PSUs in this sector of critical importance can only be explained by its doctrinaire approach to economic management: its deep-seated bias against public investment even when private investment has not been forthcoming for API production, thus confirming market failure. In doing so, the Indian government has ignored the evidence of the growing role of the public sector in many countries.

For instance, state-owned enterprises (SOEs) have increasingly gained prominence over the past decade not just in countries like China but also in several advanced countries (International Monetary Fund, IMF, 2020). Global SOE assets in 2018 were valued at USD 45 trillion, almost half of global GDP, having increased from around USD 13 trillion in the year 2000. Estimates show that SOEs accounted for 20 per cent of investment and up to 40 per cent of domestic output worldwide in 2018. Following the economic recession in 2008, many governments have used SOEs to help revive their economies (Putniņš, 2015).

In the aftermath of the Covid-19 pandemic, governments leveraged SOE capacities and delivery platforms to ensure the delivery of emergency goods and services. Governments engaged SOEs to provide medical products or services, especially when supply chains were interrupted or there were export bans on key goods. Indonesia employed its state-owned aircraft manufacturer to produce ventilators, and China provided tax incentives to companies that produced medical supplies (Qiang and Pop, 2020).

In addition to the evidence I have given, it has perhaps become imperative for the government to recognise a recently expressed view by the IMF: 'well-governed and financially healthy state-owned enterprises can help combat crises such as the pandemic and promote development goals' (Gasper et al., 2020). However, for 'well-governed and financially healthy state-owned enterprises' to become a reality in India, the central government would have to play the role it promised seven decades ago.

Notes

1 This followed the recommendations of technical teams headed by Major General S.S. Sokhey after they were deputed to visit factories in the UK, US, Canada and Europe (Lok Sabha Secretariat, 1956, p. 1).

2 The Industrial Policy Resolution stated that in future development of Schedule B industries, 'the State will increasingly establish new undertakings in these industries. At the same time, private enterprise will also have the opportunity to develop in this field, either on its own or with State participation'.

3 The other significant issues that the Hathi Committee dwelled on were the following: (i) promoting the rapid growth of the Indian pharmaceutical industry, particularly the small-scale sector; (ii) arranging the flow of new technologies into the industry and (iii) rationalising the prices of basic drugs and formulations. However, although they are important, these issues are beyond the scope of this chapter.

4 The committee also asked whether the government specifically put to IDPL that it proposed to dereserve penicillin, but the witness stated, 'No, that has not been put'.

5 www.thehindu.com/news/national/require-around-3000-crore-to-ramp-up-covid-19-vaccine-production-adar-poonawalla/article34256215.ece

6 www.thehindu.com/news/national/covishield-to-be-sold-to-states-at-400-a-dose-and-at-600-to-private-hospitals-from-may-1/article34375676.ece

7 www.thehindu.com/business/Industry/coronavirus-covaxin-priced-at-600-for-states-1200-for-private-hospitals/article34403065.ece

8 www.thehindu.com/business/Industry/serum-hails-financial-aid-from-govt-to-ramp-up-covid-19-vaccine-production/article34367000.ece
9 In 2019–20, gross fixed capital formation fell in both current and constant terms, the first time it had happened since 1958–59.

References

Dhar, B., and Joseph, R.K. (2019). The Challenges, Opportunities and Performance of the Indian Pharmaceutical Industry Post-TRIPS. In Liu, K.C., and Racherla, U.S. (Eds.), *Innovation, Economic Development, and Intellectual Property in India and China: Comparing Six Economic Sectors*. Singapore: Springer Open.

Dhar, B., and Rao, N. (2002). *Transfer of Technology for Successful Integration into the Global Economy: A Case Study of the Pharmaceutical Industry in India*. UNCTAD/ITE/IPC/Misc.22. Geneva: UNCTAD.

Gasper, V., et al. (2020, May 7). State-Owned Enterprises in the Time of COVID-19. *IMF Blog*. https://blogs.imf.org/2020/05/07/state-owned-enterprises-in-the-time-of-covid-19/.

Ghosh, A., and Keayla, B.K. (1998). *Report of People's Commission on Intellectual Property Rights*. New Delhi: National Working Group on Patent Laws.

Government of India. (1956a, April 30). *Industrial Policy Resolution*. https://dpiit.gov.in/sites/default/files/chap001%20%2013.pdf.

Government of India. (1956b). *Second Five Year Plan. Planning Commission*. https://niti.gov.in/planningcommission.gov.in/docs/plans/planrel/fiveyr/2nd/2planch19.html

Government of India. (1986). *Measures for Rationalisation, Quality Control and Growth of Drugs & Pharmaceutical Industry in India*. www.nppaindia.nic.in/wp-content/uploads/2020/07/Drug-policy-1986.pdf

Government of India. (1991, July 24). *Statement on Industrial Policy*. https://dpiit.gov.in/sites/default/files/IndustrialPolicyStatement_1991_15July2019.pdf

Government of India. (1994). *Modified Policy for Drugs and Pharmaceuticals Industry*. Press Note No. 4, 1994 Series. https://dpiit.gov.in/sites/default/files/chap006%20%206.pdf

Government of India. (1999). *De-Licensing of Five Bulk Drugs*. Press Note No. 3, 1999 Series. https://dpiit.gov.in/sites/default/files/pn13_0.pdf

Government of India, Department of Pharmaceuticals. (2019). *Assistance to Bulk Drug Industry for Common Facilitation Centre*. https://pharmaceuticals.gov.in/sites/default/files/Asistance%20to%20Bulk%20Drug%20Industry%20for%20Common%20Facility%20Centre.pdf.

Government of India, Ministry of Industry and Supply. (1948). *Industrial Policy Statement*. New Delhi: Ministry of Industry and Supply.

Government of India, Ministry of Petroleum & Chemicals. (1975). *Report of the Committee on Drugs and Pharmaceutical Industry (Hathi Committee Report)*. New Delhi.

Hamied, Y.K. (1988). The Indian Patents Act 1970 and the Pharmaceutical Industry. In National Working Group on Patent Laws. *Conquest by Patent: On Patent Law and Policy*. New Delhi: National Working Group on Patent Laws.

The Hindu. (2021, April 20). Serum Hails Financial Aid from Govt to Ramp Up Covid-19 Vaccine Production. *The Hindu*. www.thehindu.com/business/Industry/serum-hails-financial-aid-from-govt-to-ramp-up-covid-19-vaccine-production/article34367000.ece

IMF. (2020, April). *Fiscal Monitor*. Washington, DC. https://www.imf.org/en/Publications/FM/Issues/2020/04/06/fiscal-monitor-april-2020.

Keayla, B.K. (1994). Patent Protection and Pharmaceutical Industry. In K.R.G. Nair and A. Kumar (Eds.), *Intellectual Property Rights*. New Delhi: Allied Publishers.
Lok Sabha Secretariat. (1966). *Twenty Second Report of the Committee on Public Undertakings in Indian Drugs and Pharmaceuticals Limited. Committee on Public Undertakings (Third Lok Sabha)*. New Delhi.
Lok Sabha Secretariat. (1974). *Fifty-Sixth Report on Indian Drugs and Pharmaceuticals Limited. Committee on Public Undertakings (1973–74)*. New Delhi: Fifth Lok Sabha.
Lok Sabha Secretariat. (1976). *Eightieth Report on Hindustan Antibiotic Limited. Committee on Public Undertakings (1975–76)*. New Delhi: Fifth Lok Sabha.
Lok Sabha Secretariat. (1982). *Sixty-Seventh Report on Hindustan Antibiotics Ltd. on Public Undertakings (1982–83)*. New Delhi: Seventh Lok Sabha.
Lok Sabha Secretariat. (1986). *Twenty-Ninth Report on Indian Drugs and Pharmaceuticals Ltd. Committee on Public Undertakings (1986–87)*. New Delhi: Eighth Lok Sabha.
Narayana, P.L. (1984). *The Indian Pharmaceutical Industry: Problems and Prospects*. New Delhi: NCAER.
Putniņš, T.J. (2015). Economics of State-Owned Enterprises. *International Journal of Public Administration*, *38*(11), 815–832.
Qiang, C.Z. and Pop, G. (2020, July 30). State-Owned Enterprises and COVID-19: Policy Principles. *World Bank Blogs*. https://blogs.worldbank.org/psd/state-owned-enterprises-and-covid-19-policy-principles

Part IV

Quest for Security

11 Health Federalism and Women's Health Outcomes in India's 'Backward' States

Ramila Bisht

At Independence, India consciously opted for a federal structuring of her democratic polity towards forming a united and integrated political community. In the light of immense variations despite commonalities – in history, environment, society and culture – and having inherited a predominantly centralised state structure from the British, the Indian nation state sought to establish a federal structure that would balance central and regional interests.

In the field of health, the spirit of federalism was carried forward in accordance with the seminal Bhore Committee's perspectives and recommendations, which also set the tone of national health policy (GoI, 1946).[1] The Indian Constitution deemed public health a state subject, and the right to health for all citizens, irrespective of the ability to pay, was underscored as an aspirational national goal. The Constitution recognised health care as a state responsibility.[2]

Investing states with autonomous powers to make health policies and programmes and with responsibilities to implement was considered important for delivering the public good of health by ensuring egalitarian access to health services. Cooperative federalism, however, was privileged as a general principle and was reflected in the health policies including those of fiscal federalism. Along with state plans and budgets, it was envisioned that the Centre would fully fund and implement Central Sector Schemes and implement Centrally Sponsored Schemes (CSS), which were to be funded by the Centre but implemented by either the Centre or the states.

How did this Indian federal model work on the ground? What shape did cooperative federalism take in Centre–State dynamics in making and implementing health policies? In this chapter, I take a closer look at the working of federal processes in health and explore some linkages between federalism, the functioning of the health system and its impact on achieving basic women's health equity goals. The chapter is divided into four sections.

Section I provides a historical backdrop through an examination of federal processes in policy making and federal arrangements for health financing. Central perspectives on health policy and funding priorities constitute a major arena of central state interaction. I follow this up with a critical look at the state's philosophical framework in formulating women's health policy

DOI: 10.4324/9781003568711-15

and its general operation in the context of federal process. I also highlight and reflect on the regionally uneven and socially unequal policy impact.

In the second section of this chapter, I examine policy changes under the National Rural Health Mission (NRHM), its health goals including women's health and highlight the distinctive features of the new federal organisational architecture. I examine shifts in divisions of power and responsibilities between the Centre and the states, and new federal mechanisms were instituted in funding and governance. I further examine the practice of fiscal federalism, that is, how the new financial arrangements work in practice for the EAG states. The analysis is based on secondary data on allocations and expenditure patterns at the state level.

The third part of the chapter briefly captures the impact of NRHM on women's health outcomes and provides a comparative perspective on the Empowered Action Group (EAG) and non-EAG states. I based my analysis on primary data to examine the progress from the pre-NRHM period, specifically from 1998–99 to 2004–05 and during the course of NRHM implementation from 2005–06 to 2015–16.

In the final part, I undertake a case study of one EAG state, Rajasthan, to understand its continued failure to make more satisfactory progress even on the most basic indicators of women's health, even though Rajasthan is known to be an enthusiastic implementer of NRHM. Based on a review of research, I examine the realities of state health provision and the micro-realities of women's health status. I take a critical look at state policy and its implementation, consequences and experiences and end with a few conclusions.

Section I: The Federal Context, Health Policy and Women's Health

Health is a state subject in India. The central government, however, can intervene and has intervened directly in policy formulation, administration and funding. Indian federalism, as noted in a large body of literature, was centrally dominated, especially in the early post-independence decades, by a single political party. The central Ministry of Health provided the key policy and planning framework for the health sector, has played a critical role in defining national health priorities and has framed and anchored various national programs.

Fiscal federalism in health involves three tiers of government, namely Central, state and local, which together contribute to overall public-sector spending on health care. The states bear the major chunk of public health care expenditure, almost 90 per cent, but they have always been at least somewhat financially dependent on the Centre. The central government defined what would constitute major national health objectives and prioritised them in terms of funding and implementation support, and state policy implementation is subject to stringent guidelines (Saxena, 2005)

In addition to the 100 per cent centrally funded national programme of family planning, which all states are obliged to implement, the CSS health programs are partially funded by the Centre. But the schemes are designed by the central ministries and are mostly uniform across states (Rao and Singh, 2004). CSS are meant to supplement the resources of the state governments, which are responsible for the implementation of these schemes (Purohit, 2001).[3]

In Indian federalism (until 2014), there were three sources of transfers from the Centre to states. The first was the statutory transfers made on the recommendation of the Finance Commission appointed by the President of India every five years. The second was the assistance from the Planning Commission, and finally, individual central ministries designed transfers to enhance outlay on specified services in the states as desired by them (Rao and Singh, 2004).

The Bhore Committee's recommendations played a critical role in defining national health priorities, but there were notable policy shifts after some early achievements of the socially oriented welfarist approach to health in the first two post-independence decades. The emerging dominance of the elitist biomedical model of health care and of the politico-economic interests tied to it, coupled with the growing involvement of international donor agencies and the urgency of family planning, undermined the progressive universalist dimensions of the first national health policy. With economic growth prioritised, the public health sector lost priority in the budget, creating distortions that led to the subversion of the Bhore Committee model. Under the growing influence of international organisations, the central government adopted new approaches to health which were based on notions of individual benefit, voluntarism and expert training. Developments in global health in the 1970s, like the Alma Ata declaration, reiterated the original ideals of the Bhore Committee 'in a globally ratified package' (Ramani et al., 2019). However, it could not reverse the new trends.

Women's Health in the Evolving Federal Context

The Centre's role in policy formulation and fiscal federalism was reflected in the political orientation of policies related to women's health. It is known history now that the National Family Planning program, which singularly aimed to lower the fertility rate and control population growth, assumed overwhelming significance in addressing women's health. Birth control policies and strategies had enormous negative effects since women's general health was neglected. That is, both a highly centrist approach to health policy, planning and practice and wrong priorities had enormously negative consequences for the agenda of improving women's health. Women and men were converted from rights-bearing democratic citizens into state targets. The limiting effects of this myopic approach have stayed with us till today.

Despite the equality guaranteed to women in the Constitution, the national vision for women as citizens was shaped by traditional patriarchal ideologies and notions regarding their prime and "legitimate" role in the household, family and society. Commensurate with this thinking, the dominant state approach to women's health was grounded in maternalism, that is, the tendency to identify women first and foremost as mothers and beneficiaries in need of service. Women's status as current or potential mothers constituted the primary basis for their health entitlements, and maternal and child health (MCH) became a core public health programme in India. The policy imagery was of women as a "weaker sex" in need of uplift. A Central Social Welfare Board was constituted to coordinate services for women. Overall, it was a centrist policy which set the agenda for health and women's health.

Equally deleterious was that the state approach to health saw women as a monolith without taking cognisance of the divisions and hierarchical distinctions based on caste, class, gender, religion, region and tribe. It failed to take into account the enormous contributions to the economy made by women of India's labouring classes and the so-called lower castes to production and to the social well-being of communities. The interlinkages between poverty, gender and health were overlooked in policy and practice. Service development for women's health left much to be desired, and even the narrow MCH approach was relegated to an obscure, non-priority status.

Sociocultural contexts and traditional care practices were ignored, and even though the total investments in family welfare increased over the various Five-Year Plans, over time, MCH was treated as an appendage to family planning; rather, the goals of child survival and care marginalised those of maternal survival and care. Overwhelming evidence indicated that state action in public and women's health was inadequate to address the grim realities of mortalities and morbidities, especially among the poor, Dalits and Adivasis. Progress in health achievements was slow and sparse across the BIMARU states (Bihar, Madhya Pradesh, Rajasthan and Uttar Pradesh),[4] and there were wide inter- and intra-state variations. Significant caste, class, tribe and gender inequalities in health outcomes within states and regions persisted. It was only much later, under the impacts of the Indian and global women's movements and sustained campaigning against hazardous contraceptives, sex-selective abortions and coercive population control state policies, that some positive policy changes were seen (Sarojini, 2006).

The onset of structural adjustment policies in the wake of globalisation aggravated the relationship between ill health, poverty and gender and widened regional disparities. There was state withdrawal from welfare. While Centre-to-state transfers had shown general increases from the first to the sixth plans (Jeffery, 1986), they fell from 19.9 per cent (in 1974–82) to 5.8 per cent (in 1982–89) and further to 3.3 per cent (in 1992–93).[5] This had a more pronounced impact on the poorer states viz the BIMARU states and Orissa.[6] States failed to match or replace central funds, and their expenditures on public health were only about 75 per cent of those reached in 1989–90 (Purohit, 2001, pp. 87, 97). State governments were also under pressure to cut social spending in order to meet fiscal targets (Choudhury and Mohanty, 2018).

Reducing government health expenditures substantially weakened the public health systems, affecting the quality and quantity of health services. Many researchers have captured negative effects of the new policies on healthcare access to the poor.[7] Set against the long history of neglecting MCH services and depriving the rural and urban poor of good health, the new safe motherhood initiatives that were floated in the mid-1990s could only make meagre impact on women, especially in the BIMARU states.

By the mid-1990s, the poorer states faced a severe resource crunch. Inter-state disparities between advanced and the backward states widened further in this period, although all-India levels showed declining mortality rates, which had little to do with health service provision (Jeffery, 2021). While a complex range of factors must produce these variations and inequalities in health outcomes, the general situation also indicates the failure of federal health and funding policies to address the multiple inequalities based on region, gender, caste, class and tribe. State-level data and studies show that states with advanced health were generally economically better off, were ideologically and politically motivated to provide better health services and probably took the progressive aspects of national health policies more seriously. They chalked out their own paths, policies and plans to varying extents and budgeted accordingly. That is, operating federal structures have worked better for some but not for others (Ramani and Mavalankar, 2006; Joshi and McGrath, 2015; Jeffery, 2021).

The political, economic and cultural aspects of federalism in policymaking and funding patterns need to be studied further to account for the variations. As Rao and Singh (2004) pointed out, the initial diversity between the states in terms of geography (area, topography), population and economy (income levels) does not seem to have been considered under early federalism. Further explorations are needed of links between fiscal federalism and state progress in health. What role do issues such as funds transfers to the states, the exercise of discretionary powers in federal processes and discrimination in the transfer system (Bennett, 2014) play in explaining the unequal development of health services and health disparities between the states? The sociopolitical scenario grew more complex since the 1980s, resulting in disharmonies between the Centre and states. A politics of asymmetrical federalism played out in the context of multiparty systems, increased regionalisation and assertion of state autonomy, and coalition governments. (Rao and Singh, 2004; Arora et al., 2013; Aiyar and Kapur, 2019). Constitutional enactments decentralising government structures accorded greater responsibilities to local governments, including in health care.

While the turn of the century saw the formulation of two national policies, there was a policy vacuum on the ground, especially in the states in early years. There was no systematic effort at the state level to plan and monitor the delivery of health services which continued to be driven by supply rather than demand (Jeffery, 2021). Of the two national policies, the population policy, although it claimed a woman-centric approach, did not hesitate to recommend coercive birth control measures and even denied maternity benefits to poor, cash-starved women (Rao and Jain, 2001; Narayanan, 2011). The National Health Policy 2002 seemed ostensibly geared towards restoring the public health agenda of yore, emphasising increased public health investment in primary health and a new reproductive and child health (RCH) approach. However, in a by-then highly commercialised health delivery environment with a technocratic bias towards health care and a declining health system with a narrow focus on reproductive health, a tremendous amount of female morbidity was missed, with largely negative health impacts on poor women compounded by social discrimination in health access and treatment.

Part II: The NRHM: Fiscal Federalism, Central Interventions and Impacts on Women's Health

The 2005 NRHM was the flagship health care program of the newly elected UPA I government in fulfilment of its electoral promises. On paper, it signalled a back-to-basics approach that emphasised universal access to health services with a focus on women and children, disease control, sanitation and hygiene and designed with multiple schemes and programs to achieve these goals. The Mission constituted a CSS but was actually an umbrella program subsuming various centrally sponsored schemes in health and family welfare, including a newly revamped RCH II.[8] RCH II was introduced in NRHM 2005 'as the principal vehicle for reducing IMR, MMR, and TFR' (MoHFW GoI, 2005a, p. 8). It sought to create a comprehensive system to enhance expenditures, reduce interstate inequalities and in general, build rural health system capacities (infrastructural, human resources and services). The concern with women was evident in the emphasis on quality reproductive health services with more freedom and choice.[9]

The new architecture for health planning, fund disbursement and health delivery under NRHM envisaged a decentralised approach to public health. The public health service's capacity to deliver was to be strengthened by decentralising village- and district-level health planning and management, establishing new infrastructure in deficient areas and upgrading the infrastructure in the existing institutions (MOHFW GoI, 2005b). It also sought to address the interstate and interdistrict disparities through decentralised funding. Until 2014, NRHM funds were directly transferred from the Centre to the independent state societies (bypassing the state treasury) for easier administration and better utilisation of funds.[10] The central funding was channelled through the NRHM flexible pool to enable states to plan and budget according to their own priorities.[11] It also provided 0.3 per cent additionalities to subcentres through an untied fund in the high-focus states to enable local planning.

A mission steering group at the top was in charge of planning and funds. At the state level, state and district health missions were the decision-making structures, formulating plans at different levels and integrating them into the final state program implementation plan. The Mission's devolution of funds to the lower levels was sanctioned according to the plans submitted and approved as part of the state implementation plan. Special block and health offices were set up for program management. To ensure wide outreach to and greater uptake of antenatal, natal and postnatal and family planning services by women, NRHM engaged a new position called the Accredited Social Health Activist (ASHA).[12] There was a provision under the Janani Suraksha Yojana (JSY) for cash transfers for pregnant women from lower socioeconomic groups as incentive to give birth in a health facility.

Working of the New Structure

Studies of the new decentralised systems of governance planning and fiscal federalism show that expected goals have not been met. A major barrier was the stringent conditions imposed on the EAG states by the central authority in the devolution of funds.[13] These conditions presumed states' absorptive capacity to utilise the fund properly or scale up the program per their capacity (Hooda, 2013; CAG, 2017).[14]

Instead of needs-based financial allocations, the new NRHM guidelines made the ability to spend a key criterion for receiving funds, providing a continued advantage to the privileged, more well-equipped and efficient states.[15] The result was skewed disbursement of funds and continued constraints to developing health services in the EAG states. Data show that these states find it difficult to contribute and are, therefore unable to claim the transfers. The EAG states remain heavily dependent on the Centre (Planning Commission, 2011; Mukherjee, 2014; Fan et al., 2015; Rao and Choudhury, 2012). Consequently, the neediest states are the most deprived.[16]

NRHM funds have definitely resulted in progress in some states in terms of creating additional subcentres, primary health centres and community health centres; procuring equipment and recruiting personnel. However, EAG states could not overcome backlogs and structural systemic weaknesses accumulating over the years, including inadequate capacity among health societies to prepare and cost out health plans, unnecessary delays in fund transfers from one level of the bureaucracy to another and acute shortages in infrastructure and medical staff, that all impeded the sustained, quality delivery of health services. Distorted fund allocation is also a problem across states and components (CBGA, 2011; Fan et al., 2015).

Some conflicting trends in EAG state spending are also noted in the NRHM period. While health expenditures as a ratio of gross state domestic product (GSDP) declined, per capita expenditures increased. In part, this was because the poorer states were substituting central government funds for their own, especially up to 2007–08 (Berman and Ahuja, 2008). Jeffery (2021), in his analysis, shows that on average, one third of the increase is partly the result of greater fiscal transfers from the Centre. But overall, the per capita state spending has been woefully low. With the exception of Rajasthan, states with low per capita income spend less than INR 200 per capita on health from their own revenues (Mukherjee, 2014). However, states such as Madhya Pradesh (MP), Chhattisgarh, Jharkhand, Bihar and Uttar Pradesh (UP), which have some of the worst health indicators in India, do not show any significant change in their level of per capita expenditure (Rao and Choudhury, 2012; Hooda, 2013). Further, declines in the central government's public health expenditures since the completion of the first phase (2004–05 and 2009–10) of the NRHM to the subsequent period (2010–11 to 2014–15) has meant a plummeting from 13.85 per cent to -0.31 per cent in real terms (Sundararaman et al., 2016).

Section III: Women's Health Outcomes in the EAG States

In this section, I look at the progress made by the eight EAG states towards attaining better health levels during the period of NRHM implementation. I broadly define women's health as comprising total well-being and freedom from physical and mental disease and debilitation, inclusive of but not confined to maternal roles. In assessing the impact of the NRHM on women's health, I restrict my study to five key indicators of women's health that relate to reproductive functions: maternal mortality rate (MMR), total fertility rate (TFR), institutional delivery, antenatal services and female contraceptive use. While space constraints prevent a wider discussion,[17] I also hold that in a patriarchal culture in which women's childbearing is considered a 'natural' and essential part of a woman's very existence, these indicators continue to be important.

Table 11.1 presents data on health outcomes for the EAG and non-EAG states to provide a comparative focus. I look at the situation over a 10-year period of NRHM (from 2005–06 to 2015–16), treating 1998–99 as the pre-NRHM phase. Table 11.1 shows that the progressive decline in maternal mortality at the national level is mirrored in all EAG states. However, each EAG state lags the national average and is far from the NRHM targets.[18] Of the EAG states, Uttarakhand and UP fare the worst with conspicuously high maternal mortality (201 deaths), followed by Rajasthan (199) and Odisha (180). TFRs similarly declined over the ten-year period, with a sharper decline occurring between 2005–06 and 2015–16. In non-EAG states, all TFRs fell below the national average, particularly Odisha's.

The significant impact of the JSY is reflected in the increasing percentages of institutional deliveries, with MP, Odisha and Rajasthan showing conspicuous increases which are higher than the state average. Compared with the institutional deliveries, the data show very poor rates of complete antenatal care (ANC) coverage. Bihar disturbingly shows declining ANC coverage from 1998–99 to 2015–16, and UP is second from the last. Two states, Odisha and Jharkhand, register higher percentages than the national average.

Table 11.1 Maternal Mortality Rate, Total Fertility Rate, Institutional Delivery, Complete ANC Coverage and Contraception Use Among Married Women Aged 15–49

	MMR			*TFR*			*Institutional Delivery (%)*			*Complete ANC Coverage (%)*			*Any Modern Contraception Use (%)*		
EAG States	*1999–2001*	*2004–06*	*2014–16*	*1998–99*	*2005–06*	*2015–16*	*1998–99*	*2005–06*	*2015–16*	*1998–99*	*2005–06*	*2015–16*	*1998–99*	*2005–06*	*2015–16*
Bihar	400	312	165	3.7	4	3.41	14.6	19.9	63.8	17.8	17.0	14.4	22.4	28.9	23.2
Chhattisgarh	–	–	173	2.79	2.62	2.23	–	14.3	70.2	–	54.2	59.1	–	49.1	54.5
Jharkhand	–	–	165	2.76	3.31	2.55	–	18.3	61.9	–	35.9	30.3	–	31.1	37.4
Madhya Pradesh	407	335	173	3.43	3.12	2.32	20.1	26.2	80.8	28.1	40.7	35.7	42.6	52.8	49.5
Odisha	424	303	180	2.46	2.37	2.05	22.6	35.6	85.3	47.3	61.8	61.9	40.3	44.7	45.4
Rajasthan	501	388	199	3.78	3.21	2.4	21.5	29.6	84.0	22.9	41.2	38.5	38.1	44.4	53.5
Uttar Pradesh	539	440	201	4.06	3.82	2.74	15.5	20.6	67.8	14.9	26.6	26.4	22.0	29.3	31.7
Uttarakhand	–	–	201	2.61	2.55	2.07	–	–	68.6	–	–	30.9	–	–	49.3
NE States															
Assam	398	480	237	2.31	2.42	2.21	17.6	22.4	70.6	30.8	39.3	46.4	26.6	27.0	37.0
Non-EAG States															
Andhra Pradesh	220	154	74	2.25	1.79	1.83	49.8	64.4	91.5	80.1	85.4	91.5	58.9	67.0	69.4
Gujarat	202	160	91	2.72	2.42	2.03	46.3	52.7	88.5	60.2	67.5	70.5	53.3	56.5	43.1
Haryana	176	186	101	2.88	2.69	2.05	22.4	35.7	80.4	37.4	59.2	45.1	53.2	58.3	59.4
Karnataka	266	213	108	2.13	2.07	1.8	51.1	64.7	94.0	71.4	79.5	70.1	56.5	62.5	51.3
Kerala	149	95	46	1.96	1.93	1.56	93.0	99.3	99.8	98.3	93.6	90.1	56.1	57.9	50.3
Maharashtra	169	130	61	2.52	2.11	1.87	52.6	64.6	90.3	65.4	75.1	72.2	59.9	64.9	62.5
Punjab	177	192	122	2.21	1.99	1.62	37.5	51.3	90.5	57.0	74.8	68.4	53.8	56.1	66.3
Tamil Nadu	167	111	66	2.19	1.8	1.7	79.3	87.8	98.9	91.4	95.9	81.1	50.3	60.0	52.6
Telangana	220	154	81	–	–	1.78	–	–	91.5	–	–	74.9	–	–	56.9
West Bengal	218	141	101	2.29	2.27	1.77	40.1	42.0	75.2	57.0	62.0	76.3	47.3	49.9	57.0
India	**327**	**254**	**130**	**2.85**	**2.68**	**2.18**	**33.6**	**38.7**	**78.9**	**43.8**	**52.0**	**51.2**	**42.8**	**48.5**	**47.7**

Sources: MMR – Registrar General of India (SRS Estimates); all other indicators – National Family Health Survey Reports.

Note: Complete ANC Coverage for 1998–99 and 2005–06 was three or more visits, and for 2015–16 it was four or more visits

In terms of female contraception use, Bihar again shows a decline from 2005–06 to 2015–16. Three states, Rajasthan, Chhattisgarh and MP, show higher contraceptive use by women than the national average. This suggests that women continue to be targeted for family planning. This high performance in family planning stands in contrast to low levels of ANC coverage in these states.

The EAG states are slowly moving towards RCH II goals. However, they seem a long way off from significantly improving women's healthy survival. The provision of equitable life chances to them is a distant dream.

Section IV: Rajasthan-A Case Study

In this section, I aim to understand how the NRHM initiatives as practised in the state of Rajasthan have impacted women. Rajasthan is India's largest state in terms of geographical area and seventh largest by population, three quarters of whom live in rural areas and are engaged in agriculture. At Independence, the state formed through a merger of different princely states was steeped in a feudalistic mindset. The autocratic rulers in the erstwhile independent principalities cared little for the social and economic conditions of the people (Roy, 2021).

With more than 60 per cent of the state's total land being desert, it is characterised by extreme temperature, low rainfall and sparse habitation. Since 1998–99, Rajasthan has faced regular droughts, especially in the arid western region. The state is characterised by cultural diversity, and regional variations and sharp socioeconomic inequalities based on caste, class, religion, tribe and gender.

According to Census 2011, over 88.5 per cent of the population follows the Hindu faith, and Muslims constitute 9 per cent. Almost all, 75 per cent, of the state's population resides in the rural areas, of whom 18.5 per cent and 16.9 per cent, respectively, are categorised as Scheduled Caste (SC) and Scheduled Tribe (ST). The rural areas in the state are more impoverished than urban, and even within those areas, the SC and ST populations are more deprived than the other castes. Rajasthan's decadal population growth rate continues to be higher than in other states (Census, 2011; Singariya, 2012). Together, these factors adversely affected the health of the population historically and still in the early decades of the post-independence era. Over the past 20 years, Rajasthan has grown faster and reduced poverty by more than Bihar, Chhattisgarh, Jharkhand, MP, Orissa and Uttar Pradesh.[19] However, while income poverty has declined significantly, social indicators remain among the worst in India, and even among EAG states, it ranks near the bottom (World Bank, 2018).

Recognising its health challenges and the need to accelerate progress, Rajasthan has seen a spate of state-sponsored policies and programmes, as well as state- and civil society-led community-based initiatives (World Bank, 2005).[20] With the onset of structural adjustment policies, state policies have seen shifts influenced by national policy directives, especially greater engagement with the private sector (Roy, 2021). The role of the private sector and bilateral and multilateral organisations in the health sector has expanded significantly. State partnerships with the private sector in augmenting health services as well as health projects with external assistance have risen (World Bank, 2005, 2018).[21] The state of Rajasthan has thus served as an active and powerful mediator of the market in health care services, with multiple agencies and actors operating in the sector in the state.

Rajasthan has reportedly been a proactive implementer of the NRHM. Health expenditures as a percentage of GSDP was the highest in Rajasthan, higher than even in Tamil Nadu, indicating the higher priority being given to health (CBPS, 2015; Raghuraman et al., 2019). Allocations and expenditures under MCH increased between 2012–13 and 2017–18, and the average utilisation rate was around 71 per cent. The promotion of institutional deliveries was sought through schemes like Dhanwantari Scheme (2008) and Janani Express (2012).[22] Allocations for the JSY cash transfer scheme saw an average increase of 3 per cent from 2012–13 to 2017–18 (Raghuraman et al., 2019, p. 22).

The largest portion of family planning expenditure also goes towards compensation for sterilisation. Moreover, prioritisation of terminal over spacing methods is seen in the difference between the two schemes in fund allocations as well as in the disbursement of ASHA incentives. Furthermore, terminal/limiting methods are skewed towards female sterilisation (Raghuraman et al., 2019).

Finally, other cash transfer schemes (like Shubhlaxmi Yojana and Rajshree Yojana)[23] promote extremely problematic notions of girls being a "burden", which can be compensated for by the receipt of cash. Also disconcerting is the reduced funding for adolescent health programs. These have not only served a useful purpose as knowledge centres for young adults but also as platforms for addressing gender bias (Raghuraman et al., 2019, p. 119). The list of old gender biases is almost endless in state policy.

Despite the increases in MCH allocations, Rajasthan continues to register poorer MCH indicators than those of not only economically developed states like Maharashtra and Tamil Nadu but also Odisha, which is economically similar (Raghuraman et al., 2019). Moreover, the state has failed to redress the interdistrict and regional differences in the provision of services including a severe dearth of specialists and obstetricians in tribal regions. Slow implementation, lack of ground-level governance and human resources are major constraints to provision in rural Rajasthan (NRHM Rajasthan Team, 2011). Thus, imbalances and difficulties caused by the unique topography of the state, continue to keep accessibility to health services unequal and limited. Urbanised districts with higher levels of female education fare better than hill, tribal and desert districts (Iyengar et al., 2009; Raghuraman et al., 2019).

Rajasthan's "success" in NRHM implementation primarily lies in the phenomenal rise in the number of hospital births across urban and rural areas. The institutional delivery rate has tripled from 19 per cent to 63 per cent within a decade of the NRHM (Jullien and Jeffery, 2022). Studies show, however, that hospital delivery does not ensure maternal and infant safety, and there are no guarantees that deaths will be averted (Dalal et al., 2022; Unnithan, 2019; Iyengar et al., 2009).

Moreover, the JSY has given rise to new difficulties, vulnerabilities and risks for women, including for the ASHA health workers who assist birthing women (Unnithan, 2019). A large-scale survey of districts showed that success in institutional delivery is not matched by satisfactory coverage in antenatal and postpartum care (Lim et al., 2010). Availability of safe abortion services is limited, the vacuum is met by informal providers and the incidence of unsafe abortions, especially in rural areas remains high. (Iyengar et al., 2009; Unnithan, 2019; Jullien and Jeffery, 2022). Other major barriers include lack of public transport, the burden of domestic work and encountering non-supportive ASHA workers, which negatively influence the uptake of referral services among high-risk pregnant women in rural Rajasthan (Dalal et al., 2022). Anaemia is a serious health concern among poor women (Jhanjee, 2017). It has a strong direct correlation with perinatal death, along with delivery at home, multiparity and socioeconomic status (Iyengar, 2012).

In conclusion, it is important to note that whatever the quantitative gains in women's health outcomes, the wider societal context is strongly patriarchal. The state has seen a sharp decline in female labour force participation and a child sex ratio which is among the lowest in India and declining.[24] There are fewer non-farm job opportunities for women in rural Rajasthan, and very few urban women work (Iyengar et al., 2009). Strong son preference and prejudice against daughters persists; high son preference in Rajasthani society is one of the reasons for sex-selective abortions in Rajasthan. High neonatal death in the post-NRHM period is the other primary reason for the declining sex ratio. This reflects the broader state of the state's maternal health infrastructure (Arokiasamy and Gautam, 2008; Iyengar et al., 2009; Mathur and Rajagopal, 2011; Singariya, 2012; Jullien and Jeffery, 2022).

It is heartening that gender gaps in schooling are starting to close for younger girls. However, given that women's literacy influences health-seeking behaviour (Iyengar et al., 2009), that Rajasthan had the lowest female literacy rates in the country in 2011 is worrying. Further, more than 35 per cent women marry before the age of 18 years. Almost 41 per cent girls aged 15–19 years are married and childbearing; an overwhelming majority of them do not use any contraceptive method (IIPS-NFHS 4 State Fact sheet, n.d.). At the same time, older women seem to be continued victims of states' targeted approaches to family planning (Raghuraman et al., 2019). In short, the government's push towards women's health has been primarily through the channels of free care delivery and cash incentives for contraception and childcare. Most importantly, concepts of preventive health care for women are totally missing.

Conclusions

To conclude, the NRHM undoubtedly succeeded in activating action in the entire health landscape of India – at the central, state and local levels of India's federal government as well as in civil society – as perhaps no other health policy before it. New federal practices led to increased fund transfers from the Centre to the states through novel mechanisms and processes and have made quantitative dents in terms of new infrastructure and improvements in accessibility and utilisation of services. But as the case of Rajasthan shows, these have been marginal compared with the magnitude of the problem.

My examination of the NRHM's institutional arrangements and system of transfers based on the Centre's devolution norms have not created a level playing field for the EAG states and have failed to address regional and local needs and disparities. Some corrective action has ensued in terms of identifying high-priority districts in states across the country, underscoring the need for separate planning and action. But as of now, their differing and dire needs in provisioning and financing are largely unmet.

The gross indicators of women's health show that the shifts towards decentralised fund transfers and projects of multiple actors and partnerships have not been gender transformative in the EAG states. The overall state approach to women's health that has descended top down for years from the central government's family planning program appears to still provide the contemporary framework for addressing women's health issues in the EAG states, including Rajasthan. Thus, the NRHM's attempts to bring significant health benefits to these states can be said to be, despite small successes, very weak and partial. Political dimensions of Centre–State relations are also likely to be influential in the field of health, but I could not find much evidence on this issue in general or for Rajasthan. Overall, I tend to agree with critics who have noted a centrist approach despite the encouragement of state partnership and ownership in the program (Rao, 2017).

A more qualitative assessment of women's health in Rajasthan suggests that pumping funds through NRHM has not proved enough to attain even basic goals. The concurrent state pursuit of neoliberal policies in the field of health, in particular the enhanced role of varied private players in executing NRHM schemes, contradicts the spirit of public health goals articulated in the NRHM. The new federalism appears to be adapted to new structural adjustment policies more than local needs.

Moreover, what lurks beneath the plethora of "positive" attainments in women's health by the state is the continued emphasis in policy and practice of the highly constricted view of women's health. Contrary to the projection and perception of major gains in RCH outcomes, Rajasthan's camouflaged targeted approach to women's health as birth control has left little scope for processes of cultural change that would be favourable to women. While some are considering women's increased utilisation of facilities and heightened quantitative outcomes for as spectacular achievement by some, the figures hide everyday experiences of ill health, morbidities and risk and of discrimination and subordination in homes, community and health systems.

Women continue to be victims of patriarchal, gender-biased health policies and harmful technologies such as sex selection in environments that are saturated by patriarchal violence. The advanced states are not exceptions to these conditions and practices. Indeed, the NRHM's gains on the whole can be said to be piecemeal, inconsistent, superficial and contradictory for women in the EAG states. The biggest burden of NRHM's failure continues to be carried by the poorest women of these states.

I tend to agree with Williams, who argues that federalism seems inherently neither good nor bad for gender equality, that it all depends on the details of the federal systems and the contexts in which they operate. The connections between gender and federalism need to be drawn at philosophical and policy levels that concern the type of (ideal) orientation that is required of citizens in a federal system. Notions that are valuable for gender equality need to be brought in. Williams makes the important point that it is, therefore, the character of federal citizens, rather than the federal system itself, that could be inherently beneficial to gender equality (Williams, 2018).

In the design of new federal NRHM structures, such concerns have not figured at the policy level. Women's overall wellbeing is not prioritised in a health policy which is designed largely in terms of reproductive health. The EAG states have done little to modify their own approaches and attitudes. As the experiences of Rajasthan's women show, caste, tribe and gender sensitisation programs have not received central attention at the level of design. Health care can play a crucial role in reducing gender and other biases and promoting equality, provided the right approach is adopted.

Acknowledgement

I gratefully acknowledge Carol Wilson and Kumud Teresa for research assistance; Balakrishnan Nair, Aashish Gupta and Abid Fahim for statistical support and Profs Padma Velaskar and Imrana Qadeer for detailed comments on the paper. I benefitted from discussions with several other scholars who I am very grateful too, but cannot unfortunately list them all.

Notes

1 The Bhore Committee made a case for national health service: 'the state should assume full responsibility for all measures, curative and preventive, which are necessary for safeguarding the health of the nation' (Bhore Committee Vol 1:21).
2 Specifically in two articles: Article 39, which outlines employee rights to health care, and Article 246, titled "The Seventh Schedule," which outlines central- and state-level health care responsibilities.
3 Central Sector Schemes were medical education and research institutions and important national programs such as for family planning/welfare. Vertical disease control programs and components of primary health sanitation rural water

supply, which are part of the Centre's minimum needs programs, are examples of Centrally Sponsored Schemes.

4 The term BIMARU was coined in the mid-1980s by the social demographer Ashish Bose in a paper presented to the then Prime Minister, Rajiv Gandhi. It refers to the four states of Bihar (undivided), Madhya Pradesh (undivided), Rajasthan and Uttar Pradesh (undivided). The term was popularly used to point out the poorer economic and social conditions in the four northern states (www.millenniumpost.in/opinion/diving-into-details-486441.

5 This decline is most noticeable in the case of specific-purpose central grants for public health and disease control programs. The central component for public health dropped from 27.92 per cent (in 1984–85) to 17.7 per cent (in 1992–93). The latter, in the same duration, declined from 41.47 per cent to 18.50 per cent. The other component of health expenditure, family welfare, also faced a decline in central grants, from 99 per cent to 88.59 per cent of the States' health expenditure (Purohit, 2001, p. 87).

6 Between 1990–93, the revenue expenditure indices for poor states fell from 100 to 93, 98, 75, 79 and 95, respectively, for medical and public health, and its components, namely, medical, public health, prevention and control of diseases, and family welfare. The decline is at its maximum (i.e. from 100 to 75) for public health. (Purohit, 2001, p. 97).

7 Some of the key sources are (Rao, 1999; Qadeer et al., 2001; Baru et al., 2010; Ghosh, 2014).

8 RCH II stands for Reproductive and Child Health-phase II.

9 It included client-oriented, need-based, high quality, integrated services including delivery, safe abortions, treatment of reproductive tract infections and family planning services to meet unmet needs, while ensuring full reproductive choices to women. The strategy to promote male participation in family planning was also present.

10 However, in 2014–15, the union government reintroduced transferring funds to state treasury and treasury further transfers to the state NHM society (Chandrashekar and Rout, 2021).

11 The flexible pool funds were allocated according to population, with HF states receiving 30 per cent higher allocations (Rao and Choudhury, 2012, p. 21 cited in Jeffery, 2021).

12 ASHA is expected to ensure the availability and delivery of antenatal, natal and postnatal services; counselling on family planning and nutrition; safe abortion; escort for the pregnant female to hospital for institutional delivery; awareness on institutional delivery, potential danger signs and complications during pregnancy, delivery and postpartum period; and community mobilisation towards increased use of the existing health services, including serving as a link between the community and the public health system.

13 At the time of initiation of the NRHM, an MOU was signed with the states in which the states were required to contribute an additional minimum of 15 per cent of the central government's allocations or an increase of 10 per cent in their health budgets every year in the period 2007–12. (Hooda, 2013; Jeffery, 2021).

14 Though the first two instalments were released unconditionally, subsequent ones were released subject to expenditure of at least 50–60 per cent (Eleventh Plan-2007–2012). The release of funds was also conditional on the utilisation of funds in the previous year for the purpose they have been given. The Ministry inspects the performance of states through utilisation certificates and audits while deciding on sanctioning further grants. States that fail to spend their previous instalments do not receive subsequent tranches. In fact, the unspent balance of the previous year is incorporated into the next year's allocation (Hooda, 2013).

15 NRHM spending appears closely linked to a state's ability to request and spend NRHM funds rather than to a state's intrinsic need for health services. Expenditure performance of states like West Bengal, Maharashtra and Haryana is significantly better than HF states like Jharkhand, Bihar and Orissa in 2012–13 and 2014–15 (Fan et al., 2015, p. 11).

16 For instance, Rajasthan, accounting for 10 per cent of maternal deaths in 2004–06, received only 5.8 per cent of NRHM funds from 2005–2010. In contrast, Maharashtra, with 2.6 per cent maternal deaths received more than 7 per cent of the funds over the same period (CBGA, 2011).

17 While data on general health indicators is not being attempted for EAG states, in the next section, we take up wider discussion for Rajasthan state.

18 The major goals to be achieved were: reduction in MMR from 407 to 100 per 1,00,000 live births, IMR from 60 to 30 per 1000 live births and the TFR from 3.0 to 2.1 within the 7 year period of the Mission (Government of India, 2005).

19 Rajasthan's average annual per capita growth rate for the years 1994–2015 was 4.9 per cent, about 1.2 percentage points above the growth performance of the other cited states. The state's poverty rate plummeted by 19.7 percentage points, from 34.4 per cent to 14.7 per cent, during 2005–12. (World Bank, 2018).

20 In 1992, it was the only state in the country which implemented community-based distribution of contraceptives and other services. It formulated the State Population Policy in 2000 and Health Vision for Rajasthan 2025. It created autonomous societies under Section 20 of the Rajasthan Societies Act at primary and secondary hospitals to collect user fees. More recently, it started a free medicines program (World Bank Report, 2005; https://indianexpress.com/article/explained/explained-rajasthan-free-medicine-scheme-5827614/).

21 Averting Maternal Deaths and Disability Project (1999–2004), supported by UNICEF, UNFPA and Bill and Melinda Gates Foundation. Rajasthan Health Systems Development Project (2004 to 2009) (World Bank, 2005).

22 While Dhanwantari Scheme was implemented in 2008, Janani Express was initiated in 2012 (Jhanjee, 2017; Iyengar et al., 2009).

23 The Ashok Gehlot government initiated the Shubhalakshmi Yojana in 2013 aimed at reducing sex-selective abortions and improving the sex ratio in the state. The key strategy of the scheme was to provide compensation for delivering a girl child in government institutions in addition to JSY. In 2016, this scheme was revised by Chief Minister Vasundhara Raje as the CM Rajashree program, with the compensation amount raised to INR 50,000. (Jhanjee, 2017).

24 The child sex ratio in Rajasthan at 888 girls per 1000 boys in 2011 was far below the national average of 919 girls per 1000 boys (Jullien and Jeffery, 2022).

References

Aiyar, Y., and Kapur, A. (2019). The Centralization vs Decentralization Tug of War and the Emerging Narrative of Fiscal Federalism for Social Policy in India. *Regional & Federal Studies*, *29*(2), 187–217.

Arokiasamy, P., and Gautam, A. (2008). Neonatal Mortality in the Empowered Action Group States of India: Trends and Determinants. *Journal of Biosocial Science*, *40*(2), 183–201.

Arora, B., Kailash, K.K., Saxena, R., and Kham Khan Suan, H. (2013). Indian Federalism. In Suri, K.C., and Vanaik, A. (Eds.), *Political Science: Volume 2: Indian Democracy*. Delhi: Oxford Academic.

Baru, R., Acharya, A., Acharya, S., Kumar, A.K.S., and Nagaraj, K. (2010). Inequities in Access to Health Services in India: Caste, Class and Region. *Economic and Political Weekly*, *45*(38), 49–58.

Bennett, D. (2014). Kerala and the Indian Federal System: Restriction and Response. *Explorations*, *IX*, 114–126.

Berman, P., and Ahuja, R. (2008). Government Health Spending in India. *Economic and Political Weekly*, *43*(26/27), 209–216.

CAG. (2017). *Report of the Comptroller and Auditor General of India on Performance Audit of Reproductive and Child Health under National Rural Health Mission, for the Year Ended March 2016*. Union Government (Civil) Ministry of Health and Family Welfare Report No. 25 of 2017 (Performance Audit). https://cag.gov.in/uploads/download_audit_report/2017/Report_No.25_of_2017__Performance_audit_Union_Government_Reproductive_and_Child_Health_under_National_Rural_Health_Mission_Reports_of_Ministry_of_Health_and_Family_Welfare.pdf

Census of India. (2011). *Rajasthan Population 2011–2022*. www.census2011.co.in/census/state/rajasthan.html, accessed 31.8.2022.

Centre for Budget and Governance Accountability. (2011). *Budgeting for Change Series: National Rural Health Mission (NRHM)*. New Delhi: UNICEF.

Centre for Budget and Policy Studies. (2015). *Analysis of Health Budgets with a Special Focus on RCH and MCH Components of National Health Mission in Bihar, Rajasthan and Tamil Nadu*. Bangalore: Centre for Budget and Policy Studies.

Chandrashekar, S., and Rout, S.K. (2021). *Improving Government Financial Transfers for Health and Their Utilization: State Experiences*. www.hstp.org, accessed 10.6.2021.

Choudhury, M., and Mohanty, R.K. (2018). Role of National Health Mission in Health Spending of States: Achievements and Issues. *Working Papers No. 317*. National Institute of Public Finance and Policy.

Dalal, S., Nagar, R., Hegde, R., et al. (2022). Referral Care for High-Risk Pregnant Women in Rural Rajasthan, India: A Qualitative Analysis of Barriers and Facilitators. *BMC Pregnancy Childbirth*, *22*, 31.

Fan, V., Mukherjee, A., and Glassman, A. (2015). *Power to the States: Making Fiscal Transfers Work for Better Health*. Washington, DC: Center for Global Development.

Ghosh, S. (2014). Health Sector Reforms and Changes in Prevalence of Untreated Morbidity, Choice of Healthcare Providers Among the Poor and Rural Population in India. *International Journal of Health Policy and Management*, *2*(3), 125–130.

Government of India. (1946). *Report of the Health Survey and Development Committee, Vol. II Chairman: Bhore*. Delhi: Manager of Publications, GoI.

Hooda, S.K. (2013). *Changing Pattern of Public Expenditure on Health in India: Issues and Challenges*. New Delhi: ISID-PHFI Collaborative Research Centre, Institute for Studies in Industrial Development.

IIPS. (n.d.). State Fact Sheet. Rajasthan. NFHS-4 (2015–16). *International Institute for Population Sciences, Mumbai*. http://rchiips.org/nfhs/pdf/NFHS4/RJ_FactSheet.pdf

Iyengar, K. (2012). Early Postpartum Maternal Morbidity Among Rural Women of Rajasthan, India: A Community-Based Study. *Journal of Health, Population, and Nutrition*, *30*(2), 213–225. https://doi.org/10.3329/jhpn.v30i2.11316

Iyengar, S.D., Iyengar, K., and Gupta, V. (2009). Maternal Health: A Case Study of Rajasthan. *Journal of Health, Population, and Nutrition*, *27*(2), 271–292.

Jeffery, R. (1986, June). Health Planning in India 1951–84: The Role of the Planning Commission. *Health Policy and Planning*, *1*(2), 127–137. https://doi.org/10.1093/heapol/1.2.127

Jeffery, R. (2021). Health Policy and Federalism in India. *Territory, Politics, Governance*, *10*(1), 67–85.

Jhanjee, A. (2017). Access to Information and Services Regarding Maternal Health and Healthcare Within Tribal Communities Around Udaipur, Rajasthan. *Independent Study Project (ISP) Collection*, 2609. https://digitalcollections.sit.edu/isp_collection/2609

Joshi, D.K., and McGrath, K. (2015). Political Ideology, Public Policy and Human Development in India: Explaining the Gap between Gujarat and Tamil Nadu. *Journal of Contemporary Asia*, *45*(3), 465–489.

Jullien, C., and Jeffrey, R. (2022). *Childbirth in South Asia: Old Challenges and New Paradoxes*. New Delhi: Oxford University Press.

Lim, S.S., Dandona, L., Hoisington, J.A., James, S.L., Hogan, M.C., and Gakidou, E. (2010). India's Janani Suraksha Yojana, a Conditional Cash Transfer Programme to Increase Births in Health Facilities: An Impact Evaluation. *Lancet (London, England)*, *375*(9730), 2009–2023.

Mathur, K., and Rajagopal, S. (2011, June 18). No Right to Be Born in Rajasthan with Rajagopal. *Economic and Political Weekly*, *XLVI*(25), 24–25.

MOHFW GoI. (2005a). *National Rural Health Mission Broad Framework for Preparation of District Health Action Plans, August 2006*, 8–9. https://nhm.gov.in/images/pdf/guidelines/nrhm-guidelines/distt_health_action_plan.pdf, accessed 28.8.2022.

MOHFW GoI. (2005b). *National Rural Health Mission, Meeting People's Health Needs in Rural Areas, Framework for Implementation, 2005–2012*, 15–34. https://nhm.gov.in/WriteReadData/l892s/nrhm-framework-latest.pdf, accessed 28.8.2022.

Mukherjee, A.N. (2014). Fiscal Federalism and Intergovernmental Transfers for Financing Health in India. In *Working Group on Intergovernmental Transfers for Health in Populous, Federal Countries*. Center for Global Development. http://citeseerx.ist.psu.edu/viewdoc/download?doi=10.1.1.676.1443&rep=rep1&type=pdf, accessed 19.3.2021.

Narayanan, H. (2011, February 19). Women's Health, Population Control and Collective Action. *Economic and Political Weekly*, *46*(8), 39–47.

NRHM Rajasthan Team. (2011). *Report from Rajasthan 4th CRM of the NRHM-Report from Rajasthan, Jan 2011*. www.nhm.gov.in: http://nhm.gov.in/images/pdf/monitoring/crm/4th-crm/report/rajasthan.pdf

Planning Commission. (2011). *Evaluation Study of National Rural Health Mission (NRHM) in 7 States*. Programme Evaluation Organisation, Planning Commission, New Delhi. http://nhm.gov.in/images/pdf/publication/Evaluation_study_of_NHM_in_7_States.pdf, accessed 28.8.2022.

Purohit, B.C. (2001, March). Private Initiatives and Policy Options: Recent Health System Experience in India. *Health Policy and Planning*, *16*(1), 87–97.

Qadeer, I., Sen, K., and Nayar, K.R. (2001). *Public Health and the Poverty of Reforms: The South Asian Predicament*. New Delhi: Sage Publications.

Raghuraman, G., Abraham, S.M., Rao, B.V., Minni, P., and Jha, J. (2019). *Public Health Expenditure on Health in Rajasthan*. India: Centre for Budget and Policy Studies and UNICEF.

Ramani, K.V., and Mavalankar, D. (2006). Health System in India: Opportunities and Challenges for Improvements. *Journal of Health Organization and Management*, *20*(6), 560–572. https://doi.org/10.1108/14777260610702307

Ramani, S., Sivakami, M., and Gilson, L. (2019). How Context Affects Implementation of the Primary Health Care Approach: An Analysis of What Happened to Primary Health Centres in India. *BMJ Global Health*, *3*(Suppl 3), e001381.

Rao, G.M., and Choudhury, M. (2012). Health Care Financing Reforms in India. *Working Papers 12/100*. National Institute of Public Finance and Policy.

Rao, M. (1999). *Disinvesting in Health. The World Bank Prescriptions for Health*. New Delhi: Sage.

Rao, M., and Jain, D. (2001, April 21). National Population Policy 2000: Re-examining Critical Issues. *Economic and Political Weekly*, *XXXVI*(16).

Rao, M., and Singh, N. (2004). Asymmetric Federalism in India. *UC Santa Cruz: Department of Economics, UCSC*. https://escholarship.org/uc/item/0v59942g

Rao, S. (2017). *Do We Care: India's Health System*. New Delhi, India: Oxford University Press.

Roy, S. (2021). *Role of Public-Private Partnerships in Addressing Inequities in Access to Health Services: Case Studies from Rajasthan* [Unpublished PhD Dissertation, Jawaharlal Nehru University, New Delhi].

Sarojini, N.B., et al. (2006). *Women's Right to Health*. New Delhi: National Human Rights Commission.

Saxena, N.C. (2005). Central Transfers to States and Centrally Sponsored Schemes. *Working Papers id:195*. eSocialSciences. https://www.academia.edu/65902624/Central_Transfers_To_States_And_Centrally_Sponsored_Schemes, accessed 25.9. 2024

Singariya, M.R. (2012). The Demographic Dividend: Evidence from Districts of Rajasthan. *IJMBS*, 2(3), 51–54.

Sundararaman, T., Mukhopadhyay, I., and Muraleedharan, V.R. (2016). No Respite for Public Health. *Economic and Political Weekly*, *51*(16), 39–42.

Unnithan, M. (2019). *Fertility, Health and Reproductive Politics: Re-Imagining Rights in India*. London: Routledge.

Williams, S.H. (2018). Federalism and Gender Equality. *Federal Law Review*, 46(4), 491–519.

World Bank. (2005). *India – Rajasthan – Closing the Development Gap (English)*. Washington, DC. http://documents.worldbank.org/curated/en/765641468269084104/India-Rajasthan-closing-the-development-gap.

World Bank. (2018). *Rajasthan Playing to Its Strengths: A Strategy for Sustained and Inclusive Growth (English)*. Washington, DC: World Bank Group.

12 Meddling With Food Security

Political Undercurrents Affecting the Scientific Logic of Food Security

Imrana Qadeer, Sourindra Mohan Ghosh and P.M. Arathi

Introduction

A strong Centre was considered valuable in delivering welfare within a constitutional federal structure in the early years of Indian planning. To push its policies, invocation of Article 356 by the Centre to tame the 'recalcitrant' states in the 1970s and the frequent use of President's rule (Ghosh, 2020) were the initial steps towards excessive concentration of power. The ideological shift of focus from the welfare state to economic growth alone impacted welfare, particularly health, which was a state subject. Central, entitlement-based, standalone legislation such as the Mahatma Gandhi National Rural Employment Guarantee Act of 2005, the Right of Children to Free and Compulsory Education Act 2009 and the National Food Security Act 2013 helped sustained beneficiaries but could barely change lives for the better. Population health beyond medical care – food, drinking water, transport, education, work and sufficient earning – was particularly affected. This basic need of various states, especially the poorer, was set aside in the pursuit of revenue and higher growth rates beginning in the mid-1980s based on the trickle-down theory. Celebrating progress as GDP growth, the 1980s and 1990s revealed high levels of calorie protein deficiency, in urban and rural areas, 56 per cent and 58 per cent, respectively (Qadeer and Priyadarshi, 2005), and during most of the post-liberalisation era, India also experienced steady declines in calorie as well as cereal intake over the period 1993–94 to 2009–10 (Qadeer et al., 2016).

While the official propaganda welcomed the idea of a knowledge society and a shining India, neither materialised. The thrust for technological innovation and institutional transformation dominated over expanding individual capability. Shining India was ready to embrace and be guided by technological advances, big data and digital sciences to control market behaviour; leaders collected and analysed decreasing amounts of data to understand key social realities before setting policies. Ceasing plague monitoring and closing the National Nutrition Monitoring Bureau (NNMB) were mere precursors.

DOI: 10.4324/9781003568711-16

Since then, this trend has accelerated with impressive brazenness, from the handling of the Covid-19 pandemic, the counting of the dead and the hungry and junking the 75th round (2017–18) of NSS data on consumer expenditures which one could only perceive through leaks that indicated increasing poverty in a population where intake of calories and proteins had stagnated since the 1980s (Himanshu, 2019).

This process of increasing centralisation and dwindling federal features to discourage wider participation in policymaking based on adequate data has serious consequences for population health and nutrition as it often overshadows realities. The novel Indian experience of on the one hand consistently lowering the officially recommended dietary allowances (RDAs) for calories for adults (especially for men) beginning in the 1990s and on the other, long-term evidence of slow-growing or stagnant adult stature in India are among example we explore in this chapter. We look first at these two trends – in RDAs and adult heights – and then at the conceptual premises to explain their apparent contradiction, as well as the science and politics of nutrition planning and the web of connectivity of RDA. The final discussion knits together India's declining federalism and its implications for this connectedness.

Adult Calorie RDA and Human Stature and Food Intake

Studies of historical human stature as a tool to assess well-being show that since 1870, average heights have increased significantly in Western Europe but lagged in Eastern Europe and East Asia. Prior to this period the difference was not significant. For instance, Africans were relatively tall during the period studied, although many countries experienced declining height after the 1960s. People in Southeast Asia stayed relatively short throughout the period (Baten and Blum, 2014).

Other investigators identified similar trends between 1896 and 1996, where South Asia in general and India and Bangladesh in particular maintained a near plateau for those hundred years (Risk Factor Coalition, 2016). Bentham et al. (2016) reinforce these trends through their reanalysis of 1472 population-based studies, specifically of the heights of more than 18.6 million participants, to estimate mean height for 18-year-olds between 1914 and 2014 in 200 countries published in the journal *elife*. Mehta shows that for India, women's mean height increased by 5 cm from 147 cm to 152 cm over this period and that of men by only 3 cm from 161 cm to 164 cm. This is much less than in countries such as South Korea, where women grew by 20 cm and men by 15 cm over the century (Mehta, 2016). All of these researchers highlighted that a country's socioeconomic performance was closely linked to adult heights.

Currently, in addition to the historical evidence based on smaller studies, a group of researchers exploring average adult heights between NFHS-II

1998–99, III 2005–06 and IV 2015–16 found that the average height of women across age groups increased by 0.84 cm, but it declined between NFHS-III and IV in the 15–25 years age group. Among men, both the age 15–25 and age 26–50 groups showed significant decline in average height, particularly so in the poor strata and the ST (Choudhary et al., 2021). Senior scientists from the Indian Council of Medical Research (ICMR) as far back as 1960 had underlined the urgency of building data based on basal metabolic rate (BMR) and energy expenditures (EE) in different groups in India (Patwardhan, 1960).

Until 1984, the idea was resisted that conditions in India had changed enough that RDAs for calories needed to be revised (ICMR, 1984). Beginning with liberalisation, however, the RDAs for calories in India has been gradually reduced (Table 12.1) using the ranges provided by international guidelines and expert assumptions without much heed to building a reliable national database.

Moderate workers and sedentary males made marginal gains in 1990 (pregnant women were exempted), and by 2010, both moderate and sedentary women workers regained slightly while others lost further. In 2020, all RDAs were consistently lowered across work categories in both sexes. A pertinent observation is that the 1990 and 2010 experts focused on reducing RDAs for calories for heavy workers, while in 2020, the sedentary workers were affected the most.

This wavering despite the consistent use of factorial methods in the last three reports and the drastic cuts in physical activity level[1] (PAL) of all activity levels (heavy, moderate and sedentary) to bring it over time near the lower range of international guideline raises concerns about the database and the conceptual frame of analysis. The 2010 report was marked by lack of clarity about the intensity of heavy work, work and rest time ratios in occupational energy cost assessments and the assumption of an eight-hour work day for all despite evidence of long working hours for labour in India marked the 2010 report (Qadeer et al., 2018).

Additionally, seasonal agricultural work variations were treated as periods of vacation with reduced activity without considering the context. Therefore,

Table 12.1 RDAs for Calorie Intake for the Adult Indian Population

	Activity level	*1958*	*1968*	*1984*	*1990*	*2010*	*2020*
Men	Heavy	3900	3900	3900	3780	3485	3470
	Moderate	2800	2800	2800	2878	2727	2710
	Sedentary	2400	2400	2400	2420	2318	2110
Women	Heavy	3000	3000	3000	2925	2854	2720
	Moderate	2200	2200	2200	2223	2234	2130
	Sedentary	1800	1900	1900	1872	1899	1660

Source: ICMR, Reports of the Expert Group on CRDAs for the respective years.

overall EE proposed was 75 per cent of the EE in heavy agricultural work periods, an uncalled-for reduction as most landless agricultural workers and poor farmers take up non-agricultural work for survival during lean periods. In contrast to EG 1990, the report assumed lower EE on non-occupational (household) activities of heavy and moderate workers than of sedentary workers (ICMR, 2010, p. 22). This is negated by the 2020 report. These unsubstantiated assumptions heavily influenced estimation of RDAC in 2010 and raised serious doubts about the validity of its recommendations (ICMR, 2010, p. 22). Also inadequate were time-motion studies for occupational and non-occupational activities and total hours of sleep. It was expected that the next expert committee will address these issues.

With the growing economic crisis and the onslaught of the pandemic as its background, the report of the current Expert Group (EG) (ICMR and NIN, 2020) attempted this task and claimed that the previous report depended on international guidelines and did not have enough Indian data but it did not explain why it inferred from a British industrial workers study on work pattern in 1989 to calculate average physical activity ratios (PARs) for Indian worker categories. The group provided an extensive critique of the 1958 reports but not the previous two comparable EG reports. It confirmed my criticism that their earlier energy cost calculations for occupational activities were arbitrary and not supported by evidence (Qadeer et al., 2018).

The EG provided data from calorimetry studies and estimated integrated energy index (IEI).[2] However, their estimates of IEI from the reviewed EE studies are incorrect. For example, ICMR 2020 referred to activity-specific PAR – which does not consider intermittent resting time, unlike IEI – from a calorimetry study by Ramana Murthy and Balavady (1966) and apparently arrived at an IEI of 3.93 for agricultural work. The report authors do not show the underlying calculations of average PAR for various agricultural activities (like ploughing, harvesting etc.) or IEIs for overall agricultural activity considering resting time.

However, a straightforward and easy calculation of IEI for agricultural labourers from this study can easily be made in the following manner. Ramana Murthy and Balavady (1966) report an average 1730 calories of EE for 8 hours of work for agricultural labourers, which includes agricultural work (3.5 hours); obligatory activities like cattle rearing and cleaning equipment (2 hours) and resting periods (remaining 2.5 hours). With average body weight of 44.3 kg, their BMR would be 1225 calories for 24 hours (by ICMR 2020 consideration that BMR of Indians will be 10 per cent less than FAO/WHO/UNU 1985 estimates). Hence the average IEI for occupational activities of agricultural labourers according to this study would be 4.24, not 3.93 as proposed by the ICMR 2020.

The paucity of Indian studies reveals the lack of attention to this critical subject since the 1960s. Even in choosing from the Indian literature on PAL and BMR, the experts have been selective. Several aspects of this report are disconcerting, such as the use of the urban NNMB data from 2015–16, which had a small sample of 3600 households, and 32.6 per cent, 20.0 per cent and 18.0 per cent households were in service, business and labour, respectively (NIN, 2017, p. 7). The all-India (rural and urban taken together) occupational and activity structure is entirely different from the NNMB sample characteristics. Our estimates from the unit data from the NSSO employment–unemployment 2011–12 survey, which is nationally representative and sampled with a design to capture employment structure, reveals that almost 53 per cent individuals are engaged in heavy occupational activities.[3] The household intake of pulse and legume was 104.5 per cent of RDI, other than green veg 125.7 per cent and fats and oils 125 per cent of recommended intake (NIN, 2017, p. 10) in sharp contrast to the insufficiency reflected in the NSSO data we analysed (Qadeer et al., 2016); hence it is barely representative of Indian adults. This NNMB round was meant to assess diet, obesity and non-communicable diseases in urban areas of 16 states. In contrast, the EG 2010 database was the NNMB survey (2000–2001) with a rural sample tilted towards the poor. Neither focused on healthy populations as is necessary according to the FAO/WHO/UNU (WHO, 2004, p. 2).

It is pertinent that the prevalences of hypertension in men and women in the urban sample were 31.1 and 26.1, respectively (NIN, 2017, p. 17), against the NFHS-4, with 15 per cent and 11 per cent hypertension in men and women, also respectively (NFHS-4, 2017, p. 386). Additionally, 21.5 per cent and 19.4 per cent men and women respectively had diabetes in one report (NNMB, 2017, p. 18) report as against 8 per cent and 6 per cent in NFHS 4 (NFHS 4, p. 387).

With a sample from both rural and urban populations in NFHS, a subset of its sample is used to develop a regression equation for body weight to validate the use of NNMB dataset. Strict criteria for the predictors were the highest quintile of wealth index; graduate-level education; BMI of 21; haemoglobin of 12 and 13 grams for women and men, respectively; blood sugar at 100mg/dl blood and normal blood pressure that explained 87 per cent and 78 per cent of the variations in body weight for men and women respectively for different age groups; the predicted weight was the same as that proposed by the NNMB survey. NIN did not comment on which of these populations should be considered healthy, although it is known that higher weights of the urban population with high caloric intake but poor diet and being overweight are associated with low muscle mass.

This eating pattern is unhealthy, and using weight alone does not reflect body fat muscle mass ratio, which affects BMR. The sample in NNMB 2015–16 is tilted somewhat towards an obese population with oil-rich but deficient diets and cannot be assumed to be representative of the country's population without matching the predictors for which data are available in the NNMB survey. The fact remains that database for nutritional status instead of being strengthened has actually been neglected.[4]

Initially, the full growth potential of healthy Indian adults was taken to be the 95th percentile of the NNMB 4 heights,[5] and the reference weight was the corresponding median weight in the range of 95th percentile of heights with BMI in the range of 18.5–22.9. Yet NIN proposes the 50th percentile height at BMI 21 to estimate weights[6] for deriving BMR and energy costs. The argument was that standard weights can give the aspirational EE, but only existing height to calculate adult weight, BMR and RDA will help avoid over prescription and obesity. The studies to substantiate lower BMRs were selectively chosen to justify the 10 per cent reduction in estimated Indian BMR at the cost of critical work of ICMR in 2010 and that of Shetty and many others[7] (Shetty et al., 1986; Piers and Shetty, 1993; Shetty, 2005).

The BMR critical in estimating EE was reduced once by reducing the weights to the 50th percentile and twice by reducing the derived BMR by 10 per cent. Even if we agree that Indian adults have higher body fat, or there is increasing overweight and obesity, we have to recognise this as unhealthy and cannot consider them as the standard or reference, just as the short, low-body-weight, poor population is also not a reference population. We also know that increasing overweight and obesity in India are linked not to overeating but to undereating and malnourishment, reflected in the small stature of Indian adults.

This scientific exercise makes no mention of the declining pace of increase in heights or its stagnation and even declines, the conflicts of economic and nutritional priorities imposing inevitable biases, the errors in the previous report and the need to relate to the social context of high levels of under-nutrition underlined by the joint Committees of WHO, FAO and UNU reports (WHO, 2004), which recommend additional calories and improved quality of diet. The agency leaders were primarily concerned with arresting the increase in obesity and leaves multiple critical questions unanswered. Is the reduced EE in the Indian population correctly assessed? Can biological and physical shifts such as low BMR and low activity levels possibly be due to unemployment, which is significant in rural areas?[8] And can the ensuing undernourishment be considered the ideal stable state for assessing RDAs?

In other words, what does a declining RDA for calorie intake represent: is it a technological advancement that has ushered in rest and relief from excessive work and calls for eating less and exercising more or does it complete the vicious cycle of induced undernutrition by normalising low food intakes and poor stature to maintain the status quo of a suboptimal state of nutritional adaptation to food insecurity? How is this dilemma resolved?

Conceptual Premise to Resolve Conflicts Between the Two Opposing Trends

Two biological explanations have been offered to scientifically explain these opposing trends as natural, but they are problematic. Firstly, different genetic potentials among populations have undeniable impacts, but its unfolding is essentially regulated by the social factors of availability and access to adequate food and welfare. The shifting heights of the African populations and the differences in stature among different classes of the same country all show the flexibility of the upper limits of human genetic potential. Analysing NSS and NFHS data, Deaton showed that in India, as in historical data from Europe, people attain their adult height only in their 20s, several years later than in contemporary rich countries (Deaton, 2008). There is also evidence to show that Indian children growing up in the West are much taller than other migrants (Alacevich and Tarozi, 2017). To take the short stature of adults at a given point as the norm for prescribing lower RDA is therefore questionable as it denies catch up growth to young adults.

Secondly, earlier the concept of nutritional adaptation was offered to explain how populations successfully adjust to their environments without harming themselves but we now know that 'metabolic adaptation to energy restriction is not an important factor that needs to be considered when recommending energy requirements for adults in developing countries'; additionally, 'Every adaptation has its cost and there is no such thing as a "costless" adaptation' (Shetty, 2005). As early as 1987, Gopalan opined that adaptation,

> represents not a stage of normalcy but one of 'strategic metabolic and functional retreat' in response to stress, a device which may help the victim to ward off catastrophe of death but which unfortunately will not help him to 'live' life.
>
> (Gopalan, 1987)

This is where nearly half of Indians are seeking state support for survival. Several levels of adaptation are possible, with their given penalties including metabolic shifts, slowing BMR, high morbidity and low physical activity (WHO, 1985). A country decides which nutritional penalties would be socially acceptable. That is why the JCs set up by the FAO/WHO/UNU in 1985 as well as 2001 consistently underlined the importance of 'addressing the high magnitudes of energy deficiency while prescribing RDAs for developing country populations' (WHO, 2004, p. 30), RDAs being for healthy populations to maintain good nutrition. 'The correction of malnutrition – either deficit or excess – involves different energy requirements and dietary recommendations' (WHO, 2004, p. 2).

We earlier discussed (Qadeer et al., 2016) a third set of propositions – not referring to the dichotomy in question but supporting lowered RDA – offered by (Deaton and Dreze, 2009). Briefly, they argued that decreased requirements are borne out of reduced physical activity due to increased use of technology. This is probably true for a small section, but the majority of workers actually continue with increased work through multiple cropping, labour intensification and absorption of migrant labour into the expanding informal section with poor working conditions and long working hours of contractual work.

The rise in calorie intake in 2011–12 across all monthly per capita expenditures (MPCE) quintiles also questions reduction of physical activity. The reduced rural urban calorie intake between 1993–94 and 2009–10 for even the second-lowest MPCE group out of five, from the initial levels of only 1912 and 1849 k calories, respectively, underlines that the declines occurred even when intake levels were far below the new reduced norms of calorie adequacy. This could not be the outcome of reduced needs.

Another reason offered for the declining needs was better health environments leading to reduced morbidity. This too is untenable: although mortality has declined due to improved environment, the evidence according to the NSSO supports increased morbidity over 1995–2014 (Kalosona and Singh, 2017). Calorie requirements of a sick population might in fact have higher calorie requirements than the healthy; yet this sick, inactive, chronically hungry population is being mistaken for one with reduced activity due to improved conditions and access to technology. Deaton and Dreze (2009) themselves end up by accepting that 'nothing we have said justifies downplaying of calorie deficiencies among poor households'. The poor constitute over 50 per cent of the population. Though a certain proportion of the population has moved to urban jobs requiring less energy consumption, is the proportion of that shift enough to justify this level of lowering of RDA at the cost of those who stayed behind? Furthermore, with a better health environment and less physical stress, why should height as an indicator of well-being stagnate? The only explanation for simultaneous declines in average height and RDA is the official acceptance of serious nutritional penalties as normal, thus normalising suboptimal stature and using an ill-defined levels nutritional adaptation as a camouflage. Is it then a policy instrument for keeping wages low, maximising profits and rationalising weakening of food security?

To explore this question, we turn to examine the evolution of welfare policy in democratic India's hierarchical social systems with a focus on strategies to improve nutritional status. Constraints such as economic stratification, gender, caste, ethnicity, religion and education are constantly debated, but what has not been debated is how entitlements are scientifically arrived at for policymaking. Unlike visible hunger and paucity of food, the science of RDA used to arrive at entitlements is the preserve of the professional scientists.

When these scientists participate in planning and define required allowances for keeping populations within 'acceptable' limits of nutritional health, they are dealing with biases inherent in their own conceptions and methodologies and the conceptions of a neoliberal state and its priority for economic growth over nutritional health. The competing economic interests of the neoliberal system set the limits of nutritional health because the interplay of science and politics determines the weight given to population nutrition. This is where values waver – between service of the masters and the masses – in the practice of science.

Planning: The Meeting Ground of Politics and Science

It needs to be reiterated that the subjective nature of the choice between different penalties associated with adaptation is critical and that the nutrition planners have been continuously making this choice without making it explicit. The growing emphasis on revenue and GDP under the neoliberal shifts only emboldens this choice.

The initial years of planning showed the will to ensure minimum food requirements with cheap diets within the much-criticised Nehruvian planning that brought economic relief despite its low GDP (4 per cent) (Balakrishnan, 2007). This approach, however, lost its corrective façade, and cheap diets never ensured that calories were coming from balanced diets. Yet until the early 1980s, at least experts like Gopalan and Ramalingaswamy considered lowering the calorie RDAs premature (ICMR, 1984). The period over 1970–92 saw widespread entitlement failures and mini-famines leading to heightened mortality rates and fall in conception rates, both indicators of biological stresses (Chakravarti, 2001). Although, it largely went unnoticed, it was linked to the unrealized promises of freedom.

The Economic Reforms That Followed

The balance attained between a low GDP and food security achieved through agricultural policies and the public distribution system by the 1970s (Balakrishnan, 2007) could not be retained. First, the Eighth Five Year Plan proposed to 'give up activities which are not essential to its (planning's) role' (PC, 1992, Vol. 1, chapter 1, para 4). Then, the Ninth Plan transformed PDS into the Targeted Public Distribution System (TPDS), claiming thereby to sharpen the antipoverty thrust of social security within liberalisation, promoting trade in food grains and all other agricultural commodities. Policies converged on production, buffer stock operations and imports and exports of food grains. However, while food security remained an agenda, (PC, 1997, Vol. 2) altered production patterns, buffer stocks and food grain exports weakened food security.

NFSA 2013's guaranteed subsidised food to 800 million and left at least 100 million eligible persons out as their ration cards were not updated (Scroll, 2020). Calculated on the basis of the 1991 Census, for a family of 5.5, the official requirement came to 73 kg per month of cereals. TPDS could cover only part of this need (PC, 2002, Vol. 2, p. 320). Thus, the sources of cheap calories not only were short of the needed amount for those below the poverty line, those on it or just above it were left to fend for themselves with higher prices. Neither set could easily afford pulses and oils missing from the provisions. The Plan itself acknowledged that 'in the last five decades, the mortality rate has come down by 50 per cent but the reduction in undernutrition is only 20 per cent' (PC, 2002, Vol. 2, p. 290). It recognized the need to minimize the 'potential adverse consequences of globalisation on domestic production, employment and price stability of food commodities' (PC, 2002, Vol. 2, p. 316) but continued along the market-friendly path.[9] Rations, price control and building food stocks were declared wasteful in favour of market mechanisms for distribution of basic foods.

The two consecutive governments during the period of reforms, despite claiming to be the guardians of the National Food Security Act (NFSA), 2013 failed to strengthen it to control the hunger that stalked the countryside and urban slums (Patnaik, 2004). Reforms, in fact, lowered the growth rates of employment and wages and increased prices of consumables, further limiting access to food security[10] and pushing the unstated definition of nutritional health towards including severe penalties for 'adaptation'.

Redefining Entitlements

The challenge of these penalties was dealt with technically by the 10th Plan with an extended chapter on food and nutrition security opening a 'scientific route' for reform through a paradigm shift from food security to nutritional security targeting the individuals through food fortification and micronutrient distribution. At the population level, only feeding programs and TPDS remained in focus clouding the emerging negative implications of trends in wages vis-a-vis prices, targeted distribution, procurement and stocks of and trade in food grain. Within this technocentric perspective was a possible overestimation of the calorie RDA in the past, needing a quick review and its possible reduction (PC, 2002, Vol. 2, p. 325). This was a scientific task of articulating EE and RDA without societal checks such as perceived need, hunger and satiation. Only those trained in science could do this and their responsibility was great.

We know that, 'small studies in high risk or deprived settings can be biased towards certain geographies and specific populations' as observed by the Comprehensive National Nutrition Survey (CNNS) – 2016–2018 (Ministry of Health & Family Welfare, UNICEF and Population Council, 2019) and inappropriate samples are best avoided. Yet even the latest EG report does not avoid these pitfalls. The possibility of RDA becoming a source of undetectable biases in planning therefore cannot be ruled out, especially as it is not easily understood by the working people who react to hunger, paucity, rising prices and loss of work and wages but not to RDA or EE.

The 10th Plan proposed epidemiological monitoring of nutritional status and a review of RDAs (PC, 2002, Vol. 2, p. 314); only the latter was addressed in detail. Principles of nutrition science intermixed with assumed Indian realities were asserted with scarce evidence. The plan hinted that the present RDAs are flawed, based on incorrect assumptions of a high BMR, higher physical activity and hence higher PAR; in turn, the use of higher weight and height of a reference man and woman for undernourished adults leads to consuming extra calories, obesity and increasing non-communicable diseases requiring RDA revision (PC, 2002, Vol. 2, pp. 324–325).

Thus, the basis of planning for better nutrition for a largely undernourished population was undermined by the circular argument that having achieved their optimum growth potential, their requirement is of estimated average and not that recommended for persons of standard stature. The plan acknowledged the reconstituting of an ICMR Experts Group for making appropriate recommendations. From its rather conflicting exposition on theoretical and factual assumptions, the group established that, 'the energy requirement of Indians is likely to be substantially lower than the current ICMR recommendations' (PC, 2002, Vol. 2, p. 324).

These decisions were indicative of how the grey areas in nutritional knowledge about Indian populations could be geared for promoting a specific line of thought rather than clarifying them. The chair of the ICMR expert group 2010 was one of the 10th Plan advisors with a published paper on similar lines (Rao, 2005). The die was thus cast in favour of reducing RDA by the very experts expected to use science to provide food security. We examine, then, how the excessive lowering of RDA may affect tackling of poverty and welfare in India.

RDA and the Web of Its Connectivity

Poverty Estimation

Since the late 1970s, several official committees have reviewed the methodology to estimate poverty, often for streamlining welfare policies. To illustrate the implications of the shifts in the ICMR's calorie RDA on poverty estimates, we examine two of these committees that used calorie RDAs to set norms for poverty estimation.

Set up by the Planning Commission, the Task Force 1977 considered calorie requirements as the basic minimum need for estimating poverty (PC, 1979). It used the categories of ICMR's EG on nutrition – age, sex, workload – to allow for differing calorie needs for rural versus urban populations. Population weights of these categories-derived from the 27th Round of the NSS (1972–73) on employment data were applied to arrive at average calorie requirements for the entire population. Average per-capita daily requirements of 2400 Kcal and 2100 Kcal were arrived at for rural and urban populations, respectively.

Corresponding monetary equivalents to these levels of calorie intake – the MPCE – from the same round of NSS was considered the poverty line for that year. The criterion of being poor became the basis of targeted eligibility for most state welfare schemes. Hence, poverty estimates assumed much greater significance than before; from a measure of success/failure of state welfare policy, they became the determinant of its implementation.

Estimates after EG 1979 used price indices, assuming these reflected the amount of money needed to afford that same food basket. Inevitably, this methodology became contested – terrain we are not entering. The fact that the basket did not remain the same but also dwindled and varied over years and the significance of basic non-food items were recognised, and the artificial reduction of poverty estimation had to be reckoned with (Patnaik, 2008). This compelled PC to opt for a fresh estimation of poverty line and an EG was set up in 2012 for this purpose.

In 2012, for the first time since 1979, the EG 2014 unlike other committees earlier, considered calories (among other items) as a direct basis for calculating poverty line to estimate poverty (GoI, 2014). It used the methodology of the Task Force for calorie estimates based on recommendations of EG ICMR, 2010 and 68th Round of NSS on employment unemployment (2011–12) for work status and consumption. The altered calorie recommendations of the ICMR and the changed age-sex-occupational structure caused the rural average per-capita daily calorie requirement to come down to 2155 Kcal from 2,400 Kcal. The urban requirement, however, remained almost the same (2090 Kcal) because of "pronounced shift in the age-distribution towards adults with higher calorie requirements" (GoI, 2014, p. 57) that balanced out the diminishing factors.

A critical observation was that the lowering of the age-sex-activity specific calorie norm of the ICMR is responsible for 60 per cent of the reduction in the calorie requirement of the rural population between 1979 and 2011. The remaining 40 per cent of the reduction is due to a change in the structure of the population during the period (GoI, 2014, p. 57). Hence, if the degree of reduction of ICMR's RDA was less, urban average per-capita daily calorie requirement would in fact have seen a significant increase. Over and above, a reduction of calorie requirement by 10–25 per cent on the basis of adaptation was added without justification.

The estimated contribution of calorie RDA in average calorie entitlement shifts indicates how critical the need for a rigorous application of the methodology of RDA assessment is, as it silently penetrates different aspects of tackling poverty and welfare which we illustrate below.

Poverty Lines

Keeping aside the critiques of indirect methods of poverty estimates, even if we look at the official figures, the problem of underestimation is evident. The poverty line estimated by the Task force 1979 put it at Rs.61.8 per capita per month in the rural areas and Rs.71.3 per capita per month in the urban area at 1976–77 prices of food. Accordingly, the percentage of rural and urban population below poverty line (BPL) was 53 and 47 per cent (combined 51per cent) for 1977–78.[11] Later, the Tendulkar Committee on estimation of poverty was set up in 2009 (Govt. of India, 2009), using the price index estimated BPL population to be 22.0 per cent for the year 2011–12. The EG

2014 using direct methodology of the Task Force 2012 – despite the criticisms of its low estimates primarily due to its failure to use multi-dimensional deprivation measures of poverty, use of varied response periods of 68th round of NSS and, use of averages for nutrient requirements given the extent of inequality in India (Ray and Sinha, 2014; Raveendran, 2016) – estimated BPL population as 29.2 per cent for the same year. As the decision of EG 2014 was pending, the Tendulkar Committee report estimates continued to guide the policy as the official poverty estimates (NITI Aayog, 2015). The difference due to the direct method of estimation is visible, and the silent influence of RDA in the direct estimates cannot be ignored. Reduced numbers of the poor made the myth of targeted planning appear feasible.

Identification of the Poor

Poverty line based on calorie intake was the prevailing way to identify the poor until it became clear that this linear economic model alone was not sufficient alone as it gives the energy requirement of a population, not an individual. Individual requirement depends upon factors such as, age, sex, workload etc. hence, the average requirements cannot truly reflect it, nor can it reflect the magnitude of individual calorie deprivation. Thus, the problem of identifying the BPL, households remained as intractable as before, which led to a search for multipronged approaches (Mehrotra and Mander, 2009). Poverty line, however, remained a part of this new approach, and so did the use of RDA. A lowered RDA therefore continues to reduce the chances that the poor will be included despite the use of exclusionary criteria or additional features such as key expenditures on non-food items or other features of the poor.

Entitlements Under NFSA 2013

NSS 2011–12 shows that, respectively, 69.5 per cent and 65 per cent of the population in rural and urban areas were calorie deficient, and 56.0 per cent and 58.4 per cent were deficient in protein as well (Qadeer et al., 2016). NFSA 2013 therefore was enacted to secure the lives of the very poor. Although the logic of its entitlement is not clear, it provided 5 and 7 kg food grains per person per month for all BPL families and those under Antyodaya Anna Yojana, respectively. This is just about half of the actual consumption of the lowest household expenditure group, 10 per cent of the rural and urban populations, who respectively consumed 10 kg and 9.4 kg/pc of cereals a month according to NSSO 2011–12.

The average requirement according to the 10th Plan was 73 kgs per month for a family of 5.5 (13.2 kg/pc – basis 1991 Census) (PC, 2002, Vol. 2, p. 320). The inadequacy becomes explicit against the balanced diets prescribed by NIN, which proposed average monthly cereal intakes of 9.6 kg, 11.7 kg and 16.2 kg for adults engaged in sedentary, moderate and heavy activity, respectively, but with adequate quantities of pulses, milk, vegetables, fruits, fat, etc. that add calories (NIN, 2011). This underlines that despite the NFSA subsidies and TPD, the dietary gaps are significant. Lowered RDA could then only cover the depth of deprivation, not contain it.

The targeted subgroup also has a higher proportion of agricultural and industrial labourers, who mostly engage in heavy and moderate labour and have higher calorie requirements. Using the weighted average RDA as in universal PDS is therefore erroneous. The poor are cheated thrice, first by reduction in numbers, then by inadequate identification criteria and finally by ignoring the higher requirements of the majority among them. And at all levels, excessive RDA lowering has a role.

Obesity and RDA

One of the prime concerns of the experts is the rising levels of obesity (24 per cent and 22 per cent in women and men, BMI ≥25 according to NFHS–5), and they consider limiting calorie allowances as preventive. Though the higher MPCE groups with low physical activity are most affected (Kalra and Unnikrishnan, 2012), it is also found among the not so rich as an outcome of shifts in dietetic patterns and reduced energy expenditure due to changing occupations.

Rural populations moving out of heavy work into less rigorous labour in urban areas are consuming cheaper, less-balanced diets, with excess refined carbohydrates, low protein and poor-quality fats that are not easily oxidised and tend to get deposited as abdominal fat. Similar shifts have occurred within rural areas as well (Qadeer et al., 2016), with the traditional oils being replaced with cheaper palmolein and sunflower oil and the use of single oils reducing quality (Narasimhan et al., 2016). Using NFSH–3 and NFSH–4 data showed that a large proportion of overweight/obese women (BMI ≥ 25) are actually undernourished in early life, with small stature. The food transition towards more but poor-quality fats and increasingly sedentary lifestyles makes them vulnerable to overweight/obesity but a diet varied in composition acts as protection (Ghosh and Qadeer, 2020).

This obese population, apart from adequate calories, requires that its calorie sources be varied, balanced and of good quality; reducing RDA for calories for this group, then, is not the solution, and neither are micronutrients (Waijers et al., 2007). The elimination of universal PDS leaves a large proportion of population at or just above poverty line, devoid of even the subsidised cereals that would enable them to consume better-quality fats and proteins to improve their diets (Ghosh and Qadeer, 2017). In fact, the argument that RDA reduction can control obesity is misplaced for four reasons.

TPDS leaves those sitting on the poverty line or just above it unprotected and vulnerable to obesity; it does not address the critical need to improve the quality of rations. Free market economies have no mechanism for controlling consumption by the haves. The weighted-average RDA to estimate entitlement is in any case far less than the actual calorie requirement of the majority of the targeted. Could the rise in obesity then reflect the impact of the unfolding economic crisis starting with demonetisation and the shrinking prosperity of the expanding middle class and welfare withdrawal?

Weakening the Web of Food Security

The food security system in India has been significantly undermined by being linked to the market (national and international) production, distribution and procurement of food grains. Regulatory policies for all of these were meant as necessary elements of food security through conscious planning but the reforms declared these policies wasteful and inefficient and declared markets a better way for food security. As a result, both distribution of and access to basic food became limited.

Even though the trends of slow or stagnant increases in the heights of Indian adults were never a part of debate within official circles, food security policies were reformed despite knowing the vulnerability of a large section of the population with declines in calorie intakes over 1993–94 to 2009–10 after the recoveries of the initial post-Independence period. The data on consumption for 2017–18 even became a victim, with the 75th round of the consumer expenditure survey being officially rejected despite the organisation's readiness to publish it and the 'leaked data' speaking of decreasing consumption expenditures (Himanshu, 2019).

Another level of containment of welfare was when from universal distribution, the effort shifted to targeted PDS in 1997 as policies focused on revenues and financial efficiency. To manage democratic demand for inclusion and equity, the government focused on measuring poverty, identifying the poor, fixing entitlements for welfare and pushing TPDS into a cash transfer scheme. These processes of dismantling food security, we argue, used calorie RDA in different ways – appropriate and less so – given the variations in calorie RDA in population subgroups. The challenges of these uses were not unsurmountable, but they were neglected.

For example, while averaging calorie RDA across all activity groups in universal PDS was unavoidable, its use in TPDS was not fair. In fixing entitlements in TPDS while the food grains allocated were near the universal PDS that went up to 25 to 35 kg grain per family per month (Dhanaraj and Gade, 2016), the additional items of sugar, oil, kerosene and cloth, which offered financial relief and the possible addition of pulses and vegetables, were unceremoniously dropped. A population could consume diets adequate in calories but poor in quality that made them vulnerable to obesity, but this type of obesity inaccurately added to reasons for cutting the calorie RDA. That is, the ways of monitoring and streamlining food security that were intended to strengthen it ended up further undermining it. The reduced RDA for calories then becomes problematic in two ways, creating an impression that the poverty line was lower and that a substantial part of the requirement was being given to the targeted BPL families.

Not satisfied even with the financial 'efficiency' of TPD, the 10th Plan proposed a shift from the paradigm of 'food security' (with its larger connections with production, procurement and distribution), to 'nutritional security' with an emphasis on the individual, biology and technology. Interventions like fortification and micronutrient distribution as well as the idea of reducing energy expenditures on activities due to reduced biological needs were introduced. Also, the longest chapter ever written on nutrition in a plan – ineffectively supporting cuts in calorie RDA – was included.

As we noted earlier, experts common to the 10th Plan and ICMR EG 2010, proposed in the former cuts in the calorie RDA, and this finally became the ICMR recommendation. These reductions contributed to 60 per cent of the decline in average per capita daily calorie requirements calculated by the Planning Commission's EG (GoI, 2014). According to some researchers, despite a drop in adult physical activity levels, 'total energy expenditures are flat overall between 1983 and 2012'. They argued that, 'rising metabolic requirements due to increases in weight dampened the effect of falling activity levels on total energy expenditure' (Eli and Li, 2020). Yet the EG ICMR 2020 pushed the decline in RDA for calories further, firstly by assuming lower BMR across all categories of activity groups (rejecting the chosen procedure of the EG 2010 without sufficient explanation) and secondly by assuming very low occupational EE among sedentary workers (especially women) and ignoring critical household activities.[12]

These loosely argued assumptions have brought estimates of PAL at the three activity levels in India to or near the lowest ends of the international ranges.[13] Hence the present reductions in adult calorie RDA could in fact reflect acceptance of advanced penalties for human adaptation that are detrimental for health; these assumptions and RDA estimates require substantiation. The experts neglect undernutrition and overemphasise obesity without assessing the link and balance between quantity and quality of sources of calories, assumptions regarding equal hours for sleep and the nature of occupational and non-occupational work in India, as they consider very low proportions of hard work and miss key non-occupational activities for women.

Contrary to this, an International Labour Organization (2020) report points out that Indians are among the most overworked workers and earn the lowest minimum statutory wage. This makes the ICMR EG 2020 recommendations mutable. The biases reflected prompt us to argue that the only way in which the contradiction between trends of slow rates of increase in height and its stagnation and the decline in the RDA for calories over the past three decades can be explained is that rejecting the international understanding that RDAs for developing countries should be calculated on the basis of 'healthy' populations' and not their existing average general populations who are under- and malnourished. Using inappropriate samples, EG 2020 does exactly that.

Our diminishing federal framework was hit yet again by the pandemic when the Centre promulgated the Epidemic Control Act 1897 and the Disaster Management Law and issued strict guidelines to the states. Added to this was the conditional increase in the borrowing limits for the states – already burdened by the Goods and Services Tax – to implement the reforms prescribed by the Centre (Burman, 2020). Emboldened by the pandemic, this growing centralisation, apart from the economic and political push-back from the states, also disempowers their scientific institutions and scientists outside the official network. As a consequence, the biases behind scientific recommendations remain unchecked. This is why it is important to call for a review of this singularly critical scientific exercise – estimating recommended daily allowances for calories – to lay bare the technical flaws that favour the political process of planned appropriation and accumulation of wealth. The web of socio-biological connections of calorie RDA seems to have become one unquestioned pathway for undermining the food security and welfare that are crucial to health.

Acknowledgement

The authors acknowledge the support given by the Council for Social Development, especially by the librarian, Gurmeet Kaur, for the literature review as part of the background research.

Notes

1 Physical activity level is measured by the EE of a person in 24 hours using direct and indirect methods. When expressed as a ratio of BMR, it is called physical activity ratio. Thus, EE = PAR × BMR.
2 IEI is the energy cost of an activity or occupation, including the rest involved in that activity, expressed as minutes or hours calculated as a ratio of the BMR.
3 Agricultural workers, miners, construction workers.
4 The NNMB survey for monitoring nutritional status of the Indian population was stopped in 2012.
5 The 95th percentile of NMMB height was considered the full growth potential of healthy Indian adults in the given environmental context and was called an aspirational value at BMI 21 by the experts in EG 2020.
6 According to NNMB 2015–16, median weights of men were 71.8 kg and of women 60.0 kg. Using the regression equation derived from the NFHS-4 data on body weight and selected predictors of health such as BMI, wealth index, age, education, blood pressure, blood sugar and anaemia that explained 85 per cent and 75 per cent variations in weight in males and females, respectively, the reference weights for different age groups were estimated with the wealth index set at the highest quintile. The reference weight for adults was thus reduced to 65 and 55 kg for men and women, respectively.
7 According to Piers and Shetty (1993), the BMR for Indian women calculated by Schaeffer's method was 9.2 per cent lower than that of the northern populations;

Deepak (2016) in their book added that this initial difference of 10 per cent between Indian and North American and European populations was later brought down to 5 per cent by the ICMR in 2010. EG IMR 2010 evolved its own equation based on the climatic, metabolic and social differences with the southern countries to put the difference at 5 per cent. This was supported by several other studies in the literature review (Shetty, 2005). His review confirmed that metabolic adaptation to energy restriction is not an important factor in recommending energy requirements for adults in developing countries. The ICMR 2020 EG report, based on a few very small studies of selective populations, goes back to assume a 10 per cent difference without any explanation for abandoning the ICMR's earlier equation.

8 Mazoomdaar (2019) analysed the NSSO Periodic Labour Force Survey 2017–2018 report (the round of NSS data that the government declined to release) to show that casual farm labour shrank by 40 per cent since 2011–12 due to total job losses of nearly 3 crore and rise in unemployment and falling consumption for which official data has been shelved.

9 By proposing a relook at minimum support prices; decentralised competitive grain procurement and distribution; amending the Essential Commodities Act, 1955; de-licensing agro-based and food processing industries and removing restrictions on trade and export of agricultural commodities (PC 2002, Vol. 2, p. 316).

10 While 27.8 per cent of India's population lived under food insecurity in 2014–16, the proportion rose to 31.6 per cent in 2017–19 and their numbers grew from 42.65 crore in 2014–16 to 48.86 crore in 2017–19 (Bansal Vaishali, 2020).

11 Standing Committee on Finance, 2010–11: Appraisal of BPL criteria, Thirty Second Report, Fifteenth Lok Sabha, Ministry of Planning, Lok Sabha Secretariat, Ministry of Planning, New Delhi, March.

12 EG 2020, in calculating EE for commuting to work excluded cycling and considered bicycles vehicular travel along with walking. The group also did not include women's additional household work and childcare and certain tasks in rural areas: cattle rearing, wood collection and carrying water. These activities are considered important by the FAO, WHO and UNU Committees and several researchers (Rao et al., 2008; Sujatha et al., 2003).

13 The PAL ranges offered by the FAO, WHO, UNU Report 2004, was 2–2.4, 1.7–1.99 and 1.4–1.69 for heavy, moderate and sedentary work. The 2020 EG of ICMR calculated 2.3, 1.8 and 1.4, respectively.

References

Alacevich, C., and Alessandro, T. (2017, April 23). *Child Height and Intergenerational Transmission of Health: Evidence from Indian Migrants in England*. VoxEU & CEPR. https://voxeu.org/article/child-height-and-living-standards-indian-migrants-england, accessed 21.11.2021.

Balakrishnan, P. (2007, November). Visible Hand: Public Policy and Economic Growth in the Nehru Era. *Working Paper 391*. https://core.ac.uk/download/pdf/19918818.pdf, accessed 24.10.2021.

Bansal, V. (2020, August 24). More Evidence of India's Food Insecurity. *The Hindu*. www.thehindu.com/opinion/lead/more-evidence-of-indias-food-insecurity/article32424037.ece, accessed 11.3.2022.

Baten, J., and Blum, M. (2014). Human Height Since 1820. In Zanden, V., et al. (Eds.), *How Was Life?: Global Well-Being Since 1820*, Chapter 7. Paris: OECD Publishing. https://doi.org/10.1787/9789264214262-11-en

Bentham, J., Ezzati, M., and Forsner, M. (2016). Century of Trends in Adult Human Heights. *eLIFE*, *5*, 1–29, Article Id e13410, E-ISSN 2050–084X, ISSN 2050–084X, quoted in Mehta, N. (2016, July 27). Height of Indians Growing at One of the Slowest Rates in the World: Study. *Mint*, 27 July, accessed 12.9.21.

Burman, A. (2020, July 28). How COVID-19 Is Changing Indian Federalism. *Carnage India*. https://carnegieindia.org/2020/07/28/how-covid-19-is-changing-indian-federalism-pub-82382, accessed 20.2.2022.

Chakravarti, L. (2001). Biological Stress and History from Below; the Millet Zone of India, 1970–72. In Qadeer, I., Sen, K., and Nayar, K.R. (Eds.), *Public Health and Poverty of Reforms: The South Asian Predicament* (pp. 198–208). New Delhi: Sage.

Choudhury, K.K., Das, S., and Ghodajkar, P. (2021). Trends of Adult Heights in India from 1998 to 2015: Evidence from the National Family Health Survey. *PLoS ONE*, *16*(9), e0255676. http://doi.org/10.1371/journal.pone/0255676, accessed 24.4.2021.

Deaton, A. (2008, May). Height, Health, and Inequality: The Distribution of Adult Heights in India. *American Economic Review*, *98*(2), 468–474. https://doi.org/10.1257/aer.98.2.468.25.11.2021

Deaton, A., and Drèze, J. (2009). Food and Nutrition in India: Facts and Interpretations. *Economic and Political Weekly*, 42–65.

Deepak, K.K. (2016). Energy Needs of the Body, Section IV. In Talwar, G.P., Husnain, S., and Kumar Sarin, S. (Eds.), *Text Book of Biochemistry, Biotechnology, Allied and Molecular Medicine* (p. 497). Delhi: PHI Learning Private Ltd.

Dhanaraj, S., and Gade, S. (2016, June). Universal PDS: Efficiency and Equity Dimensions, Working Paper Series No. 148/2016. *Madras School of Economics*. www.mse.ac.in/wp-content/uploads/2016/10/Universal-PDS-Efficiency-and-Equity-Dimensions.pdf, accessed 14.2.2022.

Eli, S., and Li, N. (2020). *Caloric Intake and Energy Expenditures in India*. Policy Research Working Paper; No. 9309. Washington, DC: World Bank. http://hdl.handle.net/10986/34024, https://openknowledge.worldbank.org/handle/10986/34024 License: CC BY 3.0 IGO

Ghosh, A.K. (2020, September). The Paradox of 'Centralised Federalism': An Analysis of the Challenges to India's Federal Design. *ORF Occasional Paper*, 272. www.orfonline.org/research/the-paradox-of-centralised-federalism/

Ghosh, S.M., and Qadeer, I. (2017). Replacing Welfare Provisioning with Cash Transfer. *eSocial Sciences and Humanities*, 57–67. www.esocialsciences.org/eSSH_Journal/Repository/6_Replacing%20Welfare_Ghosh%20&%20Qadeer.pdf, accessed 8.12.2017.

Ghosh, S.M., and Qadeer, I. (2020, January 4). Interpretations and Implications of Increasing Obesity in India Data on Women from National Health Surveys. *Economic and Political Weekly*, *LV*(1).

Gopalan, C. (1987). Measurement of Undernutrition: Biological Considerations. In Gopalan, C. (Ed.), *Combating Undernutrition: Basic Issues and Practical Approaches* (pp. 15–16).New Delhi: Nutrition Foundation of India.

Government of India. (2009). *Report of the Expert Group to Review the Methodology for Estimation of Poverty*. New Delhi: Planning Commission.

Government of India. (2014, June). *Report of the Expert Group to Review the Methodology for Measurement of Poverty*. New Delhi: Planning Commission.

Himanshu. (2019, February 14). Why the Picture on Poverty Is Incomplete. *Mint*. www.livemint.com/news/india/why-the-picture-on-poverty-is-incomplete-11574269577580.html, accessed 14.2.2022.

ICMR. (1984). *Recommended Dietary Intakes for Indians. A Report of the Expert Group of the Indian Council of Medical Research*. New Delhi: ICMR.

ICMR. (2010). *Nutrient Requirements and Recommended Dietary Allowances for Indians. A Report of the Expert Group of the Indian Council of Medical Research*. Hyderabad: ICMR.

ICMR and NIN. (2020). Nutrient Requirements for Indians Recommended Dietary Allowances Estimated Average Requirements, A Report of the Expert Group 2020. *Department of Health Research, Ministry of Health and Family Welfare, GOI, Hyderabad.*

ILO. (2020). Global Wage Report 2020–21: Wages and Minimum Wages in the Time of COVID-19 Quoted in, the Wire Staff, 2021, the Wire. *Indians Work Longest, Earn Least with Virtually No Time for Leisure: ILO Report*, 24/FEB/2021. https://thewire.in/labour/indians-work-longest-earn-least-with-virtually-no-time-for-leisure-ilo-report, accessed 5.4.2022.

Kalosona, P., and Singh, J. (2017, August 9). Emerging Trends and Patterns of Self-Reported Morbidity in India: Evidence from Three Rounds of National Sample Survey. *Journal of Health, Population and Nutrition*, *36*, 32. https://doi.org/10.1186/s41043-017-0109-x. www.ncbi.nlm.nih.gov/pmc/articles/PMC5550946/

Kalra, S., and Unnikrishnan, A.G. (2012). Obesity in India: The Weight of the Nation. *Journal of Medical Nutrition and Nutraceuticals*, *1*(1), 37.

Mazoomdaar, J. (2019, March 21). Casual Farm Labour Shrinks by 40% Since 2011–12, Total Job Loss Nearly 3 Crore: NSSO Data Shows. *Indian Express*. https://indianexpress.com/article/jobs/casual-farm-labour-shrinks-by-40-since-2011-12-total-job-loss-nearly-3-crore-nsso-data-shows-5636734/, accessed 28.12.2019.

Mehrotra, S., and Mander, H. (2009). How to Identify the Poor? A Proposal. *Economic and Political Weekly*, *XLIV*(19), 37–44.

Ministry of Health and Family Welfare (MoHFW), Government of India, UNICEF and Population Council. (2019). *Comprehensive National Nutrition Survey (CNNS) – 2016–2018, National Report* (p. 7). New Delhi. https://nhm.gov.in/WriteReadData/l892s/1405796031571201348.pdf

Narasimhan, S., Nagarajan, L., Vaidya, R., Gunasekaran, G., Rajagopal, G., Parthasarathy, V., Unnikrishnan, R., Anjana, R.M., Moham, V., and Sudha, V. (2016). Dietary Fat Intake and Its Association with the Risk of Selected Components of the Metabolic Syndrome in Rural South Indians. *Indian Journal of Endocrinology and Metabolism*, *20*(1), 47.

National Institute of Nutrition. (2017). *Diet and Nutritional Status of Urban Population in India and Prevalence of Obesity, Hypertension, Diabetes and Hyperlipidemia in Urban Men and Women*. NNMB Technical Report No. 27. ICMR, Hyderabad. https://www.nin.res.in/downloads/NNMB%20Urban%20Nutrition%20Report%20-Brief%20%20%20report.pdf.

NCD Risk Factor Collaboration (NCD-RisC). (2016). *A Century of Trends in Adult Human Life*. https://doi.org/10.7554/eLife.13410.001, accessed 1.11.2020.

NFHS (National Family Health Survey) – 4, 2015–16. (2017). *India, Ministry of Health and Family Welfare* (pp. 386–387). Mumbai: International Institute for Population Sciences.

NIN. (2011). *Dietary Guidelines for Indians Manual* (p. 86). ICMR Centenary Year, Annexure 2.

NITI AAYOG. (2015). *Eliminating Poverty: Creating Jobs and Strengthening Social Programs* (p. 8), Paper Based on the Work of the Task Force, Task Force on Elimination of Poverty in India. www.niti.gov.in/writereaddata/files/presentation%20for%20regional%20meetings-%20NITI%20AAYOG.pdf

NNMB (National Nutrition Monitoring Bureau). (2017). Diet and Nutrition Status of Urban Population in India and Prevalence of Obesity, Hypertension Diabetes, Hyperlipidemia in Urban Men and Women. *Technical Report, 27*, 17–18. Hyderabad: NIN, ICMR.

Patnaik, U. (2004, September–October). The Republic of Hunger. *Social Scientist*, *32*(9/10), 9–35. https://doi.org/10.2307/3518206

Patnaik, U. (2008). Theorizing Food Security and Poverty in the Era of Economic Reforms. In Lechini, G. (Ed.), *Globalization and the Washington Consensus: Its Influence on Democracy and Development in the South* (pp. 161–200). Buenos Aires: CLACSO. http://bibliotecavirtual.clacso.org.ar/ar/libros/sursur/lech/12patna.pdf

Patwardhan, V.N. (1960). Dietary Allowances for Indians: Calories and Proteins. *Special Report Series No. 35*. New Delhi: ICMR.

Piers, L.S., and Shetty, P.S. (1993). Basal Metabolic Rate of Indian Women. *European Journal of Clinical Nutrition*, *47*, 586–591.

Planning Commission. (1979, January). Report of the Task Force on Projections of Minimum Needs and Effective Consumption Demand. *Perspective Planning Division Government of India*. New Delhi.

Planning Commission. (1992). *8th Five Year Plan 1992–97, Vol. 1, Chapter 1*. New Delhi: GoI. http://planningcommission.nic.in/plans/planrel/fiveyr/8th/default.htm, accessed 22.7.2017.

Planning Commission. (1997). *9th Five Year Plan 1997–2002, Vol. 2*. New Delhi: GoI. http://planningcommission.nic.in/plans/planrel/fiveyr/9th/vol2/v2c4-3.htm, accessed 22.7.2017.

Planning Commission. (2002). *10th Five Year Plan 2002–2007*. New Delhi: GoI. http://planningcommission.nic.in/plans/planrel/fiveyr/10th/volume2/10th_vol2.pdf

Qadeer, I., Ghosh, S.M., and Madhavan, A.P. (2016, March 8). India's Declining Calorie Intake: Development or Distress? *Social Change*, *46*(1), 1–26.

Qadeer, I., Ghosh, S.M., and Madhavan, A.P. (2018). Shifts in Recommended Dietary Allowances in India: The Undercurrent of Politics and Scientific Logic. *Council for Social Development, WP-CSD 2/2018*. New Delhi. http://csdindia.org/wp-content/uploads/2019/04/Shifts-in-Recommended-Dietary-Allowances-in-India-with-cover.pdf

Qadeer, I., and Priyadarshi, A.P. (2005, January 29). Nutrition Policy Shifts and Logical Fallacies. *Economic and Political Weekly*, *40*(5), 358–364.

Ramana Murthy, P.S.V., and Balavady, B. (1966). Energy Expenditure and Requirement in Agricultural Labourers. *Indian Journal of Medical Research*, *54*, 977–979.

Rao, B.S.N. (2005). *Energy Requirements of Indians* (pp. 101–109). http://nutritionfoundationofindia.org/workshop_symposia/towards-national-nutrition-security-2005.pdf/Session%203_%20Energy%20Requirements-Need%20for%20Revision_Energy%20Requirements%20of%20Indian_pages_101-109.pdf, accessed 23.7.2017.

Rao, S., Gokhale, M., and Kanade, A. (2008, March). Energy Costs of Daily Activities for Women in Rural India. *Public Health Nutrition*, *11*(2), 142–150. https://doi.org/10.1017/S1368980007000055, accessed 10.3.2022.

Raveendran, G. (2016, July). A Review of Rangarajan Committee Report on Estimation of Poverty. *Indian Journal of Human Development*, *10*(1), 85–96. http://doi.org/10.1177/0973703016648033, accessed 7.3.2022.

Ray, R., and Sinha, K. (2014, October 30). A Critical Assessment of the Rangarajan Panel Report on Poverty Measurement. *Ideas for India*. www.ideasforindia.in/topics/poverty-inequality/a-critical-assessment-of-the-rangarajan-panel-report-on-poverty-measurement.html, accessed 7.3.2022.

Scroll. (2020, April 15). 100 Million Indians Fall Through Gaps in Food Safety Net, Economists Urge Rethink on Covid-19 Relief. *Scroll*. https://scroll.in.https://scroll.in/article/959235/100-million-indians-fall-through-gaps-in-food-safety-net-economists-urge-rethink-on-covid-19-relief

Shetty, P.S. (2005). Energy Requirements of Adults. *Public Health Nutrition*, *8*(7a), 994–1009.

Shetty, P.S., Soars, M.J., and Sheela, M.L. (1986). *Basal Metabolic Rates of South Indian Males*. Report of FAO, Rome.

Standing Committee on Finance, 2010–11. (2010, March). *Appraisal of BPL Criteria, Thirty Second Report, Fifteenth Lok Sabha.* New Delhi: Ministry of Planning, Lok Sabha Secretariat. https://eparlib.nic.in/bitstream/123456789/64127/1/15_Finance_32.pdf, accessed 10.3.2022.

Sujatha, T., Shatrugna, V., Vidyasagar, P., et al. (2003). Timed Activity Studies for Assessing the Energy Expenditure of Women from an Urban Slum in South India. *Food and Nutrition Bulletin*, 24(2), 193–199. https://doi.org/10.1177/156482650302400212.

Waijers, P.M., Feskens, E.J., and Ocké, M.C. (2007). A Critical Review of Predefined Diet Quality Scores. *British Journal of Nutrition*, 97(2), 219–231.

World Health Organization. (1985). *Report of a Joint FAO/WHO/UNU Expert Consultation. Energy and Protein Requirements.* Tech Rep Ser No 724; Geneva. TRS of WHO- 724, 1985). www.fao.org/docrep/003/aa040e/AA040E03.htm#ch3, accessed 16.10.2020.

World Health Organization. (2004). Human Energy Requirements: Report of a Joint FAO/WHO/UNU Expert Consultation, Rome 17–24 October 2001. *Food Agric. Organ United Nations.* Rome.

13 Federal Polity in Communicable Disease Control in India

Reviewing the First 75 Years

T. Sundararaman and Daksha Parmar

In this chapter, we explore the sharing of authority and accountability between the Union government and the states of India with respect to the control of communicable diseases in different stages of India's development, and the implications for disease control performance. This relationship is described with relation to the development of technologies, evolutions in technical strategy, the financing of the program, and the governance of these programs. This relationship also explores the interconnections to the health systems strengthening/reform discourse of the given period and the prevailing political context with respect to the federal structure in India. We undertake this analysis across four periods: the first four decades after Independence, the health sector reform years of the 1990s up to 2005, the period of the National Health Mission (NHM) 2005 onwards and during the Covid-19 pandemic (2020–22). Then, in our conclusion, we summarise our learning across these phases.

Phase I: The Beginnings: 1947 to 1980

Under the Constitution of India as specified in the Seventh Schedule, most of health care belongs to the State List (List II). However, there is also a Concurrent List (List III), for which the Union government and the states have joint responsibility. Family planning, communicable disease prevention, medical education and research are part of List III.

This categorisation was based on the greater priority given to the family planning program and the spread of communicable diseases. The period up to the mid-1940s was marked with continuous pandemics. Plague, cholera and the flu pandemic in the first two decades and then cholera, smallpox, frequent respiratory disease outbreaks, diphtheria and whooping cough, tetanus, malaria, tuberculosis and others. The Bhore Committee Report that set the design of the health systems for India proposed a long-term system-building effort, putting in place a three- tiered hierarchy of health centres and hospitals. It also proposed a short-term program with 10-year goals that addressed the immediate priorities: disease control, population control and developing medical education so that the nation got the doctors it required for providing

DOI: 10.4324/9781003568711-17

medical services. This was perhaps one of the important reasons why the Union government retained these topics under the Concurrent List. In consonance with this understanding, the central government launched a number of National Disease Control Programs: the Malaria Control Programme in 1953, the Leprosy Control Program in 1954, the Smallpox Eradication Program of 1962 and the National Tuberculosis Program in 1962.

The National Malaria Control Programme (1953)

In terms of technology, the big game changer in communicable disease control was the arrival of dichloro-diphenyl-trichloroethane (DDT) spraying and its mass availability. Chloroquine also became available for mass treatment. Postcards and letter stocks from the postal department had a printed message asking anyone with fever to take chloroquine. In the malaria-endemic regions of the country, this drug was also distributed freely as a prophylactic measure (Dutta et al., 1979). There was high priority and backing from the newly created World Health Organization (WHO) and all bilateral and international agencies (WHO, 1976). There was a dramatic reduction in disease prevalence. From affecting 22 per cent of the entire population annually with over 8 lakh deaths, morbidity dropped to about 75 million cases per year. This encouraged the government to upgrade this as a National Malaria Eradication Programme (NMEP) in 1958 (Dutt et al., 1980; Government of India, GoI, 2016).

The main strategy was to establish a fully staffed standalone National Malaria Control Program Unit for every one million population and this unit would undertake the spraying, surveillance and treatment activities (GoI, 2016, p. 26). To build capacity in these units and for liaison with states, six Regional Coordinating Organisations were established at Baroda, Bangalore, Bhubaneshwar, Hyderabad, Lucknow and Shillong (Banerji, 1985, p. 97). Four phases were identified, preparatory, attack, consolidation and maintenance, with set time limits for completing each phase. Different parts of the country were divided into phases depending on the intensity of DDT required and the burden of the disease. Once the NMEP unit reached the maintenance phase, the medical and paramedical staff of the primary health centres (PHCs) were made responsible for conducting the surveillance work (Banerji, 1985, p. 97).

The results were even more dramatic: a spectacular decline in the morbidity and mortality due to malaria. From 1958–65, the number of cases decreased from 75 million cases per year to 0.1 million cases and mortality was zero for the years 1961 to 1965 (GoI, 2016, p. 2; Dutta et al., 1979). However, beginning in mid-1965, cases started to increase, and despite many efforts, the cases slowly climbed back to 5 million by 1976. Urban areas also saw the emergence of malaria-endemic areas.

The Centre blamed the states for not showing sustained interest, weak governance in the form of frequent transfer of leadership and not providing the required staff and poor integration with PHCs in the maintenance phase (Banerji, 1985, p. 100). Frequent stock-out of DDT, resistance of mosquitoes to pesticides and of the parasite to anti-malarials and the rising costs of insecticides also contributed to the resurgence. This fragmentation of accountability, with Centre and states holding each other responsible, remains an unchanging feature to this day.

Unlike in later decades, the same party, Indian National Congress, was dominant in the Centre and in the states for much of this period; therefore, party politics had little to do with this blame game between the Centre and the states. However, there was increasing dissatisfaction with the political governance, and in the years from 1975 to 1977, the country was placed under an authoritarian State of Emergency with the suspension of most civic rights. In the health sector, the political attention shifted entirely to a very unpopular coercive population control drive that lost the people's trust in health systems and led to neglect of all other primary health care activities. With the end of the Emergency, a revised strategy was adopted in 1977 known as the Modified Plan of Operation which was brought back as a 100 per cent Centre-funded 'centrally sponsored scheme' and later a 50–50 share with the states. In 1984, the malaria incidence had come down to nearly 2 million cases with 247 deaths (GoI, 2016), but there it has stayed through the last decade.

National Smallpox Eradication Program

The National Smallpox Eradication Program was launched in 1962. The immediate trigger was the availability of an effective safe vaccine against smallpox and India's ability to mass produce the vaccine. The goal was initially to reach 80 per cent coverage, which was raised to a target of 100 per cent coverage within a year in 1965. The Centre took on the burden of financing. The rise of cases to over 85,000 in 1967 called for a review, and the program then began to emphasize surveillance and containment in addition to vaccination.

The quality and safety of vaccines had also improved, and by the early 1970s, the problem was now limited to a few central and eastern states. Documents of that period record considerable reluctance from the states to collaborate with WHO and the Centre in these intensified search, containment and vaccination operations. WHO documents of this period posit that although it was a national goal to achieve smallpox eradication in the country, the decentralised and federal structure of the government – its states, districts, blocks and villages –presented huge challenges to the implementation of the national program (Fenner et al., 1988).

Therefore, laws and policies making vaccination mandatory were passed. Police searches for cases were encouraged nationwide and enforced by the central government with a heavy hand. Therefore, with a combination of force and persistence, by May 1975, the government could claim complete eradication of this disease (Greenough, 1995). No doubt the success of such coercive methods with persuasive service delivery, driven by the 'strong' Centre, with or without the states on board, seemed to have legitimised and encouraged the excesses of the population control program during the Emergency years.

The Leprosy Control Programs

The narrative on the National Leprosy Control Program (NLCP) is very similar to the others. Leprosy was a major public health problem in India under colonial rule, and the promise of addressing this issue was one of the commitments of Independent India. The first Five Year Plan stated that the country had an estimated one million leprosy cases (GoI, 1951). In 1954, the Government of India launched the NLCP. The technological context was the fact that there was a potential for control through mass domiciliary treatment with sulphones. Initially, it was integrated with state health systems but with central assistance. In 1969–70, this was converted into a centrally sponsored program with total expenditures borne by the Centre. In 1975, citing poor action by the states, the central government took over the control of the program from the state governments (Kotecha and Harpham, 1991, p. 82).

The National Tuberculosis Program

In the colonial period, the role of the government in tuberculosis control was limited; voluntary and private actors were the main actors. This was partly because the big epidemic diseases like cholera, plague, smallpox and malaria had the government preoccupied and also because there were no solutions for this problem. The links between tuberculosis and under-nutrition and poverty was well recognized, but even the rich were not spared, and the disease ran rampant (even Kamala Nehru, the Prime Minister's wife, died of tuberculosis).

This was to change with the discovery of streptomycin (1944), isoniazid (1952), Bacille Calmette–Guerin (BCG) vaccines and the establishment of manufacturing capacity for all of these in India by 1948. In the 1950s, the mass vaccination with BCG had begun, and many treatment centres were established, but coverage was low for both. Resources had gone to the family planning program established in 1952, but it took a further decade for the National Tuberculosis Program to be established.

From its beginning, this program was well integrated with the primary care system, but for that very reason, its fortunes depended on strong primary care systems. Since most states did not make much progress in this regard, the overall progress on tuberculosis control was very limited; this was different from the other programs for malaria, leprosy and smallpox. The strategy of the National Tuberculosis Institute (NTI) was passive case detection of the maximum number of symptomatic TB patients among outpatients attending health institutions and reliance on sputum microscopy rather than X-rays, with adequate home treatment and priority to sputum positives, and this was to happen in all health care institutions which were part of the district health system led by the district TB unit (Sivaraman, 1982, p. 82; Gupta, 1985). Services were to be free and within easy reach, with the participation of the local government (NTI, 1994; Piot, 1962). To a large extent, the states were also responsible for implementation and evaluation of the program (Nagpaul, 1989). However, the program did not do well, and much of the reason was its low priority and the weakness of state health systems.

In Summary: The First Three Decades After Independence

The immediate post-Independence period saw the rise of communicable disease programs as vertical programs designed and administered and, for the most part, fully financed by the Centre. These vertical disease control programs were actively supported by international multilateral and bilateral agencies. Each of these programs had separate work teams reporting directly to the central administration; these were parallel to the state government-supported structure. The exception was tuberculosis, for which the entire staff was to be provided by the state government, and the whole program rested on case detection and follow up in the general health service facilities.

Three important reasons seem to have driven this preference for centrally sponsored vertical programs. Firstly, disease control was in the Concurrent List of the Constitution. Secondly, for each of these diseases, new technologies had just become available in the 1940s and early 1950s which acted as a magic bullet for solving the major health problems in the short term. Further, with that came the promise of low hanging fruit, promising a quick win without having to address the bothersome issues of health system development and the social determinants of health; these were long-term issues. Thirdly, the numbers of those affected were huge, and therefore a visible impact could be made in the first two decades of Independence, thus legitimising the rule of the party that had led the country into independence with public healthcare as one of its promises.

However, by the late 1970s and 1980s, it was obvious that this strategy had reached its limits and further returns were not coming in. Smallpox had been eradicated, but all the rest of the communicable diseases saw massive resurgence. Further, these national disease control programs accounted for only about one fourth of the burden of all communicable diseases, and for the rest, neither the state governments nor the Centre had any plan. Both for the re-emergence and for the other infectious diseases, the Centre was clearly holding the states responsible, but the states did not have the technical capacity or systems development to respond.

The period from 1977 to 1985 did see some basic rethinking about the development of public health systems. Globally, the International Covenant on Economic, Social and Cultural Reforms had been adopted (1976) and signed on by India (1979). WHO moved away from vertical programs and prominently espoused the primary health care approach, and over 190 nations signed on to the 1978 Health for All by 2000 AD declaration. A new international economic order was proposed which was more egalitarian, but this failed to mobilise support. WHO adopted an essential medicines policy and a policy against infant milk substitutes, both of which were seriously objected to by international pharmaceutical and nutrition corporations and the United States of America (USA).

Within India, the authoritarian Emergency came to an end, and with that, the single-minded focus on population control also ceased. There were some bold innovations proposed by the new coalition that came to power. When the Congress returned within just a few years, as part of its Minimum Needs Program, it rolled out a substantial health system strengthening effort in the early 1980s. It also adopted the first National Health Policy 1983. All of this was short-lived. By the mid-1980s, the WHO was marginalised, and the World Bank had taken centre stage, very selective vertical interventions were back in favour but now backed by external funding, and the overall perspective towards public services became negative.

Communicable Disease Control Under Health Sector Reform: 1990 to 2005

In the early 1990s, national programs for all communicable diseases were rewritten. These now included the Revised National Tuberculosis Control Programme, the National Vector Borne Disease Control Programme, the NLEP, the National Iodine Deficiency Disorders Control Programme and the National AIDS Control Programme (NACP) for a new disease, HIV-AIDS. All of these were vertical interventions, funded in part by external donors and operating in their own silos with varying degrees of success.

The immediate political and health systems context was the structural adjustment policies followed by the government, and the resulting policies of liberalisation, privatisation and globalisation of the economy. The rationale for this policy was the fiscal crisis that resulted in part from the huge burden of debt repayments and the conditions that came with funding from international financial institutions, the World Bank and the International Monetary Fund. But there was also an internal change in policy thinking due to the fall of the Soviet Union and Soviet-style socialism and the ascendancy of the neoliberal discourse. Public services were to be kept limited to the minimum essentials, and even these minimal services were to be reformed to allow the play of market forces (Harvey, 2005).

During these years, any new public employment was discouraged, even to replace the aging public health workforce. The Centre was allowed and encouraged to protect its vertical schemes with external donor support (Kumar, 2009), and this external donor support was aggregated into a single consortium led by the World Bank, United States Agency for International Development (USAID) and the UK Department for International Development. Smaller, more responsive donors like Danish International Development Agency (DANIDA) and

Norwegian Agency for Development Cooperation (NORAD) were squeezed out. The external donors directly funded health system reform programs across 11 or more states whose aim was to restrict public health services to a very selective health care package.

A situation developed where the state budgets were adequate only for maintaining existing workforces, leaving little for internal state programs or for strengthening more comprehensive public services. The only programs they could implement were the centrally sponsored national health programs which were then the family planning program, the expanded program for immunization, the child survival and safe motherhood program (later to become Reproductive and Child Health (RCH)-1 implemented from 1997 to 2003) and then the disease control programs for TB, HIV, leprosy, and vector-borne diseases. The Centre could manage to sustain these national programs during the reform years thanks to external aid from the donor consortium. These central programs together addressed about 20 per cent of the entire disease burden, but these became the service package for primary health care, and this remained so in theory and practice until at least 2018.

For NACP-1 (1993–98), the central government negotiated a USD 85 million loan from the World Bank which was provided on the condition that a dedicated division be set up in the Ministry headed by an officer with powers equivalent to those of the secretary. State governments were obliged to set up an equivalent state office, thereby completing the vertical stand-alone design. Though the central financing supported contractual human resources for some newer functions like laboratory and supervision, the basic program of health education, case detection and treatment had to be carried out by regular state department staff. Further, functions like targeting vulnerable groups and social marketing were outsourced, quite often under central guidance. Technical support units were directly supported by the external agencies in Centre and states, and often these were implemented through major non-government, commercial agencies. NACP-3 (2007 to 2012) had a budget of about one billion US dollars.

This pattern was true of the TB, malaria and leprosy programs as well; all of them had technical support units and substantial external funding, and all had state equivalents as well. All of them had supervisory and laboratory staff paid for under the vertical project but the same pool of frontline workers as the other programs, paid for by the state. As the states had stopped recruiting staff post 1993–95, the declining number of staff had to manage an increasing number of vertical programs with their supervisors, their registers and reporting systems and cope with the service delivery requirements of each of them.

One important aspect of all these programs is the choice of program strategy, usually a uniform policy across states based on new technologies and methods that had come into vogue in the preceding decade. Superficially, the appearance of the technology could have determined the vertical nature of the program design, but it could equally be argued that program designs were favoured where technologies could be applied as if they were silver bullets solving the problem irrespective of the context and requiring a centrally managed command and control system for its deployment. Thus, in the Revised National Tuberculosis Control Program, the strategy was the Directly Observed Treatment Shortcourse, better microscopy and the blister packets of drug combinations. For malaria, it was the insecticide-treated bed nets, and for leprosy, it was drug combination therapy.

One further complication was that the RCH programs were under the Ministry of Family Welfare where the role of officers of the Central Health Services were limited and the general administrator dominated. The disease control programs were under the Ministry of Health and therefore more with the Directorate General of Health Services offices at Delhi. The powers of these two parallel ministries played out differently in the states.

In most states, the entire district workforce paid for by the states was absorbed into the centrally sponsored schemes, and within this scheme, the priority was the RCH program. In addition, because both the state health sector reform programs and the RCH programs came with financing conditions on the states, in the midst of the fiscal crisis, states could divert funds from central budgets to fulfil these conditions. Orissa, for example, took funds out of the TB and malaria programs to meet its obligations of 15 per cent contribution to the World Bank-funded Orissa health system development project (Narayana, 2008).

One massive new program in the late 1990s and early 2000s that overwhelmed all the earlier programs and pulled the staff even further from their service delivery was the pulse polio program. In states with the greatest staff deficiency, even immunization and antenatal care could not be completed, and the disease control programs could come to a halt or only be sustained at the cost of hijacking the entire district health system and even the other national disease control programs. Clearly, this effect was much greater in the central and eastern states where health systems were already very weak.

In summary, under the health sector reforms of the 1990s, the federal nature of the health sector was seriously undermined because public health services were limited to the centrally sponsored vertical programs that had been designed by the Centre in consultation with donors but with little or no consultation with states. States had to divert their staff time and resources to these central programs, but state governments could not find the funds or the policy space required to strengthen public services beyond this limited package, leaving it to the private sector to grow and fill this gap, very incompletely and at a considerable increase in societal costs.

Integrating Disease Control Under NHM 2005 and Beyond

The NHM had two important program theories (or theories of change) that contended with each other for dominance. One was that it was a scheme to finance the strengthening of state health systems. The need for such central financing was accepted, but since health was a state subject, states would submit a proposal annually which would be jointly approved. RCH and disease control programs would be integrated into this annual state plan. This approach was in tune with the federal mandate and conceived of federalism as requiring central funds as well as a dialogue between Centre and states on how best it could be spent.

The other program theory was that the vertical RCH and disease control programs would continue as the Centre's only priority. The plan of action for these verticals continued to be part of signed agreements with external funders/development partners and the states had only an implementation role. National Rural Health Mission (NRHM) was only a supplementary funding that went along with the verticals to strengthen health systems to be able to deliver these programs. NRHM funding flowed as five components: RCH, NRHM additionals, immunization, disease control programs and social determinants; this last was just a politically correct articulation, and nothing much happened under it.

The Directorate General's (DG) office and the technical wing under him saw the coming of the NHM with its logic of integrated health system strengthening as a threat. Earlier in the Ministry of Family Welfare, which managed the RCH programs, the technical wing had been marginalised, whereas in the Ministry of Health, which was in charge of the disease control verticals, they continued to have a dominant role. In 2004, just a year before the NHM was launched, the two Ministries were merged again, The NHM structure threatened to limit the DG's powers. In the states, the problem was even more acute because under the NHM, state health societies were established and placed under mission directors who were relatively junior Indian Administrative Service officers. This threatened to marginalise the roles of the Directorates of Health and Family Welfare. The issue of the encroachment of the Centre over state powers was often conflated with the encroachment of the general administrator and their multidisciplinary consultants over the Directorates and the medical leadership.

The final negotiation/understanding that emerged in practice was that the disease control programs that were under the health division and the Directorates would continue as such, and they would collect annual plans for each vertical program from each of the states and fund against that plan. Elaborate forms were sent to each state for them to complete that in effect restricted the space for any decentralised planning. In this period, the Integrated Disease Surveillance Program was also established. Here too, the architecture and every technical detail was centrally defined, though one could argue that in this case, this centralisation was necessary. Each disease control program except the leprosy program set up its own monitoring system, its own digitised monitoring system and its own supervision staff and laboratory requirements.

One development of this period was the substantial number of newer infections brought under the Expanded Child Immunization Program: hepatitis, Rota virus and pneumococcal infections, *Haemophilus influenzae* and injectable polio; among adults, Japanese encephalitis is the leading new vaccination, but only in select states. Once again, all of these were central interventions that depended on technology development and could be delivered vertically. These are imposed upon states without making any additional provision for manpower or the impacts on other programs. Many of these introductions have been questioned, but these are clearly the Centre's prerogative.

State departments on the whole have no quarrel with the verticals; and if the program does not achieve targets, the risk is minimal because accountability is so fragmented, between the Centre and states and between Directorates and NHM. In contrast, states have zero ability to develop programs for communicable disease (TB, HIV, vector-borne diseases and leprosy and the immunization program) outside the national programs. States have considerable infectious disease burdens, including hepatitis, typhoid, persistent cholera, gastro-enteritis, scrub typhus, meningococcal meningitis, other influenzas and many others, but it is unclear how these will be addressed. However, the nation as a whole must remain most concerned about what this fragmentation of authority between the Centre and states means. Other than smallpox and polio, there has been very limited success, and some diseases like TB could have worsened.

One major question in this period is when a disease reduces to a level where it is not a public health problem or priority. At this stage, the Centre would cut back the central financing and call for integrating the vertical program into the state health systems. But a critical question is how this is supposed to happen when the Centre is not investing in strengthening general state health systems. Additionally, as cases come down, interstate and interdistrict variation increases sharply, as does the need for decentralised planning, but the verticals are poorly designed for local innovation to meet changing epidemiological patterns.

The Crisis in Disease Control: Lessons From the Covid-19 Response

In the decade 2012–22, the Union government's priority shifted even further from strengthening the public sector to promoting investment and profitability in the private sector. This in turn led to greater centralisation in regulations, professional education and insurance. When public financing is the Centre's main role, federalism is a question of a Centre–state dialogue over resource allocation: to whom to give and for what. When privatisation becomes the main focus, the focus of Centre–state relationship shifts to regulations. This is best seen in the moves towards centralisation in all professional education and in health insurance.

In this distribution of resources and powers between the Centre and the states, it becomes unclear who has the primary accountability for the control of communicable diseases. States continue to lag in terms of required health system strengthening due to the lack of fiscal space, weak political will and inadequate institutional capacity. Disease control programs continue to have partial NHM funding, but without system strengthening, they fail to make much headway.

It was in this context that the Covid-19 pandemic occurred. The government was initially slow to respond, but when it finally did so in the third week of March 2020, it was a complete response. Under provisions of the National Disaster Management Act, 2005, the Centre took over much of the authority for both law and order and public health, from the states. Under that act, the Union Home Ministry could issue orders that could be seen as transgressing into two important areas in the State List: law and order and public health and sanitation. Control of disease spread across interstate boundaries is, however, already on the Concurrent List, and interstate quarantine is on the Union List.

A nationwide lockdown was announced and then implemented through a direct line to the district magistrates. The Centre took the lead in procuring the test kits, organising the testing laboratories and erecting a nationwide monitoring system. It introduced an app, Arogya Setu, for digitising contact tracing, which it could potentially monitor from Delhi. It issued the protocols for treatment and required compliance. In the first three months, these centrally driven actions were seen as immensely successful.

Three months down the line, as mass migrations and displacement broke out and despite brave assertion of the 'best control in the world' and the 'successful prevention of community transmission', it was clear that the pandemic was spinning out of control, and cases were on the rise everywhere. In the next phase, there was an effort to keep the states more visibly consulted, especially on the increasingly unpopular lock-down decisions. Eventually, this decision was left completely to the states. Relief from the Centre was 'branded' to bring credit to the Centre, whereas the responsibility of the shocks that were imposed was often passed on to the state. The Centre even began reporting on relative state performance, implying that primarily a state responsibility.

States were also uncertain of how to play it; states saw an advantage in being able to shift the accountability to the Centre, but the Centre could hit back. Central control was also a constraint if the state had an innovation that the Centre was reluctant to allow. Comparisons between states were also confusing. Kerala initially claimed dramatic success on a global scale, but as its caseloads continued to be high, it had to scale down the praise, but other states such as Uttar Pradesh and Bihar, where dead bodies were floating down rivers and mass crematoria were seen, would coolly report full control and deny any excess deaths.

Another feature of the Covid-19 response that became apparent very soon was that all preventive care and the vast majority of curative care had to be provided by the public health sector across the states. The Centre had been moving on a reform path that aimed to reposition the government as a strategic purchaser of health care services from the private sector instead of as a provider. But the empanelled private hospitals under Prime Minister Jan Arogya Yojana (PM-JAY) almost completely failed to deliver. Many were shut down and when opened did not offer the insurance cover, or they double billed both patients and the insurers with little benefit to the beneficiary.

Despite the almost unlimited powers conferred by the NDMA, used so rigorously in enforcing lockdowns on the migrant population, when it came to enforcing accountability on the private sector, even to provide the health care services they were empanelled for at the rates negotiated with insurers, they were unable to do so. Price gouging was rampant, and so was denial of even essential health services. Further, both the media and the courts were only holding the public sector accountable. Public-sector health facilities are almost completely under the state government but now are in urgent need of enhancing their infrastructure, human resources and equipment. Central support was patchy, and only the state governments with adequate pre-existing capacity could make the transition.

A good example of how Centre–state relationships played out was the *suo moto* Supreme Court hearings on this matter of Covid-19 response with a focus on vaccine procurement and supply. Initially, the Supreme Court intervened because High Courts in the states were passing orders questioning inadequacies in the pandemic response by state and central governments, and this needed to be curtailed. But when the Centre wanted to pass on the responsibility of vaccine procurement and the accountability for complete immunization against Covid-19 to the states, as well as open vaccination to private markets, the Supreme Court questioned the wisdom of this action.

Initially, some states had been keen on doing so, but soon it became clear to the states that the access to technologies in a global and national market where there were so many supply side constraints and technical capacity requirements could be handled only by the Centre. At the urging of the Supreme Court, the Centre did change its policy and took on the entire burden of vaccine procurement and logistics, ensured that vaccines were available free, while actual field-level vaccine delivery was left to the states. States did manage well, but in the process, almost all frontline staff were shifted to this work with a great setback for all the other state and central government health programs.

Conclusion

In conclusion, most disease control programs in India are effectively on the Concurrent List, but state health systems are on the State List. Since no disease control programs can be implemented without state health systems, there is a fragmentation of accountability in the area of disease control between Centre and states. This fragmentation cannot be wished away. To a large extent, it is a necessary distribution of functions.

The introduction of new technologies and changing global policies drive these programs forwards into new stages of the control program. Both these necessarily require the Centre to play the lead role, for alignment with global policy and for reasons of technical capacity: in technology assessment, patents management, procurement advantages and regulations. Financing is another important reason.

However, program implementation requires the state governments to play a role. Bypassing the state government by direct approaches to district administration and local administrations does not work and is fraught with adverse consequences in the form of disruption of essential health services and of the already weak health systems. Even if the states are consulted, the additional human resources and infrastructure that newer interventions require is seldom factored in. Since public health services are by design meant to be minimalist, leaving the rest of care to the markets, any additional burden or change can be accommodated only with loss to the existing functions. Further, if states have to keep the system in readiness for pandemic emergencies, then in normal times, states should be able to provide universal health care as well have some in-built excess capacity.

The problems of which powers to share and how accountabilities are fixed between Centre and states need both political will and dialogue to shape the design of institutions and schemes. It also requires consultations on resource requirements that states have to come up with, and the consequences to existing services if new programs are introduced without such scaling up of inputs. These would need a legal framework that defines respective roles and the financing provisions required. Federalism requires a constant engagement and dialogue between Centre and states on which are the priorities and how best to address these. There were instances when such dialogue happened, but unfortunately these are too few, and much more needs to be done to institutionalise such dialogue.

References

Banerji, D. (1985). *Health and Family Planning Services in India: An Epidemiological, Socio-Cultural and Political Analysis and a Perspective*. New Delhi: Lokpaksh.

Dutt, A., Akhtar, R., and Dutta, H. (1980). Malaria in India with Particular Reference to Two West Central States. *Social Science and Medicine*, *14D*, 317–330.

Dutta, H., Dutt, A., and Vishnukumari, G. (1979). The Resurgence of Malaria in Tamilnadu: Research Note. *Social Science and Medicine*, *13D*, 191–194.

Fenner, F., Henderson, D., Arita, I., Jezek, Z., and Ladnyi, I. (1988). Chapter 15: India and the Himalayan Area. In Fenner, F., Henderson, D., Arita, I., Jezek, Z., and Ladnyi, I. (Eds.), *Smallpox and Its Eradication* (pp. 711–806). Geneva: World Health Organization.

Government of India. (1951). *The First Five Year Plan*. New Delhi: Planning Commission, GoI.

Government of India. (2016). *National Framework for Malaria Elimination in India (2016–2030)*. Directorate of National Vector Borne Disease Control Programme, DGHS, MoHFW, GoI. New Delhi.

Greenough, P. (1995). Intimidation, Coercion and Resistance in the Final Stages of the South Asian Smallpox Eradication Campaign, 1973–75. *Social Science and Medicine*, *41*(5), 633–645.

Gupta, S. (1985). National TB Programme: Its Development, Concepts, Monitoring and Evaluation Aspects. *Journal of Communicable Disease*, *17*(2), 146–150.

Harvey, D. (2005). *A Brief History of Neoliberalism*. New York: Oxford University Press.

Kotecha, P., and Harpham, T. (1991). Can Leprosy Be Eradicated from India? *Health Policy and Planning*, *6*(1), 82–85.

Kumar, G. (2009). Introduction: Health Sector Reforms in India-Issues, Experiences and Trends. In Kumar, G. (Ed.), *Health Sector Reforms in India* (pp. 13–44). Manohar Publishers.

Nagpaul, D. (1989). India's National Tuberculosis Programme: An Overview. *Indian Journal of Tuberculosis*, *36*, 205–211.

Narayana, D. (2008). Adjustment and Health Sector Reforms: the Solution to Low Public Spending on Health Care in India? In Haddad, S., Bariş, E., and Narayana, D. (Eds.), *Safeguarding the Health Sector in Times of Macroeconomic Instability: Policy Lessons for Low- and Middle-Income Countries* (pp. 159–198). International Development Research Centre (IDRC), Canada.

NTI. (1994). *National Tuberculosis Programme in India: Yearbook 1992–93*. NTI, GoI, Bangalore.

Piot, M. (1962). Outline of a District Tuberculosis Programme. *Indian Journal of Tuberculosis*, *9*, 151–156.

Sivaraman, S. (1982). Tuberculosis in India: The Prospect. *Indian Journal of Tuberculosis*, *29*, 71–85.

WHO. (1976). *Malaria Control: Resurgence of Malaria in the South-East Asia Region: A Critical Review of the Programme in India* (Paper presented by the Government of India): Regional Committee Twenty-ninth Session Supplementary Agenda item 1, SM/RC29/11. https://apps.who.int/iris/bitstream/handle/10665/129962/sea_rc29_11.pdf, accessed 7.4.2022.

14 Surviving Covid-19 in a General Ward of a Public Hospital

A Personal Narrative

Harsh Mander

As we survive the third year of the pandemic, there is sobering admission by scientists that humankind will have to learn to continue to live with Covid-19 for the foreseeable future. I write here an account about my own personal experience in a general ward of a leading public hospital with the Covid infection, something that I struggled to do for a year after it happened, that was one of the most difficult periods of recurrent health crises in my life. I write with some hesitation. The monumental scale of suffering of literally millions of my countrywomen and men makes my own experience inconsequential by comparison. But I still do so write, if only as a direct witness to the disgraceful collapse of even elementary care and everyday humanism that I encountered in the general ward of what is widely considered the finest public hospital in the country.

I had expected to catch the Covid contagion much earlier. The eruption of mass hunger into which homeless people and urban poor people in general had been thrust overnight compelled me to descend to the streets of the city I live in, Delhi, from the second day of the first lockdown. I knew, from two decades of work among them, that there are two tenuously fragile strings that alone lift homeless people from hunger every day of their rough lives. One of these is the lowest-end, most casual, most exploitatively reimbursed, most uncertain and most unsafe employment that is unreliably available to them to help fill their bellies each day. If this employment at dirt wages does not come their way, their other social security is from religious food charities, in gurudwaras, dargahs, temples and churches in some cities (not in Delhi, I found). The punishing lockdown announced in March 2020 with four hours' notice by the Prime Minister peremptorily and mercilessly snapped both these feeble but still life-saving strings overnight. As I described at length in my book *Locking Down the Poor* (Mander, 2021),[1] this unleashed a flood of mass hunger in cities on a scale that I have not witnessed in my lifetime.

There was therefore no question: I had to be on the streets, trying to organise food (with dignity and care) to homeless persons; and the survivors of the Delhi riots of a few months earlier. So there I was, on the streets, from the second day of the lockdown, helping in a small way in distributing cooked

DOI: 10.4324/9781003568711-18

food and ration kits to homeless people who had become like sisters and brothers over the decades of our work together. I caution my reader- this was not a particularly heroic decision: it was an imperative of the heart; I could not do anything else. It was not food charity, it was food solidarity.

And I was not alone in this resolve: many of my young colleagues made the same choice and spent the next months of their lives immersed tirelessly and feverishly in organising food for those thrown by their governments and their employers so thoughtlessly and casually, indeed cruelly into mass hunger. They were answering distress calls, managing donations that poured in from every corner, making food purchases, assembling thousands of ration kits, organizing buses for migrants to return to their homes in safety, protecting homeless people in the shelters we manage, petitioning the courts and reporting the stories.

My young colleagues were aware of the risks they were taking, but for them too there was no choice. Embedded in my heart are the words of one young colleague when I asked him, 'Are you not frightened?' He replied, 'Yes, I am frightened. But much greater than my fear is their hunger. So I have to be on the streets'. Each made arrangements to try to protect their families. Some moved into the office and some into the homeless shelters for the entire duration of the lockdown. I moved into a separate bedroom of my house and stopped seeing in person my ageing father and mother-in-law. My colleagues who worked with lynching survivors and homeless people around the country pitched in heroically – in Jharkhand, Bihar, Assam, coastal Karnataka, Mewat, Western Uttar Pradesh, Madhya Pradesh, Bengal and the cities of Jaipur, Patna and Hyderabad. Together my friends distributed ten million meals.

I had quietly bargained with myself to catch the contagion early. But the virus did not come to me. My epidemiologist friends later explained that we were ironically interacting with the safest populations in these early months because the virus was carried into India mainly by the rich and middle classes who could afford international air tickets. The destitute homeless were safe because they had no occasion to interact or mingle with the middle classes. It was only after the lockdown ceased and the classes began to mix again that the virus spread to the bodies of the poorest denizens of the city.

Dismayed by how total was the denial of testing, quarantine, isolation and treatment of the homeless and the labouring poor, we decided to open our own Covid-19 centre for the homeless, in our homeless shelter on the banks of the Yamuna River in Delhi and then on the streets in homeless habitations elsewhere. It was in the course of this work that, during the second wave, we lost one of the most selfless and devoted doctors I have had the privilege of knowing, Dr Pradeep Bijalwan, to whom I paid tearful tribute in www.theindiaforum.in/sites/default/files/pdf/2021/05/07/dr-pradip-bijalwan-an-unsung-journey-for-an-equal-world.pdf. It was also in this clinic, weeks after we first opened it with Médecins Sans Frontiers in our homeless shelter that I caught the coronavirus, along with many of my colleagues.

This was some time during the month of October 2020. Everyone in our household also tested positive: my wife, my mother-in-law and our domestic helpers. As a precaution, we employed a live-in home nurse for my mother-in-law. Our symptoms were not worrying, but I have a congenital heart valve defect, and there was a worry that this might render me more vulnerable to complications. I was anxious not to become a problem to my family if my health declined, so I accepted the advice of doctor friends to check into a hospital.

I need to explain why I chose the general ward of a public hospital. I do have health insurance; in fact, we bought health (and life) insurance paid from the office for all staff as they were putting their health and lives at risk. I could have easily checked into a private hospital; beds were available at that time, and it is not as though I have in the past not used the services of private hospitals: I had on two recent occasions checked into one of the less-ostentatious private hospitals for some minor surgeries. But this moment was different. I was reading, alternating between anguish and wrath, of union ministers, chief ministers and health ministers of states, all almost without exception admitting themselves after testing positive for Covid into the most expensive private hospitals of their cities. The rage was because they clearly had no faith in the public services they were responsible for building and managing; the anguish was that they had no qualms about abandoning the poor who could not afford to enter the gates of a private hospital to these services.

I therefore decided that when Covid got to me, I would only go to a public hospital. But then the question rose: where within a public hospital? I had friends in the union health ministry from my years in the IAS, including my trainees. A phone call would have been enough at that time to get a single private room in AIIMS or Safdarjang Hospital. However, that seemed to be a cop-out because I would use my privilege to simply escape the fate of millions of my countrywomen and men in this time of the greatest health emergency of the century. So I made my decision: I would check myself into the general Covid ward of a public hospital.

My daughter, who had recovered from Covid a month earlier, drove me to the hospital. The formalities took some time. I was then asked to walk into an ambulance with some other patients. My daughter was not allowed to travel with me beyond this point. We hugged, and from the ambulance, I waved. From here on, I was on my own.

Another patient and I were driven through the traffic for some minutes to the designated Covid centre of the hospital, lodged in an entirely separate building on the opposite side of the highway. We were shown to the lift. I had carried with me a book to read, a toothbrush and paste and my phone. The lift took us to the top floor. I walked into a general ward with around 50 beds. Most of them were occupied.

I was uncertain about what I was expected to do. I looked around for a nurse. She said, 'Find an empty bed and lie down there'. I was confused:

'Won't you give me some hospital clothes to wear', I asked her. 'We don't have any', she replied brusquely. 'Find a bed, and lie down in the clothes that you are wearing'.

A little bemused, I did as I was told. I then began to size up my situation. What hit me first was the high-decibel piercing noise levels that incessantly pervaded the ward 24/7, never relenting, which became one dominant memory of the days and nights that followed. Even past midnight, the noise would not cease. One part of the clamour was of the voices of the nurses and ward boys who seemed always to shout at each other, at any time of the day or night, The second was the screams of the monitors. The monitor attached to my bed was also gutsy in its wailing; the only catch was that it was not connected to me. This meant that no one was checking my vitals. At home, at least we had an oximeter that helped monitor our oxygen levels. Here in the hospital, it was apparent that even if my oxygen levels plummeted, no one would be the wiser. And then, there was the piteous wailing of patients. At any point of time, I counted at least half a dozen patients who were convinced that they were about to die. But no family was allowed at their bedside, and none of the ward staff tried to counsel or comfort them in any way.

Between the bedlam and the hopeless grief of the wails, I tried to sleep, but this became difficult even late into the night. I thought I would chat with the ward boys, whose faces of course I could not see. They all looked like spacemen, but it was apparent that they were young men. As one spoke to me, I learnt to my shock that most of them were untrained. 'The regular ward boys of the hospital refused to work in the Covid ward', he said. 'Before the lockdown, I was a room boy in a hotel. The hotel retrenched us. My family was starving. The hospital offered work to anyone willing to work in a covid ward. I was terrified. But when you see hunger in your home, tell me what choice do you have?'

No doctor came once to see us even once in the days that I spent in the ward. And I was trapped: I now did not have the option to leave. Some days passed, maybe two, I cannot remember clearly. I begged the staff: 'You don't have clothes for me, but I am feeling sweaty and dirty. Can I at least have a bath?' After some confabulations and some more pleading, they agreed. They led me to a bathroom. This much I remember. After this, I lost my memory entirely for around ten days.

I picked up the details of some of what followed from my wife and daughter later. My wife was worried because I stopped answering my phone. She called the nurses: they said I was okay, but maybe I had slipped into a depression. My wife was very sceptical; even if I had just slipped into depression, she said, which was unlikely, I would not just suddenly just switch off, stop speaking altogether. I had after all spoken to her at length just a couple of hours earlier. But the nurses were insistent: I was okay, my Covid was under control, I maybe was in depression but there was nothing to worry about.

After another day, my wife put her foot down. She decided to insist on my discharge. It was a decision that probably saved my life. The hospital staff said it was unorthodox to let someone go who is still testing positive for Covid, but they were willing to let me go. My discharge slip reported nothing untoward.

I am told that back at home, I could not recognize my wife and daughter. When asked, I apparently said that they were nurses! I would not speak or eat, complaining all the time of a headache and nausea. A couple of more days passed when blue marks appeared on my forehead. My family and friends conferred and decided that this was possibly something serious. They took me to another hospital, where they conducted many tests. They then grimly spoke to my wife and daughter. It is not Covid. They didn't know how, but I had developed very serious brain injuries, and there was heavy bleeding in the cranium. The public hospital earlier had recommended that I take aspirin, which had further stimulated bleeding in my brain. All of this was imminently life-threatening. I would probably need immediate surgery if my life was to be saved. But that hospital did not have the expertise for this. I needed to be taken to yet another hospital.

Family and friends zeroed in on a hospital in Gurugram that was covered with my CGHS card (as I am a retired civil servant). The young neurologist took me in, and after another battery of tests, said he would like to try a few days with medicines, not surgery. I went into another Covid-19 ICU, even larger than the Covid ward in the public hospital.

It took a few more days for my memory to return, bit by bit. I recall first the vivid hallucinations. I imagined that I was cured of Covid and that people who loved me were happy and wanted me with them. In my hallucinations, I chose to first visit the people who had been released from the detention centres in Assam after our intervention in the Supreme Court. I still can recall vividly the faces of the people, the children prancing around and my conversations with them, as if all of this was real. Slowly, a part of my mind recognized that I was still in a Covid ward. I was not even permitted to go to the bathroom. How could I have travelled all the way to Assam? I struggled to take a hold of myself, and from then my memory was slowly restored.

More tragedy was in store after I returned home. My father, nearly 95 years old, was intensely, inextricably tied to me. Every day, wherever I was, I must speak to him. After Covid, he had got used to meeting me on Skype. For many years, our mutual routine had been that a day would not pass without my speaking to him. And now, ten days had passed, and I had not talked to him. He was convinced that some great harm had fallen on me. In his worry, he had a stroke, and in hours passed away. Heartbroken with the news, I pulled myself out of bed and organized his funeral, difficult in Covid times.

In the coming months, friends insisted that I meet a succession of leading neurologists. They all looked at my scans and said that how my brain was so severely injured was a mystery, more so because the hospital insisted that nothing at all had happened to me, and I had no external injuries. The doctors also all agreed that my survival, and eventual healing without changes in my personality, were nothing less than a miracle. A little longer in the public hospital, and the bleeding in my brain would surely have led to my death.

The story did not end there. My health improved a little, and I insisted on returning to the people I worked with. The crisis in their lives was too acute for me to stay away. I was back on the streets and in the shelters, and I travelled to Assam, Mewat, Western UP, Hyderabad and Bangalore. But I fell sick again, this time with raging undiagnosed fevers. I was in hospital once more, and in some time, my entire body broke out in red rashes; the doctors diagnosed one of my fevers to be adult measles.

Again after my discharge, I returned once more to my work and travels. One more time, I suddenly started losing weight with alarming rapidity, eight kilos in two weeks. I could also barely breathe or swallow. Another hospital, another battery of tests to rule out cancer and TB. The diagnosis this time was that a fungus had almost completely colonised my lungs, probably from steroids when I was being treated for my brain injury. Strong medicines and some hill air in our cottage near Bhimtaal, with my family including my three-year-old grandson, again restored me slowly back to health.

At the time I write this, I realise that my body is still ravaged, I am still to regain the fitness I had taken for granted all my adult life. Through all of this, I am also battling wild charges against me by the government, including insurrection, hate-mongering and high financial crime. I remained determined to continue to speak out against the savaging of the constitution and of freedoms, justice and fraternity. My body will take time to be restored, I realise that. But I am determined that I will not allow my voice, my spirit, my solidarity and my love – for whatever these are worth – to be vanquished by the virus, and far more dangerously by an uncaring, malign state.

As I said, I have struggled to write this dire eyewitness account for over a year. Its troubling reminders continue to haunt my memory and my conscience, of what the public good of health care had been reduced to in India, of the hell people who could not afford the extortions of for-private health care had been thrown into. And of the wages of electing a state led by people who are singularly, pathologically bereft of compassion. I still felt that however difficult, I must create this personal record for one reason, the hope that we will not allow this to ever happen to our people again.

Note

1 H. Mander (2021), *Locking Down the Poor: The Pandemic and India's Moral Centre*, Speaking Tiger, Delhi.

15 Centre–State Fiscal Relationship in Light of the National Health Mission

Is Centralisation the Answer?

Indranil

Introduction

Health care is commonly seen as a state subject in India, but in India's federal structure, roles and responsibilities are spread across the three levels of governance. Functional responsibilities across the Union, states and local bodies are outlined in the Seventh Schedule of the Indian Constitution. Major responsibilities of creating, maintaining and managing health institutions rest with the states (State List). Union and states jointly provide public health services and take care of medical education (Concurrent List). The Union's role on aspects such as family planning, health policymaking and research has been through Concurrent List. As per 73rd and 74th Constitutional Amendments local bodies are supposed to play critical roles in provision of preventive and public health services.

However, over the years, these constitutional boundaries have been blurred, and the Union government has played a greater role in areas which were perceived to be primarily state responsibilities. When the Reproductive Child Health II program gave way to National Rural Health Mission in 2005, the Union government started directly intervening into domains of health care delivery. One may interpret this as an expansion of the family welfare agenda, a Concurrent List subject. However, the government-funded health insurance schemes like Rashtriya Swasthya Beema Yojana (RSBY) and the recently introduced Prime Minister's Jan Aarogya Yojana (PMJAY) clearly operate into core areas of the State List: health care and hospital services. Recently, the Fifteenth Finance Commission-appointed High Level Group on Health Sector recommended that public health and hospitals be brought under the concurrent list under the Seventh Schedule (Finance Commission, 2019). In some way, these attempts to centralise health care policymaking and implementation intend to address issues of horizontal inequity on important national priorities. The first one decade of neoliberal reforms had clearly widened the interstate disparities in health in India. To what extent centrally sponsored schemes like National Health Mission (NHM) have succeeded in bringing in horizontal equity in public financing of health care remains an important question this chapter attempts to address.

DOI: 10.4324/9781003568711-19

India's health system is typically characterised by fragmented financing mechanisms, where people largely pay from their pocket to meet health care needs. As a result, inequities and inordinate delays in access to care, avoidable mortality, poor quality of care, dissaving, indebtedness and immiseration become part of usual household expense associated with illness (Berman et al., 2010; Ghosh, 2011). The neoliberal answer to a fragmented health system is withdrawing states from direct provisioning and introducing various purchasing arrangements using pooled resources to bring multiple disjointed private health providers into a centralised system.

The idea is that through large pools, subsidised demand and standardised care packages, issues of inequities of access and market failures would be taken care of adequately without altering the foundations of a profit-driven system. Here centralisation of financing through creation of larger pools and thus benefiting from economies of scale becomes crucial to ensure sustainability. Schemes like PMJAY or its earlier avatars like RSBY are essentially based on such delusional ideas of marriage between private greed and social need. As the US experiences (Clark & Richman 2006) with Medicare and Medicaid suggest, publicly financed, privately provided and private voluntary insurance-mediated models not only fail to address the large-scale exclusions but also lead to monopolisation of care provisioning, increasing the bargaining power of insurance agencies and provider networks. Thus, the gains from centralisation of financing remain temporary while bringing out irreversible consolidation of power and profit.

An integrated health system, as some of the advanced European country experiments suggest, needs a judicious mix of centralisation of certain functions and utmost decentralisation of some others. This understanding evolved over centuries of dealing with epidemics and public health emergencies on the one hand and political and economic transformations on the other. Division of roles and responsibilities between Union, state and local bodies, as enshrined under the Indian Constitution, was not only in line with federal political structure, it reflected some health system thinking adopted in the developed world, particularly the UK. However, there have always been efforts to undermine principles of federalism and intrusion by the Union government into roles assigned to states. Such attempts often stemmed from systemic deficiencies on the part of the states, but also were triggered by political overdrive to control states. The ideas of selective primary level care, fiscal conservatism and the squeeze of public investment, as part of neoliberal health sector reforms, contributed to centralisation and fragmentation at the same time while weakening the capacity of states and local bodies considerably to plan and deliver quality care (Qadeer, 2001).

In the 1990s, health sector reforms were introduced with the stated objective of bringing in more efficiency in financing; greater prioritisation of public health and primary care; equity in access and distribution of public subsidy and improving financial protection for the poor. Several authors have pointed out that stabilisation policies have led to considerable decline in government spending on social sector in general and health in particular (Tulasidhar, 1993; Dev and Mooij, 2002; Duggal, 1995; Reddy and Selvaraju, 1994). Studies conducted during the 1990s showed that in order to manage its fiscal deficit, the Union government resorted mainly to expenditure compression. Public expenditure as a percent of GDP fell sharply during the 1990s (Dev and Mooij, 2002; Tulasidhar, 1993; Mukhopadhyay, 2012). This resulted in a decline in combined social sector expenditures of Centre and state (as percentage of the GDP) during the early 1990s, and consequently health expenditure also declined.

One immediate impact of the squeeze in spending was observed in the decline in capital expenditure, which stagnated the expansion of health facilities and upgradation of existing infrastructure. The share of medical and public health within the health budget shrank, and thus maintenance and development of medical care services suffered. Public health programs which are preventive in nature received more severe contraction due to cuts in central transfer (Tulasidhar, 1993).

Salaries were taking up an increasing proportion of total expenditure. In a situation of expenditure contraction, items which are sacrificed, the earliest are those where spending decisions are discretionary. Thus, maintenance expenditure and spending on drugs and other consumables are initially squeezed (Tulasidhar, 1993; Mukhopadhyay, 2012). Medical care facilities which are largely financed and run by state governments suffered considerable deterioration, affecting the urban poor specifically (Duggal, 1995). At the same time, secondary health care facilities, which are mostly located in rural and semi-urban areas, have received lower shares and lacked basic amenities (Varatharajan et al., 2004). Reduced quality of secondary care in government hospitals led to increased dependence on the private sector. Cutbacks in drug spending and consequent unavailability of medicines in public facilities forced people to purchase increasing shares of prescription drugs from the private sector (Duggal, 1995). Further, freezes in recruitments in the public sector during the 1990s led to huge vacancies, especially affecting facilities serving rural areas (Varatharajan et al., 2004).

The National Health Mission was initially conceptualized to introduce bottom-up planning and flexibility of financing with the objective to develop state- and district-level capacities of planning and prioritising. However, some of the initial gains were compromised during the later years as bottom-up planning processes were undermined and budgets were cut, particularly since 2014. Introduction of PMJAY and National Health Authority, which bypasses all legislative scrutiny, are also attempts at centralisation. The Fifteenth Finance Commission-appointed High Level Working Group of Health calls for bringing public health and hospitals into the Concurrent List, highlighting the diversities of health achievements or lack of it among states.

On the other hand, there is growing evidence of gross inefficiencies in Union government procurement of TB and HIV medicines and family planning material stemming largely from diseconomies of scale and inadequate understanding of diverse realities of states. Regional differences in social sector service delivery could be reduced through regional policies or intergovernmental transfers. Intergovernmental transfers allow better state autonomy while regional policies help focus attention on some common national goals. In a vast and diverse federation like India, devising policies to suit differing needs of various sections of the population always remains a challenge, and thus intergovernmental transfers are preferred (Rao, 2016).

It has to be also noted that since 2014, a series of policy measures have been introduced in the country which had consequences for financing public services and health and lives of people, including introduction of the Goods and Services Tax (GST), demonetisation, abolition of the Planning Commission, and plan and non-plan distinction in central transfer and greater share of divisible pool of resources devolved to states through Fourteenth Finance Commission recommendation.

One of the key questions that this chapter attempts to respond to is related to the role of NHM in state finances, particularly whether NHM succeeded in reducing horizontal (interstate) inequities in public financing. We would also like to assess the effect of Centre dependency of states on resource allocations towards health services.

Material and Methods

The study for this chapter deals with the trends and patterns in public spending on health. Several sources have been used to collate public spending on health care data by state and Union governments:

- *State Finances: A Study of Budgets*; RBI (Reserve Bank of India, 2020)
- Expenditure budget, Vol I & II, Union government, various years
- Finances accounts; Various years, various state governments, Comptroller and Auditor General
- *Handbook of Indian Economy*; RBI
- National Health Mission; MIS; Quarterly Progress Report;
- *Finance Management Report*, NHM, various states
- Detailed demand for grants, various state governments

We spell out our methods used to arrive at specific outputs in the results sections and provide our sources for graphs and tables. We used MS Excel and Stata-14 to analyse the results and produce graphs and figures.

We classified states into high-focused large, non-high-focused large and North-East according to the definition used in the NRHM framework. We analysed state-level data for a period of two decades starting from 2000–01 to 2020–21. The period from 2000–01 to 2004–05 is defined as pre-NRHM and from 2005–06 to 2020–21 is post-NRHM. However, we have divided the post-NHM period into two phases: 2005–06 to 2013–14 and 2014–15 onwards.

Changing Fiscal Architecture and Flow of Funds Under the NHM

Even though public spending accounts for less than a quarter of the total health spending in India, governments have a major role in terms of planning, regulating and shaping the delivery of health services. However, the fiscal roles and responsibilities regarding various aspects of health and health care are spread across all three levels of governance: Union, states and local bodies.

As laid out in the Constitution, the major responsibilities for creating, maintaining and managing heath institutions rest with the states (State List), including public health and sanitation, hospitals and dispensaries, and water.[1] The Union's role was initially limited to family planning, health policy making and research, and the Union and states jointly provide public health services and take care of medical education (Concurrent List). Local bodies play critical roles in providing preventive and public health services.

However, over the years, these constitutional boundaries have been blurred, and the Union government has intervened in aspects where states are supposed to play key roles, often to ensure appropriate emphasis on horizontal equity in key health goals. The fiscal stance of subnational state governments in general has attained enormous focus in most public debates since the latter half of the 1980s, when states started experiencing serious fiscal imbalances (Sen and Dash, 2013). This might have led the Indian Finance Commission (FC) to recommend state-level fiscal reforms such as the rule-based framework to enact fiscal responsibility and budgetary management.

The central government, however, has a strong influence on state government expenditures via its fiscal transfers. The involvement of the central government in states' health budgets used to be confined to family planning and certain centrally sponsored disease control programmes. Beyond these, the Centre's expenditures consist of medical care in centrally administered territories, medical research and medical education in centrally funded institutions and insurance schemes for its employees. Family planning and centrally sponsored vertical programs are also administered by the states, and money is spent either through their budgets or through the different autonomous societies. Funds routed through these societies were not reflected in state budgets. This phenomenon of funds transfer through societies started in the early 2000s and different societies were formed for different Centrally Sponsored Schemes (CSS).

However, since the introduction of National Rural Health Mission (NRHM) different societies had been merged to form the State Health Societies (SHS) (GoI, 2005). NRHM funds from the Centre were directly transferred to these societies and thus do not appear in the state budgets, but the funding comes either fully or partially through matching grants from the central government. The Centre's allocation of funds to the CSS (see Figure 15.1) in different states is guided by their need, ability to absorb grants and spend them efficiently on the purposes for which they are intended and the capacity

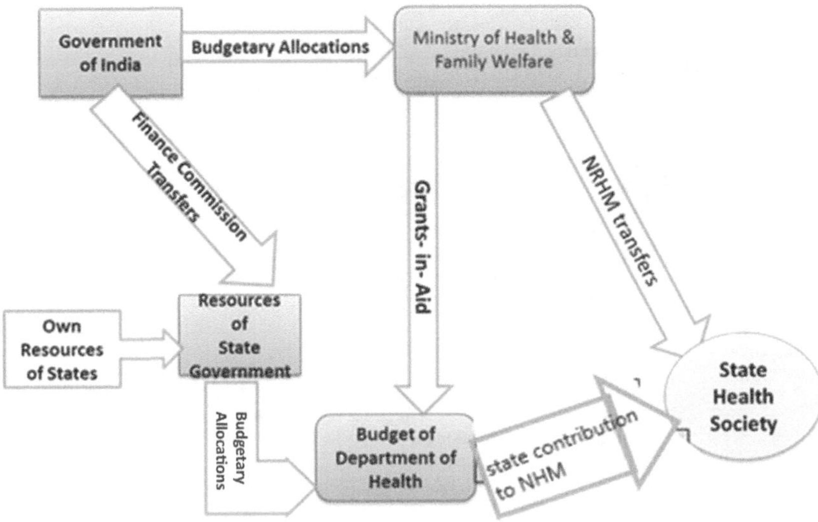

Figure 15.1 Flows of funds from Union to state governments under NHM (2005–06 to 2013–14).

and willingness to provide matching funds in the case of matching grants schemes. The share of the central government expenditure on health, including grant-in-aid to states, constitutes over a third of the combined expenditure by the states and the Centre.

From 2014–15, we observe some concrete changes in fiscal architecture. The practice of transferring funds directly to SHS have been abandoned since then; instead NHM funds are being devolved to state treasury which in turn transfer funds to SHS. Figure 15.2 displays the funds flows from the Union to states from 2014–15 onwards.

The Fourteenth Finance Commission (XIV FC) recommended considerable changes in how tax resources would be shared between Union and state governments. It recommends that the practice of plan devolution through centrally sponsored schemes be reduced and a greater share of general purpose grants be devolved to states. This essentially implies that funds devolved through the NHM would be cut while states will have greater access to tax resources. In the third section of this chapter, we study the implications of these changes for investments in health.

Trends in Union and State Government Spending on Health

In this section, we compare the trends in public spending by the Union and state governments. The years preceding the introduction of NRHM experienced stagnant public spending by both state and Union governments. As depicted in Figure 15.3; real per capita state government spending declined

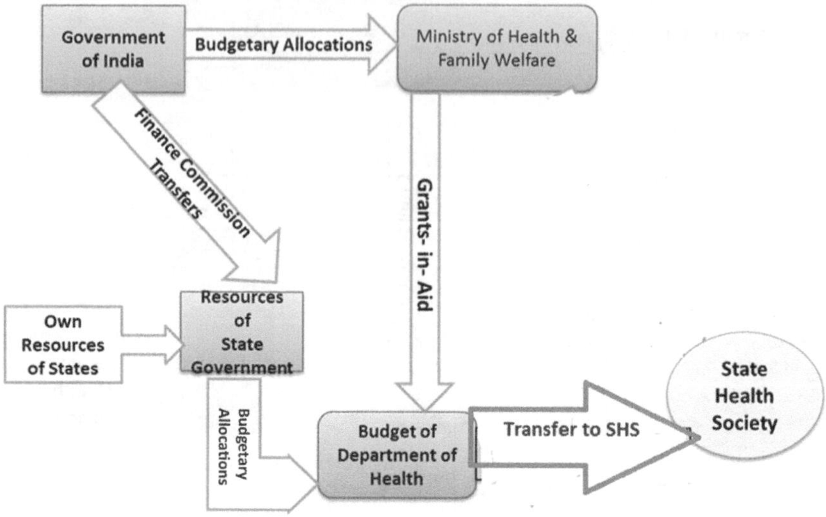

Figure 15.2 Flow of funds from Union to state government under NHM (2014–15 onwards).

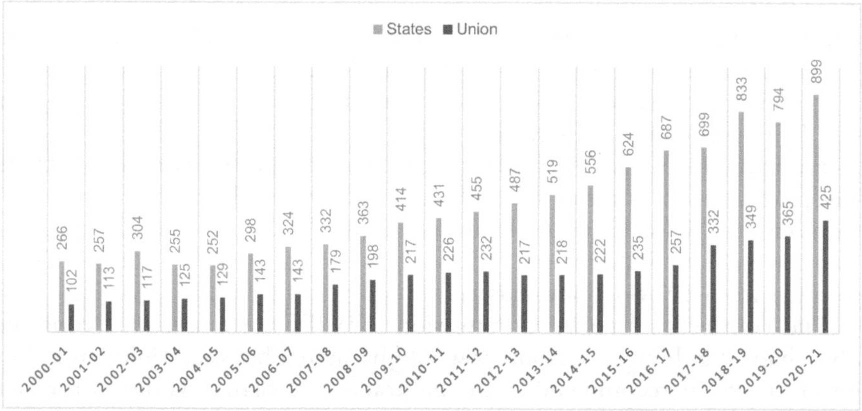

Figure 15.3 Per capita public spending on health by Union and state governments (constant prices).

Source: Public spending by states: State Government Finances; RBI; Union government spending from Indiabudget.gov.in.

between 2000–01 and 2004–05. However, we see steady growth in per capita spending by states in the subsequent period. Union government spending also grew steadily in the initial years of NRHM from 2005–06 (INR 143) to 2011–12 (INR 232). However, in the subsequent period, we see virtual stagnation until 2015–16. In fact, per capita spending by the Union government in 2015–16 was INR 235, just three rupees more than spending four years earlier.

The percentage of GSDP public spending on health by state governments increased steadily between 2004–05 and 2020–21. In fact, state spending nearly doubled as the percentage of GDP went from 0.49 per cent in 2004–05 to 0.89 per cent in 2020–21. However, Union government spending declined from 0.32 per cent in 2009–10 to 0.23 per cent in 2015–16. Although we observe some increase since then, by 2019–20 it was only 0.32 per cent, the level achieved in 2009–10. Figure 15.4 shows that both state and Union government spending increased suddenly in 2020–21, mostly because of the lockdown-induced shrinkage of GDP and the diversion of public resources to meet the health care challenges during the Covid-19 pandemic.

In terms of growth in state and Union government spending, the period since 2015–16 seems most productive. For the entire period since the introduction of NHM, state government expenditures increased by almost 9 per cent at compound annual average growth rate, while the Union government showed around 7.6 per cent growth during the same period (Figure 15.5). It is important to note that during the 2009–10 to 2014–15 period, Union government expenditures declined in real terms (-0.84), while states experienced steady growth. The sharpest cuts in Union spending took place during 2014–15 and 2015–16, the first two years of the NDA government. Given that there was a low base to start with, we see very high growth in Union expenses on health subsequently.

The Union government transfers funds to the state through various CSS like the NHM. The introduction of NRHM increased resources transferred by the Union government to states from 47 per cent of its own budget in 2004–05 to 86.5 per cent in 2007–08 (Figure 15.6). In the subsequent period, the share of transfers to states hovered around 75 per cent of total spending by the Union

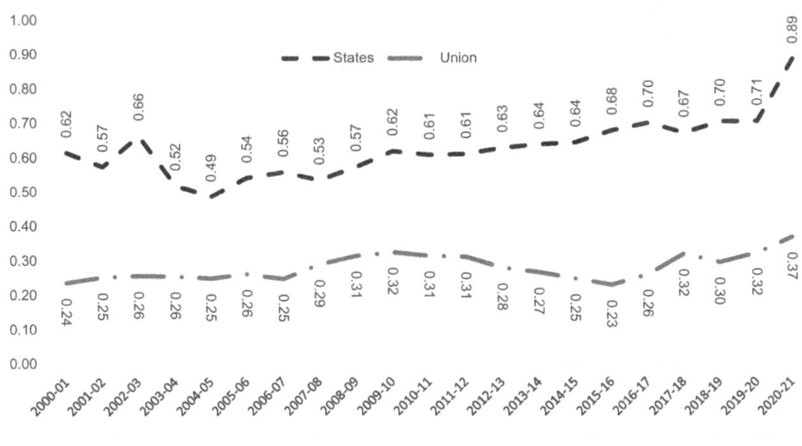

Figure 15.4 Public spending on health by Union and states as percentages of GDP.

Source: Public spending by states: State Government Finances; RBI; Union government spending from Indiabudget.gov.in; Expenditure budget vol 1 & 2, various years. Central transfers were adjusted from state budget; GDP numbers are from *State of the Economy* reports by RBI.

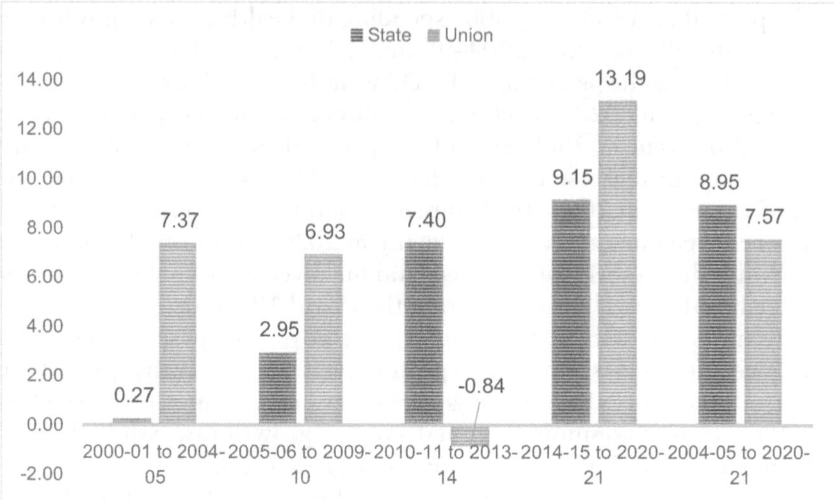

Figure 15.5 Real growth in public spending on heath by Union and states.

Source: Same as Figure 15.3.

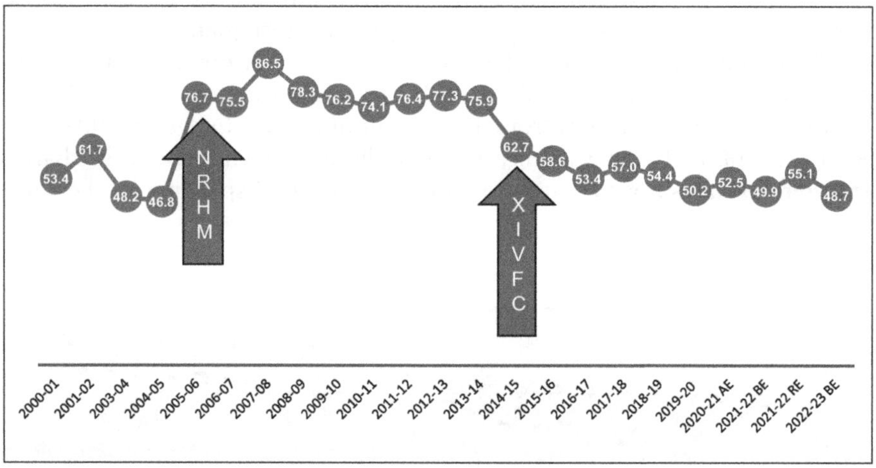

Figure 15.6 Share of transfers to states and UTs in total Union spending on health (%).

Source: Union government spending from Indiabudget.gov.in; Expenditure budget vol. 1& 2, various years. Central transfers to states have been captured from GoI: Demand for grants; major heads; Expenditure Budget vol. 1.

government (Figure 15.6). As discussed earlier, the XIV FC brought about considerable changes in the Union–state relationship, with reduced emphasis on CSS and greater devolution through untied grants under the FC. As a result, since 2014–15, devolution to states as share of total public spending on health has gone down considerably and reached below 50 per cent in the later years.

There remain considerable variations across states in shares of GDP going to public spending on health (Figure 15.7). While there are states that spend more than 2 per cent of GSDP on health, the majority spend less than 1 per cent of GDP (Table 15.1). Since 2011–12, median spending by states as percentage of GSDP has declined, depicting that only a few states are pulling up the aggregate spending as percentage of GSDP; in most states, health expenditures did not increase adequately. During the initial period of NRHM, the standard deviation in health spending as percentage of GSDP increased (Table 15.1), while in the subsequent period we observe that SD gradually declined. To better understand the trends, we need to look into interstate variations in spending, which we do next.

We have divided the period between 2000–01 and 2018–19 into four phases: 2000–01 to 2004–05 is the pre-NRHM period; the initial phase of NHM is 2005–06 to 2009–10, and then the consolidation phase between 2010–11 and 2013–14; the post-XIV Finance Commission period is after 2014–15. We observe that compared with pre-NRHM, public spending grew much faster during the various phases of NRHM/NHM (Figure 15.8a). However, growth experienced by the non-high-focus states and North-East states outstripped growth in high-focus large states (Figure 15.8b).

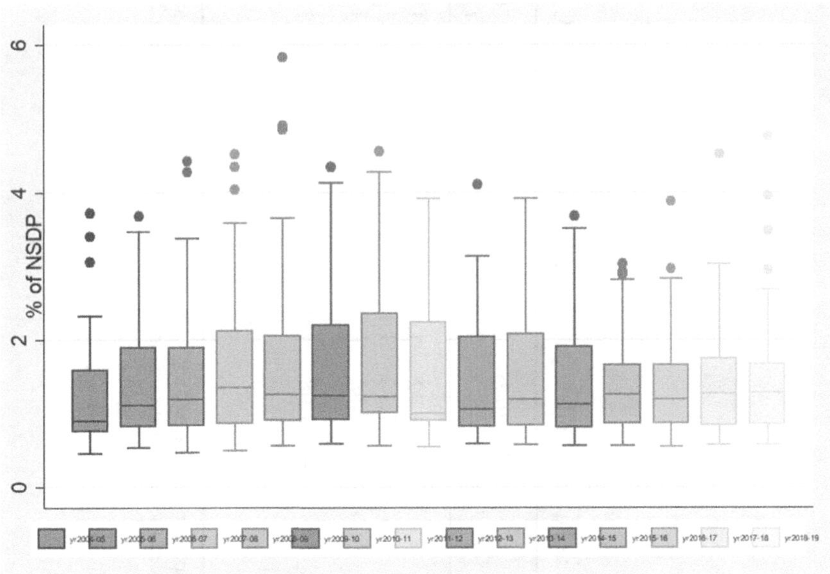

Figure 15.7 Public spending on health as percentage of GSDP (all states).

Source: Public spending by states: State Government Finances; RBI; GSDP at current market prices have been obtained from the RBI data; GDP/GSDP deflators have been used to convert nominal figures to constant prices, using 2011–12 as base year.

Table 15.1 State Public Spending on Health as Percentage of GSDP

	2004–05	2005–06	2006–07	2007–08	2008–09	2009–10	2010–11	2011–12	2012–13	2013–14	2014–15	2015–16	2016–17	2017–18	2018–19
mean	1.28	1.42	1.55	1.68	1.79	1.64	1.75	1.56	1.54	1.53	1.47	1.44	1.47	1.53	1.58
median	0.89	1.1	1.18	1.34	1.25	1.235	1.22	1	1.05	1.19	1.12	1.25	1.19	1.27	1.28
standard deviation	0.86	0.84	1.05	1.18	1.38	1.04	1.10	1.01	0.94	0.92	0.90	0.79	0.85	0.94	1.06
inter quartile range	0.84	1.08	1.07	1.27	1.16	1.29	1.36	1.35	1.23	1.24	1.1	0.8	0.8	0.91	0.82
coefficient of variation	0.68	0.59	0.68	0.70	0.77	0.79	0.63	0.65	0.61	0.60	0.61	0.55	0.58	0.62	0.67

Source: Public spending by states: State Government Finances; RBI; GSDP at current market prices have been obtained from the RBI data; GDP/GSDP deflators have been used to convert nominal figures to constant prices, using 2011–12 as base year.

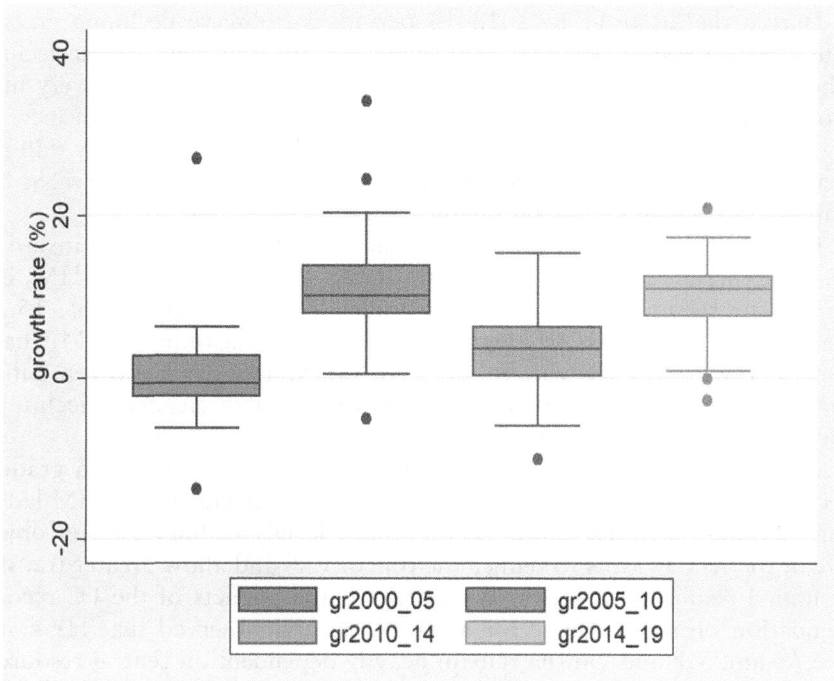

(a)

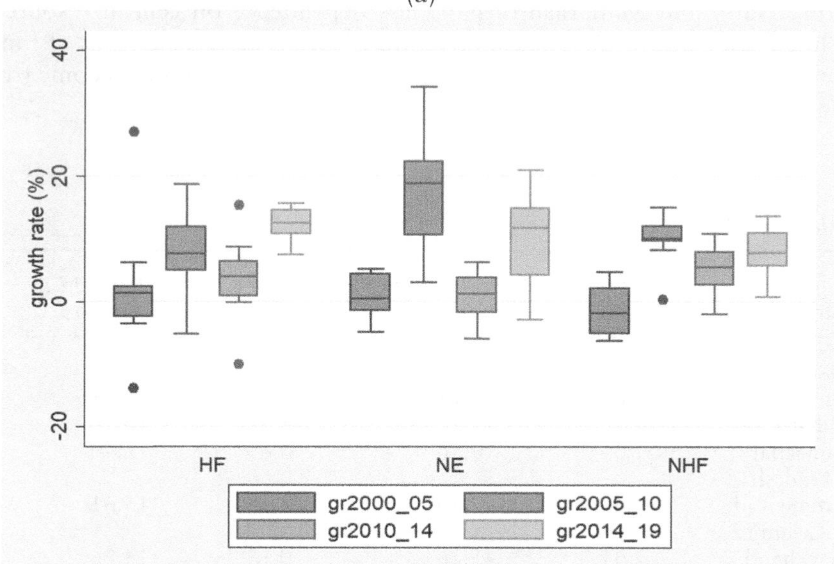

(b)

Figure 15.8 Box plots of growth rates in state spending at constant 2011–12 prices: a) by period; b) by state category (high-focus large, non-high focus, North East).

Source: same as Figure 15.7.

During the 2010–11 to 2013–14 period, we observe declining growth rates for all three category of state. The NE states saw the steepest decline, whereas after the XIV FC, after 2014–15, HF states experienced very high growth in spending. This might mean that NHM has succeeded in increasing health system capacity and created greater demand for funds within the health system. As a result, despite reductions in central share in CSS, HF states have been able to sustain public spending.

However, this story is not uniform across all HF states. For instance, Assam experienced very high growth during the first phase of NHM, but during the second phase, public spending declined steeply (Table 15.2). Among the HF states, Chhattisgarh, Odisha, Rajasthan and MP have experienced steady growth in the post-NHM phases. However, Bihar, Jharkhand and HP experienced fluctuations and often steep decline in spending.

Compared with the 1990s and early 2000s, where there was a gradual decline in the role of central resources to states, introducing NRHM led to considerable increase in central share in state level spending. One key objective of the XIV FC was to reduce the role of CSS and allow greater transfer of untied resources to states. We looked at the impacts of the FC recommendation on state finance for a few states and observed that HF states like Assam, MP and Odisha remain heavily dependent on central resources even after XIV FC recommendation (Figure 15.9). At the same time, Kerala, Tamil Nadu and Maharashtra have less dependence on central resources. While Kerala and Maharashtra have only 5 per cent to 6 per cent of funds coming from central sources, in MP, around 43 per cent of funds come from the Union government.

Table 15.2 Growth Rates in Large High-Focus States

High-Focus Large States	*2000–01 to 2004–05*	*2005–06 to 2009–10*	*2010–11 to 2013–14*	*2014–15 to 2018–19*
Assam	–1.75	34.09	–5.97	20.86
Bihar	–13.88	4.78	–0.17	14.56
Chhattisgarh	26.96	11.77	15.31	10.58
Himachal Pradesh	1.33	6.56	0.69	12.40
Jammu and Kashmir2	2.44	7.83	3.16	15.61
Jharkhand	–2.41	–5.26	–10.13	14.96
Madhya Pradesh	–3.51	7.53	6.29	9.89
Odisha	2.36	18.62	5.44	12.87
Rajasthan	–2.02	13.75	8.62	12.04
Uttar Pradesh	6.14	7.72	1.37	7.48
Uttarakhand	11.97	4.42	4.56	12.41

Source: Same as Figure 15.7.

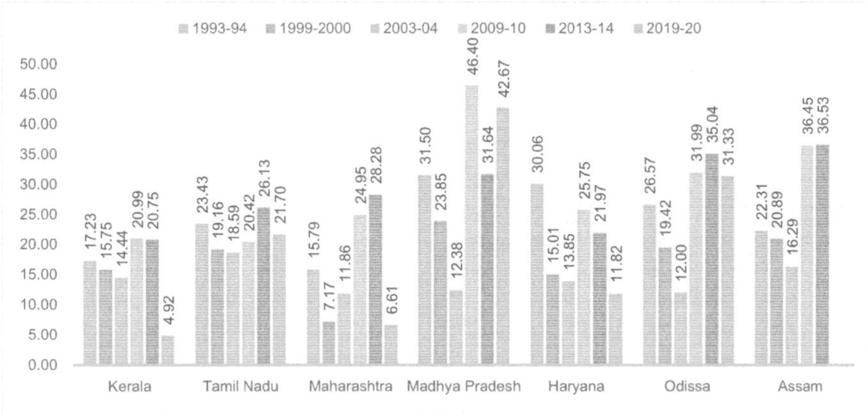

Figure 15.9 Central shares of state spending on health: selected states.

Source: Finances Accounts; Various years, various state governments; Comptroller and Auditor General.

Note: Assam did not provide a Centre–state breakdown for the year 2019–20.

Are States Converging?

Addressing the horizontal inequity between states has been a key element of NHM. The introduction of the concept of high-focus states was to provide additional financial support to states which had limited state resources and considerable health backwardness. Here we tried to assess whether states are converging in terms of per capita public spending through NHM mechanisms. The idea here is to take the mean per capita spending across states for a particular time period and generate a ratio of per capita spending of a particular state to the all-state mean. The ratio is divided into four categories: less than 0.5 (category 1); 0.5 or more but less than one (cat 2); 1 or more but less than 1.5 (cat 3); 1.5 or more (cat 4). Then we compared two time periods. For instance, in box 3.a, the columns represent the number of states whose per capita public spending ratio falls into the four categories for the pre-NHM period (2000–01 to 2004–05). The rows represent the number of states that fall into the four categories for 2005–06 to 2009–10. Thus each cell represents the transition from the earlier period to the new period.

The number 10 in Table 15.3.a means that there are 10 states that fell between 0.5 and less than 1 for both periods. There were 12 states in the same category during the pre-NHM period, and one fell back to less than 0.5 category in the first phase of NHM. Similarly, there were seven states that spent less than half the average in the pre-NHM period. However, two of them moved to the second category during the first phase of NHM, indicating some attempt to address interstate variations. In the subsequent periods, depicted in Tables 15.3.b and 15.3.c, we do not see much movement towards the average, as most states remain in the same position where they started with in the previous period.

Table 15.3 Convergence Matrices of Per Capita Public Spending by State Between Pre- and Post-NHM

3.a

		Pre NHM			
		0.5<	0.5=< to >1	1=< to >1	1.5=<
2005–06 to 2009–10	0.5<	5	1	0	0
	0.5=< to >1	2	10	0	0
	1=< to >1.5	0	1	4	2
	1.5=<	0	0	0	4

3.b

		2005–06 to 2009–10			
		0.5<	0.5=< to >1	1=< to >1	1.5=<
2010–11 to 2013–14	0.5<	5	1	0	0
	0.5=< to >1	1	11	1	0
	1=< to >1.5	0	0	5	0
	1.5=<	0	0	1	4

3.c

		2010–11 to 2013–14			
		0.5<	0.5=< to >1	1=< to >1	1.5=<
2014–15 to 2018–19	0.5<	5	0	0	0
	0.5=< to >1	0	13	0	0
	1=< to >1.5	0	0	5	1
	1.5=<	0	0	0	4

3.d

		Pre NHM			
		0.5<	0.5=< to >1	1=< to >1	1.5=<
2014–15 to 2018–19	0.5<	4	1	0	0
	0.5=< to >1	3	11	0	0
	1=< to >1.5	0	0	4	2
	1.5=<	0	0	0	4

Source: Author's calculations using RBI data and other central and state budgets to address transfer from the Union government.

Table 15.3.d compares the pre-NHM period with 2014–15 to 2018–19; it allows us to compare the transition over almost two decades, which shows 12 states in category 2, close to the pre-NHM average. The number of states in category 2 increased to 14; there were seven states in category 1, representing very low spending, and this decreased to four. These figures mean that some expenditure equalisation took place during the NHM period. However, many of these transitions took place during the first phase and not in the later period. This could be linked to gradual reductions in the central share and increase in state share under NHM. Initially it was fully Union funded. Central and state share reduced to 85:15; 75:25 and finally 60:40. This affected resource constrained states disproportionately. Table 15.4 shows the formulas we used to calculate public spending on health.

Whether a state can spend adequately on health depends on the state's ability to mobilise a larger share of total state resources available. The National Health Policy 2017 proposed to allocate 8 per cent to 10 per cent of the budget to health. There is widespread variation across states in terms of how much of the state budget is going for health. For instance, Delhi spends around 14 per cent of its budget on health, whereas Punjab spends around 4 per cent (Figure 15.10a). However, we observe here that states contribution of government expenditure in GSDP is higher are also the ones with lower per capita public spending on health (Figure 15.10.b).

Incidentally, the states where contribution of government spending is higher in GSDP are also generally poorer (UP, Bihar, Odisha, MP, etc.). Since markets remain underdeveloped and mostly informal in these states;

Table 15.4 Calculations Involved in Estimating State-Level Public Spending on Health

2005–06 to 2013–14	*2014–15 onwards*
Union Budget (U): Central Sector Programmes (A) Central Transfer to State Treasury (B) Transfer to State Health Society (C)	Union Budget (U): Central Sector Programmes (A) Transfer to State Treasury Non-NHM (B) Central Transfer to State Treasury NHM (C)
State Budget (S): 1. State Programmes (D) 2. Central Transfer to State Treasury (B) 3. State Contribution to SHS (E)	State Budget (S): 1. State Programmes (D) 2. Central Transfer to State Treasury (B) 3. Central Transfer to State Treasury NHM (C) 4. State Contribution to SHS (E)
State NHM (N) = C + E = Transfer to SHS (C) + State Contribution to SHS (E)	State NHM (N) = C + E = Central Transfer to State Health Treasury NHM (C) + State Contribution to SHS (E)
State Contribution (P) = D + E = State Programmes (D) + State Contribution to SHS (E)	State Contribution (P) = S – B – C = State Programmes (D) + State Contribution to SHS (E)
Spending at State (M) = N + P – E = State NHM (N) + State Contribution (P) – State Contribution to SHS (E)	Central Contribution to States (M) = B + C = Central Transfer to State Treasury Non-NHM (B) + Central Transfer to State Health Treasury NHM (C)
Total Spending (Union + State) = U + S – B = (A + B + C) + (D + B + E) – B = Union + State – Central Transfer to State Treasury (B)	Total Spending (Union + State) = U + S – B = (A + B + C) + (D + B + C + E) = A + S

contribution of agriculture is relatively higher and people have lesser purchasing powers, government contributions to GSDP tends to be higher. In contrast, states which are more affluent do not allocate adequate resources to health even though their per capita spending on health remains higher. This clearly indicates that unless poorer states are supported with health-specific transfers through the FC, gaps in public spending across states will not be addressed.

Fiscal Space: Post GST

Introducing the GST brought about considerable changes in the Union–state fiscal relationship. States no longer had the power to tax or decide tax rates. During the first few years of the GST, states' shares of their tax revenues as a percentage of GDP increased, while the Union government's shares declined (Figure 15.11). In fact, since the XIV FC recommendations of greater tax

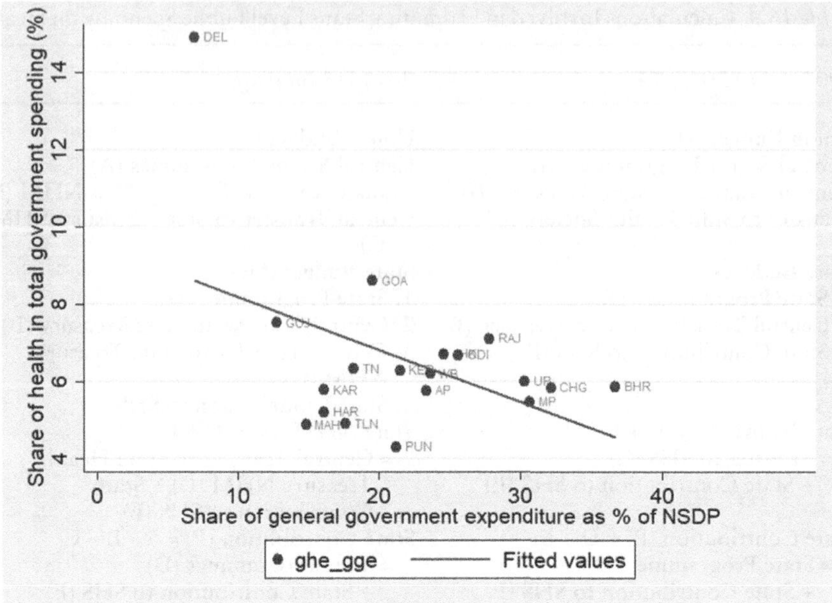

(a)

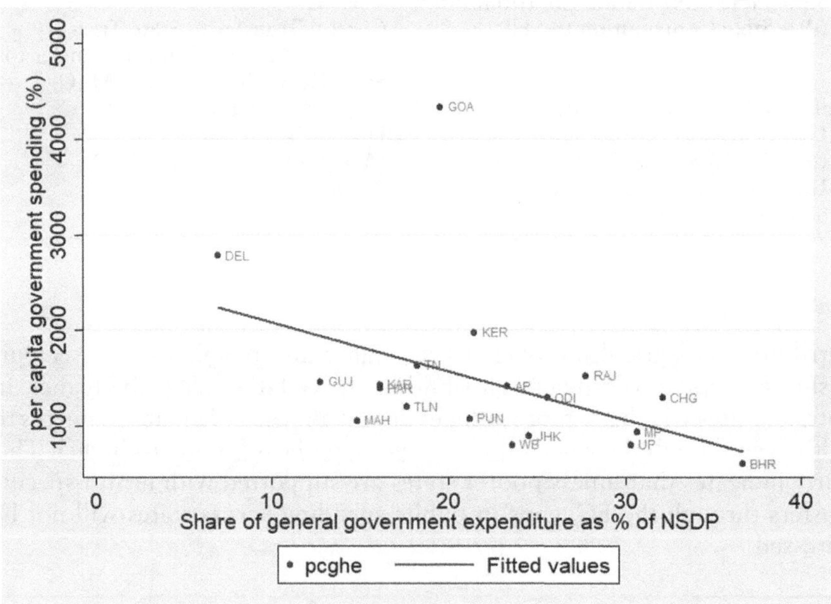

(b)

Figure 15.10 Public spending on health and budget as percentage of GDP (2018–19): general category states.

Source: Public expenditure figures from RBI.

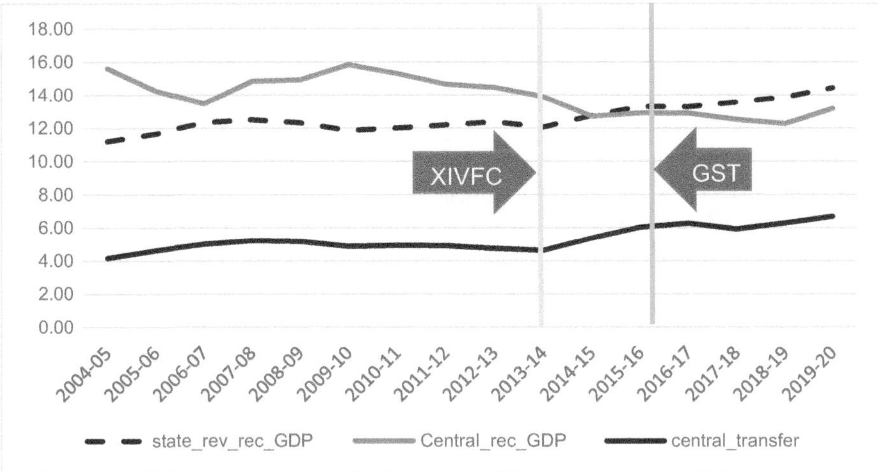

Figure 15.11 Shares of Union and state revenues and central transfers to states as percentage of GDP.

devolution to states, there was upward movement in state taxes. However, looking at the growth rates of various components of state revenue, we see consistent declines post-2014 in all the sources of revenue compared with the period of 2002 to 2014 (Figure 15.12).

In the face of a shortfall in GST collection, the Union government raised "Non-shareable taxes" and "Cesses on commodities" on excisable goods under the Union Excise Duty: petroleum products, tobacco, etc. (Mukherjee, 2022). One major concern remains sustaining the revenue stream at least at the level that was prevalent prior to GST reform to meet the expenditure demands of respective governments. Providing revenue compensation in GST helped states cope with GST shortfalls.

However, in the absence of revenue compensation, states can face revenue shocks that will affect different states' finances differently. For states, expanding the GST base by protecting the consumption base would be a major challenge given the huge consumption slump due to Covid-19-induced disruptions in the economy. As a consequence, public spending on health might have been affected along with other social sectors.

Implications of NHM on Utilization of Public Systems and Household Out-of-Pocket Spending

One of the major goals of NHM was to increase institutional deliveries in public systems; its focus has largely been strengthening public systems related to maternal and child health. Public-sector utilisation for childbirth has

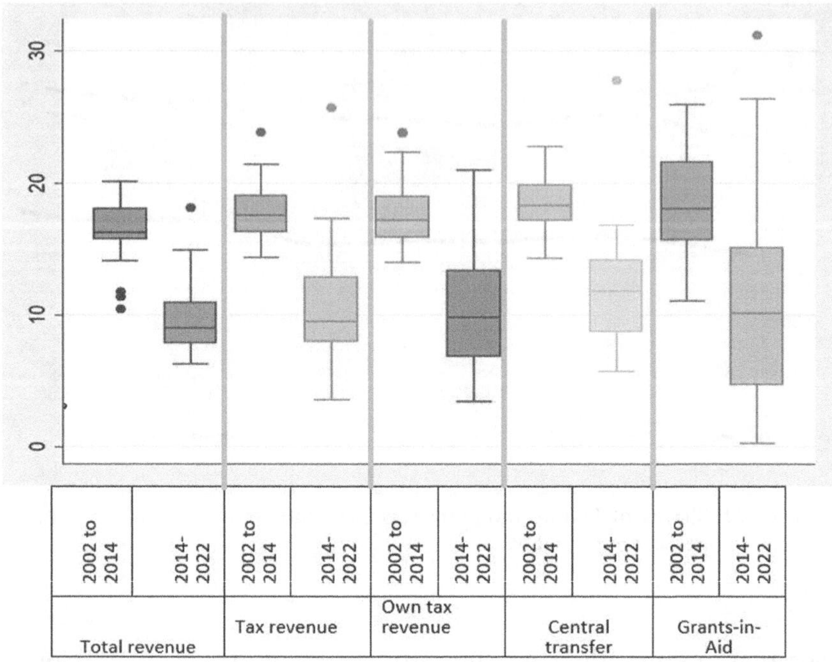

Figure 15.12 Growth rates of various revenue sources of states: 2002 to 2014 and 2014–20.

consistently increased in rural areas since the introduction of NRHM. As depicted in Figure 15.13, out of 100 childbirths in rural areas, just over half (52.4 per cent) took place in public facilities in 2004, just before NRHM, according to NSS data (MoSPI, 2019).

In the latest NSS data, for 2017–18, 75.7 per cent of the deliveries took place in public facilities. In urban areas, where most people usually depend on the private sector for institutional deliveries and other hospitalisation services, we observe modest increases in public-sector utilization. The late introduction and slow progress of NHM in urban areas, with limited interventions beyond RMNCH has led to much slower increase in public hospital utilisation in urban areas and for other hospitalisations. This also shows that if concerted efforts are made to improve public provisioning, people do trust public systems.

If we study the trends in out-of-pocket (OOP) expenditures for public and private facilities, it is clearly visible that OOPs in public facilities are low and declining, while costs in private facilities are increasing. Even though OOPs in public facilities are not strictly comparable with private ones, due to subsidies going into the public sector, it is crucial to note that over the years, care in the public sector has become cheaper, while costs in the private sector are increasing (Figure 15.14).

Discussion

The introduction of centrally sponsored programs like the National Health Mission and RSBY and subsequently PMJAY blurred the boundaries of constitutional responsibilities. Union government allocation of funds to the centrally sponsored schemes in different states is guided by their needs, ability to absorb grants and spend them efficiently on the purposes for which they are intended and capacity and willingness to provide matching grants.

In a federal context, Centre–state engagement with role clarity; areas of control and delegation to different levels of governance, ownership, responsibility divisions, accountability and autonomy at different levels are all fundamental elements that have a bearing on investments and effective health delivery. As of now, states spend more than two thirds of total public spending on health, with considerable interstate variations. States are challenged by their institutional and fiscal capacities, historical levels of investment, structural considerations and boundaries set by the Fiscal Responsibility and Budget Management Act along with a host of political economic factors.

At the same time, the National Health Mission brought about changes in practices and management principles in the Centre–state fiscal relationship. Two important reforms that NHM brought about are the concept of flexible

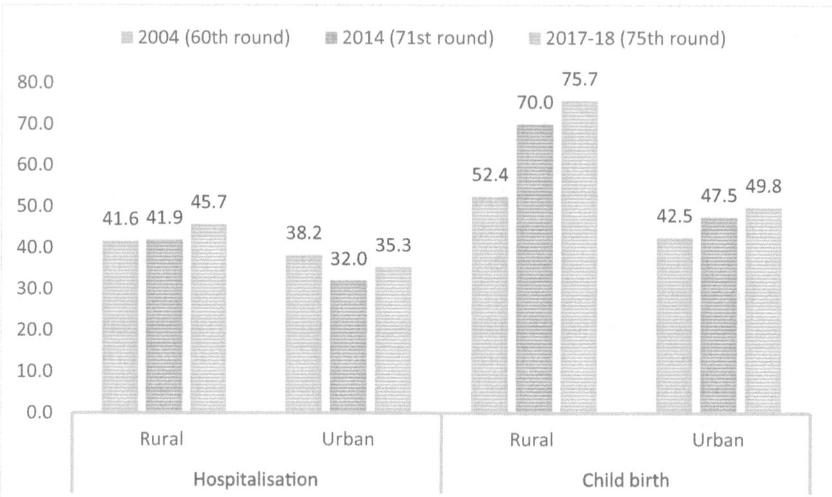

Figure 15.13 Utilisation of government facilities per 100 cases of hospitalisation and childbirth: rural versus urban.

Source: NSSO unit records, various rounds.

pool, where states are being provided lump sum funds instead of tied funds, which has been the historical practice. The other crucial change that came through was the introduction of decentralised planning. Both these innovations have had significant changes in the overall level of public spending on health and the priorities within the health sector at the subnational level, even though their implementation remains weak, and much of the potential remains un-utilised (Rao, 2017).

Apart from the inadequate expansion of public-sector hospitals and complaints about poor service quality (which is not the same as clinical quality), there has been a continuous push towards the private sector through the plethora of government-financed health insurance schemes, the latest avatar being the PMJAY. All of this together creates a situation where people, even from economically vulnerable groups, are left with no other choices but to access private institutions. That is, the private sector does not complement care provided by the public sector, and it is not the dominant provider beyond OP care; nor could the claims of free care be substantiated. On the other hand, with less investment, the public sector provides a significant part of clinical care along with an entire range of preventive care and public health services.

After the introduction of NRHM, it was observed that there has been some increase in public spending across the low-income, or high-focus, states. However, the increase was not sustained, with periods of high growth followed by slumps. The additional spending provided by the Union government led to enhancing infrastructure both physical and human power at the primary level which has already been documented in several health ministry reviews (Ministry of Health and Family Welfare, Various Years).

After the launch of NRHM, the HF states showed some improvement in institutional delivery: increased access to primary health systems and increased outreach services such as immunisation, antenatal care and contraceptive access. Institutional deliveries in almost all the states show a quantum jump during NRHM period, and most newborn children have been immunised in all the states of India. However, there are many implementation challenges that need to be improved, particularly in the context of primary care for non-communicable diseases, where programs like Health and Wellness Centres become crucial.

It has been quite evident that dependence on the private sector is iniquitous and impoverishing. As depicted in Figure 15.15, there remains an inverse relationship between per capita public spending on health and lower OOPs. Public expenditures on health is a major predictor of financial protection for health, and higher public investments in health are associated with efforts to fill human resource vacancies or create better-equipped facilities like first referral and cardiac care units or providing free medicines. States like Bihar, UP, Odisha, MP and Jharkhand which have very low per capita public investments in health are also the states with the highest OOP expenditures as shares of total health expenditures. These states also perform poorly in almost all the input indicators, be it staffing or setting up first referral units.

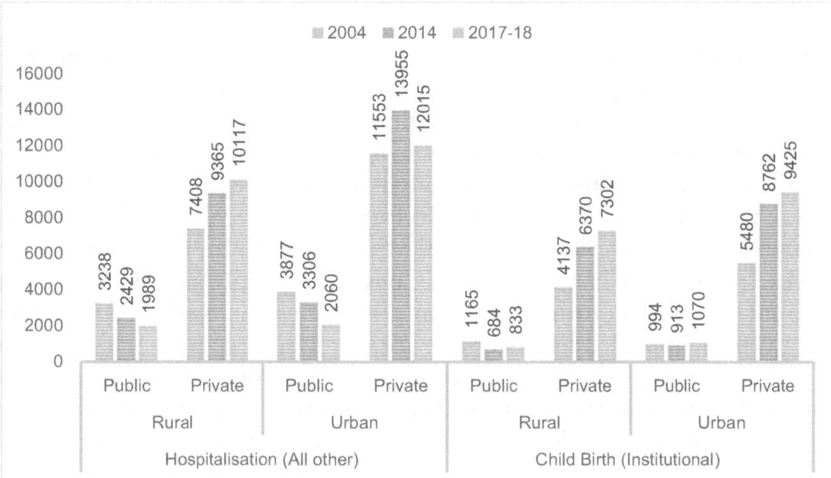

Figure 15.14 Out-of-pocket expenditure on per hospitalisation and child birth episode (INR) (constant 2004 prices).

Source: Estimated from NSS 75th-round unit-level data; CPI-AL and CPI-IW were used for price index.

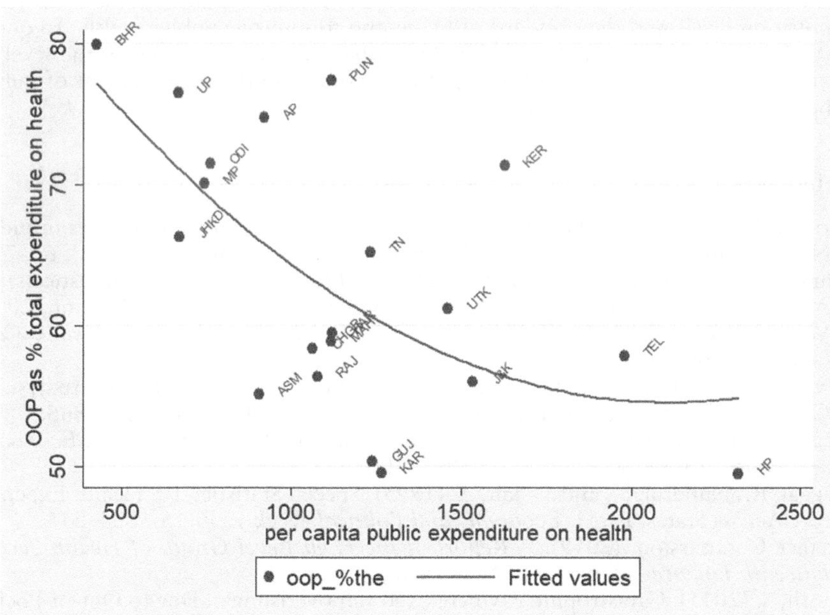

Figure 15.15 Inverse relationship between public spending and OOP expenditures: 2017–18.

Source: Authors' estimates using National Health Accounts data, NHSRC.

Conclusion

Rebuilding public primary health care is going to require not only increased investment but also creative re-organisation of services and democratisation leading to better accountability. For the public sector, it cannot be business as usual: it has to reform, but it must do so based on theoretical foundations that are completely different from what was pushed under the New Public Management and Health Sector Reform of the 1990s and later through demand-side financing discourse under Universal Health Coverage. Like the NHM experience, it has to be largely based on supply side financing, with increased investment from the Union government as well as states. However, given the lopsided fiscal capacity of states, a large part of this increase has to be financed from general taxes and come from Finance Commission grants with focus on the health sector, which was majorly expanded under the Fourteenth Finance Commission. Then only would we be able to ensure that poorer states have adequate resources and that grants are devoted to strengthening public systems in these states rather than creating dependence on the unregulated private sector.

Note

1 The Directive Principles of the State Policy in the Constitution especially enjoin the states, although they are not of course enforceable in a court of law, to increase nutrition levels and the standard of living and to improve public health. To quote the language of the Article 47, 'The State shall regard the raising of the level of nutrition and the standard of living of the people and the improvement of public health as among its primary duties'.

References

Berman, P., et al. (2010). The Impoverishing Effect of Healthcare Payments in India: New Methodology and Findings. *Economic and Political Weekly*, *45*(16), 65–71.

Clark C. Havighurst and Barak D. Richman (2006). Distributive Injustice(s) In American Health Care Source: Law and Contemporary Problems, Autumn, 2006, Vol. 69, No. 4, *Who Pays? Who Benefits? Distributional Issues in Health Care* (Autumn, 2006), pp. 7-82.

Dev, S.M., and Mooij, J. (2002). Social Sector Expenditures in the 1990s: Analysis of Central and State Budgets. *Economic and Political Weekly*, *37*(9), 853–866.

Duggal, R. (1995). Health Care Budgets in a Changing Political Economy. *Economic and Political Weekly*, *32*(20/21), 1197–1200.

Duggal, R., Nandraj, S., and Vadair, A. (1995). Special Statistics-10: Health Expenditure Across States: Part I. *Economic and Political Weekly*, *30*(15), 834–844.

Finance Commission. (2019). *A Report of the High Level Group of Health Sector, Fifteenth Finance Commission*. New Delhi, India.

Ghosh, S. (2011). Catastrophic Payments and Impoverishment Due to Out-of-Pocket Health Spending. *Economic and Political Weekly*, *46*(47), 63–70.

Government of India. (2005). *Framework of Implementation*. National Rural Health Mission, Ministry of Health and Family Welfare. www.mohfw.nic.in/NRHM.htm, accessed 12.5.2011.

Government of India. (2022). *Expenditure Budget Vol. 1& 2*. Ministry of Finance, Various Years. www.indiabudget.gov.in, accessed 15.2.2022.

Ministry of Health and Family Welfare, *Reports of Common Review Mission, NHM*, Various Years. https://nhsrcindia.org/practice-areas/kmd/common-review-mission-crm-reports; Accessed on 03.09.22.

MoSPI. (2019). *Social Consumption: Health, NSS 75th Round: Jul 2017–June 2018*. National Sample Survey Office.

Mukherjee, S. (2022, July). *Revenue Assessment of Goods and Services Tax (GST) in India*. NIPFP Working Paper No 385. New Delhi, India. https://mail.nipfp.org.in/media/medialibrary/2022/07/WP_385_2022.pdf. Accessed on 01.09.22

Mukhopadhyay, I. (2012). "Public Health Care Expenditure in India: a Study of Kerala, Tamil Nadu and West Bengal"; unpublished PhD Thesis; submitted at Centre of Social Medicine and Community Health, Jawaharlal Nehru University, New Delhi.

National Health Systems Resource Centre. (2021). *National Health Accounts Estimates for India*; Various Years. New Delhi: Ministry of Health and Family Welfare, Government of India.

Qadeer, I. (2001). Impact of SAPs on the Concepts of Public Health. In Qadeer, I., et al. (Eds.), *Public Health and Poverty of Reforms: A South Asian Perspective*. New Delhi: Sage.

Rao, M.G. (2016). *The Effect of Intergovernmental Transfers on Public Services in India*. NIPFP Working Paper No 218. New Delhi, India. https://www.nipfp.org.in/media/medialibrary/2017/12/WP_2017_218.pdf. Accessed on 01.09.22

Rao, S. (2017). *Do We Care?: India's Health System*. New Delhi: Oxford University Press.

Reddy, K.N., and Selvaraju, V. (1994). *Health Care Expenditure by Government in India: 1974–75 to 1990–91*. Working Paper. National Institute of Public Finance and Policy, New Delhi.

Reserve Bank of India. (2020). *State Government Finances*. https://www.rbi.org.in/Scripts/AnnualPublications.aspx?head=State%20Finances%20:%20A%20Study%20of%20Budgets.

Sen, T., and Dash, S.K. (2013). *Fiscal Imbalances and Indebtedness Across Indian States: Recent Trends; NIPFP Working Paper No. 119*. https://www.nipfp.org.in/publications/working-papers/?page=5; Accessed on 21-09-24

Tulasidhar, V.B. (1993). Expenditure Compression and Health Sector Outlays. *Economic and Political Weekly*, *28*(45), 2473–2477.

Varatharajan, D., Godwin, S.K., and Arun, B. (2004, August 14–20). Unimaginative Tinkering. *Economic and Political Weekly*, *39*(33), 3672–3675.

16 Decentralising the Delivery of Health Care

The Need of the Hour

A.K. Shiva Kumar

India's most notable achievement over the past 30 years has been the country's impressive economic growth record. India's GDP grew at an average rate of 5.4 per cent a year from 1991 to the early 2000s, at a much higher rate during 2004–08 when it averaged 8.8 per cent a year, and at a growth rate averaging 7 per cent to 7.5 per cent between 2009 and 2017.[1] By 2020, India was the third largest economy in the world in purchasing power parity (PPP), with a share of 6.8 per cent of global GDP[2] (after China 18.3 per cent) and the United States of America (15.9 per cent). Medium- and long-term prospects of further economic expansion remain bright despite the Covid-19 pandemic.

Under-performance in Health

India's performance in health, however, has not kept pace with the country's economic expansion.[3] High economic growth has not translated sufficiently into better health for its people, unlike in other countries even in South Asia. In 1990, for instance, India's life expectancy at birth (66 years) was lower than that of Sri Lanka and the Maldives but higher than the rest of the neighbouring South Asian countries. By 2020 (pre-Covid), India's life expectancy at birth (70 years) was still lower than that of Sri Lanka (77 years) and the Maldives (79 years) and had fallen behind those of Bangladesh (73 years), Nepal (71 years) and Bhutan (72 years).[4] This is even though India's per capita gross national income in 2021 (PPP current international dollars 7334) is significantly higher than that of Bangladesh (PPP current international dollars 6613) and Nepal (PPP current international dollars 4,261).[5]

India's health burden remains large. The burden of infectious diseases, reproductive and child health problems and nutritional deficiencies co-exists with a growing burden of chronic diseases. Non-communicable diseases (NCDs) have emerged as a leading cause of death, with the proportion of deaths due to NCDs increasing from 37.9 per cent in 1990 to 61.8 per cent in 2016.[6] High rates of tobacco consumption contribute significantly to mortality from cardiovascular diseases, cancer and tuberculosis. Of considerable concern are the increase in multidrug-resistant tuberculosis; the unacceptably

DOI: 10.4324/9781003568711-20

large numbers of malaria deaths and its resurgence in some parts of the country and the rise of viral encephalitis, dengue and chikungunya, particularly in urban areas. In addition, large gaps remain in addressing the demands of occupational health, adolescent health, mental health, geriatric care and palliative care.

This is not to undermine in any way India's achievements in health over the past 70 years. Life expectancy at birth has more than doubled since Independence, from 32 years in 1950–51 to 70 years in 2020. In 2020, the infant mortality rate (IMR) was 28 per 1000 livebirths, down from 139 in 1976. From 556 in 1990, India's maternal mortality ratio (MMR) fell to 97 per 100,000 births by 2018–20.[7] The spread of HIV/AIDS has been successfully contained. The World Health Organization (WHO) officially declared India polio free in March 2014 and free of maternal and neonatal tetanus in August 2015.

These overall achievements, however, mask large differences in morbidity, mortality and nutritional status arising out of caste, class, gender and geography. Among the more populous Indian states, Kerala's IMR in 2020 was 6 per 1,000 live births, against 38 in Chhattisgarh and Uttar Pradesh and 43 in Uttar Pradesh.[8] The MMR in 2018–20 varied from 19 in Kerala to 195 in Assam. Against 22 per cent of children under five in Sikkim and 23 per cent in Kerala who were stunted in 2019–21, the proportion was 40 per cent in Jharkhand and Uttar Pradesh and 43 per cent in Bihar.[9]

The neglect of women's health in particular is striking. The prevalence of anaemia among women 15–49 years in 2019–2021 varied from 36.3 per cent in Kerala to 71.4 per cent in West Bengal.[10] Separately, men continue to outnumber women in India. Extremely disturbing was the decline in the female-to-male ratio among children 0–6 years from 927 in 2001 to 914 in 2011, signalling the widespread prevalence of son preference and anti-female bias in Indian society.[11]

Climate change, unchecked pollution, inadequate access to safe drinking water and lack of proper sanitation and waste disposal, as well as high undernutrition pose additional health burdens on India's population. The Covid-19 pandemic has added to the health burden given that the medical impacts (including mental health concerns) are not yet fully known. Over the coming years, India is also likely to become a hotspot of zoonotic diseases.

There are several reasons for India's under-performance in health including insufficient human resources, shortage of health care services, weak management in both the public and private sectors and the neglect of the social determinants of health. With this chapter, I focus on two additional and critical factors that stand out: the neglect of primary health care and the low levels of public spending on health. Unless measures are taken to step up public investments to strengthen the public provision of health care, prioritise comprehensive primary health care, delegate responsibilities to local governments and decentralise the financing and delivery of health care, the dream of UHC is likely to remain unfulfilled.

The Neglect of Primary Health Care

The critical importance ensuring primary health care for all people was prominently underscored in the historic Declaration of Alma-Ata in 1978. The Declaration called for 'urgent and effective national and international action to develop and implement primary health care throughout the world and particularly in developing countries' by the year 2000.[12] Primary health care is

> a whole-of-society approach to health that aims to ensure the highest possible level of health and wellbeing and their equitable distribution by focusing on people´s needs and preferences (as individuals, families, and communities) as early as possible along the continuum from health promotion and disease prevention to treatment, rehabilitation and palliative care, and as close as feasible to people's everyday environment.[13]

Many countries including India have not realised that primary health care has to be the cornerstone of a strong health system and is an essential pre-requisite for accelerating progress towards universal health coverage (UHC). Evidence suggests that a primary health care approach is the most equitable, effective and efficient way to improve health. Primary care provides crucial preventive and curative services that directly save lives. Primary care also plays a critical role in promoting the conditions that make people healthy.[14]

India has not sufficiently addressed three interrelated and synergistic components of primary health care. One, there are large gaps in meeting people's health needs through comprehensive promotive, protective, preventive, curative, rehabilitative and palliative care. Evidence of this can be found, for instance, in the poor reach of immunisation coverage in India. In 2019–21, only 77 per cent of children aged 12–23 months have all basic vaccinations, 61 per cent of children with diarrhoea received oral rehydration salts, 11 per cent of breastfeeding children aged 6–23 months received an adequate diet and 67 per cent of children age 6–59 months were anaemic.[15]

Two, India has failed to systematically address the broader determinants of health (including social, economic and environmental factors, as well as individual characteristics and behaviour). The neglect of women's health is a case in point. In 2019–21, only 56.5 per cent of currently married women 15–49 years used a modern method of contraception, 57 per cent of women aged 15–49 years were anaemic and 29 per cent of ever-married women age 18–49 years had ever experienced spousal violence. Additionally, stunting is higher among children in rural areas (37 per cent) than urban areas (30 per cent), and 46 per cent percent of children born to mothers with no schooling are stunted compared with 26 per cent of children born to mothers with 12 or more years of schooling.

The prevalence of stunting decreases steadily with higher wealth quintiles, from 46 per cent of children in households in the lowest wealth quintile to 23 per cent of children in households in the highest wealth quintile. Of all social groups, stunting is also highest at 41 per cent among children belonging to Scheduled Tribes.[16] Suicide among Indian women is also a major public health concern. It is the leading cause of death among women ages 15 to 29, and rates for young and middle-aged women rank the highest among countries with similar demographics. Women in India accounted for 36 per cent of global female suicide deaths in 2016, despite making up less than 18 per cent of the world's female population.[17]

Three, India has not done enough to empower individuals, families and communities to optimise their health, as advocates for policies that promote and protect health and well-being, as co-developers of health and social services, and as self-carers and caregivers. India has focused narrowly on curative care-oriented institutions. At the same time, the institutions that provide primary health care services, namely subcentres, primary health centres (PHCs) and community health centres (CHCs), have failed to win the trust of people as so-called curative care providers at the primary level.[18]

Low Public Spending on Health

India's low public spending on health is a major cause of and an exacerbating factor in the challenges of health inequity, inadequate availability and reach, unequal access and poor-quality and costly health care services.[19]

India's public spending on health, stagnant at around 1.2 per cent of GDP[20] for almost two decades, is among the lowest in the world and falls woefully short of the commitment made in the National Health Policy 2017 to increase it to 2.5 per cent by 2025.[21] Expressed in terms of the proportion of GDP, India's government health expenditure in 2020 at 1.2 per cent may not appear to be much different from those of Sri Lanka (1.97 per cent), Thailand (3 per cent) and China (3.1 per cent). However, the differences become stark when comparing government health spending per person. In 2020, at USD 23 per capita, India's public expenditure on health was less than a third of Sri Lanka's (USD 77) and significantly lower than that of Thailand (USD 215) and China (USD 319).[22]

The low government spending on health has had three serious adverse consequences. One, a majority of Indians are forced to incur high OOP expenditures on health which at 63 per cent in 2020 is among the highest in the world,[23] significantly above the average for lower-middle income countries and much higher than in Thailand (10.5 per cent), Bhutan (15.4 per cent) and China (34.8 per cent).[24] Two, the high OOP expenditures make all segments of the Indian population, not just the poor, extremely vulnerable to catastrophic spending and impoverishment. According to the NSS 75th Health Survey Round (July 2017–June 2018), in rural India, only 12 per cent to 18 per cent of cases both rural and urban received free medicines, free X-ray and electrocardiogram and free 'other diagnostic tests.'[25] According to a recent analysis, the number of persons impoverished due to OOP expenditures increased from 77.9 million to 97.78 million between 2004 and 2014 using the Health and Morbidity Survey and from 51.48 million to 54.38 million between 2004–2005 and 2011–2012 using the National Sample Survey Organization's Consumption Expenditure Survey. Furthermore, expenditures on outpatient care including drugs led to 72 million people being pushed below poverty line in 2014.[26]

Three, low government expenditures on health have severely limited the expansion of the capacity and quality of health care services provided by the public sector. Consequently, most Indians have had no option but to access health care from a rapidly expanding private sector that has remained, by and large, unregulated. Under-investment in public health systems led the private sector to dominate service delivery and employment of health workforces and resulted in a skewed distribution of facilities, with the rural areas being severely under-served. Although roughly two thirds of India's population resides in rural areas, only one third of all health workers are in rural areas. One out of four doctors (27 per cent) and 36 per cent of nurses work in rural areas.

Of the 69,265 hospitals and close to 1.9 million hospital beds in India in 2019, 62 per cent of both were in the private sector.[27] The bulk of the health workforce is not surprisingly employed in the private sector: 65 per cent of doctors, 89 per cent of dentists, 93 per cent of Ayush d and 67 per cent of other health workers. The availability of health professionals in the public sector is further challenged by the high vacancies of sanctioned positions.[28]

In 2017–18, nearly two thirds of all ailments treated by the private sector, and only 42 per cent of even hospitalisation cases were attended to by government and public hospitals.[29] The inevitability of having to access private health care has meant much higher private out-of-pocket expenditures. For instance, in 2017–18, the average medical expenditure per hospitalisation case (excluding childbirths) at the national level was INR 4452 in government and public hospitals as against INR 31,845 in private hospitals.[30]

Under-investment by the state has also meant that many public-sector facilities tend to be under-staffed, over-crowded and poorly managed. According to the National Family Health Survey-5, in 2019–21, the most commonly reported reason for not using government health facilities at the national level was the poor quality of care (reported by 48 per cent of households that do not generally use government facilities). The second most commonly reported reason was the long waiting time at government facilities (46 per cent) followed by the fact that there is no government facility nearby (40 per cent of households).[31]

At the same time, given the virtual absence of effective regulation and oversight by the state, the quality of health care in the private sector is at best mixed and the costs are often unreasonably high. Private markets in health care are known to be grossly inefficient given the large informational asymmetry (where the profit-oriented doctor can cheat the patient by prescribing unnecessary medicines or unwanted treatment). Many so-called health practitioners do not have the requisite educational qualifications, and private medical facilities are known to over-diagnose, over-treat and mal-treat.[32] Many dispense substandard and counterfeit medicines, prescribing unnecessary drugs and tests, availing of kick-backs for referrals and manipulating hospital admissions and length of stay.[33]

Additional Features of Public Spending on Health

Six additional features reveal the importance of public spending for ensuring good health. One, in general, higher state government per capita spending on health and per capita state income tend to go hand in hand. There is high variability across Indian states in per capita public spending on health. In 2019–20, according to the National Health Accounts estimates, per capita government health expenditures among the major states varied from INR 701 in Bihar, INR 951 in Uttar Pradesh, INR 1014 in Jharkhand and INR 1249 in Madhya Pradesh to INR 2263 in Telangana, INR 2273 in Uttarakhand, INR 2590 in Kerala and INR 3829 in Himachal Pradesh.[34] States with high per capita incomes tend to spend more in per capita terms on health, and conversely, states that spend more in terms of per capita health record levels of per capita income. For instance, in 2019–20, Bihar's per capita state domestic product (SDP) was INR 45,071 against Kerala's per capita SDP of INR 221,904.[35]

Two, states with a higher per capita health expenditures, by and large, report better health outcomes. For instance, in 2020, the IMRs in Jharkhand (25), Bihar (27) and Uttar Pradesh (38) were considerably higher than in Kerala (6) and Himachal Pradesh (17).[36] Three, state governments bear a substantial burden (64 per cent) of public spending on health. Even though the Union government's financial contribution is relatively small (36 per cent),[37] the central government's influence on the delivery of health care has been substantial.

Four, there are large variations across states in terms of prioritising spending on health. For instance, government health expenditures as a percentage of general government expenditures varied from a low of 4.9 per cent in Punjab to 8 per cent in Kerala and 8.9 per cent in Meghalaya.[38] Additionally, most states spend a significantly higher proportion as revenue expenditure (on average 72 per cent of total expenditure) than as capital expenditure (28 per cent). A substantial segment of revenue expenditure is in the form of committed liabilities – such as salaries, pensions and interest payments – that states are required to pay despite resource constraints.

Five, India's public spending on primary care remains low. In 2019–20, government expenditures on primary care were only 55.9 per cent, 29.6 per cent on secondary care and 6.4 per cent on tertiary care.[39] The public spending on primary care was significantly lower than the recommendation of 70 per cent by the High Level Expert Group on Universal Health Coverage.[40]

Six, there are significant deviations between what governments budget for health spending and what they actually spend. Actual expenditures as a percentage of GSDP across 29 states tend to be far less than the budgetary commitment reflected in budget estimates and revised estimates. There is also volatility in the deviation between estimated and actual fund flow via centrally sponsored schemes (CSS). The 'one size fits all' CSS brings in serious implementation challenges in states with lower absorption capacity of central funds.

The Shortcomings of Medical Insurance

In an effort to promote UHC, the Union and state governments in India have introduced a number of publicly financed health insurance schemes for the 'poor' to improve access to in-patient hospitalisation procedures and offer financial protection to households from high medical expenses.[41] According to the NSS 2017–18 survey, before the launch of PM-JAY in September 2018, only around 14 per cent of the rural population and 19 per cent of the urban population had health expenditure coverage. Among them, about 13 per cent of rural and 9 per cent of urban population were covered by Government sponsored health insurance.[42] According to the more recent National Family Health Survey,[43] in 2019–21, health insurance coverage in India is far from satisfactory. Nearly four out of five (59 per cent) of households do not have even one member covered under health insurance or a health scheme. Only 30 percent of women aged 15–49 and 33 percent of men aged 15–49 are covered by health insurance or a health scheme. Almost half (46 per cent) of those with insurance are covered by a state health insurance scheme, and about one-sixth (16 per cent) are covered by Rashtriya Swasthya Bima Yoja-naY). Three to 6 per cent of women and 4 per cent to 7 per cent of men are covered by the employee state insurance scheme or the central government health scheme.

Indian policymakers do not seem to realise that private health care, even if properly subsidised, or private health insurance subsidised by the state, simply cannot meet the challenge of universal health coverage. To begin with, there are serious incentive-incompatibility problems with commercial insurance as interests of providers, consumers and insurance companies do not align to maximize returns to consumers.[44] Typically, insurance companies deny use, medical practitioners induce demand or encourage over-use[45] and patients themselves may misuse the facility (commonly referred to as the 'moral hazard' problem). Some hospitals and insurance companies have also resorted to anti-competitive practices by colluding and bidding for government insurance schemes[46] and adopted fraudulent measures including performing unnecessary surgeries.[47]

Medical insurance schemes tend to be inherently iniquitous. This is evident from the low coverage of a number of publicly financed health insurance schemes introduced for the poor by both the Union and state governments in India to improve access to in-patient hospitalisation and offer financial protection to households from high medical expenses.[48,49] Additionally, the availability of private facilities is strongly related to the per capita income of states and districts, which reduces access to insured services in poor states of the country.[50] Low coverage combined with high interdistrict disparity in availability of private providers makes equitable empanelment under insurance schemes difficult.[51,52] The relatively low rate of hospitalisation among the poor population and their high dependence on public facilities for inpatient care further suggest the inadequacy of government financial support in the form of health insurance schemes to the poorer sections of the population.[53]

There are distinct challenges associated with every step of the 'insurance cascade' emerging from design flaws that affect enrolment, awareness and understanding, access to and choice of participating hospitals and correct administration of the scheme. Governments admit of low awareness among beneficiaries about entitlements, denial of services by private hospitals for many categories of illnesses and oversupply of some services. Insurance schemes are not effective if they do not cover those at the highest risk of catastrophic expenditures, and beneficiaries do not find it worthwhile to learn about a scheme that is not relevant to their needs.[54]

Looking Ahead

There are several good reasons for India to step up its investments in health. To begin with, being healthy has intrinsic significance as it is an important component of a good life. Good health also has an instrumental sense to the extent that it can boost labour productivity and become a major driver of economic growth. At the same time, offering financial protection against ill-health can prevent millions becoming indebted and falling into poverty.

The benefits of good health can accrue only if India embraces the idea of universal health coverage. The commitment to UHC requires that entitlement to health care becomes independent of an individual's socioeconomic status. In other words, every individual, regardless of the ability to pay, should be entitled to a package of essential health care services without having to pay cash at the point of service delivery.

An individual should also receive essential medicines and avail of diagnostics free of cost. This requires doing away with user charges and fees for any kind for use of health care services. As is the practice in many countries, general taxation should be the principal source of health care financing. Complementing this with mandatory deductions for health care from salaried individuals and taxpayers, while possible in practice, has little potential to augment cash inflows given India's large workforce in the unorganized sector.

The principal approach of the government so far has been to (1) provide, as far as possible, universal access to free primary health care; (2) extend access to the poor and to a small set of privileged government employees to free secondary and tertiary care in public and private facilities (often through an insurance mechanism) and (3) leave the rest of the population to buy health care in the private market. The consequence of this has been the emergence of a large 'missing middle' without financial protection, a majority of whom are employed in the informal sector. The Covid-19 pandemic has only made matters worse by increasing the insecurity and precariousness in the lives of most informal sector and migrant workers.

A commitment to UHC requires decisionmakers 'to stop believing, against all empirical evidence, that India's transition from poor health to good health could be easily achieved through private health care and insurance'.[55] Switching from an insurance to a tax-financed system is the way to go. It calls for a massive expansion in government-provided health services and a reversal of the rampant and unregulated expansion of the private sector in health. India needs to accept and implement the recommendations of the XIV Finance Commission which include call for (1) increasing public health expenditure of Union and States together in a progressive manner to reach 2.5 per cent of GDP by 2025; (2) increasing health spending by States to more than 8 per cent of their budget by 2022 and (3) increasing expenditures on primary health to 66 per cent of the total health expenditures.

Strengthening community-level primary health care must become a priority within UHC. The XIV Finance Commission rightly notes that primary-level care has the potential to take care of 90 per cent of health care demands. And investment in primary health care, including prevention and health promotion, provides better health and developmental outcomes at a much lower cost.

Adopting the recommendations of the XIV Finance Commission is critical for accelerating progress in health outcomes. Centrally sponsored schemes co-financed by the Government of India should be made flexible enough to allow states to adapt and innovate. The practice of top-down mandates and guidance on program implementation has to end. The Union government should grant states considerable flexibility to tailor implementation according to local needs and realities. Financing should be provided based on bilaterally agreed compacts related to specific objectives (for example, service delivery outputs or specific outcomes) instead of exhaustively discussed implementation plans.

The XIV Finance Commission also makes a strong pitch for decentralising public spending on health. It recommended making available health grants for urban HWCs, building-less subcentres, PHCs, CHCs, block-level public health units, support for diagnostic infrastructure for primary health care activities and conversion of rural subcentres and PHCs to HWCs. These grants are to be released to local governments and should not have any pre-conditions attached to them. For all this to happen, three things are a must.

One, both the Union and state governments need to prioritise health beginning with substantially increasing public spending and strengthening the public sector for delivering on UHC. Two, there must be a concerted effort to put health in people's hands by deepening the reach of primary health care. Three, strengthening local capacities for delivering health care should go hand in hand with decentralisation funds to states. Health being a state subject under the Constitution of India, state governments are primarily responsible for the funding and delivery of health services. However, while decentralisation is good in principle, the limited competence and capacity of human resources especially at lower levels of governance poses serious problems.[56] These are not difficult to ensure for a country as well-endowed as India. What is needed is a much stronger political commitment to advancing health than what we have seen so far in India.

Notes

1 Junaid Kamal Ahmad Florian Blum Poonam Gupta Dhruv Jain (2018, October), "India's Growth Story," *Policy Research Working Paper 8599. Macroeconomics, Trade and Investment Global Practice, World Bank Group*. https://openknowledge.worldbank.org/bitstream/handle/10986/30508/WPS8599.pdf?sequence=1&isAllowed=y.
2 International Monetary Fund sourced from www.statista.com/statistics/271328/indias-share-of-global-gross-domestic-product-gdp/.
3 See, for instance, K. Srinath Reddy, Vikram Patel, Prabhat Jha, Vinod K. Paul, A.K. Shiva Kumar and Lalit Dandona (2011, February 26), "Towards Achievement of Universal Health Care in India by 2020: A Call to Action," *The Lancet*, 377, 760–768.
4 https://data.worldbank.org/.
5 The World Bank. https://data.worldbank.org/indicator/NY.GDP.PCAP.PP.CD.
6 Ministry of Health and Family Welfare (2022, February 8), "Status of Non-Communicable Diseases (NCDs) in India," by PIB Delhi, https://pib.gov.in/PressReleaseIframePage.aspx?PRID=1796435.
7 Office of the Registrar General & Census Commissioner, India (ORGI), Special Bulletin on Maternal Mortality in India 2018–2020, November 2022.
8 Office of the Registrar General & Census Commissioner, India (ORGI). Sample Registration System (SRS) – Bulletin 2020 Volume 55-I, India, 2022. https://censusindia.gov.in/nada/index.php/catalog/42687.
9 International Institute for Population Sciences (IIPS) and ICF. 2021. *National Family Health Survey (NFHS-5), 2019–21: India*. Mumbai: IIPS.
10 See note 9.
11 Ministry of Statistics and Programme Implementation. *Women & Men In India-2016*. Census of India 2011. Chapter 1 Population. https://mospi.gov.in/sites/default/files/reports_and_publication/statistical_publication/social_statistics/WM16Chapter1.pdf.
12 Declaration of Alma-Ata: International Conference on Primary Health Care, Alma-Ata, USSR, 6–12 September 1978, https://cdn.who.int/media/docs/default-source/documents/almaata-declaration-en.pdf?sfvrsn=7b3c2167_2.
13 A vision for primary health care in the 21st century: Towards Universal Health Coverage and the Sustainable Development Goals. Geneva: World Health Organization and the United Nations Children's Fund (UNICEF), 2018 (WHO/HIS/SDS/2018.X). Licence: CC BY-NC-SA 3.0 IGO. www.who.int/docs/default-source/searo/india/publications/vision.pdf?sfvrsn=9f1ad8fa_2.

14 S. Barkley, R. Marten, T. Reynolds, E. Kelley, S. Dalil, S. Swaminathan and A. Ghaffar (2020, November 1), "Primary Health Care: Realizing the Vision," *Bulletin of the World Health Organization*, 98(11), 727–727A. https://doi.org/10.2471/BLT.20.279943. PMID: 33177765; PMCID: PMC7607456.

15 See note 9.

16 See note 9.

17 See references cited in HT Chan Harvard School of Public Health. Indian women a third of world's female suicides. www.hsph.harvard.edu/news/hsph-in-the-news/india-women-suicide/.

18 Mathew George (2020, October 17), "The Fragmentation and Weakening of Institutions of Primary Healthcare: A Prescription for Their Revival," *Economic & Political Weekly*, LV(42), 2020. www.epw.in/system/files/pdf/2020_55/42/SA_LV_42_MathewGeorge_17102020.pdf (accessed 24 August 2022).

19 See, for instance, Report of the High-Level Expert Group Report on Universal Health Coverage for India (2011), Instituted by Planning Commission of India accessible at https://niti.gov.in/planningcommission.gov.in/docs/reports/genrep/rep_uhc0812.pdf and articles in the Lancet series: India – Towards Universal Health Coverage (2011) accessible at www.thelancet.com/series/india-towards-universal-health-coverage.

20 See, for instance, Centre for Budget and Governance Accountability (2020, June 5), *Numbers on the Edge: Assessing India's Fiscal Response to COVID-19*, Centre for Budget and Governance Accountability, New Delhi accessed on August 24, 2022 at www.cbgaindia.org/wp-content/uploads/2020/05/Numbers-on-the-Edge-Indias-Fiscal-Response-to-COVID-19-1.pdf, and Kumar Anurag and Sarwal Rakesh (2021), *Health Insurance for India's Missing Middle*, New Delhi: NITI Aayog. www.niti.gov.in/sites/default/files/2021-10/HealthInsurance-forIndiasMissingMiddle_28-10-2021.pdf (accessed 24 August 2022).

21 Government of India, National Health Policy 2017, *Ministry of Health and Family Welfare*. www.nhp.gov.in/nhpfiles/national_health_policy_2017.pdf.

22 WHO Database. http://apps.who.int/gho/data/node.main.GHEDOOPSCHESHA2011?lang=en.

23 Kumar Anurag and Sarwal Rakesh (2021), *Health Insurance for India's Missing Middle*, New Delhi: NITI Aayog. www.niti.gov.in/sites/default/files/2021-10/HealthInsurance-forIndiasMissingMiddle_28-10-2021.pdf (accessed 24 August 2022).

24 A.K. Shiva Kumar, Lincoln C. Chen, Mita Choudhury, Shiban Ganju, Vijay Mahajan, Amarjeet Sinha and Abhijit Sen (2011, February 19), "Financing Health Care for All: Challenges and Opportunities," *The Lancet*, 377(9766), 668–679.

25 Executive Summary on Report- Health in India, NSS 75th round accessed at https://mospi.gov.in/documents/213904/416362/Summary%20Analysis_Report_586_Health1600785338349.pdf/21af34ac-6c38-b39f-a82b-0152eb2ff1a8.

26 Roopali Goyanka, Charu C. Garg and Sheela Prasad (2019), "Impoverishment Due to Out-of-pocket Health Expenditures: Measurement and Comparison Across Different Surveys in India," *Indian Journal of Human Development*, 13(2), 121–134. www.researchgate.net/publication/335563890_Impoverishment_Due_to_Out-of-pocket_Health_Expenditures_Measurement_and_Comparison_Across_Different_Surveys_in_India.

27 Geetanjali Kapoor, Aditi Sriram, Jyoti Joshi, Arindam Nandi and Ramanan Laxminarayan, "COVID-19 in India: State-Wise Estimates of Current Hospital Beds, Intensive Care Unit (ICU) Beds and Ventilators," *The Center for Disease Dynamics, Economics & Policy and Princeton University*. https://cddep.org/wp-content/uploads/2020/04/State-wise-estimates-of-current-beds-and-ventilators_24Apr2020.pdf.

28 Anup Karan, Himanshu Negandhi, Suhaib Hussain, Tomas Zapata, Dilip Mairembam, Hilde De Graeve, James Buchan and Sanjay Zodpey (2021), "Size, Composition and Distribution of Health Workforce in India: Why, and Where to Invest?" *Human Resources for Health*, 19, 39. https://doi.org/10.1186/s12960-021-00575-2.
29 NSS 75th Round. Key Indicators of Social Consumption in India: Health http://mospi.nic.in/sites/default/files/publication_reports/KI_Health_75th_Final.pdf.
30 Executive Summary on Report- Health in India, NSS 75th round accessed at https://mospi.gov.in/documents/213904/416362/Summary%20Analysis_Report_586_Health1600785338349.pdf/21af34ac-6c38-b39f-a82b-0152eb2ff1a8.
31 See note 9.
32 See, for instance, A.K. Shiva Kumar, Lincoln C. Chen, Mita Choudhury, Shiban Ganju, Vijay Mahajan, Amarjeet Sinha and Abhijit Sen (2011, February 19), "Financing Health Care for All: Challenges and Opportunities," *The Lancet*, 377(9766), 668–679.
33 See, for instance, Samiran Nundy, Keshav Desiraju and Sanjay Nagral (Ed) (2018), *Healers or Predators?* New Delhi: Oxford University Press.
34 Government of India (2023), *National Health Accounts Estimates for India FY 2019–20*, National Health Accounts Technical Secretariat (NHATS), National Health Systems Resource Centre (NHSRC), Ministry of Health and Family Welfare (MoHFW). https://nhsrcindia.org/sites/default/files/2023-04/National%20Health%20Accounts-2019-20.pdf.
35 Reserve Bank of India (2021), *Handbook of Statistics on Indian Economy*, www.rbi.org.in/scripts/PublicationsView.aspx?id=20414 (accessed 24 August 2022).
36 Office of The Registrar General, India (2022, May), *SRS Bulletin*, Volume 55, No 1, Sample Registration System. https://censusindia.gov.in/nada/index.php/catalog/42687 (accessed 24 August 2022).
37 Government of India (2021), *National Health Accounts Estimates for India FY 2017–18*, National Health Accounts Technical Secretariat (NHATS), National Health Systems Resource Centre (NHSRC), Ministry of Health and Family Welfare (MoHFW). https://nhsrcindia.org/sites/default/files/2021-11/National%20Health%20Accounts-%202017-18.pdf (accessed 24 August 2022).
38 Government of India (2021), *National Health Accounts Estimates for India FY 2017–18.*
39 Government of India (2023), *National Health Accounts Estimates for India FY 2019–20*, National Health Accounts Technical Secretariat (NHATS), National Health Systems Resource Centre (NHSRC), Ministry of Health and Family Welfare (MoHFW). https://nhsrcindia.org/sites/default/files/2023-04/National%20Health%20Accounts-2019-20.pdf.
40 High Level Expert Group Report on Universal Health Coverage for India, Executive Summary, October 2011. https://phfi.org/wp-content/uploads/2018/05/UHC-ExecSummary.pdf.
41 For instance, the largest of them all is PM-JAY, launched by the Union government in September 2018. As of August 10, 2022, close to 125.5 million health cards had been issued, 10.9 million cases of hospitalisation were recorded and 22,796 hospitals had been empaneled. The scheme provides an annual health cover of INR 500,000 per family for secondary and tertiary care hospitalisation to over 107.4 million poor and vulnerable families (approximately 500 million beneficiaries) who form the bottom 40 per cent of India's population. There is no restriction on family size, age or gender. All pre-existing conditions are covered from day one, and benefits of the scheme are portable across the country. The scheme aims to help mitigate catastrophic expenditure on medical treatment (covering 1393 procedures) by providing cashless access to health care services for the beneficiary at the point of service, namely, the hospital. It covers up to 3 days of

pre-hospitalization and 15 days post-hospitalization expenses such as diagnostics and medicines. Public hospitals are reimbursed for the health care services at par with the private hospitals. Other schemes include Andhra Pradesh government's YSR Aarogyasri Health Scheme, the Central Government's Health Scheme, the Employees' State Insurance Scheme, Gujarat government's Mukhyamantri Amrutum Yojana, Karnataka government's Yeshasvini Health Insurance Scheme, Kerala Government's Awaz Health Insurance Scheme and Karunya Health Scheme, Maharashtra government's Mahatma Jyotiba Phule Jan Arogya Yojana, Rajasthan government's Bhamashah Swasthya Bima Yojana for the rural population, Tamil Nadu government's Chief Minister's Comprehensive Insurance Scheme and the Telangana government's Employees and Journalists Health Scheme.

42 Executive Summary on Report- Health in India, NSS 75th round accessed at https://mospi.gov.in/documents/213904/416362/Summary%20Analysis_Report_586_Health1600785338349.pdf/21af34ac-6c38-b39f-a82b-0152eb2ff1a8.

43 See note 9.

44 See, for instance, the discussion in A.K. *Shiva Kumar in Getting India Back on Track: An Action Agenda for Reform* (2014), Vintage Books/Random House India.

45 See, for instance, Sunita Reddy and Immaculate Mary (2013), 'Rajiv Aarogyasri Community Health Insurance Scheme in Andhra Pradesh, India: A Comprehensive Analytic View of Private Public Partnership Model', *Indian Journal of Public Health*, 57(4), 254–259.

46 For instance, in July 2015, the Competition Commission of India imposed a fine of INR 6.71 billion on four public-sector insurance firms after finding them guilty of involving in anti-competitive practices in bidding for Kerala government's Rashtriya Swasthya Bima Yojna. See www.livemint.com/Industry/D8um4KlhJg-4dUurPHlvSAN/CCI-imposes-Rs-671-crore-fine-on-four-staterun-insurers.html.

47 For instance, in May 2016, the Bihar Human Rights Commission directed the state government to pay compensation of around INR 150 million to 703 victims whose uterus were removed purportedly to gain incentive money under the RSBY.http://timesofindia.indiatimes.com/city/patna/BHRC-directs-govt-to-pay-compensation-for-703-uterus-removals/articleshow/52095795.cms.

48 Binod Bihari Jena and Manoj Kumar Roul (2020, September 12), 'Estimates of Health Insurance Coverage in India: Expectations and Reality', *Economic & Political Weekly*, 55(37). www.epw.in/journal/2020/37/notes/estimates-health-insurance-coverage-india.html (accessed 24 August 2022).

49 Sunita Reddy and Immaculate Mary (2013), 'Rajiv Aarogyasri Community Health Insurance Scheme in Andhra Pradesh, India: A Comprehensive Analytic View of Private Public Partnership Model', *Indian Journal of Public Health*, 57(4), 254–259.

50 Mita Choudhury, Shruti Tripathi and Jay Dev Dubey (2021, October 2), 'Experiences with Government-sponsored Health Insurance Schemes in Indian States: A Fiscal Perspective', *Economic & Political Weekly*, LVI(40). www.epw.in/system/files/pdf/2021_56/40/SA_LVI_40_021021_Mita%20Choudhury%20et%20al.pdf (accessed 24 August 2022).

51 Mita Choudhury and Jay Dev Dubey (2020), *Equity in Intra-State Distribution of Public Spending on Health: The Case of Bihar and Tamil Nadu*, NIPFP Working Paper Series, No. 315 30-July-2020, National Institute of Public Finance and Policy, New Delhi. www.nipfp.org.in/media/medialibrary/2020/07/WP_315_2020.pdf (accessed 24 August 2022).

52 Mita Choudhury and Pritam Datta (2020, April 25), 'Health Insurance in Private Hospitals: Implications for Implementation of Ayushman Bharat', *Economic & Political Weekly*, 55(17). www.epw.in/journal/2020/17/special-articles/health-insurance-private-hospitals.html (accessed 24 August 2022).

53 Mita Choudhury, Jay Dev Dubey and Bidisha Mondal (2019), *Analyzing Household Expenditure on Health from the 71st Round of Survey by the National Sample Survey Organization in India (Report submitted to the World Health Organization)*, National Institute of Public Finance and Policy, New Delhi. www.nipfp.org.in/media/medialibrary/2019/12/WHO_NSSO_report_2019.pdf (accessed 24 August 2022).

54 Sebastian Bauhoff and Nikkil Sudharsanan (2021, June 5), 'Evaluating Health Insurance Programmes: An Insurance Cascade Framework', *Economic & Political Weekly*, LVI(23). www.epw.in/journal/2021/23/commentary/evaluating-health-insurance-programmes.html (accessed 24 August 2022).

55 Jean Drèze and Amartya Sen (2013), *An Uncertain Glory: India and Its Contradictions*, London: Allen Lane.

56 http://indiabudget.nic.in/es2015-16/echapvol2-01.pdf

Index

Note: Page number in *italics* refer figures and **bold** refer tables